D0710752

Wittgenstein: Meaning and Mind

Part I: Essays

𝔅

Previous volumes of this Commentary in paperback

Wittgenstein: Meaning and Understanding, essays on the *Philosophical Investigations* (Volume 1)

G. P. Baker and P. M. S. Hacker

An Analytical Commentary on Wittgenstein's *Philosophical Investigations* (Volume 1)

G. P. Baker and P. M. S. Hacker

Wittgenstein: Rules, Grammar and Necessity, Volume 2 of an Analytical Commentary on the *Philosophical Investigations*

G. P. Baker and P. M. S. Hacker

Companion to this volume

Wittgenstein: Meaning and Mind, Volume 3 of an Analytical Commentary on the *Philosophical Investigations*, Part II: Exegesis §§243–427

P. M. S. Hacker

Volume 3
of an Analytic Commentary on
the *Philosophical Investigations*

Wittgenstein
Meaning and Mind

Part I: Essays

P. M. S. Hacker

Fellow of St John's College · Oxford

BLACKWELL
Oxford UK & Cambridge USA

First published in paperback 1993

Blackwell Publishers
108 Cowley Road, Oxford OX4 1JF, UK

238 Main Street
Cambridge, Massachusetts 02142, USA

British Library Cataloguing in Publication Data

A CIP catalogue record for this book is available from the British Library.

Library of Congress Cataloging-in-Publication Data

Hacker, P. M. S. (Peter Michael Stephan)
    Wittgenstein, meaning and mind / P.M.S. Hacker.
        p.   cm
    "Volume 3 of An analytical commentary on the Philosophical investigations." Slightly rev. and reissued separately in 2 vols.
    Includes bibliographical references and index.
    Contents: pt. 1. Essay — pt. 2. Exegesis.
    ISBN 0–631–18934–3 (pt. 1 : alk. paper).—ISBN 0–631–19064–3 (pt. 2 : alk. paper)
    1. Wittgenstein, Luwig, 1889–1951.   Philosophische Untersuchungen.   2. Philosophy.   3. Language and languages––Philosophy.   4. Semantics (Philosophy)   I. Title.
B3376.W563P53244   1993
192—dc20   93–19474
                                                                           CIP

Typeset in 10 on 12 pt Bembo by TecSet Ltd
Printed in Great Britain by TJ Press, Padstow, Cornwall

This book is printed on acid-free paper

For Sylvia

Contents

Note to the paperback edition

In 1990 I published a 575-page volume entitled *Wittgenstein: Meaning and Mind, an Analytical Commentary on the* PHILOSOPHICAL INVESTIGATIONS. It was the sequel to two previous volumes of commentary on Wittgenstein's masterpiece which I had written together with my colleague Dr G. P. Baker. The first volume, published in 1980, was entitled *Wittgenstein: Understanding and Meaning*. It covered §§1 – 184 of the *Investigations*, and consisted of analytical essays on the main topics discussed in these sections of Wittgenstein's book and detailed textual exegesis of the numbered remarks, examining the argument of each remark, explaining its role in the overall strategy, and, where it was illuminating to do so, tracing its ancestry to Wittgenstein's voluminous *Nachlass*. The seventeen essays in that volume were interspersed at appropriate places in the exegesis. The second volume, published in 1985, was a 375-page book entitled *Wittgenstein: Rules, Grammar and Necessity*. It covered §§185 – 242 of the *Investigations*. Its structure was modelled on that of Volume 1, consisting of detailed exegesis accompanied by six analytical essays. When the time came for the publication of a paperback edition, Volume 1 had to be split into two, one volume consisting of the seventeen essays entitled *Wittgenstein: Meaning and Understanding, Essays on the* PHILOSOPHICAL INVESTIGATIONS (Volume 1), and the second consisting of the original exegesis of §§1 – 184 and entitled *An Analytical Commentary on Wittgenstein's* PHILOSOPHICAL INVESTIGATIONS (Volume 1). Volume 2, being shorter, was published in paperback in the same form as the original hardback and under the same title.

Like Volume 1, Volume 3 has had to be split into two, this paperback, consisting of the original essays, and a companion paperback, *Wittgenstein: Meaning and Mind*, Part II, consisting of the original exegesis to §§243 – 427. Each can be read and used independently of the other, although they are, of course, complementary.

Apart from the structural alterations essential for the bifurcation of the original volume, the changes introduced are minimal. First, the few internal cross-references within the original text have now been replaced by cross-references to the companion volume. Secondly, the original Preface has been adapted to match it to each of the two paperbacks.

Thirdly, minor errors and typographical mistakes in the hard cover edition have been corrected.

Since I completed Volume 3, Wittgenstein's *Last Writings on the Philosophy of Psychology*, Volume 2 has been published. It contains much that is of importance to the themes discussed here, but nothing that was not available to me and, when relevant, used, with references to his manuscript volumes, in the original publication. Consequently, I have left those references as they were.

P. M. S. H.
Oxford, 1992

Acknowledgements

While writing this book I have been generously assisted by institutions, friends, and colleagues.

By electing me to a two-year Research Readership, which relieved me of teaching, the British Academy made the initial research on the Wittgenstein manuscripts easier and more efficient than it would otherwise have been. I am grateful to my college, St John's, for the many facilities it offers to its Fellows. Its support for research and the pursuit of scholarship is heart-warming. I am indebted to the Bodleian Library, in particular to the staff of the Western Manuscript Department, for many services. The publishing team at Basil Blackwell Ltd, especially Mr S. Chambers and Mr A. McNeillie, have been most helpful in planning and executing this difficult publishing project. As in the past, so too now, it has been a pleasure to work with them in close cooperation. I am most grateful to Miss Jean van Altena for the excellence of her copy-editing.

Professor N. Malcolm, Dr S. Mulhall, Professor H. Philipse, Professor J. Raz, Mr B. Rundle, Professor S. Shanker, Mr T. Spitzley, and Professor T. Taylor kindly read and commented on various drafts of essays or exegesis. Their criticisms, queries, and suggestions were of great assistance. I am especially indebted to Dr H. J. Glock and to Dr J. Hyman, whose comments on essays and exegesis alike were invaluable. Dr Glock and Mr Spitzley kindly checked my German transcriptions and translations. Participants in the university seminars which I have given together with Dr G. P. Baker over the past three years have contributed greatly to the clarification of my thoughts. Their questions were challenging and a stimulus to further efforts. I am most grateful to them all, but especially to Dr O. Hanfling, who both curbed some of my excesses and spurred me on to improve my arguments.

For various reasons it was not feasible for Dr Baker to join me in writing this third volume of Analytical Commentary. However, despite occasional disagreement in interpretation and deeper disagreement over nuance (and it is the chiaroscuro that finally makes the sketch), he read the whole manuscript and joined me in giving the university seminars. His painstaking and helpful criticisms as well as his constructive suggestions saved me from error again and again.

Thoughts reduced to paper are generally nothing more than the footprints of a man walking in the sand. It is true that we see the path he has taken; but to know what he saw on the way, we must use our own eyes.

Schopenhauer

Preface

The first volume of this Analytical Commentary was begun in 1976. Little did I then dream that a decade later I should still be struggling through the thousands of pages of the *Nachlass*, attempting to piece together a surveyable representation of the most fascinating array of philosophical arguments of the twentieth century. The task proved far more difficult and controversial, and certainly involved much greater labour, than originally envisaged. With hindsight, this is hardly surprising. For on every major issue about which he wrote, Wittgenstein undermined the fundamental presuppositions of the debate. The landscape he traversed is familiar; but the routes he took were always new, and his footsteps are not easy to follow. New solutions to received questions are difficult enough to come to terms with. New questions regarding well-worn subjects are difficult to put into fruitful perspective. But a challenge to the very presuppositions of the questions, old and new, which characterize philosophical reflection is far harder to understand and accommodate. There is no short-cut to Wittgenstein's viewpoint: one must follow his trail and look afresh at each landmark. The *Philosophical Investigations* does not aim to add a fresh theory — about meaning and understanding, about necessity or the nature of the mind — to the array of established ones. Nor is its purpose to examine opposing positions in centuries-old debates — such as realism versus nominalism, mentalism versus behaviourism, or Platonism versus formalism — in order to side with those supported by superior arguments. Its goal is to dissolve the questions themselves by showing that they rest upon illegitimate presuppositions and misguided expectations. What is legitimate about philosophical questions can be resolved by a careful description of the uses of words; the rest is illusion. As Wittgenstein observed in one of his more startling remarks, 'In philosophy, all that isn't gas is grammar' (LWL 112).

Wittgenstein: Understanding and Meaning (Volume 1 of this Analytical Commentary) laid the groundwork for understanding the trajectory of his thought. It gave due prominence to the Augustinian picture of language as an *Urbild* informing a multitude of philosophical theories about the nature of language, all of which Wittgenstein aimed to undermine. Misconceptions about the essential nature of words as names and of sentences as descriptions stand in the way of an unprejudiced view of the manifold techniques of using words and of the diverse functions of sentences in the stream of life. These misconceptions give rise to philosophical mythologies about 'the name-relation', logically proper names, sentence-radicals and semantic-mood operators, determinacy of sense, and 'the general propositional form'. They generate misguided pictures of the relationship between language and reality, and of ostensive definition as forging a connection between the two. This in turn contributes to the pervasive illusion that grammar is answerable to reality or that it reflects, and must reflect, the essential structure of the world. Against the background of Wittgenstein's demythologizing, his radical conception of philosophy was displayed. He held philosophy to be therapeutic, not theoretical. It destroys idols, but does not replace them. It is a quest for a surview of grammar, not for an armchair preview of future science. Achievement in philosophy consists in dissolution of philosophical questions, not in acquisition of new information that provides answers to them. Understanding is indeed attained; but it consists in arriving at a clear vision of what is known and familiar, rather than in grasping the articulations of a new theory about the nature of things. Theory construction lies within the province of science, and philosopy — in its questions, methods, and results — is wholly distinct from science.

Once this had been clarified, it was possible to put Wittgenstein's discussion of understanding in the right perspective. Meaning, explanation of what something means, and understanding constitute a triad of key concepts in philosophical investigations into language and the nature of linguistic representation. Reversing the direction of fit between these concepts that is presupposed by the prevailing philosophical tradition, Wittgenstein elaborated the consequences of the grammatical propositions that meaning is what is given by an explanation of meaning, and that it is what is understood when the meaning of an utterance is understood. Understanding (which is akin to an ability rather than a mental state) and the criteria of understanding assume a dominant role in his descriptions of the network of grammar in this domain. Clarification of the internal relations between meaning, understanding, and explanation also illuminates their complex connections with truth, evidence, justification, definition, rules of use, grammatical proposition, and so forth.

Wittgenstein: Rules, Grammar and Necessity, Volume 2 of the Analytical Commentary, constituted an alteration to the original plans. The complexities of §§185 – 242 of the *Investigations* needed very detailed analysis, the extensive controversies over the interpretation of Wittgenstein's intentions required the presentation of much background material from the *Nachlass,* and the generally ill-understood consequences of his account of grammar and rule-following demanded at least a fragmentary investigation of his philosophy of logic and mathematics. Hence the whole of Volume 2 was dedicated to the clarification of Wittgenstein's discussion of rules, acting in accord with a rule, and following a rule. This led to an examination of his discussion of the autonomy of grammar and of his remarks on the nature of necessity in the domains of logic, mathematics, and metaphysics.

The present paperback volume of essays takes the commentary forward from §243 to §427. These sections are no less controversial than the preceding ones. To be sure, the rocky ground already traversed should have taught one much. But as one plunges into the tropical undergrowth of the great private language arguments, it is all too easy to lose one's bearings. The path is overgrown with prevalent misinterpretations, and dark distorting shadows are cast across it by our disposition to extract theories from Wittgenstein's descriptions. The position of these arguments in the overall structure of the book needs to be clarified. Why, at this particular point, is the question of whether a private language is possible raised? To what extent are the previous remarks presupposed? Is Wittgenstein simply moving on to yet another of the 'great questions of philosophy', or is there a natural progression from the preceding argument? Why is the discussion of a private language followed by an investigation of thinking and imagining — and why is there no discussion of remembering and other faculties of the mind?

Not only is the rationale of the locus of these sections in the grand strategy controversial, but the very subject of debate in §§243ff. is disputed. What is a 'private' language? And why should anyone be interested in whether there could be a language which, unlike ordinary languages, only its speaker can, logically, understand? What is Wittgenstein's purpose? Is he trying to demonstrate the essential *social* nature of language, to show that it is an *a priori* truth that only a social creature can speak or use symbols? Is he aiming to refute a *recherché* form of scepticism about knowing what one means by one's words? Or is his target quite different?

If the subject is disputed, so too is the conclusion. Is he arguing that there can be no such thing as a 'private' ostensive definition, or rather that such a mode of assigning meaning to an expression is possible only within the context of mastery of a shared, public language? How can a philosopher who repudiates theses and proofs in philosophy go on to try to *prove* that there cannot be a private language? Or was he not trying to prove this at all?

The tactical moves are equally subject to divergent interpretation. Does Wittgenstein implicitly rely on a verification principle? Is his denial of the possibility of a private language dependent on worries about the reliability of memory? And if there is such a philosophical, as opposed to practical, worry, how could it possibly disappear in company? It is evident that he denies that sensations are 'inner objects'; but does he contend instead that they are nothing at all? He explicitly denied that he was propounding any form of behaviourism, but many have argued that his philosophy of psychology is a version of logical behaviourism. This too needs elucidation.

If the path through this terrain is shrouded in gloom, its direction is no less difficult to discern. It is clear that Wittgenstein thought that the matter of a private language bears directly on solipsism and idealism. But why is this never explicitly shown? Is the argument meant to be an implicit refutation of idealism? But is the issue not too important for such cursory treatment? Or are these venerable philosophical doctrines merely ancient idols in the jungle which are briefly illuminated as he passes by, intent upon an altogether different goal? Was Wittgenstein trying to re-orient completely our picture of the mind, so that *everything* would appear in a new light? Certainly the relation between the 'inner' and the 'outer' is as philosophically problematic, especially when viewed from the perspective of the Augustinian picture of language, as the relation between proof and truth in mathematics. Wittgenstein's treatment of the latter theme involved a radical break with all traditional approaches. It is not unreasonable to expect his discussion of the former to involve an equally startling repudiation of the very presuppositions of the debates between idealism and realism, dualism and monism, mentalism and behaviourism. Surely we should take seriously his avowal that he was destroying 'houses of cards' and 'clearing up the ground of language on which they stand' (PI §118).

The thirteen essays in this volume survey the central issues in §§243 – 427. As in Volume 1, each essay is as self-contained as possible. This goal could be achieved only at the cost of some repetition. As Wittgenstein travels 'over a wide field of thought criss-cross in every direction' (Preface, p. ix), the same landmarks are re-encountered, but always from a different direction. Each essay in this volume endeavours to represent a part of the web of the grammar of psychological concepts as he saw it. The same nodes often recur in different essays, but in each case their links with different strands are in view. The order of the essays has been determined by the sequence of remarks in the text. However, the essay on criteria found no natural location, since there is no extended discussion of the subject in the *Investigations*. It has been placed, *faute de mieux*, at the end of the book, and redeems the promissory note issued in Volume 1.

The arguments of §§243 – 427 do not constitute the 'foundations' of, let alone the whole of, Wittgenstein's philosophy of mind. But they provide essential methodical guidelines and fundamental insights. They are the route to 'the correct logical point of view — but to achieve it, one must follow the arduous trail he blazed. In the following pages I have tried to plot it as best I could. Doubtless I have erred in places, but I hope that I have captured the direction of his thought. If he is right, then the mainstream of philosophical psychology, past and present, is misguided — flowing from misconceived questions to quagmires of confused pseudo-theories. Of course, his ideas run counter to the spirit of the age, and today the will to illusion is stronger than ever. Only when philosophers wish to be cured of the sicknesses of the understanding that beset them, will they be in a position to take up the legacy of Wittgenstein.

Abbreviations

1. Published works

The following abbreviations are used to refer to Wittgenstein's published works, listed in chronological order (where possible; some works straddle many years). The list includes derivative primary sources and lecture notes taken by others.

NB   *Notebooks 1914 – 16*, ed. G. H. von Wright and G. E. M. Anscombe, tr. G. E. M. Anscombe (Blackwell, Oxford, 1961).

TLP   *Tractatus Logico-Philosophicus*, tr. D. F. Pears and B. F. McGuinness (Routledge and Kegan Paul, London, 1961).

RLF   'Some Remarks on Logical Form', *Proceedings of the Aristotelian Society*, suppl. vol. ix (1929), pp. 162 – 71.

WWK   *Ludwig Wittgenstein und der Wiener Kreis*, shorthand notes recorded by F. Waismann, ed. B. F. McGuinness (Blackwell, Oxford, 1967). The English translation, *Wittgenstein and the Vienna Circle* (Blackwell, Oxford, 1979), matches the pagination of the original edition.

PR   *Philosophical Remarks*, ed. R. Rhees, tr. R. Hargreaves and R. White (Blackwell, Oxford, 1975).

M   'Wittgenstein's Lectures in 1930 – 33', in G. E. Moore, *Philosophical Papers* (Allen and Unwin, London, 1959).

LWL   *Wittgenstein's Lectures, Cambridge 1930 – 32, from the Notes of John King and Desmond Lee*, ed. Desmond Lee (Blackwell, Oxford, 1980).

PG   *Philosophical Grammar,* ed. R. Rhees, tr. A. J. P. Kenny (Blackwell, Oxford, 1974).

GB   'Remarks on Frazer's "Golden Bough" ', tr. J. Beversluis, repr. in C. G. Luckhardt (ed.), *Wittgenstein: Sources and Perspectives* (Cornell University Press, Ithaca, 1979), pp. 61 – 81.

AWL   *Wittgenstein's Lectures, Cambridge 1932 – 35, from the Notes of Alice Ambrose and Margaret MacDonald*, ed. Alice Ambrose (Blackwell, Oxford, 1979).

BB   *The Blue and Brown Books* (Blackwell, Oxford, 1958).

LPE   'Wittgenstein's Notes for Lectures on "Private Experience" and "Sense Data" ', ed. R. Rhees, *Philosophical Review*, 77 (1968), pp. 275 – 320.

LSD   'The Language of Sense Data and Private Experience' (Notes taken by R. Rhees of Wittgenstein's lectures, 1936), *Philosophical Investigations*, 7 (1984), pp. 1 – 45, 101 – 40.

RFM   *Remarks on the Foundations of Mathematics*, ed. G. H. von Wright, R. Rhees, G. E. M. Anscombe, revised edition (Blackwell, Oxford, 1978).

LA   *Lectures and Conversations on Aesthetics, Psychology and Religious Beliefs*, ed. C. Barrett (Blackwell, Oxford, 1970).

LFM   *Wittgenstein's Lectures on the Foundations of Mathematics, Cambridge 1939*, ed. C. Diamond (Harvester Press, Sussex, 1976).

PI   *Philosophical Investigations*, ed. G. E. M. Anscombe and R. Rhees, tr. G. E. M. Anscombe, 2nd edition (Blackwell, Oxford, 1958).

Z   *Zettel*, ed. G. E. M. Anscombe and G. H. von Wright, tr. G. E. M. Anscombe (Blackwell, Oxford, 1967).

RPP I   *Remarks on the Philosophy of Psychology*, Volume I, ed. G. E. M. Anscombe and G. H. von Wright, tr. G. E. M. Anscombe (Blackwell, Oxford, 1980).

RPP II   *Remarks on the Philosophy·of Psychology*, Volume II, ed. G. H. von Wright and H. Nyman, tr. C. G. Luckhardt and M. A. E. Aue (Blackwell, Oxford, 1980).

LPP   *Wittgenstein's Lectures on Philosophy of Psychology 1946 – 7*, notes by P. T. Geach, K. J. Shah, A. C. Jackson, ed. P. T. Geach (Harvester Wheatsheaf, Hemel Hempstead, 1988).

LW   *Last Writings on the Philosophy of Psychology*, Volume I, ed. G. H. von Wright and H. Nyman, tr. C. G. Luckhardt and M. A. E. Aue (Blackwell, Oxford, 1982).

C   *On Certainty*, ed. G. E. M. Anscombe and G. H. von Wright, tr. D. Paul and G. E. M. Anscombe (Blackwell, Oxford, 1969).

CV   *Culture and Value*, ed. G. H. von Wright in collaboration with H. Nyman, tr. P. Winch (Blackwell, Oxford, 1980).

PLP   *The Principles of Linguistic Philosophy*, F. Waismann, ed. R. Harré (Macmillan and St Martin's Press, London and New York, 1965).

R   *Ludwig Wittgenstein: Letters to Russell, Keynes and Moore*, ed. G. H. von Wright (Blackwell, Oxford, 1974).

Reference style: all references to *Philosophical Investigations*, Part I, are to sections (e.g. PI §1), except those to notes below the line on various pages. References to Part II are to pages (e.g. PI p. 202). References to other printed works are either to numbered remarks (TLP) or to sections signified '§' (Z, RPP, LW); in all other cases references are to pages (e.g. LFM 21 = LFM, page 21) or to numbered letters (R).

2. *Nachlass*

All references to unpublished material cited in the von Wright catalogue (G. H. von Wright, *Wittgenstein* (Blackwell, Oxford, 1982), pp. 35ff.) are by MS. or TS. number followed by page number. Wherever possible, the pagination entered in the original document has been used. The Cornell xeroxes in the Bodleian are defective; sometimes a dozen or more pages have been omitted. Consequently, where access to the originals or to complete xeroxes has not been possible, some errors of page reference will unavoidably have occurred. For memorability, the following special abbreviations are used.

Manuscripts
Vol. I, Vol. II, etc. refer to the eighteen large manuscript volumes (= MSS. 105–22) written between 2 February 1929 and 1944. The reference style Vol. VI, 241 is to Volume VI, page 241.

Typescripts
BT   The 'Big Typescript' (TS. 213): a rearrangement, with modifications, written additions and deletions, of TS. 211, 1933, vi. pp. table of contents, 768 pp. All references are to page numbers. Where the page number is followed by 'v.', this indicates a handwritten addition on the reverse side of the TS. page.
PPI   'Proto-Philosophical Investigations'[1] (TS. 220); a typescript of the first half of the pre-war version of the *Philosophical Investigations* (up to §189 of the final version, but with many differences); 1937 or 1938, 137 pp. The shortened title form 'Proto-Investigations' is used freely. All references are to sections (§).
PPI (I) The so-called Intermediate Version, reconstructed by von Wright; it consists of 300 numbered remarks; 1945, 195 pp. All references are to sections (§).

3. *Abbreviations for works by Frege*

FA   *The Foundations of Arithmetic*, tr. J. L. Austin, 2nd edition (Blackwell, Oxford, 1959).

[1]This is not Wittgenstein's title.

GA   *Grundgesetze der Arithmetik, begriffsschriftlich abgeleitet*, Band I,
       (Hermann Pohle, Jena, 1893).
PW   *Posthumous Writings*, ed. H. Hermes, F. Kambartel, F. Kaulbach,
       tr. P. Long, R. White (Blackwell, Oxford, 1979).

4. *Abbreviations for works by Russell*

AM   *The Analysis of Mind* (George Allen and Unwin, London, 1921).
LK   *Logic and Knowledge, Essays 1901–1950*, ed. R. C. Marsh (Allen
       and Unwin, London, 1956).

5. *References to previous volumes of this Analytical Commentary*

References to Volume 1 are flagged 'Volume 1' with a page number
referring to the hardback edition. Where necessary the abbreviation MU
(with a page number) is used, referring to the paperback volume of
essays entitled *Wittgenstein: Meaning and Understanding* (Blackwell,
Oxford, 1983). References to Volume 2, *Wittgenstein: Rules, Grammar and
Necessity*, are flagged 'Volume 2'.

I

THE PRIVATE LANGUAGE ARGUMENTS

1. Preliminaries

§§243 – 315 of the *Philosophical Investigations* are commonly referred to as 'the private language argument'. The name is not Wittgenstein's, although in his notebooks he did allude to 'the discussion of a private language' (MS. 165, 101), which language no one but its speaker can understand. There is indeed such a discussion, but the received name is misleading, for these sections incorporate not one argument but many. It would be futile by now to advocate abandoning this name, but if it must be retained, it would be preferable to pluralize it and to refer to this part of the book as 'the private language arguments'. Many different but closely interwoven themes are investigated, and a wide variety of grammatical clarifications emerge. They are indeed all connected more or less directly with the *prima facie* curious idea of a language which cannot logically be understood by anyone other than its speaker. But their global purpose is to reveal the incoherence of a comprehensive picture of human nature, of the mind and of the relation between behaviour and the mental, of self-knowledge and of knowledge of other people's experience, of language and its foundations, that has dominated philosophy since Descartes. Indeed, despite the fact that we all happily avow that we are anti-Cartesians now, and are prone to view Cartesian dualism as a kind of infantile disease of philosophy which we have all outgrown, that picture, in subtle and insidious ways, still dominates contemporary thought. Central state materialism, functionalism in all its forms, and so-called 'cognitive science', despite their superficial sophistication, are as beset with the confusions which Wittgenstein diagnosed, as were rationalist, empiricist, and Kantian metaphysics of the heroic age of philosophy and behaviourism and phenomenalism earlier this century. This is not merely because contemporary philosophy still trails clouds of Cartesianism and classical empiricism in its wake. Rather the conception of the mental that informs the philosophical tradition is one to which we naturally cleave. Philosophers and non-philosophers alike, when reflecting upon the nature of the mind, on experience, or on mental states and processes, are disposed to move along these deceptively smooth tracks. We are naturally inclined to represent things to ourselves thus. Deceived by similarities of grammatical forms and oblivious to differences of use, we project characteristics of one language-game onto another. Philosophical theories give articulate form to this 'natural disposition of reason'.

The resultant picture of the mind might be dubbed 'the inner/outer conception of the mental'.[1] It stands to the philosophy of psychology somewhat as the Platonist conception of number stands to the philosophy of mathematics. Indeed, it is no coincidence that Wittgenstein hesitated as to whether to continue the early draft of *Investigations* §§1 – 189 (i.e. PPI) with his reflections on the philosophy of mathematics (RFM, Part I) or with his examination of the contour lines of the grammar of the mental (cf. Volume 2, 'Two fruits upon our tree'). For both the inner/outer picture of the mind and the Platonist conception of number, as well as their dialectical contraries, behaviourism and formalism, are rooted in the Augustinian picture of language. (Which is not to say that the philosophical theories that grow from these roots are not fed by numerous different streams.) These are informed by misconceptions about words, misunderstandings of what it is to be the name of a sensation (or experience) or to be the name of a number — the former being conceived to signify a private, mental object, the latter an abstract object. They are moulded by the illicit assumption that sentences uniformly or fundamentally serve to describe — first-person psychological sentences in the present tense being conceived to be descriptions of one's own mental states, mathematical sentences to be descriptions of relations between abstract objects.

Closely associated with — indeed perhaps indissociable from — that picture of the mental is an equally erroneous conception of language. The source of all our knowledge, empiricists argued, and of the 'materials' of thought and reasoning, is *experience*. Experience constitutes 'the given', the data of sense and introspection. According to this classical conception, the foundations of knowledge are constituted by 'ideas' given by (or derived by abstraction from) inner and outer sense. The fundamental indefinables of a language were accordingly conceived to be names of simple ideas. So language was envisaged as having its foundations in mental or subjective objects, the names of which link language to reality. (A more modern view conceives of the fundamental rules of a language as given, antecedently to experience — because innate. And the form in which they are given is imagined to be 'mental representations'.) Accordingly, the roots of language are essentially subjective or mental.

The question of whether Wittgenstein himself ever succumbed to any of these illusions is of considerable historical interest. A comprehensive case for or against such an indictment would require detailed exami-

---

[1] But how the nature of the 'inner' is conceived varies from one philosophical doctrine to another: e.g., a mental substance thinking thoughts (Descartes), subjectless impressions and ideas (Hume), images and sense-data (phenomenalists), brain states (central state materialists), and functional states with neural realization (contemporary functionalists). In all these cases an otherwise harmless, and by no means silly, metaphor is grotesquely reflected in the distorted mirror of philosophical theory.

nation of the *Notebooks 1914 – 16*, the *Tractatus*, and the writings ('Remarks on Logical Form', *Philosophical Remarks*, and the manuscript notebooks), lectures (Lee's and Moore's lecture notes), and dictations (to Schlick and Waismann) between 1929 and 1932. This would be out of place here. Nevertheless, a few schematic suggestions may be ventured. Some of the Schopenhauerian ideas in the *Notebooks*, traces of which are visible in the obscure remarks on solipsism in the *Tractatus*, can arguably be interpreted as a transcendental form of solipsism. If so, then there would appear to be in these writings elements of the general picture that Wittgenstein later strove to destroy.[2] Similarly, the preoccupation with the logical analysis of the *visual field*, evident in the *Notebooks* and prominent in the 1929 manuscript volumes and 'Remarks on Logical Form', strongly suggest a subjective, though idiosyncratic, notion of 'the given'.[3] Be that as it may, the conception of naming as effecting a connection between words and world, and of the proposition as essentially a picture or description of a state of affairs, arguably leaves no room in the framework of the *Tractatus* for any *other* account of names of sensation or experiences and of first-person experiential sentences.

That is controversial. But this much is clear: both Wittgenstein's remarks in 1929/30 about what he *used* to think concerning 'the primary', and his writings and lectures during this transitional phase involve an unambiguous commitment to numerous distortions of experiential concepts. He held that the only 'genuine propositions' were descriptions of *immediate experience*, that such propositions get compared with reality for verification and can thereby be conclusively verified and so known to be true (or false). The verification of first-person present-tense experiential propositions was conceived to be radically unlike the verification of third-person ones, and hence to differ categorially in sense, the latter being not genuine propositions, but hypotheses. His account was in effect a version of methodological solipsism,[4] a conception which he would subsequently reject as incoherent.

The change came during the academic year 1932/33 when he repudiated the idea that first-person experiential utterances are 'the genuine

---

[2] This is a controversial claim which cannot be defended here. It is briefly touched on again in 'Behaviour and behaviourism', §2, 'I and my self', §1, and 'The world of consciousness', §1. Further confirmation for it can be found in a letter of Russell's and in a coded passage in the pre-*Tractatus* notebooks (see B. F. McGuinness, *Wittgenstein, A Life: Young Ludwig (1889–1921)* (Duckworth; London, 1988), pp. 106, 225). See also Frege's letter to Wittgenstein, dated 3 April 1920.

[3] It does not follow, on such an interpretation, that the 'objects' of the *Tractatus* are sense-data. For while a coloured patch in my visual field can be considered a *phenomenal complex*, the simple objects of which it is composed, e.g. points in the visual field specified by co-ordinates (as in RLF) and unanalysable shades of colour, can be viewed as indestructible sempiternalia, beyond existence and inexistence.

[4] The terminology is Carnap's, not Wittgenstein's. Their respective positions differ, but the label is convenient provided it does not mislead.

propositions', denied that they get compared with reality at all or have a verification. Further advances in his thinking are evident in the *Blue and Brown Books* discussion of experience, mental states and processes, idealism and solipsism (1933 – 5). In the 'Notes for Lectures on "Private Experience" and "Sense Data" ' (1935 – 6), the notion of a private language makes its first appearance (see also Rhees's lecture notes from 1936 entitled 'The Language of Sense Data and Private Experience' and the 'Lecture on Privacy' (MS. 166)). By this time most of the issues which are to be found in *Investigations* §§243 – 315 were already taking shape. His ideas were further refined and developed, principally in 1937 – 9 (Vols. XV – XVII, MSS. 158, 160, 162(b)) when the skeleton of the arguments is created, and then in 1944 – 5 (Vol. XII, MSS. 124, 129, 165, 179, 180(a)) when they were completed and polished. What we see in the condensed sixteen pages of the *Investigations* §§243 – 315 is the precipitate (cf. PI, Preface) from many hundreds of pages of notes in which Wittgenstein struggled with awesome tenacity to clarify the concepts of experience and to destroy the philosophical illusions and mythologies that surround these crucial but mundane (non-theoretical) expressions that inform our lives and thought.

In Volume 2 it was argued that the suggestion that 'the real private language argument' is completed by §202 is a mistake (Volume 2, pp. 169 – 79 and Exg. §202). Wittgenstein's discussion of following rules was not meant to show that it only makes sense to talk of someone's behaviour as constituting an instance of following a rule in the context of a community of rule-followers. Rather, it was designed to show that it only makes sense to talk of following a rule in the context of a practice — a behavioural regularity — informed by normative activities (e.g. using the formulation of a rule as a standard of correctness, rectifying mistakes, justifying action by reference to a rule). Such practices, with us, are typically shared, although they need not always be, and are typically learnt in a social context, though some may be invented in solitude for one's private use. But, as Wittgenstein's numerous discussions of Robinson Crusoe, solitary cavemen, etc. demonstrate, there is no conceptual incoherence in imagining a person following a rule in an asocial context. That a language is learnt from other speakers is an important fact about the genesis of a linguistic ability, but it does not enter into the grammatical (logical) characterization of the ability (cf. PG 188; BB 12, 97; PI §495). For an ability is characterized by what it is an ability to do. The criteria for speaking a language do not require the production of a school or even a parental certificate. We would determine whether a solitary caveman or desert islander could speak or use signs quite independently of determining how he learnt to do so (cf. Exg. §243).

Had the discussion up to *Investigations* §202 been intended to prove that following a rule, like trade and barter, is only conceivable in a social group, it would not have shown that a public language in a social group is not a congruence of 'private' languages built on private ostensive definitions — as Locke explicitly, and most other empiricists implicitly, had supposed. Were Wittgenstein's conclusion at §202 merely that it is impossible to follow a rule privately (as opposed to 'privately', cf. Exg. §202), then the application of that argument to the language of sensations would not have required the association of sensation-names with, or the introduction of private ostensive definitions by reference to, 'private objects' which no one else can have or be acquainted with. For the point to be established would be that one person alone, independently of a social setting and antecedent training in a social group, could not talk about his own sensations or experiences *no matter how these concepts are defined*. The misconceived claims that different people cannot have the identical sensation and that sensations are epistemically private would be strictly irrelevant to the argument. For, even if sensations are not thus conceived, it would be impossible for a person in solitude to use a language to talk about his sensations unless he had acquired his language in a social setting. The claim that a language concerned with sensations is impossible unless shared by a community would not differ in principle from the claim that a language about physical objects is impossible unless shared by a community. In fact, Wittgenstein's concern in this strand in the web of arguments is not whether one person alone could or could not talk of his experiences in an unshared language, but whether all of us, in our normal social setting, can be conceived to be following rules constituted by mere association of a word and a mental 'object' or by private ostensive definitions. And private ostensive definitions are not ostensive definitions which other people do not happen to know about, but putative definitions (rules) which cannot be communicated to other people. It is such rules which were presupposed as the foundations of our common public languages by the mainstream of philosophy. And it is by showing that there can be no such rules, that representational idealism (and contemporary 'cognitive representationalism'), classical British idealism, phenomenalism, and solipsism can be shown to be philosophical chimeras.

Far from §§243 – 315 constituting simply an application of the account of following rules to a special problem about sensation-language, the discussion of the possibility of a 'private' language is concerned, as Wittgenstein wrote (MS. 165, 102), with idealism and solipsism, in particular with the sources of these intellectual diseases. Its global target is a misconstrual of our concepts of experience, of the nature of the mental and its relation to behaviour, that is pervasive in philosophy. These misconceptions inform philosophical, psychological, and theoretical linguistic accounts of the nature of a language, of the foundations of language in 'private' experience and 'private' rules (and so-called mental representations of rules), and of the putative foundations of knowledge.

Not only is this task not essentially completed by §202; it has barely begun.

It would, of course, be wrong to think that §§243 – 315 are independent of the preceding arguments of the book. They presuppose the antecedent clarifications of following rules, techniques of application, ostensive definitions, samples, meaning, understanding, and explanation. The crucial question which has not yet been broached is whether there can be private analogues of these, i.e. analogues within the 'private' confines of the mind. It makes sense to speak of a person's following a rule only in the context of a regularity of action involving normative activities (cf. Volume 2, p. 47) manifesting a technique of application (cf. Volume 2, pp. 161 – 5). The pertinent question in relation to a private language is not whether there can (logically) be such a thing in solitude, in an extra-social context independently of antecedent training in a social group, for Wittgenstein has shown that to be perfectly intelligible. It is rather whether there can be an analogue of following a rule[5] if, despite the person's living in a community, the putative rule which he purports to be following could not logically be followed by, or even communicated to, anyone else. For this is what would be the case were sensation-names (or, more generally, names of 'experiences') defined by private ostensive definition — and here 'private' does not mean contingently private. If anything deserves the name '*the* private language argument', it is the discussion of this crucial issue in the *Investigations* §§243 – 315, but fewer than a third of these sections are directly concerned with it, and much else is brought into view.

Ostensive definition has previously been clarified as one legitimate form of explaining the meaning of a word. It gives a rule for the use of a word, and typically introduces a sample to function as a standard of correct application. The crucial question for the idealist and representational idealist traditions is not whether one can give a private ostensive

---

[5] Wer uns die Sprache eines Volkes beschreibt, beschreibt eine Gleichformigkeit ihres Benehmens. Und wer eine Sprache beschreibt, die Einer mit sich allein spricht, der beschreibt eine Gleichformigkeit seines Benehmens und nicht etwas, was sich *ein*mal zugetragen hat.

   Aber 'eine Sprache sprechen' werde ich nur ein Verhalten nennen, das unserm, wenn wir unsere Sprache sprechen, analog ist. (MS. 124, 279)

(Someone who describes the language of a people, describes a regularity of their behaviour. And someone who describes a language which a person speaks to himself alone, describes a regularity of his behaviour, and not something that has happened only *once*.

   But I shall only call behaviour 'speaking a language' if it is analogous to ours, when we speak our language.)

This remark occurs in the MS. after a draft of PI §206(c). It is the regular behaviour (including normative activities) of a person which constitutes the criteria for saying of him (even if he speaks only to himself) that he has mastered the technique of speaking a language.

definition of a word by reference to a sample one keeps secret (i.e. does not show to anyone else), but whether one can give such a definition by reference to a 'private' sample (i.e. one which it is logically impossible to show anyone else). If not, then there can be no intelligible distinction in a 'private' language between correct and incorrect uses of signs, and hence no use of language at all.

Similarly, it has been argued earlier that the meaning of a word is not an object of any kind, but rather is given by an explanation of meaning, and an explanation is a rule for the use of a word. Understanding a word — knowing what it means — is manifest in correct use, i.e. use in accord with an appropriate explanation. It is also exhibited in correctly explaining what a word means. (If a speaker understands what he says, he must be able to say what he means, and what he means and what it means typically converge). The moot question for a private language is not so much whether one can explain to others what one means by a word, but whether one can even explain it to oneself. Hence also, not so much whether others can understand, but whether one understands oneself — indeed whether there is anything to understand at all. One could also put it thus: is the idea of an expression which it is logically impossible to explain to others and which it is logically impossible for others to understand not incoherent? If it is logically impossible for anyone else to understand, must it not also be logically impossible for oneself to understand? For does it not then follow that there actually is nothing to understand?

What Wittgenstein aimed to show is not that sensation-language, like the rest of language, is essentially shared, but that it is essentially sharable. That requirement is not met by the received accounts in the dominant philosophical tradition (or in psychology and linguistic theory). The refutation of the supposition of the possibility of a private language is, in a loose sense, a *reductio ad absurdum* of an array of deep presuppositions. For here there are and can be no rules, *a fortiori* no ostensive definitions, no samples and no techniques of application, no distinction between correctly and incorrectly following a rule, but only a *Schein-praxis* — an illusion of meaning.

This is one dominant theme in the private language arguments of §§243 – 315, but there are many others tightly interwoven in a fine tapestry of exceptional richness and subtlety of design.

2. *From grammatical truth to metaphysical theory*

Each person has 'experiences', in a generous sense of the term. He enjoys or endures sensations, perceptual experiences, emotions, and moods. People believe, imagine, and think. Just as there are physical states, events, and processes, so too there are mental ones. The experiences that a person has are, tautologically, his experiences. These are often exhibited in his behaviour. The experiences a person manifests in his behaviour are, again tautologically, *his* experiences. There is no such thing, for example, as one person manifesting the suffering of another.

Numerous psychological expressions are names of experiences which a person enjoys or endures. The word 'pain' is the name of a kind of sensation, the expressions 'seeing red' or 'having a mental image of A' are names of different kinds of experiences. If a person knows what such a psychological predicate means, he knows what it stands for. To know what the word 'pain' means is to know that it stands for a certain kind of sensation — viz. pain.

A person who has mastered a language can say what experiences he is having. His ability to do so is (typically) independent of his observation of his own behaviour, and what he says does not rest on the evidence of what he does. He cannot *doubt* whether, for example, he is in pain, wants a drink, feels dizzy, etc. Though self-deception is sometimes possible, mistake is not. When a person says how things are with him, what sensations and perceptual experiences he has, then (at least in paradigmatic cases) what he says has privileged status. There is such a thing as describing one's states of mind — an activity at which Proust, for example, excelled.

Judgements about other people's sensations, perceptions, and emotions rest on observations of what they do and say. They may say or otherwise reveal how things are with them, or they may keep things to themselves. But there is also such a thing as pretence or dissimulation, which complicates matters.

These truisms are not empirical generalizations obvious to all, but for the most part grammatical propositions partly constitutive of the constituent concepts. Philosophers, hungry for theories about the nature of the mind, typically stray from such narrow and familiar paths into the minefields of metaphysics. It is but a short step from grammatical platitudes to metaphysical theses, and from there to perdition. The following sketch indicates some of the routes.

(A) The mental realm

(i) Parallel to the public physical world, each of us enjoys access to a private realm of the mind. The mental world consists of objects (e.g. pains, images, sense-impressions, perhaps also ideas, thoughts, and beliefs), processes (imagining, remembering, thinking), and states (believing, understanding, knowing) which are logically just like physical objects, processes, and states — only mental. These are doubtless mysterious; we talk about them, but with due caution leave their nature undecided — future investigations and theories will dispel our current ignorance (PI §308).

(ii) To have an experience, for example a sensation (such as pain) or an emotion (like fear), is to stand in a certain relationship to such an object, process, or state. 'A has a pain' and 'A has a penny' (as well as 'I have a pain' and 'I have a penny') have the same logical form, the latter signifying a relation to a physical object, the former to a mental object. The nature of the mental being undecided, these objects, processes, and states may be (a) *sui generis* — essentially distinct from and irreducible to the physical; (b) neural, the experience of the subject consisting in modifications of the brain as apprehended 'from the inside'; (c) functional objects, processes, and states with a neural 'realization'.

(iii) One person cannot have the identical experience which another has, but only a similar one. I cannot have your pain, but only one just like it. So experiences are inalienable 'private property'.

(B) Names of the mental

(i) One knows what the name of a (simple) mental entity means if one knows what it stands for; e.g. one knows what 'pain' means if one knows that it stands for the sensation of pain. One can only know what such an expression means if one is acquainted with what it stands for, i.e. if one has or has had a pain. For if the meaning of a word is the thing for which it stands, to know its meaning *is* to know, i.e. be acquainted with, that thing. Alternatively, if the meaning of a word is denied to be what the word stands for, it is still plausible to argue that a word which cannot be defined by an analytical definition must be explained by an ostensive definition — and an ostensive definition of, e.g., 'pain' requires that one *have* a pain. That knowing the meaning of such words presupposes acquaintance with what they signify seems confirmed by the thought that the blind do not really know what colour-words mean because they are not acquainted with colours, i.e. lack the sensory experiences of seeing colours.

(ii) A child learns what names of experiences mean by first having the experience, and then (a) being brought to *associate* the name with his experience; or (b) being brought to give himself a mental ostensive definition by *concentrating* on the experience. Concentrating is conceived to be a mental analogue of physically pointing at an object.

(iii) Once meaning has been assigned to such a name, subsequent uses of the word can be explained (a) by causal theorists, as a matter of 'habit memory', or (b) by normative theorists, as a matter of calling up an exemplar stored in the memory. On the latter view, we link names of experiences with copies, representatives, or exemplars of the experience in question which are deposited in our 'storehouse of ideas'.

(C) Knowledge of the subjective realm

(i) Since I cannot doubt whether I am, for example, experiencing pain when I am so doing, cannot wonder whether I have a pain or not, cannot think I have a pain when I do not, therefore (a) if I have an experience, I know that I do; (b) my knowledge of my own experiences is certain; (c) my knowledge of my experiences is incorrigible.

(ii) Since having experiences is standing in a relation to mental objects, states, processes, etc., and since that relation yields knowledge, there must be an inner analogue of the corresponding relation with respect to 'outer objects', viz. perception. This analogue is *inner sense*, *introspection*, *consciousness*, or *awareness* (variously conceived and often assimilated). For, (a) when I have an experience I am conscious or aware of it — an experience of which I were not conscious would, as Kant put it, 'be as nothing to me'. I cannot have a pain, for example, and not be aware of it. 'I had a terrible pain, but I was not aware of it' is nonsense. (b) I can think about, reflect on, my current experiences — hold them, as it were, in view — and say precisely what they are like. I thus observe *in foro interno* the stream of experiences I enjoy.

(iii) Hence, one's mind is transparent to oneself. The objects, events, and processes in it are immediately known by introspection, and what is believed to be in the mind is in it. An alternative tack is to deny certainty and incorrigibility and to insist that introspection is as fallible as perception. Far from being transparent, much of the mind is opaque, and the mental states and processes in it must often be hypothesized — by psychoanalysts, theoretical linguists, and, in the fullness of time, by super-neurologists.

(iv) First-person psychological utterances are essentially descriptions of what is revealed to introspective scrutiny. What I observe, privately, *in foro interno*, I can report, for the benefit of others, *in foro externo*.

(v) Since I can describe my experiences without reference to my own behaviour, first-person psychological propositions are logically independent of behaviour. Mental states, etc. are causes of behaviour.

(D) Knowledge of others' mental states

(i) One cannot know of other people's experiences and mental states as one knows one's own, viz. by introspection. Rather, one observes their behaviour, and one infers from this what mental states or experiences are causally responsible for their behaviour.

(ii) The experiences and mental states of others are hidden, inaccessible to direct observation. For even if others tell us what they are experiencing, this is just words — and anyway, they may be lying. Similarly, even if they behave in such-and-such characteristic ways, this is just behaviour, not the experience itself — and they may be dissimulating.

(iii) The behaviour of other people consists of bare movements and the emission of sounds. The body that behaves is a physical organism subject to the causal laws that determine the movements of all physical bodies.

(iv) Since a mental state can obtain or an experience be enjoyed without any corresponding behaviour occurring, and behaviour may occur without the appropriate mental state or experience, behaviour is not logically connected with the mental.

(v) Since the experiences and mental states of others are known by inference from behavioural externalities, and since the connection between behaviour and the mental is external, the inference cannot be logical. Given the impossibility of any non-inductive identification of the inner states of others, our inferences cannot be inductive either, since inductive correlation presupposes non-inductive identification. Hence it must be either analogical or hypothetical (an inference to the best explanation).

(vi) We cannot achieve genuine knowledge of others' mental states, as we can of our own. Hence we can, at best, only *believe* that things are thus-and-so with them.

This picture has seemed to many philosophers and psychologists to be persuasive, even unavoidable. Indeed, it is obtained by seemingly minor modifications to the array of grammatical truisms previously sketched. And if the latter are not viewed as grammatical propositions, but rather as empirical platitudes, it may well seem that the theses (A)–(D) which make up this picture are merely an enrichment or further elaboration of the elementary truisms. But in fact, while the truisms are grammatical, the theses are a subtle weave of metaphysical nonsense with the occasional plain falsehood. One has only to take a few further steps from the highroad of grammar for the nonsense to explode, as it were, before one.

(a) *Scepticism about other minds*: The picture sketched out above leads convincingly to the view that we can at best attain true beliefs about other people's experiences or mental states. But the tough-minded will rightly push on. Can we even attain justified *beliefs*? If all that is available as evidence is mere behaviour (bodily movements), is any inference really licit? The analogy between ourselves and others is shaky — after all, why should I assume that the causal connections that I am aware of in my case also obtain in theirs? Maybe where I see red, for example, others see green but *call* it 'red', and so forth. An inference to the best explanation is useless if its confirmation transcends any possible experience. And is it not consistent with anything that I could experience that others are mere automatons? This, surely, we can never prove or disprove!

(b) *Scepticism about communication*: If two people cannot have the very same experience, and if the words of their languages are defined by reference to their experiences, then the supposition of mutual intelligibility is distinctly shaky. It rests wholly on hope. For although one cannot in principle know what experiences others have, one hopefully assumes that what others call 'pain' or 'red' is what one calls thus oneself; or at least, that it is very similar. And here too, it seems, nothing could definitely show that to be so.

(c) *The impossibility of communication*: A moment's further reflection shows that such hopes must be futile. For it seems *logically* impossible for another person to have what I have when I have a pain, and if I define 'pain' by reference to what *I* have then, given the assumptions about meaning which are in play, it is logically impossible for another person to know what I mean by the word 'pain'. My language must, it seems, be a radically private one, viz. unintelligible to others. For it does not even make sense to suppose that what others have when they say 'I have a pain' is similar to what I have when I have a pain. This can only be supposed if there is some operational criterion of similarity. But although I surely have one in my own case, viz. a mental *sample*, it is logically impossible for there to be one for the interpersonal case.

(d) *Collapse into solipsism*: If what I *call* 'experience' is defined in my language ('the only language I understand') by reference to what *I* have and no one else can have, then there is no longer a question of whether, for all I know, others may not be automatons. Rather, it becomes obvious that it can make no sense for there to *be* any other owners of (what I call) experience. For the supposition that there are other subjects of experience seems to be tantamount to the supposition that someone else could have *this*, which I now have. But *I* uniquely have it. So *my* experience *is* experience: there can be no other. 'I am the vessel of life' (BB 65).

Of course, no one has ever believed this. That, however, does not diminish its philosophical importance. For arguably the only reason it has not been embraced is that philosophers have found it incredible.[6] And equally, the presuppositions of their metaphysical and linguistic theories lead ineluctably to solipsism. So it must not be dismissed as ridiculous, but must be closely examined to see how we were led to this monstrosity.

---

[6] They were wrong. It is not *incredible*, but either nonsense or, alternatively, a confused recommendation to adopt a new form of representation.

3. *Deviations and dialectic*

The above picture is a simple paradigm or range of connected paradigms, an Ideal Type rather than a set of theses any one philosopher has embraced in precisely this form. The history of modern philosophy since Descartes displays many deviations from it, as well as a variety of manoeuvres to try to avoid its unwelcome consequences. Cartesianism provided the parameters for a pernicious dialectic. Successive philosophical antitheses were adumbrated, each repudiating an element in previous accounts, yet retaining cancerous components that contributed to inevitable self-destruction. For what were rejected were never the deepest origins of the incoherence. 'One keeps forgetting to go right down to the foundations,' Wittgenstein observed, 'One doesn't put the question marks *deep* enough down' (CV 62). Consequently, although metastases were excised, their source was not located, and it continued to throw off fresh malignant growths.

Descartes' dualism involved two substances in causal interaction. The Occasionalists accepted the duality, but rejected the interaction. The Idealists repudiated the Cartesian conception of body, but retained an important part of the conception of mind either with (in the case of Berkeley) or without (in the case of Hume) the attendant idea of a mental substance. For their notion of inner sense and of self-knowledge was *au fond* Cartesian, and they conceived of the relation between the mental and behaviour as external, even though these were now construed as distinct sets of *ideas* which were externally related. Materialists and, later, behaviourists repudiated the Cartesian conception of the mind, but inherited distorted concepts of behaviour and of the human body. More recently, central state materialists reverted to a form of dualism, but identified the mental with the neural, replacing mind/body dualism with brain/body dualism, and conceiving of mental properties as properties of the brain that are causally responsible for behaviour. Currently functionalists repudiate the central state materialists' type-identity thesis in favour of a token–identity thesis in which 'mental states' are held to be functional states of a human organism that are, in some way or other, neurologically 'realized'. But the fundamental *philosophical* (theoretical) picture of the 'inner' and the 'outer' is retained. The dialectic continues, but the grammar of the mental is not laid bare, precisely because the questions do not go 'deep enough down'. Instead, metaphysical doctrines and pseudo-scientific theories are advocated which are no more than manifestations of grammatical confusions about our psychological and behavioural concepts and of methodological confusions about the nature of philosophical (conceptual) investigations. The acme of absurdity is to dream of a scientific millennium in which our psychological concepts would be jettisoned in favour of 'better' or 'more correct' concepts — as if it were our *language* that is at fault!

This pernicious dialectic is also visible more locally. So, for example, 'ownership' of experience is wrongly conceived as a relation of entities, and the debate turns on *what* entities stand in this relation: are they the 'self' (a mental substance) and 'experiences' (mental objects, events, states, and processes), or the body (a physical substance) and experiences (forms of behaviour and behavioural disposition), or the brain and experiences (neural states causally responsible for behaviour). The first-person pronoun is held to be a referring expression, and the disputable question is whether it refers to the 'self', the person speaking, the body, or the brain, or whether it merely signifies a logical construction. The moot point, however, is whether its role is that of a typical referring expression at all, and whether the subject of experience can coherently be conceived to be anything other than the living human being.

Psychological expressions are held to be names of inner objects (or properties), states, events, or processes which are logically akin to names of outer ones. So the debate turns on the nature of what these expressions name, whether their nominata are mental and *sui generis* or neural; or alternatively whether they signify behavioural dispositions and their actualization or just fictions. But what goes unexamined is the distinctive use of these expressions and the conditions under which they have a use. The question that needs to be addressed, however, is whether the grammar of 'is the name of an experience' is isomorphic with that of 'is the name of an object', and whether the concepts of mental state, event, process, etc. are as similar to the concepts of physical state, event, process, etc. as their grammatical appearance suggests (viz. that the former are, as it were, 'just like' the latter, only *mental*).

It is generally agreed that first-person present-tense psychological utterances are descriptions, and the question which is typically investigated is what it is that they describe, whether and how they are known to be true. The Cartesian conception of incorrigible knowledge is rejected by many philosophers in favour of corrigible knowledge. Infallible knowledge based on introspection is displaced by the metaphor of a corrigible self-scanning device causally linked to behaviour. But the moot question is how cognitive verbs are used in the context of first-person present-tense psychological sentences. Is 'I know I have a pain' or 'I know what I think' really a cognitive claim at all? And what is it, in the practice of speaking our language, that we actually call 'self-knowledge'? Granted that there is such a thing as describing one's own state of mind, is it obvious that 'I believe what you say', 'I think he will come', 'I have a toothache', 'I want a drink' are such descriptions? The grammar of 'description' and of 'state of mind' must be clarified, and likewise the question of whether genuine descriptions of one's own state of mind are grammatically akin to descriptions of states of the room, the garden, or the economy, etc. must be answered.

The inner/outer picture of the relationship between the mental and behaviour is generally accepted, or, in the characteristic pernicious dialectic, the inner is *reduced* to the outer. What is questioned in that move is *one* half of a distorted dichotomy, but it is rarely noticed that *both* halves misrepresent our concepts. Debate turns on the character of inferences from the 'outer' to the 'inner', but what counts as 'outer' is typically taken for granted, as is the characterization of the inference as being from the observed to the unobserved. But the behaviour of a human being is not the movement of a bodily machine, and experiences are not hidden *behind* anything. Moreover, our very descriptions of the 'outer' depend upon our terminology of the 'inner'.

Wittgenstein aimed to show how we can put an end to this wearisome dialectic, not by proposing an ultimate synthesis, but by attaining clarity, so that the philosophical problems will completely disappear (PI §133). To clear the ground of misguided theories, he had to dig right down to the grammatical roots of error. In relation to the philosophical tradition, the results of his labours are as radical as his parallel investigations in the philosophy of mathematics. The presuppositions of the centuries-old debate are laid bare and rejected. Clarifications are proposed: a private language is impossible; inner states stand in need of outer criteria; avowals are not descriptions of experience; 'I know I have a pain' is not an epistemic claim; different people can have the same experience; and so on. But these are not theses, set up in competition with previous philosophical theses. They are grammatical elucidations arrived at by painstaking examination of the uses of expressions. They are not philosophical propositions asserted to be true, but epitomes of grammatical surviews. If anyone challenges them, he should be answered not by defending a thesis, but by examining how the challenger uses psychological and behavioural expressions in practice. 'The problems are solved, not by giving new information, but by arranging what we have always known' (PI §109).

The net of Wittgenstein's arguments is densely woven. He moves from strand to strand as he follows each thread until arriving at a knot. To unravel that typically requires going off in another direction before returning to pick up the thread and follow it — until the next knot is encountered. The different strands in the weave can be separated. In subsequent essays the themes of privacy, avowals and descriptions, private ostensive definition, criteria, the 'inner' and the 'outer', minds and machines, behaviour and behaviourism, are tackled separately. The price is twofold. First, one may generate the impression that the various issues are mutually independent. But the argument against the possibility of a private language is not independent of the repudiation of the traditional picture of self-knowledge. The account of first-person utterances is not independent of the insight that behaviour is a *criterion* of the mental, and that in turn hangs on a transformed conception of behaviour. This involves rejecting behaviourism and examining afresh the conception of inference from the 'outer' to the 'inner'. All these grammatical insights cannot be severed from the dramatic focal shift in the representation of the concepts of the 'inner' and the 'outer'. Secondly, by separating the interwoven strands of Wittgenstein's discussion, one's account gains in local *Übersichtlichkeit* at the cost of increasing the difficulty of obtaining a global surview. For each confusion in the history of the philosophical debate derives support from misconceptions *elsewhere* in the complex structure of psychological and behavioural concepts. (Hence removing *one* buttress, as it were, leaves the overall structure intact.) The great difficulty lies in holding all in mind simultaneously, for as light is shed upon one aspect, the others sink into shadow. The only remedy is to examine the structure from each angle again and again, to work on oneself until one can grasp the whole. Surveying the concepts we use in talking about and giving expression to our inner life is no less difficult than surveying our inner life.

II

PRIVACY

1. The traditional picture

When we reflect upon the nature of our experience and its objects, it is easy to become captivated by a misleading picture of a fundamental ontological duality which we characterize as the physical and the mental. The physical world consists of objects that exist in an objective spatio-temporal framework, that are made of matter of one kind or another, and that interact with each other in physical processes and events. But, as Frege remarked, 'even an unphilosophical man soon finds it necessary to recognize an inner world distinct from the outer world, a world of sense-impressions, of creatures of his imagination, of sensations, of feelings and moods, a world of inclinations, wishes and decisions'.[1] If we succumb to this philosophical picture of the mental as *a world*, we will be prone to populate it with objects, states, events, and processes which we conceive to be, as it were, just like physical objects, states, events, and processes, only immaterial or ethereal (BB 47).

Corresponding to this distinction, a further, metaphysical, duality is characteristically introduced. Objects in the physical world are independent existences. They belong to the public domain, can be perceived by all who are appropriately situated, can often be owned, shared among several owners, or exist unowned. But objects in the 'inner world' are *essentially* owned: 'It seems absurd to us that a pain, a mood, a wish should go around the world without an owner independently. A sensation is impossible without a sentient being. The inner world presupposes somebody whose inner world it is.'[2] Not only are these inner objects essentially owned, they are also essentially untransferable and unshareable. Each person's inner world is metaphysically private property (LPE 277).

To someone who thinks thus, yet another duality, this time an epistemological one, will seem fitting. If the inner world is private property, it is natural to suppose that its owner has privileged access to it. It seems that he can know in a unique way what objects, states, or processes are in it. For while anyone can perceive the public objects in the physical world by means of his senses, only the owner of an inner world can apprehend its occupants by means of introspection. 'Internal sense'[3] or 'inner-sense'[4] is the source of our knowledge of the subjective objects

---

[1] G. Frege, 'Thoughts', repr. in B. McGuinness *Collected Papers on Mathematics, Logic, and Philosophy*, ed. B. McGuinness (Blackwell, Oxford and New York, 1984), p. 360.
[2] Ibid.
[3] Locke, *An Essay Concerning Human Understanding*, Bk. II, Ch. i, Sect. 4.
[4] Kant, *Critique of Pure Reason*, A22/B37.

in our private inner world, and it gives us an *immediate, non-inferential, acquaintance* with them, which contrasts with the inferential, perception-mediated knowledge that we strive to attain of objects in the public domain.

When I see the sun, I am often aware of my seeing the sun; thus 'my seeing the sun' is an object with which I have acquaintance. When I desire food, I may be aware of my desire for food; thus 'my desiring food' is an object with which I am acquainted. Similarly, we may be aware of our feeling pleasure or pain, and generally of the events which happen in our minds. This kind of acquaintance, which may be called self-consciousness, is the source of all our knowledge of mental things. It is obvious that it is only what goes on in our minds that can be thus known immediately.[5]

Not only is our knowledge of the inner immediate, according to this venerable picture, it is also certain. Descartes argued that as long as we restrain ourselves from imputing the character of our current experiences to anything 'outside the mind', then our sensations and thoughts (*cogitationes*) are 'clearly and distinctly perceived',[6] and hence *indubitable*. Unlike the physical world, the inner world is *transparent* to its owner:

Since all actions and sensations of the mind are known to us by consciousness, they must necessarily appear in every particular what they are, and be what they appear. Everything that enters the mind, being in reality a perception, 'tis impossible anything should to *feeling* appear different. This were to suppose that even where we are most intimately conscious, we might be mistaken.[7]

To the dualities of the physical and mental worlds, and of the public and private, there correspond epistemological dualities of the dubitable and indubitable, the corrigible and incorrigible. 'I cannot doubt that I have a visual impression of green, but it is not so certain that I see a limeleaf. So . . . we find certainty in the inner world, while doubt never leaves us in our excursions into the external world.'[8] It seems therefore that the private is better known than the public. It is a striking, if somewhat paradoxical, feature of philosophers of the post-Cartesian, materialist era to have argued persistently that mind is better known than matter.

Wittgenstein subjected this traditional philosophical picture to critical scrutiny. In every respect he found it a distortion of grammar in the flawed mirror of metaphysics. His resolution of the tangle of philosophical problems in this domain is not a version of 'logical behaviourism' or a form of 'verificationism'. Indeed, it does not lie on the traditional map of possibilities at all. Rather, he aimed to undermine the whole range of

[5] B. Russell, *The Problems of Philosophy* (Oxford University Press, London, 1967), pp. 26f.
[6] Descartes, *The Principles of Philosophy*, Pt. I, Sect. 68.
[7] Hume, *A Treatise on Human Nature*, Bk. I, Pt. iv, Sect. 2, ed. L. A. Selby-Bigge, rev. P. H. Nidditch (Clarendon Press, Oxford, 1978), p. 190.
[8] Frege, 'Thoughts', p. 367.

received options, leaving behind, as it were, 'only bits of stone and rubble' (PI §118).[9]

2. Private ownership

One source of the misconceptions of the classical picture lies in the idea that another person cannot have my experiences: you cannot have my toothache or feel my anger; nor can you have my mental images, for they lie before my mind's eye — they are inner objects in my subjective world. This claim seems to say something about the nature of experience — not something physiological or psychological — but rather something metapsychological or metaphysical. It seems to pinpoint the essence of personal experience that is antecedent to its causal connections with other phenomena (LPE 277). Two people can jointly own the same house; or one can own it first and then sell it to another. Two people can *have* the same room in college, can share it, occupy it simultaneously or successively. But 'Nobody else has my pain. Someone may have sympathy with me, but still my pain belongs to me and his sympathy to him. He has not got my pain, and I have not got his feeling of sympathy.'[10]

Of course, we do say that two people can have the same pain, e.g. a throbbing headache in the temples. But, the philosopher will add, this means that the pains are exactly alike, not that they are identical. 'It would be a contradiction to speak of the feelings of two different people as being numerically the same; it is logically impossible that one person should literally feel another's pain.'[11] This seems plausible, for surely if A and B each have a headache, there are *two* headaches, not one! After all, two people cannot *share* a headache as they can share a room or an umbrella, or as two households can share a telephone line or a garden! Another man's headache is, *ex vi termini*, another headache (cf. FA §27). Their respective sensations are qualitatively identical but numerically distinct.

We are tempted to think thus in as much as we project the grammar of names of physical objects onto expressions signifying experiences. If we think of each person's experiences as objects in a particular inner, subjective world, we will also think that an object in one inner world can no more migrate to another inner world than it can enter the public world of physical objects. Not only can you not have my pain while I

---

[9] This essay is concerned only with two common presuppositions underlying the traditional conception, viz. the privacy of 'ownership' and epistemic privacy. Others are discussed in later essays. The discussion of private 'ownership' of experience rectifies a mistake in Volume 2, pp. 270f. and 279 (amended in the 2nd impression of the paperback edition). Cf. also Exg. §253.

[10] Frege, 'Thoughts', p. 361.

[11] A. J. Ayer, *The Problem of Knowledge* (Penguin, Harmondsworth, 1956), p. 202.

have it, since pains are unshareable, but you cannot even have my pain after I no longer have it. If I do not have the pain that previously belonged to me, then that pain has passed, it no longer exists. It cannot enter the inner world of another person, for there is, as it were, no point of contact between distinct subjective worlds. It is part of the nature of experiences to belong to a subject. For the very identity of these inner objects is bound up with the inner world to which they belong.

> States or experiences, one might say, *owe* their identity as particulars to the identity of the person whose states or experiences they are. From this it follows immediately that if they can be identified as particular states or experiences at all, they must be possessed or ascribable . . . in such a way that it is logically impossible that a particular state or experience in fact possessed by someone should have been possessed by anyone else. The requirements of identity rule out logical transferability of ownership.[12]

The inclination to think thus may be strengthened by the unreflective assumption that the location of a sensation is a criterion for who has it. A's pains, one wants to say, are the pains in A's body. If there is a pain in A's knee, it is A's pain. B may have a similar pain in his own knee, but since B's knee cannot be in the same place as A's knee, his pain cannot be in the same place either. So their respective pains are qualitatively identical, but numerically distinct.

In response to this, Wittgenstein invites us to 'consider what makes it possible in the case of physical objects to speak of "two exactly the same", for example, to say "This chair is not the one you saw here yesterday, but exactly the same as it" ' (PI §253). Evidently we draw such a distinction by reference to spatial location: one chair cannot be in two places at the same time, and two chairs cannot simultaneously occupy the same location. Is it not the same with pains? Since A's pain is in *his* body and B's pain in his distinct body, they are, by parity of reasoning, numerically distinct.

The reasoning is confused, for two different language-games are being crossed. There are many different uses of 'in' ('in the afternoon', 'in the army', 'in the story', 'in heaven', 'in the mind', 'in a sentence', etc.), and among them different senses of location (BB 8) — in the drawer, in the book, in the crowd, in the picture. The expression 'a pain in the leg' has a quite different grammar from 'a pin in the leg', even though both determine locations, and we generate confusion by construing the former on the model of the latter. If an object is in X (as a penny may be in my pocket), it can be taken out of X. It must be smaller than X, otherwise it will not fit and will, at best, be half in, half out. It can be perceived to be in X by, for example, opening X. But while it is true that you cannot perceive the pain in my leg, as indeed you cannot see the pin

---

[12] P. F Strawson, *Individuals* (Methuen, London, 1959), pp. 97f.

in the closed pin-box, the pain is not *in* my leg in the same sense. Even if you open up my leg, you will not find my pain inside it. It cannot be extracted or removed (any more than can a cut in my leg), and although it can be made to go away by an analgesic, when it goes away, it does not go elsewhere. A pain in my finger is neither larger nor smaller than my finger, although it may be the whole of my finger that throbs painfully or only the middle joint. If I have a pain in my foot and my foot is in my shoe, I do not have a pain in my shoe (and the same applies to having a cut in my foot), whereas if I have some money in my purse and my purse is in my pocket, I do have some money in my pocket. In short, 'pain in my leg' does not determine a location in the same way as 'penny in my pocket' does. Hence we should be suspicious of the claim that since A's pain is in his foot and B's pain is in *his* foot, therefore their pains are in different places.

It is noteworthy that it is not quite right to claim that if A has a pain, it *must* be 'in' his body, for this is liable to be misconstrued. An amputee will commonly locate a phantom pain where the amputated limb would have been had it not been removed; but it manifests confusion to suggest that in these anomalous cases the person who has the pain is mistaken about where his pain is. For it would be incoherent to argue that his pain is actually located elsewhere, in a part of his body which does *not* hurt, e.g. the stump of the amputated limb! Where it hurts is not necessarily where the injury or infection is, as is evident also from the case of reflected pains. The criteria for the location of a person's pain are where he points to or where he says it is. These normally coincide, i.e. if he says that his leg hurts, then he also points at his leg to indicate where it hurts. So too, the pain is located in the place he assuages, in the limb he limps on or nurses and so on (PI §302). Phantom pains are anomalous, for there is no such thing here as assuaging the place to which the amputee points. Similarly, he may say that his foot hurts, even though he has no foot, and he points not at his foot but at the place where his foot would have been. But although this exception could not become the rule, it does not stretch the concept of pain-location to the breaking-point, since the person did have a limb where he points. We may say that he is wrong in saying that his foot hurts, but right in saying that he has a pain 'there ↗', where his foot would have been. This degree of conflict of criteria can be accommodated. It is a rule of grammar that a person's pain is where he indicates, avows, etc., not a truth of metaphysics that pains are *in* bodies. But the behavioural regularities which give point to our grammatical convention that a person's identification of the location of his pain is authoritative, i.e. a criterion for the location of his pain, consist in the fact that he assuages his injured limb, clutches the part of his body that hurts, and so forth. If a person were systematically to insist that his pains were outside his body, we would not understand him, not because he was *mistaken*, but because the concept of pain-location would be stretched beyond the breaking-point.

The concept of pain-location is parasitic upon the concept of the sufferer from pain, for the location of a pain is where the sufferer says it is. The person who has a pain is he who *manifests* or expresses the pain (or would do so but for such-and-such reasons). Hence it can be misleading to say that A's pains are the pains in A's body, for that may wrongly suggest that the location of a pain determines the possession of a pain, as if 'Where is it?' were prior to 'Whose is it?' or 'Who is hurt?' But, on the contrary, we can only ask *where* a pain is if we can say *who* is suffering. If two people have a pain in their left thumb, we say that they have a pain in the same place. The fact that their thumbs are in different places no more implies that their pains are in different places than the fact that they are sucking their swollen thumbs implies that they have a pain in their mouths. Consequently, it is wrong to say that two people *cannot* (metaphysically!) have a pain in the same place, and mistaken to infer that two people cannot have the same pain *because* their pains must be in different places. (For a discussion of the Siamese twins' pain at the point of juncture, see Exg. §253.)

The source of confusion lies in the superficial similarities between the grammar of expressions signifying, roughly speaking, experiences and the grammar of names of objects. Unmasking further differences should dispel the temptation to think that the foregoing arguments are indecisive. We speak of sensations, sense-impressions, feelings, and moods (but not so much emotions) as *things that we have*. In philosophical discourse we talk of the 'owner' of experiences, and insist, as Frege did, that while ownership of objects is contingent and transferable, possession of experiences is essential and inalienable (i.e. the experiences only 'exist' in as much as they belong to someone). If a person owns a car, a certain relationship obtains between two objects. Is it not the same when a person has a headache? Of course, in the first case, the related objects are independent existences in that the same car may be owned by someone else or by no one at all. Whereas 'subjective objects', as Frege called them, are dependent existences. But that is precisely the difference between objects in the physical world and objects in the inner world! Since my pain is an object in my inner world, no one else can *have* my pain — and does that not mean that I stand to this pain in a relation which no one else can have to it? So, despite the previous clarifications, does it not follow that since you manifestly cannot have my pain, your pain cannot be identical with mine, but only exactly similar?

We are deceived here by the *form* of our language, and need to be reminded of the wide range of different logical categories that are represented in the grammatical form of ownership. We speak of having a car, and here there is a relation between a person and a chattel. The car I have belongs to me, but I might sell it to someone else. Indeed, I might have — be in possession of — a car which belongs to my friend, for he may have lent it to me. We also speak of having a wife or a son, and although this signifies a relationship between two particulars, it is not one of ownership at all, but of being married to or being the parent of a person. We also speak of having a duty or an obligation, and this too may signify a relationship, not a relationship between a person and an object called 'a duty' or 'an obligation', but rather a relationship (e.g.) to a person to whom the duty is owed or to whom a promise was made. Similarly, we talk of having a cold, a sharp tongue, or a sense of humour, and in these cases no relationship between a person and an object of any kind is signified. There is no such thing as having a cold and wondering whether it belongs to one — though one might wonder from whom one caught it. Finally, we talk of *having* a relationship to something or someone, and here it is perspicuous that we are employing the form of ownership bereft of any content at all. For to have a relation to something is not to be related to a relation. If we say that the pen has or stands in the relation of *being to the left of* to the ruler, we do not mean that the pen has two relations, one to the ruler and the other to the relation of being to the left of.

Is having a pain a matter of standing in a relationship to an object (an identifiable particular)? And if so, what relationship is masked here by the form of ownership? An obvious answer is suggested by the grammar of 'pain', for do we not speak of *feeling* pain, as we speak of feeling a pin or feeling the warmth of the fire? And is feeling something not standing in a certain relation to an object, viz. a perceptual relation? Grammar is deceptive here. Feeling a pain is not a form of perception. One can feel a pin in the sofa only if there is a pin to be felt; but if there is no pin there, it may *seem* to one that one feels a pin. Furthermore, there may be a pin, and one may feel *for* it with one's fingertips and yet *fail* to detect it. But to feel a pain *is* to have a pain — one cannot feel it and not have it, nor can one have a pain and not feel it. Nor can it *seem* to one as if one has a pain although one has none. Although 'having' here is replaceable by 'feeling', neither expression signifies a relation any more than 'pain' signifies a relatum. To have a pain is to be in pain, to suffer. It is not to *own* anything. It makes no sense to wonder whether the pain I have belongs to me or to someone else. Neither 'It belongs to me' nor 'It does not belong to me' has any sense when what I have is a headache. Two people with migraine may suffer in exactly the same way, viz. both have a splitting headache. And then we say that they have the same pain. Is it then numerically the same? No — it is neither numerically the same nor qualitatively the same. That distinction belongs to the domain of objects and has no application here. The question 'Whose pain?' is answered by identifying the person who manifests pain. The question 'What pain?' is answered by specifying the intensity, phenomenal characteristics, and location of the pain as indicated by the sufferer. And two people who suffer from the same illness may indeed have the same pain, just as two chairs may have the same colour.

A final objection may be raised. Pains, after all, are not like colours. If an abstract painting consists of two red squares on a blue ground, one could call it 'A study in two colours' but not 'A study in three colours'. But if I have a pain in my foot and a similar pain in my hand, surely I have two pains, not one! We may grant this; for in so far as we count pains, difference of location in the subject's body implies *another* pain, and to that extent we do have a thin analogue of the numerical/ qualitative identity as applied to objects. But it does not follow that if you have a headache and I have a headache, then there are two headaches or even one headache (as opposed to two aching heads) in the room, since headaches are not *in the room* at all. Rather, there are two people in the room suffering from headache — which may be the same or different. To the extent that pains are countable, countability is limited to each person.

The grammatical form of ownership characterizes not only our discourse about sensations, sense-impressions, and feelings, but also about ideas, opinions, beliefs, and thoughts. Labouring under the illusion that two people cannot have identical pains, sense-impressions, or feelings, but only exactly similar ones, we may, like Frege, hasten to ensure that two people *can* have, think, or entertain the *identical* thought. For, we may argue, if discourse is to be intelligible, surely what A thinks must be communicable to B; it must be possible for B to grasp the very same thought that A entertains. Indeed, if logic is to govern our discourse, then if A thinks and says that *p* and B says that not-*p*, they must be contradicting each other — which will only be the case if one and the same thought, viz. that *p*, is in question, affirmed by A and denied by B. Hence it is tempting to insist, as Frege did, that thoughts are like experiences in not being perceptible objects in the physical world, but unlike them in not being subjective objects in the inner world that is private to each subject of experience. Like objects in the physical world, thoughts do not need an owner. They are objective, independent existences, like substances, only not spatio-temporal. And one may even go so far as to postulate a 'third realm' for them to exist in, together with numbers and other abstract objects. This seems to ensure that it is intelligible that two people may grasp the very same thought.

This Platonizing myth-making is both incoherent and redundant. It is incoherent in as much as it would only make sense to talk of different people thinking the numerically identical thought if it made sense to talk of them thinking qualitatively identical, but numerically distinct, thoughts. But it does not; for that distinction, which applies to the domain of objects, no more has application to thoughts than it does to experiences. It is redundant, since the apparent difficulty this manoeuvre was designed to meet is itself illusory. Frege was right to deny the psychologicians' thesis that different people's thoughts can at best be qualitatively identical, but misguided to think that the only alternative is to reify thoughts in order to ensure the possibility of the numerical identity of different people's thoughts. (For further critical analysis of 'private ownership' of experience, see Exg. §253.)

3. *Epistemic privacy*

The idea that since no one else can have the very same experience as I have, then no one else can really know what it is like is robbed of part of its force by Wittgenstein's clarification of the concept of having an experience and having the same experience. Nevertheless, the supposition that when I have, say, a pain, I know that I do, and moreover know this with certainty, is still firmly entrenched. After all, I am *aware* of the pains I have, I *feel* them, and if I sincerely say that I am in pain (have such-and-such a visual impression, want this, or intend that), no one can gainsay me. The mainstream of philosophy has insisted upon this fundamental principle — indeed typically taking it as an inexplicable datum of experience:

> When a man is conscious of pain, he is certain of its existence; when he is conscious that he doubts or believes, he is certain of the existence of those operations.
> But the irresistible conviction he has of the reality of those operations is not the effect of reasoning; it is immediate and intuitive. The existence therefore of those passions and operations of our minds, of which we are conscious, is a first principle, which nature requires us to believe upon her authority.
> If I am asked to prove that I cannot be deceived by consciousness — to prove that it is not a fallacious sense — I can find no proof. I cannot find any antecedent truth from which it is deduced, or upon which its evidence depends. It seems to disdain any such derived authority, and to claim my assent in its own right.[13]

This infallibilist conception of 'inner sense' did not go unchallenged. If 'inner sense' is a form of self-observation yielding knowledge, if awareness of, for example, pain is akin to awareness or consciousness of objects by means of a perceptual faculty, then it is, as Reid admitted, a mystery that it is infallible. As long as the putative infallibility was viewed as a fact of nature, it was bound to be challenged. Comte argued that 'this pretended direct contemplation of the mind by itself is pure illusion', on the ground that 'The same organ' (viz. the mind) cannot simultaneously perceive, feel, or think, and observe itself so doing: 'The thinker cannot

---

[13] T. Reid, *On the Intellectual Powers of Man*, Essay VI, Ch. V, in Sir William Hamilton (ed.), *The Works of Thomas Reid*, 6th edition (Edinburgh, 1863), Vol. I, p. 442.

divide himself into two, of whom one reasons whilst the other observes
him reason. The organ observed and the organ observing being in this
case identical, how could observation take place?'[14] Mill responded by
insisting

that a fact may be studied through the medium of memory, not at the very moment of
our perceiving it, but the moment after: and this is really the mode in which our best
knowledge of our intellectual acts is generally acquired. We reflect on what we have
been doing when the act is past, but when its impression in the memory is still fresh.
Unless in one of these ways, we could not have acquired the knowledge which
nobody denies us to have, of what passes in our minds.[15]

James agreed with Comte that 'No subjective state, whilst present, is its
own object; its object is always something else,'[16] and with Mill that in
practice, memory may always be legitimately invoked. But, he stressed,
memory is fallible. To be in a mental state is not sufficient for
knowledge, otherwise babies would be infallible psychologists. One
must not only *have* one's mental states, one must also 'report them and
write about them, name them, classify and compare them and trace their
relations to other things. . . . And as in the naming, classing, and
knowing of things in general we are notoriously fallible, why not also
here?' He concluded that 'introspection is difficult and fallible; and that
the difficulty is simply that of all observation of whatever kind.'[17]

The arguments were reasonable, given the incoherent premises that
saying what one feels or thinks, reporting one's mental states, etc. rest on
observation of some kind, and that awareness of one's sensations or
emotions is of the same category as awareness of objects. Seeing and
hearing are ways of acquiring knowledge about one's environment. But
having a pain, feeling cheerful, thinking something are not ways of
acquiring knowledge about one's pains, feelings, or thoughts. To be
aware or conscious of a pain, a mood, or of thinking does not belong to
the category of perceptual awareness, let alone to 'inner perception', but
to the categories of capacity, in particular of capacity to say how things
are with one, of receptive attention, and (in certain cases) of realization.[18]

---

[14] Auguste Comte, *Cours de Philosophie Positive*, Vol. I, pp. 34–8; quoted in W. James,
The Principles of Psychology (Dover, New York, 1950), Vol. I, p. 188.
[15] J. S. Mill, *Auguste Comte and Positivism*, 3rd edition (1882), p. 64.
[16] James, *Principles of Psychology*, Vol. I, p. 190.
[17] Ibid., pp. 189f.
[18] Recent writers have recapitulated the confusions of the nineteenth century in
challenging the classical thesis of the infallibility of introspection as *factually false*. One
example, commonly adduced, demonstrates the muddle: a man being tortured expects
another searing pain; his torturers place a piece of ice on his back, and he screams. Did he
not believe, falsely, that he had a pain? We might ask the victim why he screamed. He could
answer in two ways: (a) because it hurt frightfully — in which case we have discovered that
in these circumstances a piece of ice can cause as much pain as a red-hot iron; (b) because he
thought it was going to hurt, and screamed in alarm and anticipation. Could he not venture

Wittgenstein's response to the traditional picture of self-knowledge was radical, indeed revolutionary. He denied that we *know* about our current experiences. Contrary to the empiricist, rationalist, and even Kantian conceptions of the 'inner', he insisted that it is wrong, even *nonsense*, to say 'I know I have a pain' (PI §246, pp. 221f.). Such an utterance can be a grammatical assertion, or merely an emphatic affirmation, but not, as philosophers typically take it to be, an epistemic claim. And if it is philosophers' nonsense to claim that I know that I am having such-and-such an experience, it is *a fortiori* absurd to say that in inner sense we have paradigms of propositions that are known with certainty, let alone that they exemplify incorrigible knowledge. Wittgenstein repudiated the very idea of 'inner sense' as an analogue of perception, and denied that an avowal (*Äusserung*) of experience is a report of one's observations or a description of what has been observed *in foro interno*. Our talk of 'introspection', of 'inner vision', is merely a metaphor (Vol. XVI, 61), and the idea of privileged access, viz. that I can 'see' within me, where no one else can, is an absurdity. And even the more modest claim that I must be in a better position than anyone else to say what I am experiencing is brought into question (LPE 279). Consequently, in so far as there is such a thing as self-knowledge, it does not consist in knowing the truth of an array of first-person present-tense experiential propositions, such as 'I have a toothache', 'I have a visual impression of red', or 'I intend to go soon'. ,

Wittgenstein's arguments, if correct, overturn centuries of consensus. It should, however, be borne in mind that, faithful to his methodological principles, he was not propounding new theories in opposition to antiquated ones. He did not contend that we are ignorant about our own states of mind, or that our 'introspective investigations' are in fact subject to doubt. In denying that we have privileged access to our own mental states, he was not suggesting that we have unprivileged, indirect access. In each case a proposition of traditional philosophy is rejected, not because it is *false* and its denial true, but because it is nonsense — or does not mean what philosophers typically take it to mean. In all cases his manoeuvre is to draw our attention to rules of grammar and to show

---

a different answer, viz. that he thought he was in agony, but was mistaken? No — for this would invite the question 'How did you find out that you were wrong?' Did the sensation change after a few seconds? — in which case he *was* initially in agony, but it then subsided. Or was the sensation the same? — in which case, he initially misidentified it. But that would make sense only if there were available to him criteria of identity for pain in his own case, which he applied incorrectly, private criteria which determine for himself alone whether what he 'has' is a pain or not. That, however, makes no sense (see 'Private ostensive definition'). There is no room in our grammar for a sensation's *seeming* to its owner to be a pain but not really being one. Did it *feel* like a pain, even though it was not one? This is patent nonsense, for there is no 'seeming' here at all. There is no room in our grammar for thinking, rightly or wrongly, that one is in pain; and if we try to make room for this grammatical articulation, the language-game collapses into incoherence.

how we mistakenly construe a grammatical connection or exclusion for an empirical or 'super-empirical' one about the essential nature of the mental.

It makes sense to say of a person that he knows that such-and-such is the case only if it also makes *sense* to deny that he does. For 'A knows that *p*' is meant to be an empirical epistemic proposition, and hence to exclude an alternative. But if there is no such thing as A's being ignorant of *p*, i.e. if it is unintelligible that *p* should be the case, yet A does *not* know it, then 'A knows that *p*' says nothing about A's knowledge. So if the form of words 'A was in pain but he did not know it' is ruled out, i.e. if it does not describe a specifiable possibility, then 'A was in pain and he knew it' is likewise excluded. So too, 'I know I am in pain' can only be conceived as an epistemic utterance if 'I do not know whether I am in pain' is held to be intelligible. But there is no such thing as being ignorant of whether one is in pain; someone who said 'Maybe I am in agony but I do not know whether I am' would not be understood. There is room for indeterminacy ('I am not sure whether the sensation I have is to be called "a pain" or just "a dull ache" '), and, in appropriate cases, e.g. one's thoughts, for indecision ('I don't really know what I think about X'), but not for ignorance.

It might be urged that there is a difference between being in pain and knowing that one is in pain, for in the latter case, over and above the pain, one must recognize that what one has *is* a pain. And, one might add, that is why we do not say of animals that they *know* they are in pain for they are not 'self-conscious' creatures as we are. This is doubly wrong. First, it makes sense to talk of recognizing only if it also *makes sense* to talk of not recognizing or misrecognizing (LSD 111f.). But it does not make sense to say 'I had a pain, but I did not recognize it', let alone to say 'I had a pain, but I thought it was a pleasant sensation'. If someone were to manifest normal pain-behaviour and later say 'I had a pain, but I did not recognize it', we would not know what he was trying to tell us. Secondly, while it is true that we do not say of animals that they know they are in pain, we do not say that they do not know whether they are in pain either. And when our pet is manifestly suffering, we do not console ourselves with the thought that although it is in pain it mercifully does not know it. The simple truth is that animals do not *say* they are in pain, whereas human beings do. The fact that they do not say so does not show that they are ignorant, and the fact that we do does not show that we are better informed. What it shows is that we have learnt to manifest our pain in ways unavailable to animals, whose behavioural repertoire is limited to pre-linguistic behaviour.

The verb 'to know' belongs together with a large group of related epistemic verbs. It makes sense to talk of knowing that *p* where it makes sense to talk of finding out, coming to know, or learning that *p*. But when I have a pain, I do not find out. If one knows that p, one can answer the question 'How do you know?' by citing grounds, e.g. evidence for p or saying that one perceived that p. But when I have a toothache, there is no such thing as my inferring this from evidence, nor is there any such thing as my perceiving my toothache. If it makes sense to talk of knowing that p, it also makes sense to talk of guessing, surmising, and conjecturing that p, and hence too of confirming or disconfirming one's guess or conjecture. But these too make no sense in the case of 'I am in pain' or 'I intend to go'.

Misled by metaphors (e.g. 'the mind's eye') and by homonyms (e.g. '*feeling* pain'), the prevailing tradition in epistemology has confused the *grammatical exclusion* of ignorance with the presence of knowledge. But the exclusion of ignorance, viz. the senselessness of 'I do not know whether I am in pain' also excludes knowledge. 'I know I am in pain' is not an epistemic statement; 'I feel a pain' is not a perceptual claim; and 'I am aware of a pain' is not a cognitive judgement.

Hence too the venerable thesis of the transparency of the mind is confused. It makes sense to say that something appears thus-and-so to a person and that it is as it appears, only if it also makes sense for it to be other than it appears. But it does not make sense to say 'It seems to me that I have a pain, but actually I don't have one', or 'You think you have a pain, but you don't really have one'. So one cannot argue that it is a peculiarity of the mental that things are as they appear and appear exactly as they are, and that *therefore* we know, without a doubt, how things are in the 'inner world' that belongs to us alone. For if there are no 'appearances' in the domain of the mental (from the subject's point of view), then appearances are no guide to knowledge, let alone an infallible guide. So much the better, one might think; for if there is no gap between appearance and reality, then believing that things are thus-and-so with me is a sufficient condition for knowing that they are. But that is mistaken; for it only makes sense to believe that things are empirically thus-and-so if it makes sense for one's belief to be false. Believing truly is inseparable from the possibility of believing falsely. But there is no such thing here as believing falsely; 'He believes he is in pain, but he is wrong' is nonsense. Hence there is no such thing as *believing* that one is in pain.

A similar confusion occurs in the case of certainty and incorrigibility. It is true that I cannot doubt whether I am in pain, but that is not because whenever I am in pain I am certain that I am. It is not that I am *unable*, however hard I try, to doubt whether I am in pain. Rather, nothing counts as *doubting* that one is in pain. Doubt is excluded by grammar, not refuted by grounds for certainty. It makes no sense to say 'I may be in pain or I may not, I am not sure'. Of course, I may be uncertain as to whether the sensation I have qualifies as a pain or is just a rather unpleasant feeling, but *that* doubt does not stem from ignorance, and it is not to be resolved by gathering further information. The apparent incorrigibility of avowals of pain is a distorted reflection of the grammatical exclusion of error. 'I thought I was in pain, but I was mistaken' is nonsense (although 'I screamed because I thought it was going to hurt' is perfectly in order). It is true, as Reid put it, that 'I cannot be deceived by consciousness' in the matter of my sensations; but that it is not because I am so perceptive or because that of which I am conscious is so easy to recognize, but rather because there is no such thing as deception of this kind in this particular language-game. 'I cannot make a mistake' here is like 'I cannot be beaten at patience'. (But *self-deception* is, of course, common when it comes to such 'inner states' as emotions and attitudes – whereon hangs another tale.)

Locke argued that it is 'impossible for anyone to perceive without *perceiving* that he does perceive. When we see, hear, smell, taste, feel, meditate, or will anything, we know that we do so.'[19] That is misconceived: I may see that A sees something, hear what he is manifestly listening to, apprehend what he is thinking, and find out what he wants. But I cannot see that I see something or perceive that I hear a noise – there is no such thing. James observed glibly that 'The word introspection need hardly be defined — it means, of course, the looking into one's own mind and reporting what we there discover. *Everyone agrees that we there discover states of consciousness.*'[20] But I can no more *look into* my mind than I can look into another's, and we often have more insight into the mind of another than into our own. The perceptual metaphor bound up etymologically with the word 'introspection' is profoundly misleading in philosophy and psychology. We confuse the ability to say how things are with us, what we are feeling or perceiving, what we think or want, with the ability to *see* — with the mind's eye, of course — and *therefore*, we think, we can say what is 'within' us.

This picture of our capacity to give verbal expression to our experiences, desires, thoughts, and intentions is distorted by the perceptual model of introspection. For to be able to say that one has a pain when one has one is not to have access to anything, let alone *privileged* access, and an avowal of pain is not the report of an observation. Of course, one can report one's pains, as when one tells the doctor that one's pain this morning is not so severe as yesterday and that the throbbing has subsided. But the cry 'Ow, I've hurt my finger' is not such a report. Similarly, there is such a thing as observation in this domain, as when I record the course of my pains in a diary for medical purposes; but it can be misleading to characterize this as 'observation', since it is not based on *observing* anything (RPP II §177). To say to another 'I'm furious with

---

[19] Locke, *Essay Concerning Human Understanding*, Bk. II, Ch. xxvii, Sect. 11.
[20] James, *Principles of Psychology*, Vol. I, p. 185.

you' is typically to express my anger, not to describe something accessible to me alone by introspection, just as to say 'I love you' is to avow one's affections, not to describe oneself or one's emotion. Hence too it is not necessarily the case that I am in a better position than others to say what I see, feel, or think. If I am semi-delirious and in severe pain, I may be unable to do more than groan inchoately, but the doctor, familiar with the disease, may be able to describe my pains in detail. If I am in a fit of rage or ecstasy of delight, words may fail me, and my ability to express my feelings in words, as opposed to deeds, may be less than that of a bystander. And when I have difficulty in expressing my thoughts, someone else may articulate them much better than I could, and I may say 'Yes, that's exactly what I meant'.

What *is* true, but wholly distorted by the traditional picture of self-knowledge and self-awareness, is that *my word* has a privileged *status*. This is not because I have access to a private peep-show and so can describe what I see in it, whereas others cannot. Rather, it is because what I say is an expression or manifestation of my experience, whereas what others say of me is not. 'I have a headache' is typically a manifestation of pain, and comparable to a groan; 'I've decided — I'll go' is an expression of intention, and 'I think that such-and-such' is not a *description* of anything 'inner' but typically (in an appropriate context) an expression of opinion. The privileged status of my utterances is *grammatical*, not epistemic, and it is constituted by the fact that my utterances are *criteria* for how things are with me. They are not statements or reports of what I know, but expressions of what I think, manifestations of my will and purpose, and avowals of what I feel or perceive. (But one must not forget that we have here a whole spectrum of cases, which Wittgenstein described in detail; see 'Avowals and descriptions', §4.) There is indeed such a thing as self-knowledge and self-consciousness; but it does not consist of an array of reports and descriptions of one's sensations, perceptions, thoughts, and feelings. We say of a person that he is highly self-conscious if he has a heightened awareness of his own emotional life, reflects deeply on the character of his reactions, the pattern of his desires, and the subtle nuances of his motives. To attain authentic self-knowledge is typically far more difficult, not easier, than to achieve knowledge of the character, motivation, and personality of others.

Is there *no* use at all for 'I know . . .' in this domain? Does Wittgenstein's contention not fly in the face of linguistic usage? He anticipated this objection: 'If you bring up against me the case of people's saying "But I must know if I am in pain!", "Only you can know what you feel", and similar things, you should consider the occasion and purpose of these phrases. "War is war" is not an example of the law of identity, either' (PI p. 221). One may say 'I know I am in pain' as an emphatic assertion that I *am* in pain (PI §246), as one may say 'I know I intend to go to London' as an exasperated concession to someone who is nagging. Or one may use such expressions as grammatical statements to emphasize that doubt or uncertainty is senseless (PI §247). Of course, we also say such things as 'I don't know what I want (think, intend)'; but this is not an expression of ignorance to be resolved by more careful introspection. Rather, it is an expression of the uncertainty of indecision, and what is requisite is not information about my desires (thoughts, intentions), but resolution. We also say 'I know what I want (think, intend), but I'm not going to tell you'; but that is just to say that I do indeed want (think, intend) something but I am not going to say what it is, or to declare that my mind is made up but that I am going to keep my decision to myself. Wittgenstein was not legislating about linguistic usage, but rather pointing out that these expressions do not belong to the language-game to which they superficially appear to belong:

> If I say 'This statement has no sense', I could just point out statements with which we are inclined to mix it up, and point out the difference. This is all that is meant. — If I say 'It seems to convey something and doesn't', this comes to 'it seems to be of this kind, and isn't'. This statement becomes senseless only if you try to compare it with what you can't compare it with. What is wrong is to overlook the difference. (LSD 130)

If we take 'I know I am in pain', 'I know what I see', or 'I know what I want' as epistemic statements, as are 'I know he is in pain', 'I know what he sees', or 'I know what he wants', then we cross language-games and produce philosophers' nonsense (cf. PI p. 221). One should remember that it does not follow from the fact that one is playing a game on a chessboard and has a queen on the board that one is playing chess.

Objections come from various quarters. Surely, one may respond, one can lie about one's plans. But to lie is to know that *p* and to assert that not-*p* with intent to deceive. Does this not show that it *must* make sense to know that one has a pain? Equally, one remembers that one was in pain; but to remember is to know what one previously knew and not to have forgotten it. Does it not follow that if one can remember being in pain, one must have known that one was in pain? If I know that you know such-and-such, then surely I too know it, for are we not eyes and ears to each other? So if I know that you know that I am in pain, do I not therefore know that I am in pain? Surely, if there are nine other people in the room, I may know that no one in the room is in pain (if, e.g., we are all making merry). Does that not imply that I know that I am not in pain?

And finally, one might question the claim that I have no grounds for saying that I am in pain. For, after all, I have the best justification for saying so, namely that I feel the pain!

Wittgenstein anticipated these objections, or at least showed how they may be rebutted. To insist that one can lie about one's pain yet cannot know that one is in pain seems to imply that one can lie about something of which one is ignorant, which is absurd. But the complement of the grammatical observation that there is no such thing as knowing that one is in pain is that there is equally no such thing as not knowing (being ignorant of the fact) that one is in pain. To lie about one's pain is to be in pain and to say that one is not, or not to be in pain and to say that one is (LPE 280). Similarly, to remember that one was in pain is to have been in pain and not to have forgotton it, to know now that one was in pain – not to know now something one knew before. Only dogmatic adherence to a form of analysis (explanation) forces one to construe the recollection of pain as a retention of acquired knowledge. So too, I may, of course, realize that you know that I am in pain; but I neither need nor can use your authority to assure me that it is indeed true that I am in pain, since there is no such thing as my being sure that, or unsure whether, I am in pain. Your knowledge is authoritative for me only if it makes sense for me not to know what you know; but 'I don't know whether I am in pain or not, please tell me' is nonsense.

Although my sincere avowal of pain is authoritative, i.e. constitutes a criterion for others to say of me 'He is in pain', that is not because I have a special epistemic authority with respect to my pains, but because my avowal of pain is an expression of pain, just like a groan. Again, from the fact that I know that no one in the room is in pain, it does not follow that I *know* that I am not in pain, but only that *I* am not in pain and that I know that the other nine people are not either (cf. Exg. §§408f.). Finally, one may insist that one said one had a toothache because one felt it, not because one was acting – i.e. in order to draw that contrast (LPE 315, 319). But feeling a toothache is not a justification for saying one has a toothache as feeling a penny in one's pocket is a justification for saying that there is a penny in one's pocket. For to feel a toothache *is* to have a toothache. One may justify an utterance by citing evidence, but that I have a pain is not evidence for my having a pain. One may also justify an utterance, e.g. 'The curtains are ultramarine', by reference to a sample. But the only sample that could, as it were, justify saying 'I have a pain' would be a 'private' one, and there is no such thing (LPE 293; cf. 'Private ostensive definition', §3). It is, of course, true that I do not say that I have a toothache on the grounds of observing my behaviour (as others do), but it does not follow that I say it on any other grounds. I say it without justification, and rightly so (PI §289; MS. 166, 25f., 44f.).

4. *Only a first step*

The suggestion that first-person psychological utterances of the kind under consideration are not expressions of knowledge goes against the grain of centuries of philosophical reflection. To accept it involves as dramatic a re-orientation of philosophical thought as does Wittgenstein's parallel argument that propositions of mathematics are not descriptions of a realm of abstract entities, but rather rules of representation, and that accordingly 'knowing', 'believing', 'being certain', etc. in the domain of mathematics have a quite different grammar from that of knowledge, belief, and certainty in the empirical domain (cf. Volume 2, 'Grammar and necessity', §4). That we possess knowledge of our own subjective experience, that we know with absolute certainty how things are with us, has been the common ground of agreement between sceptics and their opponents ever since philosophical debates about the extent and possibility of human knowledge began.[21] It could be challenged, philosophers thought, only in a fit of madness, for here at least our knowledge is secure; we cannot err about our current sensations and feelings, about our sensory experiences, i.e. about how things sensibly seem to us to be. And the debate raged for centuries over how, if at all, we can infer from this solid foundation any knowledge about the 'external' world or about the states of mind of other people.

It was altogether characteristic of Wittgenstein to seek to disentangle the knots in our philosophical understanding by questioning precisely what seemed unquestionable, what was taken for granted virtually before debate began. It seems to have been an almost instinctive maxim of his that where philosophical debate has polarized between a pair of alternatives that seem exhaustive, the appropriate method to follow is not just to examine the conflicting arguments on each side and then opt for the seemingly stronger ones. Rather we should find out what was *agreed* by all participants in the centuries-old debate and reject that.[22]

Of course, rejecting the cognitive conception of first-person present-tense psychological utterances does not mean accepting the view that we do not know but merely believe that things are thus-and-so with us. Indubitable knowledge is not repudiated in favour of dubitable knowledge or mere belief, for, as we have seen, *both* are ruled out. To insist that avowals are made without any grammatical justification is not to insist that they stand in need of justification. Rather, we must come to see that justification in this domain makes no sense, and to view such utterances as none the worse for that. We must learn to see these

[21] Ibid.
[22] Cf. F. P. Ramsey, *The Foundations of Mathematics* (Kegan Paul, Trench, Trubner and Co. Ltd, London, 1931), pp. 115f.

language-games from a different perspective, just as in the philosophy of mathematics we must view mathematical propositions from a different perspective than the customary one.

The clarification of the confusions of private ownership of experience and of epistemic privacy with its attendant conceptions of introspection and the subjective transparency of the mind is only a first step. The classical pictures of the mind and their contemporary dialectical antitheses are held in place, as has been suggested, by numerous further misconceptions. Hence subsequent investigations will explore the incoherence of private ostensive definition as a means of assigning sense to psychological predicates. The picture of the relation between behaviour and mental state as a relation of 'outer' to 'inner' must be shown to rest on misunderstandings of metaphors and misconstruals of grammar. The distinctive uses of psychological expressions must be brought to light in order to clarify how different they are from the superficially similar uses of names of physical objects and their properties. Only when these further steps have been taken can one break the spell of the mythology of the mind that bewitches us.

III

PRIVATE OSTENSIVE DEFINITION

1. A 'private' language

Anyone can keep a diary in which he records his pains and other sensations, perhaps to report to his doctor the course of his illness. He can also register his feelings, emotions, and moods for his own private purposes. The language in which he writes his diary may be English, a language known to many. And if other people read this diary, they will understand it. To forestall this, the diarist might write in code, in which case others will not understand it unless he explains the code to them. But a code is not a language, let alone a private one. There can be languages which only one person in the world speaks, such as the language of the last Mohican. And it is possible to invent a new language, which no one apart from its inventor understands until he teaches it to others, e.g. Esperanto. There is nothing philosophically problematic about the privacy of such languages.

One can even imagine human beings who spoke only in monologue (PI §243), so that their languages were never employed in interpersonal communication at all, but only in talking to themselves. The idea is far-fetched, but not unintelligible. How they might have learnt their private languages is irrelevant to an account of their linguistic capacity (MS. 124, 214). But the languages of such monologuists might come to be understood by a sufficiently patient and ingenious anthropologist (PI §243). Robinson Crusoe, who learnt English at home, spoke his language in isolation, and we can imagine a caveman using a picture language in solitude (MS. 165, 74, 103ff.; MS. 124, 213f., 221f.). One can even imagine beings born with innate linguistic capacities (cf. PG 188; BB 12, 97; PI §495). These imaginary cases are not conceptually awry. One might perhaps have qualms about the intelligibility of a languageless creature's *inventing* a language, on the grammatical ground that 'to invent a language' is only predicable of one who already speaks a language. But no such objection applies to the idea of innate linguistic capacities. All Wittgenstein's imaginary cases exemplify languages which are, in one innocuous sense or another, private. These languages *could* be taught to others, and might be translated into our language (cf. Volume 2, pp. 172 – 9, and Exg. §243).

A 'private language' in the sense pertinent to Wittgenstein's discussion in *Investigations* §§243 – 315 is private in a more radical (and, ultimately, incoherent) way. It is a language the subject-matter of which is exclusively the subjective experience of the speaker. The words of the language refer to (PI §243) or are the names of (PI §§244, 256f.) sensations (PI §244), feelings and moods (PI §243), sense-impressions (PI §§272 – 7; LSD 4, 128; LPE 291), or sense-data (LPE 316; LSD 128f.). Of course, this makes it very unlike any natural language, for our languages abound with names of physical objects, public events, observable properties of objects, sounds, smells, and so on. But it is very like what many philosophers have made of our ordinary languages. For, generally speaking, this is how Descartes, Locke and his empiricist successors, and, more recently, the phenomenalists conceived of the underlying nature of our languages. This conception of a language is a philosophical fiction. The task Wittgenstein undertakes is to expose it for what it is – a tangle of conceptual confusions.

What is 'private' about a language thus conceived? In the first place, the nominata seem to be private in two respects. First, they seem to be privately 'owned'; for do we not say 'You can't have my experiences'? Secondly, the items named seem to be epistemically private. For if another person cannot have my experience, but only a similar one, he cannot know what it is really like. It is important to note at the outset that both these forms of privacy are bogus (PI §§246 – 8, 253 – 4). In so far as it is true that sensations are private, it does not follow that you cannot have the same pain as I have. Nor does it follow that you cannot really know whether I am in pain, what my pain is like, or whether I see red when I look at a ripe tomato. However, on these common philosophical assumptions of privacy, the consequences for the envisaged language are radical. Not only are its objects private, but the language itself is private in yet a further sense, viz. that no other person could (logically) understand it. Of course, neither the Cartesians nor the empiricists, who argued that 'words in their primary or immediate signification stand for nothing but the ideas in the mind of him that uses them'[1], typically imagined that they were explaining what it is for words to have a meaning in a language unintelligible in principle to anyone but the speaker. They thought they were explaining the nature of our ordinary languages which in general we use successfully to communicate with each other. Equally, non-philosophers who conceive of subjective experience as being 'private' in the specified senses do not suppose that, on their assumptions, what they say about their experiences must be unintelligible to anyone else.

The consequence of incommunicability, however, flows *perspicuously* from the further assumption that names of experiences (in the requisite sense) are given a meaning, i.e. are explained, by reference to the items they name, and from the misleading principle that to understand such

[1] Locke, *Essay Concerning Human Understanding*, Bk. III, Ch. ii, Sect. 2.

names is to know what they stand for.[2] On the resultant conception, names of subjective experiences are not tied up with the natural behavioural manifestation of the experiences (PI §256), and recognition of these manifestations is irrelevant to knowing what sensation-words mean.

There are different routes to these suppositions, which originate in the Augustinian picture of language. If it is held that the meaning of a word *is* the object it stands for, and if what the words of the envisaged language stand for are experiences conceived as privately 'owned' and epistemically private, and if, finally, the link between a word and its meaning is associative, then indeed no one else can understand the language. This is a straight and relatively naïve route – a direct consequence of that very simple *Urbild*. But one might deny that what names of private experiences stand for are their meanings, yet still insist that these names are indeed given a meaning by reference to such 'private experiences', even though experiences are not meanings. A refinement of the Augustinian picture would suggest (a) that the names are given a meaning not by association with objects which are their meaning, but by a kind of ostensive definition, and (b) that the private experience is a defining sample or paradigm for the use of such a name.[3] But since the sample is inaccessible to and unknowable by all save its owner, i.e. not contingently but essentially private, no one else could come to know what the names in such a language mean. If the 'names of simple ideas' or the 'primitive indefinables' of a language are given a meaning by private ostension involving *essentially* private samples or exemplars, then the language is a radically private one. For, 'The essential thing about private experience is really not that each person possess his own exemplar, but that nobody knows whether other people also have *this* or something else' (PI §272).

It might seem that as soon as one has shown that such a language cannot be a means of interpersonal communication, all interest in this philosophical monstrosity should lapse. After all, it might be said, it is obvious – and surely needs no argument – that our ordinary language is typically understood by speakers and hearers, is teachable and learnable. The question of whether there could be a language which is in principle

---

[2] To say that the word 'pain' stands for the sensation of pain is trivially correct, but says nothing at all about what this 'standing for' consists in, i.e. what it means to say '*that in the technique of using the language*' this word corresponds to, or is the name of, that sensation (cf. PI §51).

[3] Something like this is nicely articulated by Locke: 'Such precise, naked appearances in the mind, without considering how, whence, or with what others they came there, the understanding lays up (with names commonly annexed to them) as standards to rank real existences into sorts, as they agree with these patterns, and to denominate them accordingly' (*Essay Concerning Human Understanding*, Bk. II, Ch. xi, Sect. 9.

intelligible to no one other than its speaker seems uninteresting and of no relevance to any philosophical concern. Yet Wittgenstein spends hardly any time on the issue of incommunicability, taking that to be perspicuous, and focuses primarily on the question of the conceivability of a radically private language.

The explanation is straightforward. It is correct to argue:

A radically private language is not a means of interpersonal communication.

The language I speak is a means of interpersonal communication.

∴ The language I speak is not a radically private one.

But this in unhelpful. For there are immense philosophical pressures which make the ideas that together constitute the notion of a private language seem compelling. It is, after all, no accident that those ideas have dominated the mainstream of philosophy during the last few centuries. What could be more plausible than to hold that I know what 'pain', 'fear', or 'cheerful' mean simply by experiencing such feelings and naming them, just as I learn the names of objects in the 'external world' by encountering them. After all, when I say I have a toothache, I do not have to see whether I am clutching my cheek. My use of names of experiences here seems wholly independent of the behavioural manifestations of my experiences. And surely, when I have a pain, I know that I do – I could not have a toothache and not know it! And someone else cannot know that I have a toothache as I do – for I *feel* it! But no one else can feel my toothache! Although it is primarily philosophers who go further and insist that names of material objects must ultimately be defined in terms of names of subjective experiences, this does not, at first blush, seem too extravagant. For as most good empiricists will insist, objects are not *given* – it is experiences that are given, and objects are inferred! The foundations of language and the foundations of knowledge alike seem to rest upon private experiences.

A philosopher, a psychologist, or a linguist who succumbs to these pressures can equally argue:

The language I speak is private.

Other people do typically understand what I say.

∴ A private language is intelligible to others.

If the first premise seems irresistible and the second a truism, the obvious conclusion to draw is that, after all, there must be something wrong with the incommunicability claim. And this, after all, is what the mainstream of philosophers since Descartes have, explicitly or implicitly, taken for granted.

Characteristically, Wittgenstein presses home his attack at the point which seems altogether unquestionable. The crucial issue is, can *I* understand 'a language which describes my inner experiences', on the assumptions that my experiences are privately 'owned', epistemically private, and determine the meanings of their names? The thrust of his argument is not that *others* cannot understand a radically private language, hence such a language is of no great use or interest, but rather that *I* could not understand such a putative language. Consequently, there is no such thing, in this sense, as a private language – it is but a phantasmagoria of philosophy.

2. *Names, ostensive definitions, and samples – a reminder*

The arguments that demonstrate that the concept of a private language is incoherent turn on the interrelated notions of names, naming, ostensive definitions, and samples. These were discussed in Volume 1 in detail ('Augustine's picture of language', 'Explanation', 'Ostensive definition and its ramifications'). Here the salient points that bear upon the matter of a private language will be summarized.

The Augustinian *Urbild* conceives of all words as names – of objects, properties, relations, etc. Names are combined to form sentences the essential role of which is to describe how things are. Learning a language consists in learning the names of things, and inventing a language consists in giving names to things. The meaning of a name is thought to be its bearer, and the grammar of a name is conceived to be a consequence of its meaning, i.e. it flows from the nature of the entity named. Once we assign a name to a thing, we can go on to talk about it, to refer to it in speech. What it is to talk about or refer to a thing is determined by the name-relation which is fixed by the mere act of naming.

This, Wittgenstein argued, is wholly misguided. While it is true that with respect to any expression 'N', one can typically find a form of words ' "N" signifies N', this does not reveal the uniformity of 'the name-relation' or of the functions of words. It says that 'N' has a use, but does not say what use it has. It merely demonstrates a constant form under which we can subsume an endless diversity of grammatically distinct types of expression with different functions. What it is for an expression to be a name, to signify or refer to something, depends upon the grammatical category of the expression, and hence on the rules for its use. There is no such thing as *the* name-relation; rather there are as many 'name-relations' as there are grammatically distinct kinds of name. There is no *one thing* called 'talking about' or 'referring to' things; rather what is called 'referring' varies according to the grammatical category of the expression in question and the character of the language-game being played. The bearer of a name is not the meaning of the name, although what a name means is sometimes explained by pointing to its bearer. The grammar of a name does not flow from the character of the object named but consists in the rules for the use of the name. Assigning a name to a thing does not determine the use of the name, but is preparatory to its application in accord with the grammatical rules for its use. Hence naming presupposes stage-setting in the language which fixes the grammatical category of the expression. It is no coincidence that in Vol. XI and the 'Big Typescript', §27(a) of *Investigations* was followed by §257. We do, to be sure, name sensations and talk about them; but that says nothing about what it is for an expression to be the name of a sensation and indicates nothing about the nature of the stage-setting in the language that is presupposed for the very possibility of giving a sensation a name.

A natural outgrowth of the pre-philosophical Augustinian picture of language is the idea that expressions in a language fall (very roughly) into two broad classes; definables and indefinables (or, in more archaic terminology, names of complex ideas and names of simple ideas). In its simplest form this conception represents definitions as intra-linguistic substitution-rules, the paradigm of which is *Merkmal*-definition. The network of definable expressions rests upon an array of indefinables, and it is the latter which are correlated with objects and properties in the world. Indefinables, according to this view, link language with reality.

But definition is only one form of explanation of meaning, and *Merkmal*-definition only one kind of definition. Though philosophers since Plato have been mesmerized by formal definitions, the latter have no explanatory, normative privilege. It is a philosophical confusion to suppose that the meaning of an expression is uniquely given by specification of a formal definition, and that inability to give such a definition betokens lack of understanding or mere 'tacit' understanding – as if inability so to define an expression constitutes an inability to say what it means, so that one's understanding, manifest in correctly using an expression, outstrips one's ability to say what that expression means and what one means by its use. Formal definitions are *one* form of explanation of meaning, but there are many others which are equally legitimate. Explanations by listing examples, by exemplification, paraphrase, or contrastive paraphrase likewise specify how an expression is to be used, and so too does an ostensive definition. Explanations (including formal definitions) are rules, setting standards for the correct use of expressions. An internal relation obtains between the explanation and the application of an expression, and is manifest in and constituted by our own use of the explanation as a measure against which to judge the correctness of the application of the expression. Consequently, anything that constitutes an explanation of meaning must be reproduceable; a measure (like a yardstick) that disappears irretrievably as soon as it is canonized is no measure. Equally, for something to constitute a standard

of correctness there must obtain a technique of applying it, a method of
projection from the expression of the rule onto its extension. Explanations have a role in our linguistic transactions in so far as they are
employed in determinate ways to teach, justify, and distinguish correct
from incorrect applications of expressions.

It is hardly surprising that Wittgenstein associated ostensive definition
with the Augustinian conception of language (BT 25; cf. PLP 94). It is
natural to conceive of ostension as the mechanism linking language with
reality – as if the intra-grammatical network of definables were connected to things in the world by pointers. Ostension, it seems, correlates
words with things, and this bare correlation suffices to establish meaning, for is the thing pointed at not what the word means? If so, it will be
natural to assume that the grammar of the word flows from the nature of
the object picked out. In this sense ostension seems to lay the foundations
of language; it correlates words with things and thereby gives content to
the network of definables. If it is to fulfill this august role, the correlation
must be unambiguous and infallible. But pointing with one's hand does
not satisfy this requirement; it is not unambiguous and it can be
misinterpreted. What one *means*, however, when one points is wholly
unequivocal for *oneself*. Indeed, pointing is only necessary to explain to
others what an expression means. For oneself, meaning *this* is quite
enough. So the fundamental form of correlation of words with things is
mental ostension. Indeed, this must be the only form of correlation when
the expressions thus correlated are names of sensations, feelings, or
sense–data.

This conception is a philosophical mythology, an emblematic picture
akin to the story of Adam's naming the beasts in the garden of Eden. The
competence of ostensive definition is not restricted to so-called indefinables, for many expressions can be explained both by *Merkmal*-definition
and by ostension. Objects, properties, relations, and even numbers can
correctly be defined by ostension. One can indeed point at an object, its
colour, shape, texture, or number. But this is not by way of mysterious
mental acts of *meaning* the one rather than the other. That one means the
colour when one points at a poppy and says 'That is red' is manifest in
what one counts as another person's understanding one's ostensive
definition, i.e. what one counts as his going on to apply the word 'red'
correctly to other things. An ostensive definition, like any other explanation of meaning, is misinterpretable. It can be clarified by making
explicit the grammatical category of the defined expression, e.g. 'This
colour is red'. This may avert misunderstanding and ensure uptake,
provided the concept of colour is understood. An ostensive definition
presupposes the grammatical category of the definiendum. In this sense it
is merely one rule among others for the use of a word, for the
grammatical place of the word in the language-game must be prepared.

The object or feature pointed at is not the meaning of the defined expression and cannot determine its grammar.[4] Indeed, it is a confusion to suppose that ostensive definition links language to reality at all. Like *Merkmal*-definitions, it is a grammatical rule and remains within language. It links a word (in certain cases) with a defining *sample* or *paradigm* – and samples are best considered part of grammar. They belong to the means of representation. This is manifest in the fact that just as a *Merkmal*-definition is a rule licensing substitution of definiens for definiendum, so too the sample, ostensive gesture, and utterance 'This' are substitutable for the definiendum (e.g. 'The curtains are this ↗ colour', said while pointing at the sample). It is an illusion to suppose that concentrating one's attention (performing an 'act of meaning'!) determines what is being defined, or that it constitutes a kind of subjective pointing. It is the technique of using the explicit ostensive definition as a criterion of correct use that fixes the grammatical category of the expression defined, the way in which the sample is to be employed as a standard or measure of correct application.

That an object pointed at functions as a sample of a colour, shape, texture, etc. is not an intrinsic feature of the object but of its use in our practices of explaining the meanings of words and justifying their application. An object can be used as a sample only in so far as it represents what it is a sample of (thus one cannot use the sky as a sample of green) and can be copied or reproduced. Its primary role is that of an object for comparison, for it must be capable of measuring other things for identity or difference. Hence it must be possible to 'lay a sample alongside reality' for match or mismatch. So a sample must be perceptible, and there must be a method of comparison, a technique of projection, which determines what counts as matching the sample or failing to match it. This will vary from one grammatical category to another.

The contention that a private language is impossible, i.e. that this very concept is incoherent, turns on the claims that merely associating a name with a nominatum does not suffice to endow the sign with a use, that there is no private analogue of public ostensive definition, that there is no such thing as a mental sample, and that there is no such thing as a technique of applying an expression in accord with a rule which is in principle incommunicable to anyone else.

---

[4] It is easy to see why this *Bedeutungskörper* conception is appealing. Unless the word 'red', for example, is used correctly as a colour-word, we will be inclined to say that the speaker has not correlated the word with the right thing, does not know what it stands for. So if he does know what thing it stands for, he will use it correctly. So, it seems, the correct use of the word, its grammar, is determined by the thing it stands for!

3. The vocabulary of a private language

Having clarified the confusions underlying the notions of epistemic privacy and private ownership of experience, Wittgenstein reverts in *Investigations* §256 to the putative private language: 'Now, what about the language which describes my inner experiences and which only I myself can understand?' Experiences here (PI §§256 – 7) are conceived to lack any natural manifestation in behaviour, and so the putative names of experiences are not tied up with any expressive behaviour. This picture conforms to the Cartesian and empiricist conceptions of names of ideas, impressions, or sense-data. In the absence of a connection with expressive behaviour (e.g. by way of substitution in the first-person case and by way of criteria in the third-person case), what form of connection between name and sensation is envisaged? Wittgenstein explores various possibilities.

The most commonly supposed nexus is associative: 'I simply associate names with sensations and use these names in descriptions' (PI §256). If I wish to keep a diary about the recurrence of a certain sensation, all I have to do is to associate the sensation with a sign, say 'S', and enter the sign in the diary whenever I have the sensation (PI §258). What justifies my writing 'S'? Well, surely the fact that I have S! I am justified by what is, in fact, the case!

But this is wrong. What is in fact the case is what makes 'I have S' true (or false), not what justifies its assertion.[5] We are concerned here with a *grammatical* justification – and that is given by a *rule* (LPE 293). But associating a sign with a sensation does not give the sign a grammar, for no conventions of use are established by this association (LSD 4). To be sure, saying 'alpha' when one has a particular impression looks like an act of christening; but genuine acts of christening (in a church) or name-giving (when launching a ship) take place in a complex social setting governed by an array of conventions which determine a particular language-game in which the name has a subsequent use (LSD 4; LPE 290). Making a noise while concentrating one's attention on a sensation does not make the noise a name of anything, for it does not normatively determine what to do with this noise on subsequent occasions. It does not lay down a norm of correct use.

In order to establish a name-relation we have to establish a technique of use. And we are misled if we think that it is a peculiar process of christening an object which

---

[5] That *p* is the case cannot *justify* the assertion that *p*. Evidence for *p* justifies asserting that *p*, and such evidence may be inductive or criterial. Or an ostensive definition, a rule, may be adduced to justify the use of a word. As will become clear, in the case of 'I am in pain', there is *no* justification for its utterance; and if it is an avowal (*Äusserung*) of pain, it makes dubious sense even to talk of it *being made true* by one's being in pain.

makes a word the word for an object. This is a kind of superstition. So it's no use saying that we have a private object before our mind and give it a name. There is a name only where there is a technique of using it. – That technique can be private, but this only means that nobody but I knows about it . . . (MS. 166; cf. Volume 2, p. 178)

To be sure, a definition establishes a technique of use. So can one not enrich the bare idea of association with that of definition? For surely I can give myself a kind of ostensive definition of 'S', not by pointing with my hand, of course, but rather by concentrating my attention on the sensation (meaning the sensation) and as it were pointing *inwardly* (PI §258). This determines what 'S' is to stand for, and 'once you know *what* the word stands for you know its whole use' (PI §264). Moreover, when one thus concentrates on the sensation, one can inwardly undertake to call it 'S' in the future (PI §262).

This is mere charade. Concentrating one's attention is not a kind of pointing. It seems as if it is, because when one speaks to someone else one occasionally looks intently at an object, and one's gaze functions as a kind of pointing for the other person – but not for oneself (Vol. XII, 189; LSD 38). Concentrating one's attention on something (no matter whether it is a sensation or a colour) is not to give an explanation of the meaning of a word. For 'Explanation is something which shows us how to use a word at some other time as well' (LSD 39). But staring or concentrating does not do that, for neither of these determines a rule or fixes a method of comparison. Contrary to appearances, they have no role in any language-game, not even in one which I might play by myself (a private game). This will become evident in what follows.

Furthermore, as already argued, the object for which a word stands is not its meaning. The essence (*Wesen*) of an object is determined by grammar, not by nature (cf. PI §§371, 373). So the use of the word does not follow from the object it names. Finally, concentrating on a sensation does not suffice for undertaking to use the word as the name of *this* sensation in the future (PI §263). For, (a) what is the *this* upon which one concentrates? One no more determines a criterion of identity by concentration than one does by emphatic stressing of the word 'this' (cf. PI §253). (b) To be the name of a *sensation* requires a specific technique of use, quite unlike the technique of use for colour-names for example. It is of no avail to say that one is going to use the word 'in a certain way' in the future, unless one can spell out *which* way (cf. PI §262). Of course, one way of so doing is to display a sample and explain its role. But, (c) can an impression or sensation be used as a sample? This question is *logical*, not epistemological or sociological. What is the technique of use of such a private sample? How is it to be used as a measure – as an object of comparison (LSD 105)? Is it even logically *possible* so to use it?

A philosopher defending the supposition of the intelligibility of private ostensive definition might reply that there is no difficulty at all here. For the grammatical post at which the sign 'S' is to be stationed is given by the concept of *sensation*. If one can disambiguate a public ostensive definition by saying 'This colour is sepia', why can one not articulate the grammar of a private ostensive definition by impressing upon oneself that this *sensation* is S? But 'sensation' is a word of ordinary language, not a word of a private language intelligible only to oneself (PI §261). The private language theorist is not at liberty to help himself to expressions which are linked to behavioural manifestations of the mental, on pain of relinquishing his claims to the privacy of his putative language. And to argue that 'sensation' too is defined by private ostensive definition will not resolve his difficulty, but compound it. Of course, he might be tempted to a more nebulous fall-back position, viz. to claim that 'S' (or 'pain', as be construes it) means or refers to a *certain phenomenon* (LSD 42), a *certain impression* (LPE 290), or a *certain experience* (LSD 108). But these blank cheques can only be used if they can be cashed in the currency of 'Namely *this* ↗' – and that is not possible here (LSD 42, 105). He might be inclined to insist that 'S' or 'pain' means or refers to *something*, which he *has*. But 'have' and 'something' are likewise words of ordinary language with a determinate use (PI §261). To this he may respond indignantly that surely pain is not a *nothing*! Of course not, Wittgenstein replies. Pain is neither a something nor a nothing; the point is rather that a nothing will serve just as well as a something about which nothing can be said (PI §304).

In order to give a name to a sensation or sense-impression in a putative private language, the private language theorist must show how the name is to be defined or explained. For a sign is a name only in so far as it is given a rule-governed use, and the role of a definition is to determine for future occasions how the expression is to be used (LPE 291). In explanations of word-meaning by public ostensive definition, a sample typically plays a crucial normative role in this respect. Having a sensation, say a toothache, seems to provide one with a mental sample which will function as a standard for subsequent applications of the word 'toothache'. One is indeed tempted to say that someone who has never felt pain could not know what the word 'pain' means (PI §315). Can one not imagine someone having a toothache for the first time and exclaiming 'Now I know what "toothache" means!'? This seems to betoken the availability of a sample which defines 'toothache' (LSD 9).

This, Wittgenstein argues, is an illusion. 'The private experience is to serve as a paradigm, and at the same time admittedly it can't be a paradigm' (LPE 314). Why not? A sample must function as a standard of comparison for subsequent applications, must be preservable or reproducible; and it must be possible to lay a sample alongside reality for match or mismatch. Hence it must be possible for there to be a technique of projection manifest in the use of the sample as a standard of correct use. These requirements are not satisfied in the case of sensations or impressions – although they seem to be.

There can be no such thing as preserving a pain for future use. One cannot take a photograph of it, as one can of pain-behaviour (LSD 42). One can preserve a sample of red, ultramarine, or sepia on a colour-chart and consult it on later occasions; but one cannot preserve an impression of a colour for future use (LSD 42). A sample (of colour, for example) is something which persists, can be examined again, looked at for a time and shown to others (LSD 110).

The private language theorist will concede that one cannnot show others a mental sample, but will insist that there are adequate analogues of the preservability or reproducibility of samples. (a) Could one not imagine a *persistent* sensation, such as a constant pain in one's hand? Could that not function as a private sample? (Of course, the theorist will admit, we do not typically have such persistent sensations; but his point, at the moment, is to break the log-jam of objections!) (b) Not all samples are persistent anyway – it suffices that they be *reproducible* (e.g. samples of musical notes are reproducible by means of a tuning-fork). So cannot one reproduce a sensation of pain, say, simply by pinching oneself to remind oneself what the word 'pain' means? (c) Not all expressions in our ordinary language that are *defined* by reference to samples are *applied* with the aid of samples. It suffices that one remember what they mean (e.g. 'red'). So if one defines 'S' by reference to a certain sensation, it is surely possible to remember the sensation and, if doubt arises, to *recall* this defining sample! Can one not, as it were, store it in one's memory and reproduce it as an image which then functions as a private sample? So even though the sensation passes, what persists is its copy in the reproductive imagination (LSD 33ff., 113).

Persistent samples: One can have relatively persistent sensations. But neither ephemeral nor persistent sensations can function as samples. For, first, persistent samples, such as colour-charts or the standard metre-bar (for, remember, it is the *bar*, not its *length*, that is the sample), have independent criteria of identity. One can detemine whether one's colour-chart, left in the sun, has faded or been stained, or whether the standard metre-bar (or one's own metre-rule) has been bent, snipped, or stretched. In such cases, one will cease using that object *as* a sample; far from being at the mercy of samples, we are free to abandon any given object that has been used as a sample and to adopt or make a new one. For whether something is a sample depends on whether we use it as one (see Volume I, 'The standard metre', §4), and that is up to us. But in the case of a sensation, there is no distinction between the sample and the feature which it represents on the model of the distinction between the metre-bar and the length of which it is a defining sample. So there are no analogous criteria for the sameness or difference *of the sample*. But a sample which can change without making any difference makes no difference! Consequently, if a sensation is to function as a sample, it would have to be akin not to a persistent sample (such as a colour-chart or metre-bar) but to a reproducible one (such as a note produced by a tuning-fork). This will be examined below.

It is natural to object that surely a person must notice whether his sensation is the same or not! If that means that one can say whether one's toothache is still acute and stabbing or whether it is no longer so severe, but a dull, throbbing ache, then that is indeed correct. But these are *descriptions*, and they presuppose the concepts they employ. It is a cardinal error to confuse a sample (a standard of measurement) with a description (the result of a measurement) (LPE 320). One can derive a description from a sample; but when we describe our toothache as being still the same or as having changed thus-and-so, we are not describing the sameness or difference of a sample (in contrast with saying that the metre-bar is bent), nor are we deriving our description from *any* sample. What the subject sincerely says, given that he generally manifests mastery of the technique of using the sensation-name, is the sole criterion (for others) for the sameness or difference of his sensation. *He* has no independent means of determining whether his sensation is still the same or not – he just says so. But this means that the thought that he could use his sensation as a persistent private sample is misconceived, for he would have no way to determine whether the sample had changed or not. But there must always be a difference between a sample's being the same and its being believed or asserted to be the same. *That* distinction collapses here, although it seems not to, because, given the concept of, say, toothache, one *can* say whether one's toothache is the same or not.

Techniques of comparison: Suppose I have a persistent sensation in my hand and I want to define the word 'pain' by using it as a sample. So I go through the motions of giving myself a private ostensive definition. Can I then say that I have a pain in my head, and justify this by claiming that what I have in my head *is* what I have in my hand? After all, I can define the word 'red' by pointing at a colour-chart and saying 'This ↗ is red', and I can describe the roses as being *this* ↗ colour, viz. red.

There is no genuine analogue of this in the case of sensations. (a) I cannot (logically) *perceive* my sensations as I can perceive both the sample of red and the roses and see that the roses are that colour. (b) I cannot (logically) point at my sensation as I can point at the colour-sample, either for others or for myself alone. (c) I cannot (logically) compare a sensation in my hand with a sensation in my head (or in my other hand) for match or mismatch as I can compare an object with a sample.[6] When I compare the roses with the colour-chart or when I measure the table with a yardstick, I can make a mistake – i.e. compare rightly or wrongly. I can check my judgement by looking again in better light or measuring a second time, more carefully. I can ask someone else, who may be more skilful than I at fine discrimination. But there is no such thing as judging that I have a pain in my head by comparing what I have in my head with what I have in my hand. There is no method of projection or technique of comparison here. I cannot, as it were, lay my *hand* alongside my head (as I can lay a yardstick alongside the table) in order to judge whether what I have in my head *is* that sensation (as I can judge that the table is that length).

The private language theorist may accept the first two points, (a) and (b), but have qualms about the third, (c). Though having a pain is not perceiving a pain, is it not enough to have a pain in one's hand in order for it to function as a sample for a pain elsewhere? After all, one *can* have a pain in one's hand and the same pain, e.g. a rheumatic one, in one's other hand; and one may *say so*! That is correct. But there is no such thing as saying so *on the basis of comparison with a sample*. For where there is a comparison with a sample, there is a possibility of making a mistake, i.e. it makes *sense* to compare wrongly. But it makes no sense to say 'I thought I had a pain, but I was mistaken', let alone 'I thought what I had in my head was what I have in my hand, but I was wrong' (as one can say 'I thought the curtains were this ↗ colour [pointing at a sample], but I was wrong'). Furthermore, the question of how one can *apprehend* that what one 'has' in one's head is what one 'has' in one's hand is not answered by saying that one can *feel* that they are the same, for feeling a pain *is* just having a pain; nor can it be answered by saying that one *has* it, for having a pain is not a mode of apprehending its identity with or difference from a sample. In short, it means nothing to say that what I have in my hand *is* that certain phenomenon which I have in my head and which I call 'pain', unless that is just a garbled way of saying that I have the same pain in my hand as in my head. The unintelligibility of there being a technique of comparison is a definitive objection to the idea of private ostensive definition.

Reproducible samples: Granted that we do not typically have persistent sensations, nevertheless we can surely *reproduce* sensations, like notes on a tuning-fork. So if one wants to make sure what the word 'pain' means, can one not simply stick a pin in one's hand? – That does not tell one what the word means! Of course, one is tempted to say that it does – that

---

[6] Of course, I can compare today's headache with yesterday's *in saying* that it is not so bad now. But I cannot employ yesterday's headache as a standard by reference to which to judge whether what I now have is to be *called* 'a headache', for there can be no *technique of comparison*.

it reminds one what one calls 'pain'. For does one not *recognize* the sensation? The temptation must be resisted. (a) It only makes sense to talk of recognizing where it also makes sense to talk of not recognizing or misrecognizing. For 'recognize' is a success-verb, and success presupposes the possibility of failure. But it makes no sense to talk of not recognizing or misidentifying a sensation as a pain, as a headache or backache (as opposed to identifying a pain as angina pectoris). (b) If what one is supposed to recognize here is a *sample* of pain, then, as we have seen, it can make no sense to talk of recognizing it as a pain (or as painful). For if it is to determine the concept of pain, it cannot at the same time be said to fall under it, just as the standard metre-bar cannot be said to be a metre long (cf. Exg. §50, and Volume 1, 'The standard metre'). A sample is a measure; something recognized is something measured. Can't one recognize the sample? No, for as argued, there can be no independent criterion for recognizing it correctly here. One cannot put a British Standards Authority stamp on a putative sample of pain, and putting it on the pin with which one pricks oneself is of no avail. For 'pain' does not mean the same as 'Whatever A feels when he pricks himself with a standard pin'! True enough, one might object; but equally 'C-flat' does not mean 'whatever note is produced by striking such-and-such tuning fork'! So is 'pain' not on the same level as the name of a sound defined by reference to such a method of reproducing a sample? Not so; for we can admit that a tuning-fork is defective. As long as the discriminatory abilities of sensitive hearers persist, a defect in the tuning-fork is perceptible. But pains are not perceptibilia, and there is no such thing as being more or less skilful in distinguishing the sameness or difference of a pain. One can reproduce a sound which can function as a sample, precisely because sounds are perceptible, can be compared for sameness and difference, can be recognized or mistakenly misidentified. (c) Admittedly, pricking oneself with a pin typically gives one a pain. But what one needs is the *concept* of pain or a sample of pain that will be associated with a technique of application to constitute a rule for the use of the word 'pain'. And one has not got that here (cf. Z §§548 – 6; for further ramifications, cf. Exg. §288).

Remembering the sample: Why can one not define a sensation-word 'S' by reference to a certain sensation S and simply *remember* the defining sample. When in doubt, all one has to do is to bring to mind an image of S.[7] After all, one can remember the meanings of colour-words and conjure up mental images of, say, sepia or ultramarine when one wants to remind oneself what these names mean. Isn't it the same with

---

[7] It is unhappy, in English, to talk of 'an image' of pain (see Exg. §300). Not so in German; and the argument would not differ in substance if one were talking of mental images of colours allegedly functioning as private mental samples.

sensation-words? Not at all. One can memorize what words mean, e.g. that 'Tisch' means table. One can learn what colour-words mean by studying a colour-chart and impressing upon oneself the connections between words and samples. And when trying to remember what 'sepia' means, one might call to mind a mental image of sepia. But 'if you say he *learns* this, then you distinguish between a correct and a wrong remembering; if not, there is no learning' (LSD 114). One can 'impress upon oneself' the connection between a name and what it names, but that means that this process brings it about that one remembers the connection *correctly* in the future. That in turn presupposes a criterion, i.e. a standard, of correctness (PI §258). One can remember that 'Tisch' means table or think wrongly that it means fish, and one can check which is correct in a dictionary. Can one not, however, have a *mental dictionary*, one which exists only in the reproductive imagination? After all, one can appeal from one memory to another. Someone with an eidetic memory can think that he remembers what a word, e.g. 'Tisch', means, and check his memory against his mental image of the page in the German/English dictionary. That is correct – but only if *there is* a German/English dictionary. The mental image of the page in the dictionary can only confirm one's recollection of the meaning of a word if it itself can be tested for correctness against the actual page. Otherwise one is checking one's memory of the meaning of a word against one's memory of its meaning, which is like buying several copies of the same newspaper to confirm what is written in it (PI §265).

This argument has seemed to some philosophers to be an expression of scepticism about memory. But that is quite wrong; it is rather a demand for the intelligibility of a distinction between remembering correctly and remembering incorrectly what a word means:

> I cannot remind myself in my private language that this was the sensation I called 'red'. There is no question of my memory's playing me a trick – because (in such a case) there can be no criterion for its playing me a trick. If we lay down rules for the use of colour-words in ordinary language, then we can admit that memory plays tricks regarding these rules. (LSD 8)

Wittgenstein's concern is not whether one can *in fact* find out whether one has remembered rightly (after all, one often cannot in ordinary daily life), but rather whether anything could logically *count* as remembering correctly or incorrectly. For, 'Looking up a table in the imagination is no more looking up a table than the image of the result of an imagined experiment is the result of an experiment' (PI §265). But could one not *guess* the right application of 'S', and might it not be a fortunate fact that normally one guesses correctly? No – 'There is nothing to guess at' (MS. 166, 21). For one can only guess if something *counts* as guessing right, and that requires an independent standard of correctness.

The idea that a mental image can function as a sample is compelling, precisely because one *can* have a mental image of a sample, as when one memorizes a colour-chart. And if the colour-chart is then destroyed, that surely does not mean that suddenly one cannot use the words one previously learnt, such as 'sepia', 'indigo', or 'violet'. So why can't one give a name to a sensation and then, as it were, store a copy of the sensation in one's memory? One's image will then function as a sample of S, as does one's image of sepia. For is a mental image not something like a *picture*? And a picture, to be sure, can function as a sample or a paradigm! Of course, a mental image is a private picture – but why should that matter, since its role is that of a private standard for the use of its owner alone?[8]

This is misconceived. (i) 'Memory can be compared with a storehouse only so far as it fulfils the same purpose. Where it doesn't, we couldn't say whether the things stored up constantly change their nature and so couldn't be said to be stored at all' (MS. 166, 33). Again, the point is not the fallibility of human memory and the consequent fear of error, but rather the absence of any criterion for remembering correctly, hence the collapse of any *distinction* between remembering correctly and remembering incorrectly. Hence it is no use supposing that one might *recognize* the image as an image of S (MS. 166, 26) or *believe* that it is the image of S (cf. PI §260). For this recognition and belief presuppose (a) the concept of S – which is precisely what is in question; and (b) the possibility of misrecognition or believing falsely (LSD 110). But if 'whatever is going to seem right to me is right . . . that only means that here we can't talk about "right" ' (PI §258), hence not about recognition or belief either.

(ii) It is true that a picture can function analogously to a sample. One can (and does) explain what the word 'horse' or 'duck-billed platypus' means by pointing at a picture just as well as by pointing at the animal. A coloured picture of a tomato can replace a ripe tomato in an ostensive definition of the word 'red'. But a mental image is not a picture, even though in certain cases a picture can correspond to it (PI §301). One can imagine sepia and paint what one imagines. What one paints can then function as a paradigm (and can also serve to explain what it was that one imagined). But 'The image of pain is not a picture and *this* image is not replaceable in the language-game by anything that we should call a picture' (PI §300 and Exg.). One can imagine pain, but that presupposes, and so cannot explain, the concept of pain. For one cannot explain what 'pain' means by pointing at, let alone painting, a picture or a paradigm of a pain (LSD 39f.), as opposed to one of pain-behaviour (PI §300).

---

[8] Note that even if this move were valid, the private language theorist would still be confronted with the insurmountable objection that there can be no method of comparison here.

The use of sensation-names in the first person resembles the use of colour-words in certain respects. In neither case are the expressions used on the basis of evidence. There are no criteria for saying 'That is red' or for avowing 'I have a pain'. Here, in a certain sense, one says what one says without (evidential) justification (cf. PI §§289, 381). In typical uses of 'red', 'green', or 'blue', one employs no samples at all, and one employs no sample when one says 'I have a toothache'. But the language-games with colour-words are essentially, grammatically, bound up with samples used in teaching, explaining, and justifying (LSD 121). Not so in the case of sensation-words. 'The impression of a "private table" in the game arises through the *absence* of a table, and through the similarity of the game to one that is played with a table' (Z §552).

4. *Idle wheels*

Wittgenstein was well aware that his arguments demonstrating that the sensation of pain does not enter the language-game with the word 'pain' as a sample of sepia, say, enters the language-game with colour-words gives the impression that he is denying the existence of pain. One is inclined to say that one's justification for moaning is having *pain*, and that one can point inwardly at what one has (LPE 312). Surely *this*, one wants to say, is the important thing (PI §298). After all, 'there is *something* there all the same accompanying my cry of pain. And it is on account of that that I utter it. And this something is what is important – and frightful' (PI §296). One wants to object: 'You seem to deny the existence of something; on the other hand you say you don't deny any existence: why should it seem as if you did? You seem to say: "There is only . . .". You deny, it seems, the background of the expression of sensations. Doesn't the expression point to something beyond itself?' (MS. 166, 35f.). Wittgenstein conceded that it looks like this. 'The "private experience" is a degenerate construction of our grammar (comparable in a sense to tautology and contradiction). And this grammatical monster now fools us; when we wish to do away with it, it seems as though we denied the existence of an experience, say, tooth-ache' (LPE 314). How can this false appearance be dispelled?

Of course, Wittgenstein insisted, there is all the difference in the world between pain-behaviour accompanied by pain and pain-behaviour with-out pain; indeed it is precisely the difference between manifesting one's suffering and pretending to suffer (cf. PI §304). But it is misleading in this context to represent that difference as the difference between behaviour plus an accompaniment and behaviour without an accompa-niment. Where a form of behaviour is an *expression* of something, it is misconceived to think of what it expresses as a hidden accompaniment that lies behind the behaviour. For it is not hidden, but manifest; it does not lie 'behind' the behaviour (there is no 'behind' here), but infuses it; and it is no accompaniment, for that concept is appropriate only where the items said to accompany each other are logically independent (MS. 166, 16; PI §296; Vol. XVII, 7ff.). But it is true that people sometimes have a pain and do not show it and that sometimes they pretend to be in pain.

So is Wittgenstein agreeing that when someone who is truthful says that he sees red or has a pain we can take his word for it? Of course; we believe that what he experiences is as he says it is, *according to the method of projection appropriate to the case* (MS. 166, 34f.).[9] But an incommunicable private object plays, and can play, no role in grammar in either case. Moreover, the genuine sensation of pain (or the mental image of red) has no place *in the grammar* of the word 'pain' (or 'red'). We say of another person that he has a pain on the grounds of his behaviour, and *he* says that he has a pain on no grounds at all and without any (grammatical) justification; rather he gives expression to, or manifests, his pain. Of course, here too there are criteria for whether he knows what the word 'pain' means.

In a final effort to shake the grip of the private object that apparently functions as a private sample for the use of a word and as a private justification, Wittgenstein constructs a *reductio ad absurdum* (Vol. XV, 87ff.). Suppose that at birth everyone were given a table of colours which no one else is allowed to look at. We teach these children the use of colour-words as usual, and tell them to enter the colour-names in their private tables. Before they apply colour-words to objects, they always glance at their tables. They come to use colour-words as we all do. Now suppose we find that on their tables they have written 'red' under the green sample, 'green' under the red one, and so on. Further, we find that a child, before he says that the ripe tomatoes are red, looks at his colour-chart and puts his finger on the green sample and then says 'They are red'. And equally, when we ask him to explain what 'red' means, he looks at his chart, puts his finger on the word 'red' beneath the green sample and then points at a ripe tomato and says 'That colour is red'. Clearly, the private table is an idle wheel in the mechanism of his language. Even if we suppose that when we remove his private chart he falls into confusion and can no longer use colour-words correctly, it is still evident that *grammatically* the chart plays no role in his use of language. And now suppose that this chart exists only in his imagination. Does it now make any difference? A free-wheeling cog does not engage with a mechanism by being transposed into the imagination.

---

[9] What is appropriate for 'red', viz. the use of a public ostensive definition, is inappropriate for 'pain'. And if someone avows severe pain in his foot, but laughs and behaves normally, does not limp or assuage his foot, etc., we would say that he is joking.

A similar argument occurs in *Investigations* §271: ' "Imagine a person whose memory could not retain *what* the word 'pain' meant – so that he constantly called different things by that name – but nevertheless used the word in a way fitting in with the usual symptoms and presuppositions of pain" – in short he uses it as we all do' (cf. PI p. 207; MS. 166, 18 and 36f.). One is tempted to reply that one *could not* make such a mistake here, that one *could not* misidentify one's sensation (irrespective of the matter of a private sample). That is both right and wrong; it is true that one could not make a mistake, but not because one always, as a matter of fact, identifies one's sensation correctly. Rather, because there is here neither an identification nor a misidentification, neither a recognition nor a misrecognition (cf. PI §270). The supposition of a private object that gets identified correctly and which is then described by saying 'I have a pain' is the absurdity which Wittgenstein is rejecting. An expression of pain (*Schmerzäusserung*) no more involves the antecedent identification of an inner object than the expression of amusement by laughter involves the identification of an inner feeling of amusement which one then expresses!

'I have a pain' is an expression of pain, just as 'I am frightened' is an expression of fear and 'I am tired' an expression of weariness. These utterances are themselves forms of behaviour that constitute criteria for saying of a person that he is in pain, frightened, or tired. They are learnt extensions of natural expressive behaviour and are essentially bound up with those forms of behaviour.[10] In our philosophical reflections on 'self-knowledge' and 'self-awareness' we are prone to confuse the grammatical exclusion of misidentification or misrecognition with the presence of infallible identification or recognition. Similarly, we are impressed by the fact that an avowal of pain does not rest on any public criteria, for in truth we do not look to see whether we are groaning before we say that we have a toothache. So we wrongly suppose that there must be an inner, private justification. The irony is that if, per *impossibile*, there were an inner justification, e.g. a private mental sample justifying the use of the word or a private object *described* by 'I have a pain', then doubts would be intelligible:

if we cut out human behaviour, which is the expression of sensation, it looks as if I might *legitimately* begin to doubt afresh. My temptation to say that one might take a sensation for something other than what it is arises from this: if I assume the

---

[10] That is not to say that all avowals are substitutes for natural expressive behaviour. Some sensations have little if any form of pre-linguistic manifestations, e.g. heartburn or 'butterflies in the stomach'. But 'I have heartburn' and 'I have butterflies in the stomach' are expressions of *sensation* and to that extent bound up, indirectly, with the natural manifestations of sensation. Such avowals are learnt extensions of the verbal expressions of sensations that are partial substitutes for natural expressive behaviour. Fresh branches may grow from a conventional graft. (Cf. Exg. §244, 2.1(vi).)

abrogation of the normal language-game with the expression of a sensation, I need a
criterion of identity for the sensation; and then the possibility of error also exists.
(PI §288)

Clearly, that is unintelligible in our language-games with sensation-
words. If someone were to say 'Oh, I know what "pain" means; what I
don't know is whether *this*, that I have now, is pain', we would not
know what he was trying to tell us. 'That expression of doubt has no
place in the language-game' (PI §288). This is made vivid in Wittgenstein's example of a genuine diary entry of a real sensation-word 'S'.
Suppose I discover, by inductive correlation, that whenever I have a
certain sensation my blood-pressure, as measured by a manometer, has
risen. So I can keep a diary to register the rise and fall of my
blood-pressure without reliance on the manometer. Here it *seems quite
indifferent* whether I have recognized the sensation rightly or wrongly; for
even if I regularly misidentify it, it does not matter. For I predict
correctly the rise in my blood-pressure. Does that show that I correlate
the rise in blood-pressure with my *believing*, rightly or wrongly, that I
have the sensation in question? On the contrary, it shows that any
supposition of recognition, error, identification or misidentification in
the case of sensations, is mere show. There is no such thing as believing
that one has a pain, for then it would make sense to say 'I had a pain, but I
did not believe I did' or 'I believed I had a pain, but I was mistaken'. But
these make no sense (cf. Exg. §270).

The word 'pain' is not defined by reference to a 'private object'; nor is
it defined by reference to a public *object*. And 'I have a pain' is not a
description of an inner experience which is *made true* (and justified) by
reference to the occurrence of a particular indefinable experience. To
achieve a surview of this part of the grammar of psychology, one must
jettison altogether the model of explanation appropriate to words for
physical objects and perceptual properties, and with it the mythology of
experience as private and incommunicable – i.e. of a 'world' of private
experience. Only when these dense mists of language are blown away
can we hope to see aright the grammar of experience and its expression.

IV

MEN, MINDS, AND MACHINES

1. Human beings and their parts

'It comes to this: only of a living human being and what resembles (behaves like) a living human being can one say: it has sensations; it sees; is blind; hears; is deaf; is conscious or unconscious' (PI §281). This grammatical remark crystallizes a crucial array of connections in Wittgenstein's philosophy of psychology. Its consequences, both within philosophy and without – in psychology and neurophysiology, as well as in so-called cognitive science – are dramatic.

A wide range of expressions are predicable literally or primarily only of human beings and of creatures that behave like them. For the criteria for the application of such expressions consist in behaviour patterns in specific contexts against a background of widely ramifying complex capacities manifest in behaviour. Among these expressions are psychological terms such as sensation-names and perceptual verbs, the large vocabulary of thought and belief, consciousness and attention, desire and will, as well as emotion, mood and attitude, decision, motive and intention.

The first and paramount corollary is that it makes no sense save metonymically, metaphorically, or in a secondary use (cf. Exg. §282) to ascribe sensations, perceptual capacities and their exercise, thought and experience either to parts of the human body or to the body itself. This principle is a grammatical one, not an empirical generalization or a metaphysical necessity. It is not a matter of fact that it is the human being who is hungry, not his body – which needs food, or his stomach – which is empty. It is not a metaphysical principle, due to the essential nature of bodies and thought, that it is the person who thinks, ponders, and reflects – and not his brain. It is grammar that excludes attributing toothache to the brain or good eyesight to the 'visual' striate cortex. No sense has been given to these forms of words, no conditions of application have been laid down for the correct use of 'His brain has toothache' or 'His brain's eyesight is deteriorating'. One may be tempted to ask whether our grammar is right, whether it may not be unjustified? Could it not be overtaken by scientific progress?

A fuller answer will emerge below, but for the moment we should bear in mind some of Wittgenstein's arguments previously discussed (cf. Volume 2, pp. 329 – 38). Grammar is not justified by the facts; indeed there is no such thing as justifying grammar by reference to reality on the model of verifying an empirical proposition by reference to what makes it true. Grammar consists of rules for the use of words and has no such justification. It determines what we count as possible descriptions of how things are in reality, fixing a logical space which the facts, so to speak, may then occupy or fail to occupy. Grammar is autonomous, not answerable to, but presupposed by, factual propositions. In this sense, unlike means/ends rules, it is arbitrary. But it has a kinship to the non-arbitrary. It is moulded by human nature and the nature of the world around us. Facts about us and about the world condition the language-games we play and give point to our employing the concepts we have. Radical changes in us or in the world could rob our language-games of their point. But they could not show our concepts to be correct or incorrect, since there is no such thing. (The concept of a unicorn is not defective because there are no unicorns.) But concepts may be more or less useful for certain purposes, more or less appropriate relative to certain goals and concerns.[1]

It follows that although we are at liberty to introduce new words and new uses of words into our language, we cannot justify these grammatical innovations by reference to facts to which they correspond. For there is no such thing as such a correspondence between concepts and reality, nor can any empirical discovery contravene grammar and show it to be 'incorrect'. In the customary use of our psychological vocabulary, these expressions have no application to the body and its parts (or to inanimate things), save in metonymical, metaphorical, figurative, or secondary uses, which are severally explained by reference to the primary application of the terms to human beings and to what behaves like them. Hence the latter cannot be appealed to in order to license the literal application of these expressions beyond the bounds fixed in our grammar. If neurophysiologists, psychologists, artificial-intelligence scientists, or philosophers wish to change existing grammar, to introduce new ways of speaking, they may do so; but their new stipulations must be explained and conditions of application laid down. What may not be done is to argue that since we know what 'to think', 'to see', or 'to infer' mean and know what 'the brain' means, therefore we must know what 'the brain thinks, sees, and infers' means. For we know what these verbs mean only in so far as we have mastered their existing use, which does not license applying them to the body or its parts, save derivatively. Nor may one cross the new 'technical' use with the old one, as, for example, neuroscientists typically do in their theorizing. For this produces a

---

[1] The concept of phlogiston proved to be useless, but not incorrect, for the purposes of chemistry. It was the *theory* of combustion which employed the concept of phlogiston that proved to be incorrect. Of course, many theoretical concepts in science are embedded in a theory, in as much as they are wholly explained by reference to other theoretical terms. Nevertheless, the fact that the theory proves false or incorrect does not show that the concept is incorrect, for *concepts* neither correspond nor fail to correspond with reality.

conflict of rules and hence incoherence *in the neuroscientists' use* of these terms.

Typically, such extensions of the psychological vocabulary by scientists or cognitive scientists is not explained *de novo*, but is held to be justified, i.e. rendered true or correct, by scientific discovery or theory. This is the first error. Further, the new application is held to be wholly transparent by reference to existing use. This is the second error. Failure to apprehend these mistakes results in a blindness to the consequent incoherences in the novel applications of the terms. These incoherences do not lie simply in failure to conform to the ordinary use of the psychological terms, but rather in the conflict, *in the innovators' use*, generated by the extension of the application of the vocabulary beyond what existing grammar licenses, coupled with reliance upon existing grammar (i.e. existing rules for the use of the terms) to explain what these expressions mean (cf. RPP I §548). Scientists could, of course, introduce wholly new terminology; but it is no coincidence that they do not. Were they to do so, they would have to explain its use from scratch. Moreover, it would lack the explanatory force which appears to cling to their extended use of our existing vocabulary. For their aim is to explain what thinking, perceiving, etc. are by reference to the 'thinking' or 'interpreting', 'inferring' or 'hypothesizing', allegedly engaged in by the brain and its parts (or by a machine). We shall return to these matters in §4 below.

Parts of the body: One may hurt one's hand, but it is not the hand that *suffers*; it is the injured person. My hand may hurt, but it does not hurt itself; it hurts *me*, and it is I who have hurt myself. I may have a pain in my hand, but my hand does not have a pain in its thumb. I may be conscious of a throbbing pain in my hand, but my hand is neither conscious nor unconscious of it.

This is how we speak. And if we cannot logically justify it, if there is no such thing as that sort of justification here, we can nevertheless display the roots of our style of discourse. For in an important sense these articulations of grammar are not arbitrary, but reach deep into our instinctive behaviour. 'It is a primitive reaction to tend, to treat, the part that hurts when someone else is in pain' (Z §540), but 'if someone has a pain in his hand, then the hand does not say so . . .[2] and one does not comfort the hand, but the sufferer: one looks into his face' (PI §286). This sort of behaviour is *pre-linguistic* – 'a language-game is based *on it*, . . . it is the prototype of a way of thinking and not the result of thought' (Z §541). Just look at a mother tending her injured child, and equally at a child's reaction to his mother's having hurt herself. One is

---

[2] Wittgenstein added in parenthesis '(unless it writes it)' – which is, I take it, a (rather poor) joke.

filled with pity for the person, not for the person's hand (PI §287)! It is the *person* who expresses or manifests pain, *in his behaviour*. It is he who cries out, contorts his face with pain, weeps, and nurses his injured hand. His pain-avowals are an extension of his primitive pain-behaviour. We commiserate with him, ask him whether his pain is getting less, try to cheer him up, distract his attention from his suffering, and make allowances for him because he is in pain.

What goes for pain goes, *mutatis mutandis*, for other psychological expressions too. It is human beings, not their sense-organs, that see, look around, watch, and observe what is in view. A person sees *with* his eyes, and we can say whether he sees and what he sees by noting how he keeps a moving object in sight, avoids impediments in his path, or looks for things. His behaviour constitutes the criterion for saying 'He sees, looks, has noticed . . .'. Similarly, it is human beings and animals that can be said to be conscious or unconscious, awake or asleep. They, and not some parts of them, regain consciousness after having been stunned or anaesthetized. And so too it is the *person* who expresses his thoughts, opinions, and beliefs in his utterances and manifests them (defeasibly) in his deeds (cf. PI §360). His emotions are exhibited in his face, tone of voice, bodily responses, and in his behaviour.

Of course, there are some predicates that apply, in certain contexts, to a person and to parts of his body interchangeably. 'A gripped the hilt' and 'A's hand gripped the hilt' *generally* mean the same. We say of the blind that they are sightless, and we also speak of sightless eyes. But sightless eyes are not eyes that cannot see, they are eyes with which a person cannot see or eyes of the dead. We talk of warnings falling on deaf ears, but it is not the ears that cannot hear, but the person who refuses to listen. Numerous metonyms and secondary uses of expressions involve applying psychological verbs to parts of the body: 'My eyes have seen the glory of the coming of the Lord', we say; we speak of the heart aching with grief – but it is the person who sees or grieves (and this use of 'ache' is a secondary one). We say that someone has a good brain (i.e. is intelligent), urge someone to use his brain (i.e. to think), and wonder what is going on in his head (i.e. what he is thinking). In extra-theoretical contexts such turns of phrase are harmless. But unless taken figuratively, metonymically, or as secondary uses, as they often are not in psychology or cognitive science, they are typically nonsense. And if they are taken figuratively, metonymically, etc., then it is wholly futile to appeal to them to vindicate psychologists' or neuroscientists' exten-sion of the application of psychological predicates to the brain as part of a theory which purports to explain vision or thought. For the criteria justifying the literal application of psychological verbs are characteristic forms of behaviour of a person. Eyes, ears, hearts, and brains do not *behave* as human beings. Hearts beat and pump blood, but they do not fall in love and express it in amorous glances, shy blushes, or in writing sonnets to their mistresses. Eyes respond to, i.e. are causally affected by, light, but do not look for their friends in a crowd; and although they may twinkle with glee, the glee is not the eye's. Ears respond to sound-waves, but they do not answer what their owner hears, do not tap feet to heard rhythms, do not listen attentively and smile in response to what is heard. And brains do not think; for there is no such thing as a brain expressing a thought or manifesting those distinctive patterns of behaviour and action in the circumstances of life that constitute criteria for thinking.

The body: There are predicates which can be applied indifferently both to people and to their bodies. 'A is bitten all over with mosquito bites' and 'A's body is bitten all over' in most contexts mean the same. 'She is beautiful' and 'Her body is beautiful' are sometimes interchangeable. This cuts no metaphysical ice, but only shows that in certain sentential contexts 'A' and 'A's body' are inter-substitutable. But not, typically, in psychological contexts. It is true that 'I ache all over' and 'My body aches all over' are interchangeable; but it is not my body that feels ill – I do, and I have aching sensations all over my body – but my body does not *have* aching sensations all over *its* body. It makes no sense to say 'A's body is thinking (is in pain, is conscious)', for behaviour, *pace* behaviourists, is not an attribute of a body (cf. 'Behaviour and behaviourism', §4). We are prone to forget how *peculiar* is the locution 'A's body' (and 'my body') and how it differs from genitives applied to other physical objects, e.g. 'A's bodkin'. Of course, here too we can envisage a different grammar. Instead of 'A is in pain', one might say 'A's body is in pain', and instead of 'I have a headache', it would be said 'My body has a headache'. But this shift in grammar would ramify (BB 73): rather than saying 'A must take an aspirin and lie down, should consult a doctor and work less hard', one would say 'A's body must take an aspirin, lie down, etc.'. One would not say 'I am going to London', 'I am thinking (expecting, hoping)', or 'I would like (want, prefer, etc.)', but rather 'My body is going to London (is thinking, etc.)'. And instead of 'A is in pain, but isn't showing it', one would say 'A's body is in pain, but his body is not showing it', and so on. And it will be A's body that speaks, that compliments my body for the work it has done or insults my body for the offence it has caused. Bizarre as this seems, it again makes little difference, *as long as one does not cross this new form of representation with the old one*. It will not be licit to say 'I can say what I feel (think, want) without observing my behaviour', for the correct form of expression will be 'My body can say what it feels without observing its behaviour'. In this form of representation, certain uses of 'my body' will have as privileged a position in grammar as 'I' does in our form of representation, and significant distinctions we draw will be obliterated or obscured.

2. The mind

It is in general wrong to ascribe psychological predicates to the body and its parts, save metonymically or metaphorically. It does not follow that it is correct to apply them to the mind. Notoriously, Descartes did just that, attributing all psychological properties to an immaterial substance, the mind or soul, which he thought to be only causally related to the body. It is, he held, the mind which has sensations, sees (or seems to see), hears (or seems to hear), is angry or pleased, thinks and doubts, has desires, intends and decides. This conception, which has dominated philosophical reflection for centuries, is incoherent in many respects. For present purposes we need to recall how the expression 'the mind' is actually used in our language, and so to bring the word back from its metaphysical use to its common-or-garden employment. We do not use the word 'I' as we use the phrase 'my mind', and although 'His mind is preoccupied (in a turmoil)' means the same as 'He is preoccupied (in a turmoil)', we cannot typically replace 'he' by 'his mind' in the generality of contexts of verbs of sensation, perception, emotion, thought, and will.

Puzzled about the nature of the mind, philosophers and psychologists raise the question 'What is the mind?' and endeavour to answer it by offering a definition. Or they paraphrase it immediately by 'What sort of entity is a mind?' and wonder whether it is an immaterial entity in causal interaction with the brain or is actually identical with the brain or stands to the brain as a programme to a computer. But 'What sort of entity is a mind?' is as pernicious a question as 'What sort of entity is a number?' Substantives are substance-hungry, but abstinence is to be recommended. 'How is the word "mind" used?' is the question we should address if we wish to clarify the nature of the mind (cf. PI §370). It is tempting to answer it by offering a definition. It has been suggested that the mind is the capacity to acquire intellectual abilities, i.e. abilities to engage in activities which involve operating with symbols.[3] This is illuminating, connecting the notion of a creature which has a mind with that of a creature with concept-exercising abilities and with the capacity to acquire them. But it is wrong; for it provides no standard of correctness for such (licit) uses of the word 'mind' as 'A thought crossed my mind', 'He has a quick (devious, dirty, small) mind', 'I have made up my mind', etc. And although these phrases are largely restricted to concept-employing creatures, it is not awry to say of a horse that it has a mind of its own when it stubbornly refuses to obey the will of its rider. To search for a *Merkmal*-definition of 'mind' is arguably as futile, and

---

[3] A. J. P. Kenny, 'The Origin of the Soul', in A. J. P. Kenny, H. C. Longuet-Higgins, J. R. Lucas, and C. H. Waddington, *The Development of Mind*, Gifford Lectures 1972/3 (Edinburgh University Press, Edinburgh, 1973), p. 46.

certainly as unhelpful for philosophical clarification, as searching for a definition of number. What is needed is a description of the use of the word 'mind' that will provide a surview of its grammatical articulations. Here only a pen-sketch will be essayed.

The English word 'mind' is connected primarily with the intellect and the will. At the most general level it is associated with intellectual faculties: a person is said to have a powerful, agile, subtle, or devious mind if he is skilful, quick, ingenious at problem-solving, or if his solutions, plans, and projects display subtlety or cunning. Hence too it is connected with corresponding intellectual virtues and vices: a person has a tenacious, idle, vigorous, judicious, or indecisive mind according to the manner in which he grapples with problems requiring reflection and according to the typical upshot of his reflections. (Curiously, however, we do not characterize a person's *mind* as wise, intelligent, or foolish.) A person is of sound mind if he retains his rational faculties, and is said to be out of his mind if he thinks, proposes, or does things that suggest unreason where reason is meet.

Numerous ordinary uses of 'mind' are bound up with (a) thought, (b) opinion, and (c) memory. (a) One turns one's mind to something when one starts to think about it, and one puts one's mind to it when it needs resolving. Ideas come to mind, flash through one's mind, or lurk, just out of reach, in the back of one's mind. And sometimes, when one cannot think or recollect, one's mind goes blank. (b) To know one's mind is to have formed one's opinion, and to tell one's mind is to express it. To give someone a piece of one's mind is to tell him harshly what one thinks of him, and to be of one mind with another person is to agree in opinion or judgement. (c) To keep or bear something in mind is not to forget it, and to call to mind (and *remind* oneself) is to recollect. Something out of mind is forgotten or not thought about ('Out of sight, out of mind'), and someone who is absent-minded is forgetful and inattentive.

Other connections are with the will. To make up one's mind is to decide, whereas to be of two minds is to waver between alternatives; to change one's mind is to withdraw one's previous opinion, judgement, intention, or decision and form one afresh. To have a mind to do something is to be inclined or tempted to do it, and to have half a mind to do something is to be sorely tempted, perhaps against one's better judgement.

Other uses fade off in other directions, e.g. broad- (or narrow-) minded, small- and petty-minded, having a dirty mind, having a mind like a razor, displaying presence of mind, having things on one's mind and hence no peace of mind, and so on. But this brief sketch suffices for drawing some morals.

Numerous pictures are bound up with this rich terminology, pictures of space (in, out of, through, or across the mind), of room (broad, narrow, small), and so of parts (half a mind, one's whole mind), of agency (quick, agile, powerful), and hence of virtues and vices (tenacity, indolence). But these pictures are not a theory of the mind, and our uses of these phrases no more commit us to a theory than does our talk of sunrise and sunset. Our terminology no more presupposes that 'the mind' is an 'entity' of any sort than our talk of numbers commits us to the view that numbers are 'entities'.

On the rebound from Cartesianism, it is tempting to argue that in talking of the mind we are indulging in a fiction, pretending that there is an entity of a strange sort, an immaterial homunculus or a non-physical space occupied by ethereal things (ideas, sense-data, or experiences). But this is as misguided as the supposition that in talking of numbers, we pretend that there exist Platonic objects in an abstract realm. 'What sort of entity is a mind?', like 'What sort of entity is a number?', can only be answered by insisting that a mind, like a number, is not an entity of any sort – not even a fictional or 'pretend' entity. This may seem drastic: for does that not mean that there are no minds, that minds do not exist? That too is confused, as is the thought that if one denies Platonism, then one is committed to the view that numbers do not exist. The moot question is rather: what does it mean to say that minds (or numbers) exist? To be sure, decisive people have a mind of their own, and quick-thinking people have agile minds. There can be no question but that when pondering, thoughts cross one's mind, and that when imagining things, one has things before one's mind's eye. These are not 'ontological commitments' or metaphysical revelations, but humble grammatical propositions. All they commit us to are uses of words.

It is philosophy and psychology (of scientific folk) that misconceive the *pictures* embedded in ordinary languages, misinterpret these pictures as theories, and construct alternative and equally absurd theories in response to their own misinterpretations of these pictures. The idiom of inspecting one's mind, seeing with the mind's eye, or searching one's mind for this or that, of introspecting, etc., if misconstrued, fosters the philosophical mythology of the transparent mind and its counterpart, the elusive mind, as well as the misconceived psychological methodology of Wundt's introspective psychology. In response to these confusions, psychological behaviourism denied the existence of the mind and held our ordinary discourse to be ridden with primitive fictions. Similarly, some contemporary philosophers look forward to a scientific millennium in which our current psychological vocabulary is replaced by something truer to the facts, e.g. a neuroscientific language embodying a true theory of human organisms. These muddles stem, *inter alia*, from adverting to pictures as if they were theories and disregarding their (wholly atheoretic) uses. The task of philosophy here is to describe the grammar of the mental. The task of psychology is to construct empirical theories (where theorizing is appropriate) within the framework of well-understood psychological concepts (including technical terminology where it is required). It is not errors in our language that are responsible for absurd theories of the mind (although that is not to say that new terms and distinctions are not needed in empirical psychology). It is our misconstruals of the uses of our expressions, our asking misconceived questions and trying to answer rather than to dissolve them.

Does this mean that the mind is just an aspect of the body? 'I'm not that hard up for categories,' Wittgenstein replied (RPP II §690). Height, weight, and build are aspects of the body – not having a thought in mind, making up one's mind, or having a mind of one's own. But equally, thinking, perceiving, having emotions, wanting, intending, and resolving are *not, pace* Cartesians, properties of, or activities performed by, the mind. It is living human beings (and what behaves like them) that reflect, ponder, and cogitate. It is people who love or hate, hope or despair. It is not my mind that makes up its mind, steels its will, and acts – it is I.

3. *Only in the stream of life . . .*

That people have such-and-such sensations is manifest in their behaviour: in their cries and groans of pain, the grimaces of their faces, their scratching, their rubbing and assuaging their limbs, and in their articulate avowals. That people see is evident in their looking, watching, scrutinizing, and reacting to what is visible; that they hear is manifest in their listening and responding to what is audible, etc. Their wants, intentions, and purposes are expressed in their tryings, strivings, and goal-directed behaviour and speech. These are grammatical propositions that characterize human life; and the use of the rich and variegated psychological vocabulary is part of our form of life, not part of an explanatory theory that might prove false and be rejected. Psychological and neurophysiological theories may come and go, but the propositions that people love and hate, make up their minds and pursue their aims, have things in mind and call things to mind, are no more theoretical than that white is lighter than black or that colours can be seen but not heard. It is not a matter of *opinion* that people have minds (cf. PI p. 178).[4] For what could show that *people* lack minds? Of course, we employ these psychological expressions in explanations of behaviour; we say that someone cried out because he hurt himself, moved aside because he saw the impediment in his path, jumped because he was frightened. Such explanations may, in

---

[4] 'Ich habe nicht die *Meinung*, dass er eine Seele hat'. There is no precise equivalent of 'mind' in German. 'Mind' is more restricted than 'Seele' or 'Geist', and so too is 'soul'.

their context, be right or wrong; but they are not part of a verifiable or falsifiable *theory* of human behaviour. And the use of 'I have a pain', 'I am frightened', 'I want (wish, expect, etc.)' are not reflexive applications of a theoretical vocabulary, any more than 'I cried out in pain', 'I ducked because I saw it coming', or 'I jumped with fright' are *theoretical* explanations.

Our psychological vocabulary has behavioural, species-specific roots and highly acculturated branches, foliage, and fruits. The expressions we employ in characterizing other people's thoughts, feelings, and experiences and in explaining what they do and say in terms of their experiences, beliefs, desires, and purposes have a use only in the stream of human life. Our use of psychological words in manifesting and avowing our own experiences or in giving expression to our thoughts and opinions is part of the weave of our life; it is constitutive of human life and not simply part of a theory about it.

These expressions make sense only in this complex weave, 'For concepts are not for use on a single occasion' (Z §568):

> How could human behaviour be described? Surely only by sketching the actions of a variety of humans as they are all mixed up together. What determines our judgement, our concepts and reactions, is not what *one* man is doing *now*, an individual action, but the whole hurly-burly of human actions, the background against which we see any action. (Z §567)

It is important to stress that 'One pattern in the weave is interwoven with many others' (Z §569). One cannot, as it were, isolate one pattern in this tapestry by removing a number of the threads.

> The concept of pain is characterized by its particular function in our life.
> Pain has *this* position in our life; has *these* connections. (That is to say: we only call 'pain' what has *this* position, these connections.) (Z §§532f.)

The concept of pain is bound up not just with characteristic pain-behaviour in circumstances of injury or illness, but also with pity and commiseration, fear and anxiety, cruelty and mercy. It is interwoven with special attitudes towards the sick (both care *and* disdain), with *concepts* of health and welfare and hence with that of the good of a being. And *this* example is a relatively simple one: 'Only surrounded by certain normal manifestations of life [*Lebensäusserung*] is there such a thing as an expression of pain. Only surrounded by an even more far-reaching particular manifestation of life, such a thing as the expression of sorrow or affection. And so on' (Z §534). It only makes sense to say of a creature that it feels pain if it is a creature which can (logically) manifest it in behaviour. Hence the concept gets a firm grip with respect to humans and mammals, but starts to slip with lower creatures (RPP II §659) and has no application to the inanimate. And a far more complex setting of behaviour and behavioural manifestations of sophisticated capacities is necessary for the concepts of dissimulating or pretending to be in pain (cf. Exg. §249).

If that is so, how much more complex a behavioural setting is required for us to attribute fear, hope, expectation, and relief, let alone expecting, hoping, wanting, or wishing for something not here and now, but tomorrow, next week, or at the end of the year.

> We say a dog is afraid his master will beat him; but not, he is afraid his master will beat him tomorrow. Why not? (PI §650)

> Why can a dog feel fear but not remorse? Would it be right to say 'Because he can't talk'? (Z §518)

> Only someone who can reflect on the past can repent. But that does not mean that as a matter of empirical fact only such a one is capable of the feeling of remorse. (Z §520)

These emotions, and hosts of other experiences, are intelligibly predicable only of language-using creatures. 'There is nothing astonishing about certain concepts only being applicable to a being that e.g. possesses a language' (Z §520). Only of creatures with a far more complex repertoire of behaviour than dogs have, in particular only of those who have mastered the techniques of using a language, does it make sense to say that they have opinions, wonder whether, reflect or ponder on, guess or surmise that something is the case. Here the weave of life must be dense and rich – as it is with us. A creature that can hold opinions, reflect on problems, come to or sometimes jump to conclusions is a creature that can behave in endlessly variegated, subtly differentiated ways. It must be capable of expressing its opinions (or keeping them to itself), of articulating its reflections, and of acting on its conclusions. It must be a creature who can say to itself, and of whom it can be said, that it is justified or unjustified, has good grounds or lacks them, makes mistakes and occasionally corrects them, resolves to act on its conclusions. It must have goals, take pleasure in attaining them, and be disappointed at failure. The applicability of such concepts as opining, reflecting, wondering, guessing, surmising, etc. is not severable from the applicability of a wide range of other concepts – of desire and will, motive and intention, satisfaction and disappointment, etc. For the criteria for the application of the former involve the application of the latter.

4. Homunculi and brains

The asymmetry between first- and third-person psychological utterances and the assumption that first-person present-tense psychological utterances are uniformly descriptions of inner states uniquely accessible to their owner induces the thought that psychological predicates signify attributes of the mind rather than of the whole human being. Further pressures are generated by scientific reflections on the nature and mechanisms of perception. If vision is explained by the production of a retinal image of what is in view, and if that image is conceived as being transmitted to some part of the brain and, in some sense, reconstituted there, it is tempting to think that for a person to see an object, it is necessary that something other than the person, viz. his mind or soul, should see an internal picture of that object. Descartes argued that the retinal image, by stimulating the optic nerve, causes an image to be reproduced on the pineal gland. He rightly warned that although, in his view, the picture generated in the brain resembles the object perceived, the resultant sensory perception is not caused by that resemblance, for that would require 'yet other eyes within our brain with which we could perceive it'.[5] It is obviously futile to try to explain what it is for a human being to see (or to think, reason, or infer) by reference to something else's seeing (thinking, reasoning, or inferring). For this both generates a regress and demands an explanation of what it is for this other thing (mind or brain) to see (think, reason, or infer). Descartes' warning, which is apt, might suggest that he carefully avoided the 'homunculus fallacy'. But this would be wrong. For he erred in two respects: first, he held that it is in the pineal gland that 'the two images coming from a single object through the two eyes . . . can come together in a single image or impression before reaching the soul, *so that they do not present to it two objects instead of one.*'[6] But since the soul does *not see* what is on the pineal gland, it is not necessary that there be there one image as opposed to two or none. Whatever is there is not the *object* of perception. Secondly, no matter what is registered on the pineal gland or for that matter in the 'visual' striate cortex – no matter whether it is an image, a 'map', or any other so-called internal representation – it is not something that can intelligibly be said to be 'presented'. For to whom is it 'presented'? In short, it is a conceptual confusion to attribute sight to the soul or mind.

Where Descartes misguidedly ascribed perceptual and intellectual predicates to the soul, contemporary psychologists and neurophysiologists ascribe them to the brain. Three examples make this vivid:

[5] Descartes, *Optics*, in *The Philosophical Writings of Descartes*, tr. J. Cottingham, R. Stoothoff, and D. Murdoch (Cambridge University Press, Cambridge, 1984), Vol. 1, p. 167 (*Oeuvres de Descartes*, eds. Ch. Adam and P. Tannery, rev. edn (Paris, Vrin (C.N.R.S.), 1964 – 76. Vol. VI. p. 130). Hereafter AT followed by volume and page numbers.
[6] Descartes, *The Passions of the Soul*, in *Philosophical Writings*, Vol. I, p. 340 (AT XI, 353).

we can thus regard all seeing as a continual search for the answers to questions posed by the brain. The signals from the retina constitute 'messages' conveying these answers. The brain then uses this information to construct a suitable hypothesis about what there is . . .

. . . it is the cortex that asks meaningful questions, and so dictates the whole scanning process through its connections with the mid-brain . . . the real problem is to find out how the cortex uses the message it gets from the retina to answer the questions and to ask others. This is the serial process that we call visual perception.[7]

Impressed by Helmholtz's incoherent idea that 'perceptions' are 'unconscious inferences', scientists find themselves

driven to say that such neurons [as respond in a highly specific manner to, say, line orientation] have knowledge. They have intelligence, for they are able to estimate the probability of outside events – events that are important to the animal in question. And the brain gains its knowledge by a process analogous to the inductive reasoning of the classical scientific method. Neurons present arguments to the brain based on the specific features they detect, arguments on which the brain constructs its hypothesis of perception.[8]

Suspicious of the Cartesian conception of the mind, scientists are prone to substitute the brain. Hence, seeing is held to be

probably the most sophisticated of all the brain's activities: calling upon its stores of memory data; requiring subtle classifications, comparisons and logical decisions for sensory data to become perception.[9]

If it is nonsense to say that a person's mind has toothache, smells the scent of roses, or intends to go to London, it is 'nonsense on stilts' to suppose that a brain classifies and compares, asks questions and answers them, constructs hypotheses and makes decisions. These are predicates of human beings, applied on the basis of sophisticated behaviour and presupposing complex capacities. It is no more the brain that sees than it is the mind.

Nothing which a brain can intelligibly be said to do constitutes a behavioural manifestation of pain. It is not brains that feel pain, but people (and animals) who have brains and manifest pain in their behaviour. If one replies that surely, when a person is in pain, the C-fibres in his brain are firing and this is a criterion for being in pain, one merely manifests further confusion over the concept of behaviour in general and the criteria for pain in particular. Brains do not groan or cry

[7] J. Z. Young, *Programs of the Brain* (Oxford University Press, Oxford, 1978), pp. 119, 124.

[8] C. Blakemore, *Mechanics of the Mind* (Cambridge University Press, Cambridge, 1977), p. 91.

[9] R. L. Gregory, 'The Confounded Eye', in R. L. Gregory and E. H. Gombrich (eds), *Illusion in Nature and Art* (Duckworth, London, 1973), p. 50.

out; they do not limp on their sprained ankle or rub their bruised shoulder. My brain does not ask for an analgesic, excuse its inattention by reference to a headache, ask to be left alone, or call for a doctor. The firings of C-fibres are not a behavioural manifestation of the brain's being in pain, but at best an inductively discovered condition for the possibility of a person's having a pain.

A *fortiori* it makes no sense to say that a brain calculates, constructs hypotheses, asks or answers questions. These are intelligibly predicable only of language-users, not of a *part* of a creature who has mastered the techniques of using a language. A brain cannot speak or write – not because it is dumb or illiterate, but because it makes no sense to say 'His brain spoke (or wrote)'. The brain can neither use nor misuse a language. There is no such thing as a brain expressing an opinion ('I think it is going to rain') or acting on a belief (e.g. taking an umbrella), let alone arguing, disputing, hypothesizing, or conjecturing; nor does it make sense to attribute to a brain misunderstanding or reactions to other people's opinions and beliefs such as indignation, resentment, or delight.

But scientists do speak thus of the brain. Can it not be argued that these are derivative or secondary uses? Not so. 'He has a good brain' means the same as 'He is intelligent'. 'My brain isn't working today' means the same as 'I can't think clearly today'. These and many other phrases are quite harmless. But the claims that the brain asks and answers questions, makes subtle classifications, comparisons, and 'logical decisions' are not metonymical. These are not the questions and answers, comparisons and decisions, of a person; indeed, they are not held to be anything of which the person is aware. Rather they are putative explanatory hypotheses which are meant to explain perception, much as the theories of certain theoretical linguists, who attempt to explain how we can understand what we hear, are prone to suppose that the brain engages in complex logico-linguistic analysis of acoustic inputs. Far from being harmless *façons de parler*, these are pernicious; for they are low-grade nonsense in the guise of high-powered theory.

5. Can machines think?

It might seem that the above arguments are refuted by the simple observation that we talk of *machines* as calculating, computing, and even thinking, say that they have more or less powerful memories, and speak, in relation to such machines, of artificial intelligence. Artificial-intelligence scientists insist that they are already building machines that can think and see, recognize and identify, make choices and decisions. Chess-playing machines can 'beat' chess-masters, and computers can 'calculate' far more efficiently and quickly than mathematicians. If all this is to be taken at face value, it seems to show, first, that the grammatical remark that these predicates, in their literal use, are restricted to human beings and what behaves like human beings is either wrong *simpliciter* or displays 'semantic inertia' that has been overtaken by the march of science, for machines actually do behave like human beings. Secondly, if it makes literal sense to attribute epistemic and even perceptual predicates to machines which are built to simulate certain human operations and to execute certain human tasks, it seems plausible to suppose that the human brain must have a similar abstract functional structure to that of the machine design. In which case, surely, it must make sense to attribute the variety of psychological predicates to the human brain after all. And if that is so, then are not the answers to the centuries-old philosophical questions about the relation of mind to body and about the nature of thinking or consciousness to be found in physiological psychology and artificial-intelligence theory?

Philosophical problems stem from conceptual confusion. They are not resolved by empirical discoveries, and they cannot be answered, but only swept under the carpet, by conceptual change. Fifth-generation computers will doubtless be able to execute astonishing tasks. But their existence will do nothing to clarify the question of whether it makes literal sense to attribute psychological predicates to machines that are not, and do not really behave, like human beings. The fact that we now apply a limited range of epistemic verbs to our gadgets no more shows an enlightened 'semantic momentum' stemming from insight into the true nature of the mental than does the fact that we have always applied these expressions to dolls or spirits and ghosts (PI §282).

Wittgenstein addressed the question briefly in the 1930s and obliquely in the *Remarks on the Foundations of Mathematics*. In the *Blue Book* he wrote:

'Is it possible for a machine to think?' (whether the action of this machine can be described and predicted by the laws of physics or, possibly, only by laws of a different kind applying to the behaviour of organisms). And the trouble which is expressed in this question is not really that we don't yet know a machine which could do the job. The question is not analogous to that which someone might have asked a hundred years ago: 'Can a machine liquefy a gas?' The trouble is rather that the sentence, 'A machine thinks (perceives, wishes)' seems somehow nonsensical. It is as though we had asked 'Has the number 3 a colour?'. (BB 47)

Wittgenstein's point is not that thinking, being in some sense ethereal, gaseous, non-physical, cannot be a property of a machine because it must, of its nature, be a property of something that has a 'spiritual nature', viz. the mind. On the contrary, he had already repudiated that in *Philosophical Grammar* (PG 106):

In the consideration of our problems one of the most dangerous ideas is the idea that we think *with*, or *in*, our *heads*.

The idea of a process in the head, in a completely enclosed space, makes thinking something occult. . . .
    It is a travesty of the truth to say 'Thinking is an activity of our mind, as writing is of the hand'. (Love in the heart. The head and heart as loci of the soul.)

As argued above, it is not a person's mind that thinks for him, nor does he think with it. But replacing that Cartesian idea by the supposition that it is the brain that thinks is equally awry. It makes no more sense literally to attribute thinking to the brain than to assert (or deny) that the number 3 is green. One may say 'Hush! I'm thinking. Don't disturb me!', but not 'Hush! My brain is thinking. Don't disturb it!' One may add, 'Wait a moment and I'll tell you', but not 'Wait a moment, and my brain will tell me, and then I'll tell you'.

    Nor is Wittgenstein's point that thinking is an emergent property of sufficiently complex material structures, whether biological or electrophysical. For it is not as if, once the 'machinery' of the brain becomes exceedingly complicated, a super-physical 'world' of experience springs into being. He noted that

It seems to us sometimes as though the phenomena of personal experience were in a way phenomena in the upper strata of the atmosphere as opposed to the material phenomena which happen on the ground. There are views according to which these phenomena in the upper strata arise when the material phenomena reach a certain degree of complexity. E.g., that the mental phenomena, sense experience, volition, etc., emerge when a type of animal body of a certain complexity has been evolved. (BB 47)

He added that there is obviously something right about this. Clearly, psychological faculties are empirically related to cerebral development, 'for the amoeba certainly doesn't speak or write or discuss, whereas we do' (ibid.). Nevertheless, the picture of the mental as an emergent 'world', as it were, is wholly misconceived (see 'The world of consciousness', §2). And although neurological complexity (crudely speaking) is empirically requisite for possession of perceptual, volitional, and cognitive faculties, the kinds of features and the nature of their 'complexity' (if any) that underlie and constitute criteria for attributing such faculties and their exercise to a being are quite different from this. Psychological concepts are not concepts of ethereal properties or processes, and the presuppositions and conditions of their application concern issues logically independent of neurological complexity, or indeed of the 'computational' complexity or power of a machine.

    Has Wittgenstein not been overtaken by scientific progress? Are computers not precisely prosthetic organs of thought (cf. Z §607)? Or, if not *organs*, at least machines that can think for us, faster and more efficiently than we can? Can't we say, when we press the appropriate keys on our computer and wait for an answer to flash upon the screen,

'Now it's thinking'? Yes, we can joke thus; as we can pat our dear old car and say 'She's temperamental today'. But the *behavioural* criteria *in the circumstances of life* for saying of something that it is thinking can no more be exemplified by a computer than a number can turn green. It is not, and does not behave like, a human being, and what it does is not a criterion for saying that it is thinking.

It might seem that the 'Turing test' circumvents this objection. If a computer could be so programmed that the typed answers displayed on its machine screen were indistinguishable from those a human being might type out in response to questions, is the machine not behaving precisely as a human being? Not so! It takes more – but not *additively* more – to perform a speech-act than to make a noise or generate an inscription. Human beings are no more uncomprehending programmed typing-machines than computers have a form of life. The appearance of typed messages on a screen may be the *product* of human behaviour or of a machine programme put to certain human purposes. But it is not a form of human behaviour.[10]

It is now known that Wittgenstein read Turing's famous paper 'On Computable Numbers'. His only *direct* comment on it is brief and bewildering: 'Turing's "machines". These machines are *humans* who calculate' (RPP I §1096). It is possible to make sense of this enigmatic remark, however, by reference to the presuppositions of Turing's discussion and other remarks of Wittgenstein on the concepts of calculation, following rules, and mathematics.[11] Accepting a version of Church's thesis, viz. that all effective number-theoretic functions (viz. algorithms) can be encoded in binary terms and that these binary-encoded functions are machine-computable, Turing sketched an abstract notion of a computing machine by analogy with human beings calculating:

We may compare a man in the process of computing a real number to a machine which is only capable of a finite number of conditions $q_1, q_2, \ldots, q_R$ which will be called 'm-configurations'. The machine is supplied with a 'tape' . . . running through it, and divided into sections . . . each capable of bearing a 'symbol'. At any moment there is just one square, say the r th bearing the symbol G(r) which is 'in the machine'. We may call this square the 'scanned symbol'. The 'scanned symbol' is the only one of which the machine is, so to speak, 'directly aware'.[12]

---

[10] Similarly, the pattern in a carpet may be the product of a human being making the carpet or of a Jacquard loom, but it is not a form of behaviour.

[11] The following discussion is indebted to S. G. Shanker's 'Wittgenstein versus Turing on the Nature of Church's Thesis', in *Notre Dame Journal of Formal Logic*, 28, No. 4 (Oct. 1987), pp. 615 – 49.

[12] A. Turing, 'On Computable Numbers, with an application to the *Entscheidungs-problem*', §§1 – 2, *Proceedings of the London Mathematical Society*, 42 (1937), pp. 230 – 65.

Using the expression 'computer' to mean a person computing, Turing continues:

The behaviour of the computer at any moment is determined by the symbols which he is observing, and his 'state of mind' at that moment . . . Let us imagine the operations performed by the computer to be split up into 'simple operations' which are so elementary that it is not easy to imagine them further divided. Every such operation consists of some change of the physical system consisting of the computer and his tape. We know the state of the system if we know the sequence of symbols on the tape, which of these are observed by the computer . . . and the state of mind of the computer . . . The simple operations must therefore include:
(a) Changes of the symbols on one of the observed squares.
(b) Changes of one of the squares observed to another square within L squares of one of the previously observed squares . . .
The operation actually performed is determined . . . by the state of mind of the computer and the observed symbols in particular, they determine the state of mind of the computer after the operation is carried out.
We may now construct a machine to do the work of this computer. To each state of mind of the computer corresponds an 'm-configuration' of the machine . . .[13]

Notwithstanding the crudity of Turing's conception of a *state of mind* and of his notion of determination, he successfully demonstrated that given binary encodability, recursive functions are ideally suited to mechanical implementation by means of electrical circuitry. But given that we can now construct, partly due to Turing, ingenious machines to relieve us of computing tasks, does it follow that computers (in the contemporary sense of the term) can calculate, let alone think? Or is it rather that by using our machines, we can now arrive at the results of complex calculations without anyone (or anything) literally calculating, as we can now find out what is happening on the other side of the moon without anyone (or anything) going there to look (viz. by means of spacecraft television cameras)?

Calculating devices were invented long before computers, ranging from the humble abacus to the slide-rule and the mechanical calculating machines invented in the nineteenth century. No one was tempted to say that these gadgets could literally calculate or think. Are electronic computers in principle any different? It is tempting to insist that they are, not merely because the tasks that they can be used to undertake are so much more complex, but also because they surely follow rules. For do we not programme them with ever more sophisticated algorithms, and do they not follow these instructions meticulously? No; one can no more literally instruct a computer to do anything than one can instruct a tree, though one can make a tree grow in a certain way, and one can make a computer produce the result of vastly complex calculations. One can

[13] Ibid., §9.

replace a complex rule with a sequence of simpler rules compliance with which will ensure the same outcome, and human beings can typically follow such simple rules quite mechanically, i.e. without reflecting (RFM 422). But a machine cannot follow a rule mechanically, no matter whether the rule is simple or complex, since it makes no sense to talk of a machine *following* a rule.

This grammatical remark should be obvious from previous discussions of following rules (cf. Volume 2, 'Rules and grammar', 'Accord with a rule', 'Following rules, mastery of techniques and practices'). A machine can execute operations that accord with a rule, provided all the causal links built into it function as designed and assuming that the design ensures the generation of a regularity in accord with a chosen rule or rules. But for something to constitute following a rule, the mere production of a regularity in accord with a rule is not sufficient.

A being can only be said to be *following* a rule in the context of a complex practice involving actual and potential normative activities (cf. Volume 2, pp. 44 – 8, 254 – 69) of justifying, noticing mistakes and correcting them by reference to the relevant rule, criticizing deviations from the rule, and, if called upon, explaining an action as being in accord with the rule or teaching others what counts as following the rule. The determination of an act as being done *correctly* in accord with a rule is *logical*, not causal. For transformations of signs to constitute calculating or inferring, the nexus must be normative. Must it not be deterministic? Must not the consequences flow with the inevitability of a machine? To this one might reply ironically with Wittgenstein, 'What sort of machine? One constructed of the usual materials – or a super-machine? Are you not confusing the hardness of a rule with the hardness of a material?' (RFM 220). A causal nexus determines an outcome causally, not normatively; but the determination that underlies the steps in a calculation or in a logical inference is not causal.

'We are calculating only when there is a *must* behind the result.' But suppose we don't know this *must*, is it contained in the calculations all the same? Or are we not calculating, if we do it quite naïvely?

How about the following: You aren't calculating if, when you get now this, now that result, and cannot find a mistake, you accept this and say: this simply shows that certain circumstances which are still unknown have an influence on the result.

This might be expressed: if calculation reveals a causal connection to you, then you are not calculating.

Our children are not only given practice in calculation but are also trained to adopt a particular attitude towards a mistake in calculating, towards a departure from the norm.

What I am saying comes to this, that mathematics is normative. (RFM 424f.)

The transformation of signs constitutes calculating or inferring only in so far as it is normative. And such transformations are normative only if they have a function apart from the transformation – viz. as determining a sense and as constituting a measure ('This is how things *must* be!'). What makes a sign-game into mathematics is the use of the signs *outside* mathematics: 'Just as it is not logical inference either, for me to make a change from one formation to another (say from one arrangement of chairs to another) if these arrangements have not a linguistic function apart from this transformation' (RFM 257). The point is vividly made by imagining calculating machines occurring in nature, in impenetrable caskets. 'And now suppose that . . . people use these appliances, say as we use calculation, though of that they know nothing. Thus e.g. they make predictions with the aid of calculating machines, but for them manipulating these queer objects is experimenting' (RFM 258). No matter how reliable the resultant predictions, the people are not making calculations with the machines, any more than one makes calculations with a crystal ball. And could one say that the machines are making calculations independently of human beings? No, no more than one can say that the revolving globe tells the time independently of human beings' conventions of time-measurement.

The internal relation between a rule and what correctly accords with it is manifest in the employment of the rule in the practices of life, in using the rule as a canon of correctness. There can be no accord with a rule if there is no following of that rule, and following a rule requires regularities of behaviour in the context of normative activities. One can programme a machine to execute an algorithm. If its parts do not malfunction, its causal connections will ensure the correct output. But what makes the output *correct* is not the causal inevitability with which it is produced. In what seems almost to be a direct reply to Turing, Wittgenstein wrote:

> Does a calculating machine *calculate*?
> Imagine that a calculating machine had come into existence by accident; now someone accidentally presses its knobs (or an animal walks over it) and it calculates the product of 25 × 20.
> I want to say: it is essential to mathematics that its signs are also employed in *mufti*. (RFM 257)

But, one could add, our calculating machines are always in uniform, never in *mufti*. We use these machines (computers) to save us the tedious labour of calculating; but it does not follow, and is indeed nonsense to assert, that the machine infers or draws conclusions. One could readily build a computer from a very large toy railway-set with a huge number of switch-points and storage depots for different types of carriages to be shunted into until called upon for further operations (i.e. a 'computer memory'). This computer would be cumbersomely large and slow, but in essence its operations would not differ from the latest gadgetry on the computer-market. Would any one say, as hundreds of trains rush through complex networks of on/off points according to a pre-arranged timetable (a programme), depositing trucks in sidings or depots and collecting others, 'Now the railway-set is calculating', 'Now it is inferring', or 'Now it is thinking'? Does it make any difference if the 'railway-set' is miniscule and the 'trains' move at the speed of electric current?

Turing conceived of a human being computing a real number as having his behaviour *determined* 'by the symbols which he is observing, and his "state of mind" at that moment . . .'. In particular, it is these that 'determine the state of mind of the computer after the operation is carried out'. It is clear that Turing was thinking here of causal, psychological determination, and that he failed to see that the determination of the correctness of a computation cannot be causal. Again, Wittgenstein identified the crux of the matter:

> *There are no* causal connections in a calculation, only the connections of the pattern. And it makes no difference to this that we work over the proof in order to accept it. That we are therefore tempted to say that it arose as the result of a psychological experiment. For the psychical course of events is not psychologically investigated when we calculate. (RFM 382)

One might say that Turing's philosophical speculations (as opposed to his mathematical insights into computability) conflated a human who is, as it were, a calculating machine with a human calculating mechanically.

> A human calculating machine might be trained so that when the rules of inference were shown it and perhaps exemplified, it read through the proofs of a mathematical system (say that of Russell), and nodded its head after every correctly drawn conclusion, but shook its head at a mistake and stopped calculating. One could imagine this creature as otherwise perfectly imbecile. (RFM 258)

Of this creature one could not say that it knows any mathematics, understands mathematical notation, calculates, or draws inferences. But we might use it to save us the labour of calculating and checking proofs. And in a society which used logical and mathematical formulae and derivations (only valid ones!) solely as decorations for wallpaper, this human calculating machine might be used to check whether the wallpaper was 'correctly' decorated (cf. LFM 34ff.)! Of course, *we* can do calculations mechanically, without reflecting (RFM 422), but – and here we come full circle to Wittgenstein's sole direct remark on Turing's machines – 'if calculating looks to us like the action of a machine, *it is the human being* doing the calculation that is the machine' (RFM 234).

A creature that can calculate mechanically can also calculate thoughtfully or reflectively. If it can think, it must also make sense to say of it that it ponders, mulls over, and reconsiders (but it makes no sense to consider or reconsider *mechanically* (RPP I §560)); hence that it is, from time to time, pensive, reflective, or in a contemplative mood. It is a creature which can be said to be collecting its thoughts before it speaks, to be wrapt or engrossed in thought. It must be capable of having beliefs and opinions, hence it must make sense to say that it is incredulous or opinionated, open-minded or bigoted. It may be of a sceptical cast of mind or tentative and hesitant. It may be shrewd, prudent, and wise or short-sighted and poor in judgement.

This array of attributes and dispositions is in turn embedded in a wider network. For this battery of psychological predicates can only be applied intelligibly to a being who can manifest such features and dispositions in behaviour, express its thoughts, beliefs, and opinions in speech and action. ('What a lot of things a man must do in order for us to say he *thinks*' (RPP I §563).) And that in turn makes sense only in the context of richly differentiated behaviour within a form of life.

Intellectual and cognitive capacities cannot be severed from conative and affective ones, and these in turn are bound up with perception, pleasure, and pain. We, who can think, reason, and conjecture, hold opinions and beliefs, also place trust in certain judgements on which we act, rely on what we are told for our plans and projects, have hopes and expectations. We are pleased at certain outcomes, disappointed at others, surprised or amazed at the turn of events. We not only act in pursuance of our goals, but also set ourselves goals. The achievement of our ends affects our welfare and prosperity, and we respond to our successes or failures with joy, pleasure, and delight or with grief and distress.

What prevents the literal applicability of concepts of thought, reason, and inference to our calculating devices are not deficiencies in computational power, which may be overcome by fifth-generation computers. Rather, it is the fact that machines are not alive. They have no biography, let alone autobiography. The concepts of growth, maturation, and death have no application to them, nor do those of nutrition, health, and reproduction. It makes no sense to attribute to a machine *will* or *passion*, *desire* or *suffering*. The concepts of thinking and reasoning, however, are woven into this rich web of psychological faculties. It is only of a living creature that we can say that it manifests those complex patterns of behaviour and reaction within the ramifying context of a form of life that constitute the grounds, in appropriate circumstances, for the ascription of even part of the network of psychological concepts.

Thought, inference, and reason are capacities of the animate. And these capacities are bound up with a vast network of further faculties, of perception, pleasure and pain, emotion and volition, which are exercised and exhibited in endlessly varied behaviour within the stream of life. Could we not imagine an inorganic being with behavioural capacities akin to ours, a being which manifests perception, volition, pleasure and pain, and also thought and reasoning, yet neither grows nor matures, needs no nutrition and does not reproduce? Should we judge it to be alive for all that, to have a life, a biography, of its own? Or should we hold it to be an inanimate creature? There is surely no 'correct' answer to this question. It calls for a decision, not a discovery. As things are, we are not forced to make one, for only what is organic displays this complex behaviour in the circumstances of life. But if we had to make such a (creative) choice or decision, if Martians were made of inorganic matter, yet displayed behaviour appropriately similar to ours, it would surely be reasonable to disregard the distinctive biological features (absent in the Martians) and give preference to the behavioural ones. If in the distant future it were feasible to create in an electronic laboratory a being that acted and behaved much as we do, exhibiting perception, desire, emotion, pleasure, and suffering, as well as thought, it would arguably be reasonable to conceive of it as an animate, though not biological, creature. But, to that extent, it would not be a machine, even though it was manufactured.

Machines, unlike living creatures, do not *have* a body, although they are bodies (cf. 'Behaviour and behaviourism', §4). Only what can (logically) die can have a body.[14] Machines and their parts have purposes and functions: viz. those which they were designed to fulfil. The organs of a living creature have functions the non-fulfilment of which adversely affects the normal (species-specific) capacities of the creature. But its body has no intrinsic function or purpose. A living being may be used by another for a purpose or to fulfil a function, as we use animals and other human beings for purposes that are not their own. But it does not itself have an intrinsic purpose, even though it may, unlike a machine, be capable of adopting purposes and goals. Human beings, in particular, can set themselves ends; and in so doing, they manifest preferences, likings, and dislikings. In pursuit of their ends they exhibit motives and intentions the fulfilment of which is marked by satisfaction and pleasure. In the achievement of their ends, their welfare is typically affected and their happiness sometimes augmented. It is only of living creatures, not of machines, that we say that they have a good, and only of such creatures can it be said that they flourish or prosper. Circumstances can beneficially or deleteriously affect the condition of a machine, be good or bad *for* it. But they cannot affect the welfare or the good of a machine, since it makes no sense to say of something that has no life that it is well or that it is doing well. What is lifeless has no welfare.

---

[14] Of course, a car has a body attached to its chassis; but that is not the sense in which an animal (but not a plant) has a body. Plants, unlike machines, can die, but they do not have bodies. A dead plant is not a corpse, for a living plant is not sentient.

Thinking is a capacity of the animate, manifest in the behaviour and action characteristic of its form of life. We need neither hope nor fear that computers may think; the good and evil they bring us is not of their making. If, for some strange and perverse reason we wished to create artificially a thinking thing, as opposed to a device that will save us the trouble of thinking, we would have to start, as it were, with animality, not rationality. Desire and suffering are the roots of thought, not mechanical computation. Artificial intelligence is no more a form of intelligence than fool's gold is a kind of gold or counterfeit money a form of legitimate currency.

V

AVOWALS AND DESCRIPTIONS

1. Descriptions of subjective experience

The classical picture of the relation between the mental and the physical represents a complex web of grammatical structures as delineating two co-ordinate worlds, the world of 'subjective experience' and the world of physical objects (see 'Privacy', §1). The former is conceived to be private, directly accessible only to its owner, the latter to be public, accessible to all. The objects, events, and processes in each domain can be described, for do we not distinguish between descriptions of objects of experience that are in the physical world and descriptions of our experiences of objects? Indeed, there is much more in the subjective domain than perceptual experiences of objects; for we experience sensations, emotions, and moods; we have desires and intentions; and we think, believe, and form judgements; and these too, and much more, we represent in words.

Perception is our source of knowledge of the world around us. We find out how things are by looking, smelling, listening etc. We, so to say, perceive the facts, read off their description from what we thus perceive, and portray what we apprehend in words, in accord with rules (cf. PI §292). It is altogether natural to think that the inner, subjective world is likewise perceived; and here too, it seems, we read off a description, e.g. 'I have a toothache', 'I think it is raining', 'I want a drink', from the facts accessible to us alone. Of course, perception of the inner does not involve a sense-organ, but we do talk of *being aware* of our pains, of rising anger or feelings of joy, just as we talk of being aware of the ticking of the clock or of a curious smell in the room. So it seems as if, despite the absence of sense-*organs*, we have a faculty of inner sense whereby we can apprehend how things are with us subjectively. We dub this faculty 'introspection' and conceive of ourselves as reporting events and processes in our subjective world by introspective scrutiny of the facts, which we then represent for the benefit of others (or for our own future use) in descriptions.

Many further factors induce the picture of first-person psychological utterances as descriptions of states of affairs in an inner world. After all, one is inclined to say, propositions such as 'A has a toothache' ('is angry', 'wants a drink', 'intends to go', etc.) are surely descriptions of a person, characterizing his mental state. If A says sincerely 'I have a toothache', that provides adequate grounds for describing him as having a toothache, i.e. for saying 'A has a toothache'. And if the latter sentence is a description, so too is the former first-person utterance. For surely 'I have a toothache' said by A says *of* A just what 'A has a toothache' says of him. The former symmetry between first- and third-person psychological sentences seems to make this an inescapable conclusion. Indeed, a natural inclination to cleave to the pre-theoretical *Urbild*, the Augustinian picture of language, that words are names and sentences *au fond* descriptions of states of affairs makes it natural to imagine that 'I have a pain' describes exactly what 'He has a pain' said of me describes.

Not only is there a first/third-person symmetry to induce this thought, but there is also an equally obvious tense symmetry. For does not 'I had a pain yesterday' express exactly the same proposition as 'I have a pain' said yesterday? And does not 'I had a pain yesterday' describe how things were with me? It is, after all, just what I might say in response to the doctor's query 'How were things yesterday?'.

Further weight is given by the equally natural thought that truth consists in correspondence with the facts, for a true proposition, after all, is a proposition which describes things as they, in fact, are. The proposition that A has a pain is true if and only if A has a pain, i.e. if that is how things are, i.e. if it is a fact that A has a pain. But equally, A's utterance 'I have a pain' may be true or false, for A may be lying. It is true if and only if he has a pain, so one and the same fact makes the two assertions true. Indeed, some philosophers have argued that the two utterances express the same proposition or make the same statement. Surely then, they describe the very same fact and are true in virtue of what they thus describe.

These considerations emphasize a logical symmetry between first- and third-person psychological sentences. But the price that has to be paid for conceiving of both alike as descriptions is high. For if one thinks of, e.g., 'I have a pain' as a description after the manner of 'He has a pain', then it seems that it is one which is *justified* by the facts. So I am in a position to assert such a proposition only in so far as I know or believe it to be true. I must compare it with reality, i.e. verify it. This, it seems, I can do, for it is I who have the pain; indeed, am I not in a uniquely privileged position to do so? The justification here appears to be private, in as much as only the subject really knows whether his description is true. For only he can compare the proposition directly with the reality that makes it true (or false).

This conception of the descriptive status of first-person psychological utterances generates a fundamental epistemological asymmetry side by side with the apparent logical symmetry. For while 'He is in pain', for example, allegedly describes the same state of affairs as 'I am in pain' said by him, one who asserts the former is not in a position to compare it directly with the facts. The grounds upon which he asserts third-person psychological propositions consists in what people do and say. From their 'external' behaviour he must infer the existence of their mental state, which, if it obtains, makes his assertion true. Hence judgements about the mental states of other people are essentially conclusions of inferences from the observed to the unobserved. The character of such inferences has been variously construed by philosophers. One common strategy is to claim that the argument is *analogical*, that we attribute mental states to others by analogy with our own case. An alternative is to represent the arguments as *theoretical*, as a matter of an inference to the best explanation. Postulating inner states, unobservable to outsiders, as it were, provides the best available explanation of the manifest behaviour. A more radical option (methodological solipsism) is to argue that other people's states of mind are second-order logical constructions.

In this essay we are concerned with only one strand in this web of confusion, viz. the mischaracterization of avowals of experience (*Äusserungen*) as descriptions of experience and the misconception of avowals and reports of experience as a matter of reading a description off the facts presented to one in introspection.

2. *Descriptions*

One paradigm of description which Wittgenstein often employed as an object of comparison is giving a word-picture of perceptible states of affairs, events, or objects. Here one characteristically observes what lies within one's perceptual field and depicts it in words, as it were reading the description off the facts. What one says may be true or false, accurate or inaccurate, detailed or rough-and-ready. To be sure, there are many different language-games that constitute describing, and they are less alike than one might think. Many different things in different contexts count as describing what one sees; contrast describing a scene with describing a painting of a scene, or describing a scene, whether actual or painted, with describing the impression it makes. Even when the words used are the same, e.g. in describing a scene and in describing a corresponding dream, the difference of context shows that the use to which the words are being put is wholly different, as is evident from the different kinds of criteria of success or failure, correctness or mistake, etc. which apply to the descriptions in these distinct contexts. Describing what one hears is importantly different from describing visibilia, and describing what happened *at* a play is altogether unlike describing what happened *in* the play. Furthermore, describing what one perceives is unlike describing how something ought to be or ought to be done, as different as a picture is from a blueprint. Again, the description of a blueprint is quite different from the description of a fictitious episode in a novel. And numerous further specific language-games with descriptions have distinctive features of their own, e.g. describing one's dreams, describing something from memory, or describing how one imagines something. In each case, what is called 'describing' or 'a description' interlocks with quite different grammatical joints. What counts as improving or refining one's description, checking it, correcting it, varies from case to case.

This diversity is important (PI §291), but for present purposes it will suffice to contrast the simple paradigm of describing what is visible before one, e.g. the room in which one is sitting, with a range of first-person present-tense psychological propositions, such as an utterance of pain, an exclamation of anger, or an expression of intention. This will serve to highlight the differences between the language-games and to cast doubt upon the traditional supposition that such utterances as 'I am in pain' are standardly and uniformly employed as descriptions of a state of affairs. Subsequently, reminders of what we actually call 'describing one's state of mind' and 'describing one's pain', as well as 'reporting how one feels', will be adduced.

The activities (and the concepts) that belong to the language-game of describing one's surroundings are, in the first place, observing, scrutinizing, examining, and investigating (LW §51). Here too there must be room for the ideas of perceptual competence and observational conditions: if one has poor eyesight, one may put on spectacles to see more clearly, and if it is dusk, one may turn on the light to improve visibility. The upshot, in certain cases, is identifying (or misidentifying) and recognizing. In giving a description of a room, one strives for accuracy (Is the table mahogany or teak?), and one may refine one's description on closer scrutiny. One may make mistakes and correct them after further investigation (Actually, it is padouk!). It makes sense here in many cases to consult authorities (Is the Piranesi print one of the *Vedute* series or not?) and to elaborate one's description accordingly. Hence too, one may ask others for their considered judgement. It makes sense here to answer the challenge 'How do you know?' and also 'Why do you think that?', for in certain cases one has grounds or evidence for one's identifications and characterizations. And one may be certain (and yet wrong) or tentative and unsure of one's attribution or identification. In respect of certain features there is such a thing as expertise, and some people are better than others in carrying out the task of giving a detailed and accurate description.

The contrast between this simple paradigm and many typical first-person present-tense psychological utterances is marked. 'I have a toothache', 'I intend to go', 'I think he is in London', 'I am furious with you', 'I expect him to come' are very different kinds of sentences. But they have in common the following feature: used spontaneously in an appropriate context, they diverge dramatically from the paradigm of description just spelled out. First, such utterances are not grounded in perception. If asked how one knows that there is an octagonal table in a certain room, one may reply 'I saw it'. But one does not perceive one's toothache, intention, thought, anger, or expectation. Of course, it is tempting, especially in the case of sensations, emotions, and moods, to say 'I know that he has a pain (is angry, is cheerful) because I see how he behaves, but I know that I have a pain (etc.) because I feel it'. But to feel pain, angry or cheerful is just to have a pain, be angry or cheerful. So 'I know I have a pain because I feel it' amounts to 'I know I have a pain because I have it', i.e. because it is true, i.e. because I am not lying (LSD 13). But that I am not lying is neither a source of knowledge nor a ground for my assertion. Secondly, in as much as such utterances are not based on observation, it makes no sense to speak here of conditions of observation; one cannot, as it were, improve the conditions of visibility so that one may better apprehend one's toothache. There are no organs for perceiving one's pains, emotions, or thoughts, and one cannot be more or less skilful is feeling toothache or in feeling cheerful. Thirdly, one does not identify or recognize one's sensations, thoughts, or intentions, although one may realize that the pain in one's chest is angina pectoris or that one's intentions are disreputable. Consequently, there is no room for misidentification of the sensation, but only for mischaracterization of the cause of the pain (e.g. it is indigestion, not angina). For 'I thought I had a pain in my chest, but I was mistaken' makes no sense. Fourthly, there is no such thing as checking what one has said by looking more closely, comparing one's sensation, emotion, or thought with paradigms. It makes no sense to consult others or to look up authorities to find out whether one has a sensation, what one intends to do, or what one thinks. Fifthly, one's utterance does not rest on evidence, and it is senseless to ask 'How do you know that you have a toothache?' or 'Why do you believe that you intend to go?'. For finally, knowledge and ignorance, certainty and doubt, have no place here – but only indecision (see 'Privacy', §3).

These grammatical differences cast doubt on the suppositions that such first-person utterances are parallel to the corresponding third-person propositions, that they describe one's 'inner world' as observation statements describe the 'public world'. These doubts are strengthened by the fact that the supposition that they are such descriptions must in the final analysis rest on the intelligibility of private ostensive definition, on the independence (in these cases) of truth and truthfulness, and on the thought that the relevant psychological concepts are names of private objects, events, and processes. These misconceptions are assailed by Wittgenstein in the private language arguments.

3. *Natural expression*

The traditional philosophical conception of first-person psychological utterances is so natural, so firmly rooted in superficial analogies of form, in similes and metaphors that are in constant (and harmless) use, that it can only be combatted by showing that it is eminently avoidable. We are not *forced* to conceive things thus by the very facts of the matter, any more than we are forced to conceive of mathematical propositions as descriptions of relations between abstract objects that are real but non-actual. We are constrained only by our natural disposition to advert of similarities of form and to overlook differences in use, to theorize rather than to describe, to explain instead of clarifying the rules for the use of our expressions.

The classical picture conceives of the language-game with 'I have a pain' as beginning with the sensation, which the sufferer observes *in foro interno*, identifies, and then represents in a description which communicates to others what is directly accessible only to him. But on the contrary, Wittgenstein argued, this language-game begins with natural expressive behaviour in certain circumstances (PI §§244, 290). We cry out when we injure ourselves, groan and scream; we grimace and clutch the part that hurts, assuage the injured limb. It is in these primitive, instinctual forms of pre-linguistic behaviour that the language-game with 'pain' is rooted, not in observations of private objects in an ethereal realm. We do not ask a child who has hurt himself how he knows that it hurts or whether he is quite sure that it does; we comfort him.

Note that something similar holds for a wide range of rudimentary psychological states, reactions, and conditions – although not for all, and not for more developed forms. A child who wants a toy reaches for it and tries to get it. The child's anger is manifest in striking out, contorted features, and screams of rage. If the child expects to be given a piggyback, he jumps up and down in eager anticipation; if he is frightened, he blanches, cries, and runs to Mummy. We do not wonder whether the child who tries to reach his toy and screams in frustration has correctly identified his desire. And we do not query, of the frightened child, whether he has recognized his feelings. These are primitive forms of behaviour characteristic of our species. They are antecedent to our language-games and provide the behavioural bedrock for them.

The exclamation 'It hurts', the groan 'I have a toothache', the cry 'I've hurt myself' are manifestations (*Äusserungen*) of pain, not descriptions; they are comparable to moans or screams of pain rather than to descriptions such as 'He has a toothache' or 'He has hurt himself'. Avowals of pain are learnt extensions of natural expressive behaviour, and are themselves forms of behaviour: 'words are connected with the primitive, the natural, expressions of the sensation and used in their place. A child has hurt himself and he cries; and then adults talk to him and teach him exclamations and, later, sentences. They teach the child new pain-behaviour' (PI §244). The importance of this observation is not as a contribution to (armchair) learning theory, but rather as a way of pinpointing and illuminating crucial features of the grammar of such utterances. An avowal (*Äusserung*) of pain, such as 'It hurts' or 'I have a pain', no more rests on 'introspective evidence' than does a scream or a groan of pain, and it is no more a description of an observed inner state than is a moan. For in the most rudimentary case, 'It hurts' is simply a partial replacement of a cry, groan, or scream of pain. The spontaneous avowal, like a moan, is an expression of pain, as crying out in alarm is an expression of fear or laughter of amusement. Like natural, non-linguistic forms of pain-behaviour, an avowal of pain is a criterion for others to assert 'He is in pain'. It is not an empirical discovery, established by inductive correlation, that when people hurt themselves, they typically cry out, clutch their injured limb, and assuage the pain. There is no such thing as non-inductive identification of pain other than by reference to pain-behaviour; for in one's own case one does not identify one's pain at all, one has a pain which one (typically) manifests in behaviour. The behavioural manifestation of pain, whether natural or linguistic, is not a *symptom* of pain. We learn the use of 'pain' by learning to say 'He is in pain' when someone behaves in these characteristic ways in circumstances of injury or illness and by learning to extend our own natural pain-behaviour by using such sentences as 'It hurts' or 'I have a pain'.

To view avowals of pain as forms of pain-behaviour akin to moans or cries of pain is not to identify pain with pain-behaviour. To moan is not to say 'I moan', and to cry out 'I have a pain' is not to say 'I am manifesting pain-behaviour'. We do not use the word 'pain' as we use the phrases 'manifestation of pain' or 'expression of pain'. Indeed, it is an essential aspect of this language-game that someone can be in pain and not groan or moan, and so too that one can hurt oneself and not cry out 'It hurts'. Conversely, one can pretend and dissimulate, groan or exclaim 'I have a pain', and yet not be suffering at all. This makes it appear as if pain and its manifestations are logically independent. But that is not so: unless injury and illness were associated with these forms of behaviour, we should have no use for the concept of pain (cf. LPE 286). For pain-behaviour *is* logically connected with pain, not, of course, by way of entailment, but rather by pain-behaviour's constituting a criterion for a person's being in pain. It makes no sense to say 'Here is pain, and here is behaviour – it just happens that they are associated' (cf. LSD 10). While pretence is sometimes possible, it is absurd to suppose that all pain-behaviour might be pretence. For the very concept of *pretending to be*

in pain is parasitic upon the concept of *being in pain*. There are criteria for
pretending to be in pain no less than for being in pain. Pretending to be in
pain must be *learnt*, and the prototype for pretending to be in pain is
manifesting *pain*. Numerous concept-involving capacities and skills must
be acquired by a human being before it can intelligibly be said of him that
he is pretending to be in pain. The idea that a new-born child might be
pretending thus is absurd, for his behaviour lacks the necessary articulations, his capacities are too limited, and the weave of his life is as yet too
simple (cf. Exg. §249).

As with a moan, so too with an utterance of pain, it makes no sense to
ask 'How do you know?' or 'Why do you believe that?'. One does not
learn or find out that one has a pain; there can be no question of error or
mistake, and so too no room for knowledge or ignorance, certainty or
doubt. Hence the concept of justifying an utterance of pain has no
application in the manner in which a description of a feature of a room
can be justified. It makes no sense to justify one's avowal by reference to
perception; nor does it make sense to cite evidence. One cannot justify
what one says by producing a sample as one can justify saying that the
curtains are eau-de-Nil by displaying a sample of that colour. One can,
of course, insist that one said one was in pain because one *was* in pain, as
opposed to acting the role of someone injured or to reading out a text.
Here one draws a contrast between language-games, but that is not a
ground for assertion.

It is important to emphasize that Wittgenstein was not *assimilating*
avowals to the natural expression of 'inner states'. An avowal of pain is
not *just like* a groan, and it would be as misleading to say that it has the
same logical status as a groan as it is to assimilate it to a description
(LSD 11). For there are differences as well as similarities. An utterance
(*Äusserung*) of pain, unlike a moan, is articulate; it is a linguistic
expression consisting of words in grammatical combination. A sentence
that can be used in a spontaneous avowal has other uses too. It can be
embedded in the antecedent of a conditional, it has an intelligible
negation, and there are tense transforms of such a sentence. These cases
are not expressions or manifestations of inner states and must be treated
differently. Similarly, while the spontaneous use of such sentences in
appropriate circumstances is a form of expressive behaviour, they can
also be used coolly in reports or explanations (see below).

These features, however, must not blind us to the distinctive grammatical differences between avowals and descriptions, differences that
remain significant even in reports and genuine descriptions of how one
feels, of one's pain, or one's own mental states. It is evident that the
connection between the word 'pain' and the sensation of pain is
altogether unlike the connection between the word 'red' and the colour
or the word 'dumb waiter' and the piece of furniture. One can say that

the word 'pain' is the name of a sensation, as one can say that the word 'red' is the name of a colour or 'dumb waiter' the name of an article of furniture. But the expression 'is the name of a sensation' is as unlike 'is the name of a colour' or 'is the name of a piece of furniture' as 'is the name of a number' is unlike 'is the name of a numeral'. One can explain what 'red' or 'dumb waiter' means by ostension. One can label a colour-sample 'red' and hang a name-plate from a dumb waiter. But there is no such thing as a mental sample of pain, and the notion of a private ostensive definition of 'pain' is a philosophical misconception. One cannot stick a label on a sensation of pain, and this name/object model has no application to sensations. Rather ' "pain" is the name of a sensation' amounts to no more than ' "I have a pain" is an expression of pain (*Schmerzäusserung*)' (RPP I §313). For the word 'pain' is connected to the sensation of pain by way of its connections with behavioural expressions of pain, and one such connection consists in the fact that 'I have a pain' *is* an expression of pain (PI §244).

Just as the name/object model is inappropriate for sensation-names, so too the central paradigm for '"w" refers to . . .' has no genuine use here. Of course, one can say 'The word "pain" refers to the sensation of pain', as one can say that the word 'red' refers to the colour red. But in the latter case one can point to the colour and add 'Namely *that*'. The move from talking of referring to physical objects or their perceptible properties to talking of referring to sensations is a shift in language-games, which calls out for a fresh explanation of what is meant here by 'referring' (cf. Z §434). The tempting idea that the speaker knows exactly what he refers to when he says 'I have a pain', since he can, as it were, cast a sidelong glance at the private sensation, is a piece of philosophical mythology (PI §274). But, of course, one can say: 'The word "pain" refers to the sensation of pain, not to pain-behaviour' – this is a grammatical remark, and it draws an important distinction.

This schematic account of the rudiments of the grammar of 'pain' can and should be generalized, but not mechanically. It does not provide, as it were, a blueprint for the grammar of sensation-words in general, let alone for all psychological expressions. Although it is illuminating to compare the spontaneous utterance 'I have a pain' with a groan and to view it as a partial substitute for and learnt extension of this natural pattern of pain-behaviour, one cannot say the same of the report 'I have a dull nagging pain in the lumbar region' or 'I have a throbbing pain in my knee'. There is no natural expressive pain-behaviour that differentiates dull, nagging pains from throbbing ones. Numerous bodily sensations, e.g. of pressure, of swelling, sensations of tingling, of a hot flush, of heartburn, etc. have little if any distinctive, differentiating natural expression. Their primary behavioural manifestation *is* linguistic. (Does it make sense to say of a mouse that it has tingling sensations, feels nauseous, has a nagging ache in its shoulder?) Nevertheless, these more refined forms of verbal expressive behaviour are rooted in the more primitive ones. Once the primitive linguistic extension is grafted onto the natural expressive behaviour, further linguistic extensions grow. For the mastery of a language opens up the possibility of ever more subtle, refined, and linguistically differentiated pain-*behaviour*.

It may seem *prima facie* curious to suggest that the possibility of experience should be conditioned by the possibility of its expression. For we are inclined to think of experience as *given*; and whether it can be expressed and how it is expressed seem to be further matters. But this is obviously misconceived, as is evident as soon as one recollects that the criteria for having a certain experience lie in what a creature does (and *says*), and hence that the possibility of enjoying a given experience (and the intelligibility of ascribing or denying such-and-such an experience to a creature) turns upon the possibility (intelligibility) of its expression. It makes sense to say that a dog wants a bone now, but not that it now wants a bone next Sunday, for nothing in the behavioural repertoire of a dog would count as the expression of a desire to have a bone next Sunday. But the child who learns to use the exclamation 'Want!' in conjunction with a pointing gesture, instead of reaching for an object and crying, and who subsequently learns a tensed language becomes able to want things which it *could not* previously want, e.g. a new teddy bear for Christmas. The vast majority of our desires have no natural, pre-linguistic behavioural expression; but their expression is nevertheless rooted in the primitive behaviour of striving to get or crying for something or other.

4. *A spectrum of cases*

The affinity between spontaneous avowals and natural expressive behaviour must not mask the fact that the uses of first-person psychological sentences are heterogeneous. Some approximate to primitive cries and gestures, and others are far removed from those paradigms. Wittgenstein was not suggesting that there is no such thing as reporting, informing, telling others how things are subjectively with one. But what is called 'telling someone what one feels', 'describing one's state of mind', or even 'observing one's emotional state' are much more unlike reports, descriptions, and observations of the physical world than one thinks.

The uses of first-person psychological sentences constitute a whole spectrum of different cases. At one end of this spectrum there is a disparate cluster of exclamations, such as 'It hurts!', 'How nice to see you!', 'What a surprise!', that merge with spontaneous avowals such as 'I have a toothache', 'I'm furious with you!', 'I'm delighted', 'I do hope he'll come'. Here too are expressions of desire and intention, such as 'I'm hungry', 'I want a drink', 'I'll go', and avowals of thought and belief. Despite negative affinities (viz. *not* constituting descriptions, reports, observations, etc.), there are great differences. A groan of pain may be wrenched from me, but 'I'm furious with you!' is a flash of anger, and 'I am delighted' may be a gesture of pleasure. 'I want a drink' is often a request, and 'I prefer red wine', said when offered a mixed tray, is the expression of a choice. 'I don't believe it!' is often a cry of incredulity'; 'I think it is getting late' may be a suggestion that it is time to go, and 'I believe . . .' may be used as a polite denial, a tentative judgement, a confession of faith, or a passionate commitment. 'I feel great joy' and 'I'm so happy to see you!' are expressions of joy and delight, not statements of inner observations. But does 'joy' not designate (*bezeichnen*) something inner? 'No, "joy" designates nothing at all. Neither any inward nor any outward thing' (Z §487). The model of 'object and designation' is altogether inappropriate here (cf. PI §293).

The diversity is indefinitely large, and how we draw distinctions will be partly determined by our purposes in so doing. Relative to a given purpose, our differentiation of cases will depend upon the circumstances of utterance, the sentential context, and the accompanying behaviour – the tone of voice, facial expression, and gesture. But in all these cases the concept of *description* gets no grip. These fragments of expressive behaviour are no more assertions about one's state of mind than are such corresponding exclamations as 'You swine!', 'Water!', 'Red wine, please', 'No!', or 'Let's go!'. Of course, one can make inferences from them about the speaker's feelings, desires, attitudes, and beliefs, but that does not show that they are true or false descriptions. For one can make similar inferences from the corresponding exclamations, and no one would call those 'descriptions' (cf. RPP I §463). Indeed, the concepts of truth and falsehood are typically out of place here, although dissimulation and deception are possible in such contexts, as indeed they are with groans, smiles, or laughs. Similarly, the more such utterances approximate to exclamations, the less room there is for evaluating them as sincere or insincere; for this dimension of evaluation gets a firmer grip in relation to the articulate expression of one's inner life, confessions, and telling others how one feels or what one thinks. The innocent and the sincere are they who interpose nothing between their inner life and its outward articulation which would censor or distort.

Of course, these sentences can be used differently; but whether they are employed as articulate expressions of feelings, emotions, or attitudes or as reports is not determined by investigating what 'want', 'believe', or 'think' signify:

> We ask 'What does "I am frightened" really mean, what am I referring to when I say it?' And of course we find no answer, or one that is inadequate.
> The question is: 'In what sort of context does it occur?'

I can find no answer if I try to settle the question 'What am I referring to?', 'What am I thinking when I say it?' by repeating the expression of fear and at the same time attending to myself, as it were observing my soul through the corner of my eye. (PI p.188)

The roles of these expressions in our language-games cannot be clarified by 'semantic investigations' or by thinking about what stands *behind* them, what they report or describe. For in numerous contexts they do not report or describe anything. We need to look around, not behind – at the context and circumstances of use in the stream of life.

Between exclamations, avowals, and expressions on the one hand and genuine descriptions of mental states on the other lie hosts of intermediate cases of reports, articulations of thought, feeling, and attitude. I may vent my feelings so that you should appreciate my response to your behaviour, as when I say 'I'm very angry with you for breaking your promise'. This is not a spontaneous reaction of anger, but it is not a description of my state of mind either. 'I'm looking for my book', 'I intend going to London next Sunday', or 'I should like to spend next summer in Rome' are not spontaneous avowals but are uttered with the intention of conveying information. But they are not descriptions; nor do they rest on observation or evidence (RPP II §§176f.).

'I'm frightened' may be an exclamation of fear; but in a different context it may be uttered as a piece of information or as an explanation of why my hands are shaking. It can even be said with a smile as one wryly confesses one's trepidation (LW §§17, 20f.; PI p. 174). One can report what one thinks or intends, and such a cool confession of what one has in mind is not a spontaneous expression. Nevertheless, it is not a description of anything either. To tell you what I think is not to describe an inner object or process with which I am uniquely acquainted (RPP I §572); for what I think is no object, and I am not 'acquainted' with my thoughts. If one insists that it is perfectly licit to talk about describing one's thoughts, Wittgenstein will issue no prohibitions, but only draw one's attention to grammatical differences:

> If someone wants to call the words the 'description' of the thought instead of the 'expression' (*Ausdruck*) of the thought, let him ask himself how anyone learns to describe a table and how he learns to describe his own thoughts. And that only means: let him look and see how one judges the description of a table as right or wrong, and how the description of thoughts; so let him keep in view these language-games in all their situations. (RPP I §572)

My expression of my thoughts may be faulty, but not because I am insufficiently observant – rather because I am insufficiently articulate. What I say may be wrong, but not because I have misidentified my thought. My confession of my thoughts may be inadequate, but not because I have made a mistake – rather because I have been untruthful or have held something crucial back, have exaggerated or understated.

Informing, telling, confessing, and reporting states of mind, sensations, and attitudes may be truthful or untruthful. One may lie about one's pains, feelings, and thoughts. But a lie about what one feels or thinks is unlike a lie about what another person feels or thinks. I tell a lie about A if I know him to be upset and assert that he is not, with intent to deceive. But I lie about my feelings or thoughts if I feel or think such-and-such and deny that I do, with intent to deceive. Moreover, when I say what I think or feel, my sincere confession is a criterion for my thoughts and feelings. But when I say, in all honesty, that A is upset, that does not guarantee (*ceteris paribus*) the truth of what I say.

In cases of confessing, reporting, or telling what one thinks, intends, or feels, one can typically answer the questions 'Why did you say that?' or 'What did you mean by that?'. But unlike similar questions asked of descriptions of objects, the answers here do not rest on observation and do not allude to features of an object being described. Rather, they characterize the point of the utterance, not its grounds, for it has none. Or they paraphrase the utterance to render it more perspicuous (PI p. 188).

Describing one's state of mind is indeed something one can do: but it is a much more specialized language-game than one might initially think (LW §50). Such descriptions are likely to be more accurate, refined, and observant in proportion to one's degree of self-consciousness or self-awareness. But self-consciousness is not consciousness of a 'self'. Whether a use of a form of words counts as a description of a state of mind is dependent upon the context and manner of utterance, e.g. upon antecedent discourse and upon the tone of voice of the speaker, his intentions and purposes (LW §43). The concept of a *state* of mind is far more restricted than philosophers typically assume. Intending, believing, thinking, for example, are not states of mind; and to say what one intends, believes, or thinks is never to describe one's mental state. States of mind have genuine duration (RPP II §722); hence they are typically described in the imperfect or continuous tense, interwoven with descriptions of what one did, how one reacted, what one was thinking about. 'I can't keep my mind on my work today; I keep on thinking of his coming' (PI §585); 'I have been afraid of his arrival all day long . . . immediately upon awakening I thought . . . then I considered . . . time and again I looked out of the window . . .' (RPP II §156); or 'I have been hoping for the whole day . . .' (RPP II §722) can legitimately be called 'descriptions of a mental state'.

A highly self-conscious person is one who attends to his emotional and conative life, who registers the ebb and flow of his passions, reactions, and attitudes. Such a person reflects upon his responses, analyses them, and searches for patterns that inform them. His descriptions of his mental states will typically be sensitive, detailed, and articulate. But even here, at this end of the spectrum of first-person psychological propositions, the relevant descriptions are very unlike descriptions of the 'outer'. They may be observant, but do not generally rest on observation. They may, in various ways, be inadequate or defective, but not because of misperception. Their typical flaws are likely to be forms of *self-deception*, rooted in a defect of the will rather than of the intellect, let alone of the senses. One who deceives himself about his state of mind, his motives, or intentions may or may not also deceive others. But if he does, it will not be because he is truthfully reporting a mistaken observation, but because he is being untruthful – with himself, and so too with others. There is no such thing as self-deception with respect to sensations, but our emotional life and avowals of motivation are run through with the distorting influence of the will and fantasy. So here, unlike the case of sensations and spontaneous avowals that are expressions of the 'inner', there is room for knowledge and error, i.e. self-knowledge properly speaking, and self-deception or failure to realize the pattern of one's reasons and desires. But this kind of knowledge, ignorance, and error is altogether unlike knowledge, ignorance, and error regarding what is 'outer'.

The spectrum of uses of first-person psychological sentences to which Wittgenstein drew attention involves subtle gradations. A corollary of that fact is that one often cannot say of a particular utterance that it lies at this or that point on a scale – for avowals, reports, and descriptions may occur in blends. If someone were to say 'I have spent the whole day in fear [and here he might elaborate in detail] . . . and now too I am full of anxiety', it would be misguided to try to classify his utterance as either avowal or report or description. 'Well, what should we say', Wittgenstein remarked, 'other than that here we have the use of the word "fear" in front of us?' (RPP II §156).

VI

BEHAVIOUR AND BEHAVIOURISM

1. *Behaviourism in psychology and philosophy*

Behaviourism in empirical psychology originates with the work of J. B. Watson in the USA during the 1910s. Reacting against W. Wundt's introspective psychology on the Continent and against E. B. Titchener and William James in the USA, Watson repudiated the prevailing orthodoxy that psychology is the study of consciousness. On the contrary, he insisted, 'the subject matter of human psychology is the behaviour of the human being'.[1] Psychology is a purely objective branch of natural science, and its ultimate goal is the control and prediction of behaviour.

Not only is consciousness not the subject-matter of psychological science, but the very concept of consciousness is unusable. The committed behaviourist, Watson declared, will drop 'from his scientific vocabulary all subjective terms such as sensation, perception, image, desire, purpose, and even thinking and emotion as they were subjectively defined'.[2] This is not merely because these concepts are insufficiently sharply defined for 'scientific purposes'. Rather, there is no such thing as consciousness as traditionally conceived. 'The belief in the existence of consciousness', he wrote contemptuously, 'goes back to the ancient days of superstition and magic.'[3] The scientific psychologist 'can do without the terms "mind" and "consciousness", indeed he can find no objective evidence for their existence'.[4] Hence 'the behaviourist recognizes no such things as mental traits, dispositions, or tendencies'.[5]

For psychology to mature into a natural science, it must confine itself to what can be observed, viz. behaviour. Like physics, its explanations and predictions must rest on functional dependencies between observable data. Customary explanations of human action in terms of 'subjective' psychological concepts are dismissed as pre-scientific mythology.[6] The

---

[1] J. B. Watson, *Behaviourism* (Kegan Paul, Trench, Trubner, and Co., London), p. 2.
[2] Ibid., pp. 5f.
[3] Ibid., p. 2.
[4] Ibid., p. 18.
[5] Ibid., p. 98. It is noteworthy that Watson equivocated between the radical claim that consciousness, the mind, mental traits, etc. are fictions, the claim that there is no evidence for their existence, and the claim that 'scientific', 'objective' psychology need pay no heed to them. His repudiation of the dualist (Cartesian) confusions of introspectionist psychology led him to embrace a distorted conception of behaviour, of what is or is not observable, and of what is 'objective'.
[6] B. F. Skinner was subsequently to refer to ordinary explanations of actions in terms of desires, reasons, and motives as 'explanatory fictions'.

data of psychological science are environmental stimuli on the one hand and movements of the organism on the other – not only movements of the whole body, but also changes in respiration, blood pressure, and retinal reactions. Although Watson indignantly rejected the criticism that the behaviourist is merely 'a muscle physiologist',[7] he saw no incongruity in claiming that the glands are organs with which we *behave*, since the action of the glands is no less a response to stimuli than the movement of the limbs or the utterance of a sentence.[8] Behaviour amounts to any movement of or in an organism. The crudity of this conception of behaviour unsurprisingly gave rise to conceptual difficulties in demarcating the domain of psychological investigation and in characterizing what is to count as a legitimate description of its data.

Behaviourist psychology, according to Watson, aims to discover scientific laws correlating external stimulus and behavioural response. Subsequently, psychologists were to distinguish *molar behaviourism*, which restricts its investigation to functional relations between stimulus and 'gross observable reactions' of organisms, and *molecular behaviourism*, which would, it was hoped, explain the laws discovered by molar behaviourist science in terms of underlying physiological laws. Intentions, purposes, and desires were bypassed as explanatory fictions, and explanations of behaviour were ventured in terms of stimulus conditioning, 'drives', etc. Speech was explained not by reference to thought, but in terms of causal conditioning:

The fact that every object and situation in the external environment is *named* is of vast importance. Words not only can and do call out other words, phrases and sentences, but when the human being is properly organised they can call out all of his manual activity. The words function in the matter of calling out responses exactly as did the objects for which the words serve as substitutes.[9]

Knowledge was held to be no more than causally generated 'verbal habits'; and self-knowledge, far from involving 'introspecting' one's mind, was argued to be no different in kind from knowledge of other people.

The capacity for thought and the traditional association of thinking and consciousness constituted a locus of forceful objections to the behaviourist programme. Watson tried to forestall them by denying that

---

[7] Watson, *Behaviourism*, p. 14.

[8] Ibid., p. 77.

[9] Ibid., p. 233. Here Watson cleaves to an almost pure and primitive version of the Augustinian picture of language. He continued thus: 'Wasn't it Dean Swift who had one of his characters who couldn't or wouldn't speak carry around in his bag all the objects of common use so that instead of having to say words to influence the behaviour of others he pulled out the actual object from his bag and showed it? The world would be in this situation today if we did not have this *equivalence for reaction* between objects and words.' The reference is to *Gulliver's Travels*, Pt. III, §2, 'A Voyage to Balnibarbi'.

thinking is an incorporeal mental activity. It is, he argued, nothing more than talking to oneself – i.e. sub–vocal word–behaviour.[10] The muscular habits learned in overt speech are responsible for implicit or internal speech – which is what thinking is. This claim was held to be an empirical thesis supported by evidence derived from the observation of children's behaviour:

> The child talks incessantly when alone . . . Soon society in the form of nurse and parents steps in. 'Don't talk aloud – daddy and mother are not always talking to themselves.' Soon the overt speech dies down to whispered speech, and a good lip reader can still read what the child thinks of the world and of himself . . . The great majority of people pass on to the third stage under the influence of social pressure constantly exerted. 'Quit whispering to yourself', and 'Can't you even read without moving your lips?' and the like are constant mandates. Soon the process is forced to take place behind the lips. Behind these walls you can call the biggest bully the worst name you can think of without even smiling.[11]

Rather surprisingly, Watson considered this sub-vocal talking to be a form of 'word-behaviour',[12] presumably because he thought it to be a matter of laryngal movements. Even more curiously, he held that the deaf and dumb, who speak by means of manual sign-language, 'use the same manual responses they employ in talking in their own thinking', and even that in their dreams they talk to themselves using finger-language with great rapidity![13]

Such confusions are rife in Watson's writings. Nevertheless, the official ideology was to view the mental as primitive mystification, rather as contemporary cognitive scientists view what they call 'folk psychology'. Similarly, all teleology was to be swept away in favour of the mechanics of bodily behaviour. The advance of science was identified with the elimination of final causation and its replacement by efficient causes in proper explanations of phenomena. In parallel with the physicist or engineer, 'It is part of the behaviourist's scientific job to be able to state what the human machine is good for and to render serviceable predictions about its future capacities whenever society needs such information.'[14] Refinement and sophistication were added to this theory of human conduct by Hull and Skinner, but the spirit of behaviourism remained essentially the same.

The immediate impact of Watson's behaviourism upon philosophy is evident in Russell's *Analysis of Mind* (1921), which Russell had given to Watson for comments while in manuscript (AM 6). In the Preface he

---

[10] Ibid., pp. 238ff.
[11] Ibid., pp. 240f.
[12] Ibid., p. 243.
[13] Ibid., p. 241. The muddle is exemplary. To think is not to talk to oneself, and to make finger-signs while asleep is neither to think nor to talk to oneself.
[14] Ibid., p. 271.

wrote 'I think that what has permanent value in the outlook of the behaviourists is the feeling that physics is the most fundamental science at present in existence.' This idea was to bear fruit in Carnap's physicalism in the 1930s and in the Vienna Circle's dream of 'unified science'; but because of Russell's neutral monism, it is in fact far less prominent in the book than one would expect from his declaration. His stance was a curious admixture of classical empiricism with Watsonian behaviourism, tenuously held together by neutral monism. Unlike Watson (in his more radical pronouncements), he did not deny the existence of consciousness, although he agreed that consciousness is not definitive of the mental. Rather, it is to be analysed in terms of mental imagery, its meaning relation to what it is an image of, and belief or expectation.[15] Both mind and matter, he argued, are logical constructions. Laws of physics and laws of psychology alike are causal, but the latter are distinguished from the former by their concern with *mnemic* causation, which may have neural foundations. The raw data out of which both mind and matter are constructed are appearances, which, viewed subjectively, are sensations.

The unhappy synthesis of empiricism and behaviourism is evident in Russell's account of desire: ' . . . desire, like force in mechanics, is of the nature of a convenient fiction for describing shortly certain laws of behaviour' (AM 32). All that can actually be observed in animals or in other human beings consists in bodily movements, physiological processes, and emitted sounds (AM 43f.). Mechanical movements depend only upon properties which animal bodies share with matter in general, but 'vital' movements depend for their causation upon the special properties of the nervous system (AM 47). The explanation of animal action in terms of desire is behaviourist; e.g. a hungry animal is restless until it finds food, when it becomes quiescent. That which brings a restless condition to an end is said to be what is desired (AM 32). The concept of desire in the case of animals is explicable in terms of behaviour cycles, viz. 'a series of voluntary or reflex movements of an animal, tending to cause a certain result, and continuing until that result is caused, unless they are interrupted by death, accident, or some new behaviour cycle' (AM 65). The 'purpose' of a behaviour cycle is the result that terminates it in a condition of quiescence, and the animal is said to 'desire' the purpose while the behaviour cycle is in progress.

In his account of *human* desire, however, Russell immediately introduces familiar empiricist apparatus. What sets a human behaviour cycle in motion is a sensation (for which no behaviourist account is offered), of discomfort, discomfort being a causal property of a sensation to induce movements likely to lead to cessation of that sensation (AM 68). Unconscious desire is merely a tendency to a certain behaviour

---

[15] AM, Ch. XV; Russell's account here is reminiscent of Hume's.

caused by sensations of discomfort. Conscious desire, however, is desire accompanied by a true belief as to its 'purpose' (AM 72), i.e. as to what state of affairs will cause quiescence. The traditional view that we have immediate knowledge of our own desires which does not depend upon observation of our actions is false. 'I believe that the discovery of our own motives can only be made by the same process by which we discover other people's, namely the process of observing our actions and inferring the desire which could prompt them. A desire is "conscious" when we have told ourselves that we have it' (AM 31). But a belief as to the purpose of our own desire 'may very well be erroneous, since only experience can show what causes a discomfort to cease' (AM 72). (It is unclear whether 'false consciousness' is or is not meant to instantiate what he called 'conscious desire', for he was evidently pulled both ways.)

An equally curious admixture of crude behaviourism and classical empiricism is visible in Russell's account of language and meaning. The essence of language, he held, lies in the use of fixed associations in order that a sensible sign may call up the idea of something else. That of which it is intended to call up the idea is said to be the meaning of the sign; and the salient puzzle which Russell addresses is 'what is the relation of the word to the individual which makes the one mean the other?' (AM 191). His answer is that this relation 'is of the nature of a causal law governing our use of the word and our actions when we hear it used' (AM 198). In four respects, understanding words can, he argued, be given a behaviourist analysis. Active understanding is merely a matter of suitable circumstances making a person use the relevant word properly (AM 197, 199). Passive understanding consists in the hearing of the word causing a person to behave appropriately. One is further said to understand a word if one associates it with another word (say, in a different language) which has the same stimulus effects on behaviour, and if one associates the word with the object it 'means', so that the word acquires some of the same causal efficacy as the object.

Does understanding not require that a person know, i.e. be able to say, what the word means? Not so, Russell insisted (in company with Watson). Understanding language is more like understanding cricket than it is like knowing dictionary definitions (AM 197): 'It is a matter of habits, acquired in oneself and rightly presumed in others. To say that a word has a meaning is not to say that those who use the word correctly have ever thought out what the meaning is: the use of the word comes first, and the meaning is to be distilled out of it by observation and analysis.' Indeed, 'There is no more reason why a person who uses a word correctly should be able to tell what it means than there is why a planet which is moving correctly should know Kepler's laws.' This behaviourist understanding 'may be reduced to mere physiological causal laws' (AM 199).

With respect to two important domains of language-use, Russell parted company with Watson and cleaved to his empiricist forbears. Memory-statements and imaginative narrative, he held, must be accounted for in terms of mental imagery. Moreover, these two functions are of the essence of *thinking*, since it is only thus that words, through their connection with images, 'bring us into touch with what is remote in time or space' (AM 203). In understanding a word, 'there is a reciprocal association between it and the images of what it "means". Images may cause us to use words which mean them, and these words, heard or read, may in turn cause the appropriate images. Thus speech is a means of producing in our hearers the images which are in us' (AM 206). The meaning of a word 'is wholly constituted by mnemic causal laws' (AM 210). As Wittgenstein was later to picture this classical empiricist conception, 'Uttering a word is like striking a note on the keyboard of the imagination' (PI §6).

Analysis of Mind constituted an unhappy half-way house between classical empiricism and logical behaviourism. The latter emerged, under the title of 'physicalism', in the Vienna Circle. In *Der Logische Aufbau der Welt* (1928), Carnap attempted a wholesale reconstruction of empirical concepts and knowledge on a methodological solipsist foundation. He held that from the purely logical point of view of 'construction theory' a materialist foundation which reduces the psychological to the physical (behavioural) was perfectly possible. Indeed:

A materialistic constructional system has the advantage that it uses as its basic domain the only domain (namely, the physical) which is characterized by a clear regularity of its processes . . . Since the task of empirical science . . . consists, on the one hand, in the discovery of general laws, and, on the other hand, in the explanation of individual events through their subsumption under general laws, it follows that from the standpoint of empirical science the constructional system with physical basis constitutes a more appropriate arrangement of concepts than any other.[16]

He noted (not quite accurately) that the behavioural psychology of Watson, Dewey, and others (referring to the bibliography in Russell's *Analysis of Mind* for more details) reduced all psychological phenomena to the physical, i.e. observable behaviour. 'Thus a constructional system which is based upon this position would choose a physical basis . . . such a system would be quite possible and practicable.' However, Carnap himself opted for a constructional system with a phenomenalist or, as he called it, 'an autopsychological basis', on the grounds that it should conform to the epistemic order of propositions. Consequently he gave a *logical* behaviourist analysis of the heteropsychological, arguing that

[16] R. Carnap, *The Logical Structure of the World*, tr. R. A. George (Routledge and Kegan Paul, London, 1967), §59.

propositions about other people's experiences, etc. are second-order logical constructions, reducible in the first instance to propositions about their behaviour. The autopsychological, however, was not reduced to the behaviour of the subject, but constructed out of the 'given' – i.e. bare 'unowned' sense-data.

In 1932, however, under pressure from Neurath, Carnap shifted ground. The principle of the unity of science (methodological monism) and the demand for 'intersubjective verification' triumphed over the epistemological rationale for choosing a phenomenalist base for construction. In two articles in *Erkenntnis*, 'Die physikalische Sprache als Universalsprache der Wissenschaft'[17] and 'Psychologie in physikalische Sprache',[18] he defended the thesis that 'all sentences of psychology describe physical occurrences, namely, the physical behaviour of humans and other animals'.[19] This, he argued, 'coincides in its broad outlines with the psychological movement known as "behaviourism"'.[20] The general physicalist thesis that 'physical language is a universal language', i.e. that all empirical sentences are translatable into physicalist ones, when applied to psychology, yields a form of *logical behaviourism*.

Unlike radical versions of psychological behaviourism, Carnap's logical behaviourism did not imply that mental states, etc. are fictions – i.e. that there really are no such things. Rather, the claim was that all psychological sentences are translatable into an array of 'physicalist' ones. Accordingly, Carnapian physicalism stands to psychological behaviourism somewhat as linguistic phenomenalism[21] stands to idealism. A corollary of physicalism was that the laws of psychology are actually physical laws, and it seemed reasonable to suppose that they might ultimately be deducible from general physical laws that apply to inorganic matter.[22]

The supposition of the reducibility of third-person psychological propositions to behavioural ones was already defended in *Logische Aufbau* and 'Pseudoproblems in Philosophy' (1928). In 'Psychology in Physical Language', Carnap argued that such propositions are equivalent to assertions that there exists a physical microstructure of the person's body which is responsible for certain kinds of behaviour and behavioural disposition. This significantly modified the behaviourist analysis, since it admitted into the analysans not only propositions about behaviour, but

[17] Carnap, *Erkenntnis*, II (1931), pp. 432 – 65, published in English as a monograph *The Unity of Science*, tr. M. Black (Kegan Paul, London, 1934).
[18] Carnap, *Erkenntnis*, III (1932/3), repr. as 'Psychology in Physical Language', tr. G. Schick, in A. J. Ayer (ed.), *Logical Positivism* (Allen and Unwin, London, 1959), pp. 165 – 97.
[19] Ibid., p. 165.
[20] Ibid., p. 181.
[21] 'Linguistic phenomenalism', as opposed to Mill's modal phenomenalism.
[22] Carnap, 'Psychology in Physical Language', p. 167.

also propositions about physiological changes within the body (as, indeed, Watson had) and essential reference to (as yet unknown) states of the central nervous system. This did not, however, prevent members of the Vienna Circle from referring to the doctrine as 'logical behaviourism',[23] with the proviso that the term 'behaviour' must include 'internal behaviour'[24] and dispositions to behave in certain ways.

The most significant change relative to *Logische Aufbau* lay in the account Carnap now gave of first-person present-tense psychological sentences. These, he claimed, are reducible to sentences about one's bodily state, behaviour, and behavioural dispositions. The argument was thin, to say the least, and the range of examples amounted to a starvation diet. The sentence 'I now am excited' in the so-called *system-language* was alleged to be rationally supported by the protocol sentences 'I feel my hands trembling', 'I see my hands trembling', 'I hear my voice quavering', etc. It has, Carnap insisted, precisely the same content as 'My body is now in that condition which, both under my own observation and that of others, exhibits such and such characteristics of excitement'.[25]

From the point of view of Wittgenstein's response to behaviourism, it is not necessary to trace the story any further. But it is clear enough what different routes remained to be explored. A stricter psychological behaviourism (molar behaviourism) would disregard physiology and concentrate upon searching for laws correlating stimulus and behavioural response. A stricter logical behaviourism would search for analyses which restrict the analysans of psychological statements to specifications of behaviour and behavioural dispositions. Materialists would go in the other direction, identifying the mental with states of the central nervous system. Carnap himself later opted for yet another line of attack, suggesting that scientific psychological concepts are not dispositional, but are 'hypothetical constructs' within a theoretical structure.[26] This in turn, cross-fertilized with the mechanist thesis derived from Turing and Craik, led to contemporary computational functionalist theories (see 'Men, minds, and machines', §5).

2. *Wittgenstein: first reactions*

When Wittgenstein resumed philosophy in 1929, behaviourism was definitely in the air. There is no evidence to suggest that he read Watson's

---

[23] See C. G. Hempel, 'The Logical Analysis of Psychology' (1935), repr. in translation in *Readings in Philosophical Analysis*, ed. H. Feigl and W. Sellars (Appleton, Century, Crofts, Inc., New York, 1949), p. 381.

[24] See Carnap, 'Logical Foundations of the Unity of Science' (1938), repr. in *Readings in Philosophical Analysis*, ed. Feigl and Sellars, p. 412.

[25] Carnap, 'Psychology in Physical Language', p. 191.

[26] Ibid., p. 197, and *idem*, 'The Methodological Character of Theoretical Concepts', in H. Feigl and M. Scriven (eds.), *Minnesota Studies in the Philosophy of Science*, Vol. 1.

book, but he certainly read Russell's *Analysis of Mind*, in which Watson's ideas are discussed. It seems likely that at some stage he at least looked at Carnap's *Logische Aufbau*,[27] and he definitely read the first of the *Erkenntnis* articles in 1932, which occasioned a quarrel. Wittgenstein accused Carnap of plagiarism, and held that Carnap's ideas concerning physicalism were derived from the *Tractatus*, conversations Wittgenstein had held with Waismann and Schlick in which Carnap had participated, and reports of Wittgenstein's new ideas circulated to members of the Vienna Circle by Waismann. He abruptly severed relations with Carnap.

The quarrel is *prima facie* puzzling, as Wittgenstein never went so far as to give a 'physicalist' or 'logical behaviourist' account of first-person present-tense psychological utterances. It is true, of course, that in 1929/30 he gave a kind of logical behaviourist analysis of third-person psychological propositions. But Carnap had done something very similar in *Logische Aufbau*, long before he met Wittgenstein. Until the full correspondence with Schlick and Carnap is published, it will be impossible to be certain about the details of this quarrel. The following is, therefore, a conjectural reconstruction.

The *leitmotif* of Carnap's first *Erkenntnis* article is the 'unity of science', i.e. the claim that 'all empirical statements can be expressed in a single language, all states of affairs are of one kind and are known by the same method'.[28] This thesis involved three corollaries: (a) That there are no philosophical propositions, and no special domain of philosophical knowledge, since the whole task of philosophy consists 'in clarifying the notions and statements of science'.[29] (b) Statements in logic and mathematics 'are tautologies, analytic propositions, certified on account of their form alone. They have no content, that is to say, assert nothing as to the occurrence or non-occurrence of some state of affairs.'[30] (c) 'Contentful' (empirical) statements do not divide into mutually irreducible kinds (e.g. physics, biology, and the *Geisteswissenschaften* – psychology, history, and the social sciences); rather, 'all statements in Science' (i.e. all cognitive statements) can be translated into, and are reducible to, the intersubjective language of 'physics'. It is noteworthy that the details of Carnap's thesis of the reducibility of psychological propositions to behaviouristic ones are *not* discussed in *The Unity of Science*, but are

---

[27] It is referred to explicitly in PLP 197, 270, 407, and perhaps in a conversation with Waismann in 1931 (WWK 182). It is possible, however, that the latter allusion is *not* to *Logische Aufbau* but to conversations with Carnap. Had Wittgenstein read it before 1932, the quarrel with Carnap would perhaps have been precipitated before publication of Carnap's first *Erkenntnis* article.
[28] Carnap, *Unity of Science*, p. 32.
[29] Ibid., p. 33.
[30] Loc.cit. To be sure, this is an oversimplification of Wittgenstein's view of the propositions of mathematics, since he did not claim that they were either tautologies or analytic, but rather that they were pseudo-propositions (TLP 6.2).

explicitly[31] postponed for discussion in the subsequent paper, 'Psychology in Physical Language', which was published a year later. In a letter to Schlick[32] dated 8 August 1932, Wittgenstein remonstrated that Carnap's central ideas were taken without acknowledgement from him. Certainly the only acknowledgement was to Neurath, who had coined the term 'physicalism' and who had, Carnap wrote, persuaded him to abandon the methodological solipsist base of *Logische Aufbau*. It seems that Carnap had said, or written, to Schlick that Wittgenstein had not touched on the matter of physicalism. Wittgenstein objected: 'Dass ich mich nicht mit der Frage des "Physicalismus" befasst hätte, ist unwahr (nur nicht unter diesem – scheusslichen – Namen) und in der Kürze, in der die ganze "Abhandlung" geschrieben ist.' ('That I had not dealt with the question of "physicalism" is untrue (only not under that – horrible – name), and with the brevity with which the whole of the *Tractatus* is written.') Moreover, he continued, Carnap's account of ostensive definition was derived from conversations at which Waismann was present. His conception of a hypothesis likewise came from Wittgenstein and not, as Carnap had insisted (presumably in a letter to Schlick), from Poincaré and Reichenbach, whose notions of grammar and proposition were quite different. The distinction between formal and contentful forms of speech (*inhaltliche Redeweise*), Wittgenstein remonstrated, went not one jot beyond his own work, and he expressed incredulity that Carnap could pretend that he had not understood the concluding propositions of the *Tractatus* on the proper method of future philosophy, but had arrived at that conclusion independently.

It seems that Wittgenstein thought (with some justice) that the general principles of 'the unity of science' or 'physicalism' were explicit in the *Tractatus*.[33] That he paid no attention to Carnap's reduction of first-person psychological propositions to behavioural ones is not surprising, since this programme was not carried through in the first *Erkenntnis*

[31] Carnap, *Unity of Science*, p. 72.
[32] See M. Nedo, *Wittgenstein: sein Leben in Bildern und Texten* (Suhrkamp, Frankfurt, 1983), pp. 254f.
[33] He was surely right that the conception of philosophy as logical analysis of propositions of 'natural science', i.e. empirical propositions, and as exposure of the nonsensicality of metaphysical propositions originates in the *Tractatus* (e.g. TLP 6.53). The claim that *all* empirical propositions are analysable into truth-functional combinations of elementary propositions can be taken to be equivalent to the thesis of the unity of science, but is non-committal with respect to a physicalist basis as opposed to a methodological solipsist (or phenomenalist) one. It is evident that a version of the latter emerges explicitly in the *Philosophical Remarks*. What remain very unclear are Wittgenstein's references in 1929 to a distinction between 'primary' and 'secondary' languages, which he had previously advocated and now repudiated. For if the secondary is not reducible to the primary, then the thesis of unity must have been abandoned. It is noteworthy that his remarks on primary and secondary language are not only obscure but are also equivocal, sometimes repudiating the distinction and sometimes using it (PR 51, 58, 84, 88, 100, 103, 158, 168, 267).

article. The analysis of third-person psychological propositions in terms of observable behaviour, however, was arguably implicit in the *Tractatus*, and had been explicitly advocated by Wittgenstein since 1929 (WWK 49f.; PR 88 – 95). The general thrust of this quasi-behaviourist account is evident in Waismann's *Thesen* (1930/31), which, it is plausible to assume, Carnap had read:

> A proposition cannot say more than is established by means of the method of its verification. If I say 'My friend is angry' and establish this in virtue of his displaying a certain perceptible behaviour, I only *mean* that he displays that behaviour. And if I mean more by it, I cannot specify what that extra consists in. A proposition says only what it does say and nothing that goes beyond that. (WWK 244)

The behaviourist pressure was premised upon the suppositions that first-person psychological sentences express genuine propositions, that these are verified by reference to immediate experience, and that psychological concepts such as pain are systematically ambiguous. Wittgenstein clarified the predicament with a nice example:

> Suppose I had stabbing pains in my right knee and my right knee jerked with every pang. At the same time I see someone else whose leg is jerking like mine and he complains of stabbing pains; and while this is going on my left leg begins jerking like the right though I can't feel any pain in my left knee. Now I say: the other fellow obviously has the same pain in his knee as I've got in my right knee. But what about my left knee, isn't it precisely the same case here as that of the other's knee? (PR 93)

Consequently, he concluded:

> The two hypotheses, that others have pain, and that they don't and merely behave as I do when I have, must have identical senses if every *possible* experience confirming the one confirms the other as well. In other words, if a decision between them on the basis of experience is inconceivable. (PR 94f.)

Of course, what this means is not that we can never know whether others are really in pain, but rather that to ascribe pain to others is not really to talk of anything over and above their behaviour. This would be made explicit in a different form of representation in which one never, for example, attributed toothache to other people, but only characterized their behaviour as being akin to one's own when one has toothache oneself. Of course, one would then talk in pitying tones of people who display toothache-behaviour (but are not said to have toothache), and one would differentiate genuine toothache from simulated toothache by reference to behaviour (cf. PR 93). The central point is that one cannot traverse the bounds of sense, e.g. attributing what I have – my toothache – to others, in thought. 'Philosophers who believe you can, in a manner of speaking, extend experience by thinking, ought to remember that you can transmit speech over the telephone, but not measles' (PR 95).

The misunderstanding of the radical asymmetry between first- and third-person psychological propositions is a source of both solipsism and behaviourism. These doctrines are the opposite of each other (LWL 112), each apprehending correctly that one member of any pair of such propositions is logically unlike the other, and each doctrine misconstruing that insight.

The logic of our language is so difficult to grasp at this point: our language employs the phrases 'my pain' and 'his pain', and also the expressions 'I have (or feel) a pain' and 'He has (or feels) a pain'. An expression 'I feel my pain' or 'I feel his pain' is nonsense. And it seems to me that, at bottom, the entire controversy over behaviourism turns on this. (PR 94)

Later in the 1930s, when his own views had changed dramatically, Wittgenstein was to compare behaviourism and finitism in mathematics:

we want to see the absurdities both of what the finitists and of what their opponents say – just as we want in philosophy to see the absurdities both of what the behaviourists say and of what their opponents say.
   Finitism and behaviourism are as alike as two eggs. The same absurdities and the same kind of answers. Both sides of such disputes are based on a particular kind of misunderstanding – which arises from gazing at a form of words and forgetting to ask yourself what's done with it . . . (LFM 111)

Here Wittgenstein was thinking primarily, if not exclusively, of psychological behaviourism, rather than of logical behaviourism. This is evident from the later remark 'Finitism and behaviourism are quite similar trends. Both say, but surely, all we have here is . . . Both deny the existence of something, both with a view to escaping from a confusion' (RFM 142). Psychological behaviourism misguidedly denied the existence of experiences (pains, desires, emotions, etc.) in order to escape from the confusions of introspective psychology which conceived of the mental in Cartesian, dualist terms. But both alternatives are absurd. In *Philosophical Remarks* Wittgenstein had sought to escape from the horns of this dilemma by construing third-person propositions as 'hypotheses' the symptoms of which are behaviour (see 'Criteria', §1). Subsequently he was to find a quite different resolution.

Two features of Russell's quasi-behaviourist drift in *Analysis of Mind* caught Wittgenstein's attention when he returned to philosophy, viz. Russell's account of desire (and related intentional concepts) and his rudimentary causal theory of meaning (which was also mooted in Carnap's *Erkenntnis* article). Wittgenstein's objections were rooted in ideas concerning the pictoriality of the proposition which originated in the *Tractatus* and persisted in modified form despite abandonment of the picture *theory* of the proposition. In both cases the criticisms apply with equal force to psychological behaviourism as conceived by Watson.

The key defect in Russell's theory of desire is that an internal relation, viz. between desire and its fulfilment, is taken to be an external relation. There is an internal relation between a proposition and the fact that makes it true, and so too there is an internal relation between a desire and what fulfils it:

> for me, there are only two things involved in the fact that a thought is true, i.e. the thought and the fact; whereas for Russell, there are three, i.e. thought, fact and a third event which, if it occurs, is just recognition. This third event, a sort of satisfaction of hunger (the other two being hunger and eating a particular kind of food) could, for example, be a feeling of pleasure . . . (PR 63)

The consequences of Russell's account are the following absurdities: (a) that we often do not find out what we wanted until our desire is satisfied, i.e. until the behaviour cycle has terminated in a state of quiescence; (b) that we are often mistaken about what we wanted (e.g. it would make sense to say 'I thought I wanted to go to London, but I actually wanted a piece of cake'); (c) that if we do know what we want, our knowledge must rest on induction from past experience (e.g. 'This feeling of dissatisfaction has, in the past, been alleviated by an apple, so I must want an apple'); (d) that if one wants something one has never had before, one cannot know what one wants.

The postulated causal, external, connection between desire and its fulfilment is what produces these incoherences. 'I believe Russell's theory amounts to the following,' Wittgenstein wrote (PR 64); 'if I give someone an order and I am happy with what he does, then he has carried out my order. (If I wanted to eat an apple, and someone punched me in the stomach, taking away my appetite, then it was this punch that I originally wanted.)' On Russell's theory it makes no sense to say 'I wished for an apple, but a pear has satisfied me', for if the pear has satisfied me, then what I wished for was really a pear (BB 22). But this is absurd, since we distinguish between fulfilling a wish or desire and producing gratification that may ameliorate an unfulfilled wish or desire. Furthermore, on Russell's account, it is not a tautology, but an empirical truth, that if someone sincerely says that he wants an apple, then his desire will be satisfied by an apple (PLP 117). But saying 'I should like an apple' does not mean 'I believe that an apple will quell my feeling of discomfort'; and this latter proposition is not the expression of a wish or desire at all (PI §440).

By contrast, Wittgenstein insisted that the connection between a proposition and what makes it true, a desire and its satisfaction, an expectation and its fulfilment, and an order and its execution is in every case *internal*:

> The fulfilment of an expectation doesn't consist in a third thing happening which you could also describe in another way than just as 'the fulfilment of the expectation', thus for example as a feeling of satisfaction or pleasure or whatever.

For expecting that *p* will be the case must be the same as expecting that this expectation will be fulfilled; whereas, if I am wrong, expecting *p* would be different from expecting that this expectation will be fulfilled.

Isn't it like this: My theory is completely expressed in the fact that the state of affairs satisfying the expectation of *p* is represented by the proposition *p*? And so, not by the description of a *totally* different event. (PR 65f.)

Describing an expectation by reference to what is expected is to give an internal description (PR 68); and if there were only an external connection, then no connection at all could be described, since we only describe the external one by means of the internal one (PR 66). With Pavlovian behaviourism obviously in mind, Wittgenstein added 'Salivation – no matter how precisely measured – is *not* what I call expecting' (PR 70).

He connected this insight explicitly with his earlier ideas in the *Tractatus*:

Expecting is connected with looking for: looking for something presupposes that I know what I am looking for, without what I am looking for having to exist.

Earlier I would have put this by saying that searching presupposes the elements of the complex, but not *the* combination that I was looking for.

And that isn't a bad image: for, in the case of language, that would be expressed by saying that the sense of a proposition only presupposes the grammatically correct use of certain words. (PR 67)

With the abandonment of the metaphysics of logical atomism, however, the apparent metaphysical harmony between language and reality is disclosed to be a harmony *within language* (see Volume 2, 'Accord with a rule', pp. 86 – 91). Desire and the characterization of its satisfaction, expectation and the description of its fulfilment, make contact in language. For 'the desire that *p*' = 'the desire that is satisfied by *p*'s being the case'. The articulate expression of a desire (wish, expectation, or command) contains a 'picture' of what will fulfil it. It makes no sense to suppose that one only finds out later what one really wanted or to think that one's expression of desire is a hypothesis confirmed or disconfirmed by a later experience of gratification. The failure to discern this internal relation, to apprehend the unintelligibility of the primary characterization of a desire or expectation other than in terms of its fulfilment, vitiates the Russellian and causal, behaviourist theory of desire.

A similar flaw lies at the heart of the behaviourist theory of meaning. Wittgenstein was willing to concede that language learning is rooted in training that antecedes explaining what expressions mean (PLP 111 – 14). Such training is not unlike setting up a causal mechanism by way of stimulus conditioning, which approximates to the behaviourist conception. It does not follow, however, that in general 'the pronouncing of a word is now a stimulus, now a reaction' (PLP 113f.) as Watson and, with qualification, Russell suggested, let alone that its meaning consists in 'a causal law governing our use of the word and our actions when we hear it used' (AM 198). Suppose we trained a dog to behave in such-and-such a way or built a machine (a calculating machine) to perform such-and-such a task, given the stimulus of a sign 'p'. Now contrast (a) The sign 'p' means the same as the command to do so-and-so and (b) The animal (or machine) is so conditioned (or constructed) that the occurrence of the sign 'p' brings about so-and-so. The causal account of language in effect reduces the explanation of meaning given in (a) to the description of a causal nexus given in (b). But (a) specifies a convention, a rule for the use of the sign 'p' – an explanation within the 'calculus' (network of rules) of language; whereas (b) describes a causal mechanism. The truth of (b) is wholly independent of the truth of (a), and the convention is independent of the reactions of the dog or machine. A dog, however well trained, may misbehave, and a machine, however well constructed, may malfunction. But that what it does *is* misbehaviour or malfunctioning is determined by reference to the stipulated convention of meaning. Otherwise, what meaning a sign has would always be a matter of a hypothesis about what reaction it will call forth, and its meaning would not be determinable in advance of the behavioural consequences of its use from occasion to occasion. Hence too, one could not determine that the machine was malfunctioning, since what 'p' means would just be whatever response it produces (PLP 114 – 16).[34]

The meaning of an expression, Wittgenstein argued, is not its effect. It is what is given by an *explanation* of meaning. And explanation consists in a move *within* language; it is a rule for the use of a sign, an articulation within the grammatical network of the language. Although training in the rudiments of word-use may be behaviouristically conceived, it rapidly progresses to explanations of meaning, to asking and being given answers to the question 'What does "x" mean?', and hence to progressive mastery of a *normative*, not a causal, structure. (At this stage, Wittgenstein favoured comparing it with a *calculus* of rules, a simile which he later progressively relinquished.) Moves within this structure are justified by reasons, not causes, and it is these normative connections that constitute the meanings of expressions. The meaning of an expression is the correlate of understanding, for one is said to understand an utterance when one knows what it means. The criteria of understanding include both *correct use*, which is not a causal concept, and *giving correct explanations*, e.g. by paraphrase, examples, ostension, or exemplification, which are rules for the use of expressions. The correctness of use is

---

[34] This contrast between a causal and a normative connection lies at the heart of Wittgenstein's response to the idea of a 'Turing machine' (see 'Men, minds, and machines', §5). It is also a pivotal point in the contrast between experiment and calculation in mathematics (RFM 194 – 9, 364 – 6, 379 – 82, 389 – 92).

determined by the practice of measuring applications against the yard-stick of explanations.

Although Russell's comparison of understanding a language with understanding cricket (AM 197) is apt, since in both cases a technique is mastered and a practical skill is acquired, his claim that understanding is independent of knowing what the expressions one understands mean is incoherent – as absurd as the idea that one might know how to play cricket without knowing the rules. Russell remarked that there is no more reason why a person who uses a word correctly should be able to tell what it means than there is why a planet which is moving correctly should know Kepler's laws (AM 199). This reveals his conflation of the nomic with the normative. Planets do not move *correctly*, whereas people do use expressions correctly or incorrectly. But it only makes sense to say of a person that he uses a word 'correctly' if there is a standard of correctness which he satisfies; and that is what is given by accepted explanations of meaning. The first steps in the rudiments of language learning may be mere training (which antecedes understanding). But the introduction of explanations of meaning, questions about what expressions mean, criticisms of use as incorrect, etc. transform behavioural regularities (which can (perhaps) be represented in terms of stimulus and response according to causal connections) into normative behaviour justified by reasons (which cannot intelligibly be so conceived). Contrary to what Russell asserted (AM 197), the supposition that the meaning of a word is 'to be distilled out of [its use] by observation and analysis' is incoherent. For whatever causal connections between utterance and behaviour are established by training (or stimulus/response condition-ing), they cannot determine the logical (grammatical) consequences of the use of a symbol, as opposed to its putative causal consequences. Hence they cannot determine the differentiation of correct from incorrect use; and so they bypass the question of the meaning of an expression altogether.[35]

3. *Crypto-behaviourism?*

A crucial development in Wittgenstein's thinking occurred in 1932/3 when he abandoned the view that first-person psychological utterances are the 'genuine propositions', denied that they get compared with reality (viz. immediate experience) for verification, and repudiated his earlier view that they are objects of knowledge or ignorance. Instead he came to view them as expressions (*Äusserungen*) or manifestations of the

---

[35] Wittgenstein was equally critical of Russell's associationist explanation of meaning in terms of imagery and 'mnemic causal laws', but this theory and its flaws do not belong to a discussion of behaviourism.

'inner' and to see their occurrence not as a *symptom* for a hypothesis, but as a *criterion* of the mental. The ramifications of this change are explored in other essays ('Privacy', 'The inner and the outer', 'Men, minds, and machines', and 'Criteria').

That Wittgenstein repudiated psychological behaviourism is obvious enough. He did not argue that pain, for example, is a mere fiction, but rather that pain, conceived as a 'private object' that lies behind pain-behaviour, is a *grammatical* fiction (PI §307). He acknowledged the difference between pain-behaviour with pain and pain-behaviour without pain and denied that pain is a mere nothing (PI §304). But, more enigmatically, he also denied that pain was a something and justified this *prima-facie* obscure remark as a rejection of 'the grammar which tries to force itself on us here'. He also repudiated the picture of an inner process associated with, for example, the notion of remembering (PI §305). Contrary to the empiricist tradition, he denied that feeling or 'experiencing' pain is a pre-condition for understanding the word 'pain' (PI §315), and that clarification of the meaning of the verb 'to think' requires any introspective scrutiny of thinking (PI §316). One might harbour the suspicion that his repudiation of psychological behaviourism goes hand in hand with acceptance of a form of *logical* behaviourism.

The case for such an interpretation seems to be strengthened by closer examination of the transformation in Wittgenstein's philosophy in 1932/3 when he abandoned his earlier conception of first-person psychological sentences. For did he not insist that what appear to be reports of an inner realm of mental objects are in fact merely verbal *behaviour*? The verbal expression of pain, he argued, is new pain-behaviour which replaces crying (PI §244). The utterance 'Now I understand' or 'Now I know how to go on' is not a description of a mental state, but a signal (PI §180) or an exclamation that corresponds to an instinctive sound or a glad start (PI §323). The words with which one expresses one's memory are a *memory-reaction* (PI §343), and the expression of expectation is a *verbal reaction* (Z §53). Is this not a logical-behaviourist account of first-person psychological propositions?

In *Philosophical Remarks* Wittgenstein surely gave an analysis of third-person psychological propositions in terms of behaviour. Although he subsequently claimed that behaviour is a criterion of the inner, did he not continue to insist that third-person psychological propositions are verified, and can at least on occasion be conclusively verified, by reference to behaviour? It is characteristic of those who oppose logical behaviourism to claim that the subject of experience knows directly and with certainty what experiences he is having, whereas others know or perhaps only believe on the basis of indirect evidence. But that is precisely what Wittgenstein denied. It is nonsense to say 'I know I have a pain', and others often do know, with certainty, that I am in pain (cf. PI

§246); furthermore their evidence – viz. my behaviour – is *not* indirect (LPE 278). Did Wittgenstein not claim that the *body* is the best picture of the soul (PI p. 178), and that if one sees the *behaviour* of a living thing one *sees its soul* (PI §357)? But remove the poetry from these remarks, and do we not have before us a form, indeed an extreme form, of logical behaviourism? Small wonder that the *Philosophical Investigations* and *Concept of Mind* have seemed to many bemused philosphers to be sisters under the skin.[36]

There is no denying that Wittgenstein's philosophical psychology shares significant features with behaviourism. Negatively, like (logical) behaviourists, Wittgenstein repudiated the traditional philosophical conception of the inner. Experience is not hidden behind behaviour; nor does it accompany behaviour as music which only I hear can accompany my singing. The mental is not a private world accessible only to its owner, and experiences are not private ethereal objects inhabiting such a realm. The subject does not have a privileged access to his mental states and does not know better than others how things are with him (indeed, in typical cases it makes no sense to talk either of knowledge or of ignorance). Like the (psychological) behaviourists, Wittgenstein was willing to accept the idea that language-learning with us is founded on brute training, which presupposes for its success a variety of natural forms of behaviour and reactions.[37] Far from first-person present-tense psychological utterances being reports of parades upon an inner stage, he conceived of them as extensions of, and often partial substitutes for, natural, primitive, expressive behaviour. Contrary to the empiricist tradition, he did not conceive of language-use as a translation, for the benefit of others, into 'word-language' from language-independent thoughts. On the contrary, 'our language-game is behaviour' (Z §545), and the capacity to think is in general parasitic upon the capacity to express one's thoughts in utterance and behaviour. Parallel to logical behaviourism, Wittgenstein argued that the ascription of psychological predicates to other people is *logically* connected with behaviour; we would have no use for these expressions if they were not bound up with behavioural criteria (LPE 286). The inner is indeed verified by reference

---

[36] This is in fact doubly erroneous. First, Ryle's *Concept of Mind* is mischaracterized as 'logical behaviourist'. Secondly, Wittgenstein's account differs extensively from Ryle's, both on numerous points of detail (e.g. doing mental arithmetic, tunes going through one's head, imagining) and on general issues of principle (the explanation of first-person psychological utterances and the characterization of self-knowledge).

[37] This seems to be an empirical claim, and to that extent lies outside the bounds of logical grammar. Arguably Wittgenstein would have held it to be a platitude, a remark on the natural history of human beings, not a novel curiosity but an evident truism (cf. PI §415). Though he would have repudiated Skinnerian theories of language, Chomsky's argument in favour of an innate knowledge of universal grammar as a *sine qua non* of language-learning would, I suggest, have struck him as yet another house of cards.

to the outer, and doubts about the inner, e.g. over dissimulation, are settled by reference to more evidence consisting of the outer. For even a person's sincere avowal is a form of behaviour. Behaviourists were surely right to note the importance of the fact that avowals license predictions; if people's avowals of understanding were not in general followed by successful exercises of appropriate skills, these forms of words would have no use. And if people's expressions of pain were not integrated into more general patterns of pain-behaviour, their words would be meaningless. Finally, Wittgenstein, like the behaviourists, denied that the empirical study of human psychology is to be pursued by 'introspection', i.e. by noticing what goes on in one's own case when one thinks, is angry, or desires this or that, and describing what one observes for the benefit of the psychologist. Nor is it a study of the inner at one remove – an examination of unobservables by means of registering their effects, like particle physics. Everything suggests that he would have repudiated as incoherent the classical conception of psychology as the investigation of a special 'realm of consciousness'.

Despite these important converging lines, it is fundamentally misguided to classify Wittgenstein's descriptions of the grammar of psychological expressions as a form of logical behaviourism. The convergence is explained by the common repudiation of (roughly speaking) Cartesianism and the classical empiricist Cartesian inheritance. To escape from these confusions, the radical psychological behaviourist denies the existence of the mental, and the logical behaviourist reduces the mental to behaviour. Wittgenstein did neither. To a first approximation, what he did was to explore the grammar of the expression or manifestation (*Äusserung*) of the inner. In his detailed examination of the relation of behaviour to what it is a manifestation of, of the logical status of avowals of experience, of thinking and imagining, of intention and desire, and of the very *concepts* of body and behaviour (i.e. of what *counts* as behaviour), his account diverged dramatically from logical-behaviourist strategies.

In *Investigations* §571 Wittgenstein pointed out that it was misleading to suggest that psychology treats of processes in the psychical sphere just as physics does in the physical. The physicist observes the phenomena (e.g. movements of bodies) that he theorizes about, but the psychologist observes the *Äusserungen*, i.e. the expressive behaviour, of human beings. This is an apt warning against introspectionist psychology. But does it then follow that the psychologist deals only with behaviour and not with the mind (PI p.179)? Not so; for although the utterances (*Äusserungen*) of human beings are *also* forms of behaviour, they are uses of language too – and they are not *about* behaviour. Wittgenstein developed this theme at greater length in the *Remarks on Philosophical Psychology*:

So does psychology deal with behaviour (say), not with human states of mind? If someone does a psychological experiment – what will he report? – What the subject says, what he does, what has happened to him in the past and how he has reacted to it. – And not: what the subject thinks, what he sees, feels, believes, experiences? – If you describe a painting, do you describe the arrangement of paint strokes on the canvas – and *not* what someone looking at it *sees*?

But now how about this: The observer in the experiment will sometimes say: 'The subject said "I feel . . .", and I had the impression that this was true.' – Or he says: 'The subject seemed tired.' Is that a statement about his behaviour? One would perhaps like to say: 'Of course, what else should it be?' – It may also be reported: 'The subject said "I am tired" ' – but the cash value of these words will depend on whether they are plausible, whether they were repeating what someone else said, whether they were a translation from French, etc.

Now think of this: I recount: 'He made a dejected impression.' I am asked: 'What was it that made this impression on you?' I say: 'I don't know.' – Can it now be said that I described his behaviour? Well, can one not say I have described his face if I say 'His face became sad'? Even though I cannot say what spatial alterations in the face made this impression?

It will perhaps be replied: 'If you had looked closer, you would have been able to describe the characteristic changes of colour and position.' But who says that I or anyone could do this? (RPP I §287)

The report 'He was dejected' is about both behaviour and state of mind, but not side by side, as if one were an accompaniment of the other. Rather, about one in one sense and the other in another (RPP I §288).[38] The dejected look is not a *sign* of sadness, as a flushed face is a sign (an empirically correlated symptom) of fever (RPP I §292). It manifests, makes visible, the person's mood.

The relations of behavioural expression to what it is an expression of are not external. The inner is not related to its outward manifestations as an unobservable entity to its causal effects (e.g. as an electron is to its traces in a cloud chamber). The relation is internal or grammatical. But the mental is not, *pace* logical behaviourists, reducible to behaviour. 'He is in pain' does not *mean* 'He is behaving (or is disposed to behave) thus-and-so'. Nor is pain-behaviour related to pain as symptom to hypothesis. Rather, it is a *criterion* of pain. It is possible for pain to occur without being manifest, and it is possible for pain-behaviour to be displayed without there being any pain. This grammatical relation, though distinct from entailment, nevertheless allows for certainty, although it is defeasible (see 'Criteria').

A verbal utterance which constitutes the expression of an inner state, etc. is *also* a kind of behaviour; but it is not *only* a kind of behaviour. It is

---

[38] PI p. 179 rephrases this: 'aber nicht im Nebeneinander; sondern vom einen durch das andere'!

an articulate use of language. The utterance 'I have a toothache' is not *about* my clutching my cheek or about my groanings and wincings. It is akin to a cry of complaint; but the complaint is not about my behaviour, it is about my toothache, which is a sensation. And sensations are not patterns of behaviour. Nevertheless, the grammar of 'about' in the context of an *Äusserung* is unlike the grammar of 'about' in the context of a description – it signifies what the *Äusserung* is an expression of. Such an avowal is not uttered on the grounds of my observations of my own behaviour (*pace* Carnap's logical behaviourism), and I do not *know it to be true* on the same grounds as others, since I cannot be said to know or to be ignorant of its truth. It is *groundlessly* uttered, and it is not *verified* by reference to behaviour or *anything else*! The verbal manifestations of pain, joy, or desire are not *correlated* with what they manifest. For one cannot say '*This* is pain, and *this* is pain-behaviour – they normally go together, therefore . . .'. The logic of expression (*Äusserung*) is not the logic of correlation of distinct domains, and the grammar of psychological words used in verbal manifestations of the mental is not the grammar of names of objects (PI §293). One might say that behaviourism, no less than dualism, failed to appreciate the grammatical (logical) significance of the fact that 'I have a pain' is an *expression* of pain.

4. *Body and behaviour*

The Cartesian sundering of mind from body constituted *inter alia* a methodological demarcation of the domain of the physical sciences. Bodies as such belong within that domain. What differentiates a corpse from a living human being (as opposed to a living animal, which is merely a 'biological machine') was held to be the fact that the living human being is animated by a mind. Here lies the gap in the otherwise seamless web of efficient causation in nature. For the mind can control, via the pineal gland, the movements of the body. Although the total quantity of motion in the physical universe, like the quantity of matter, is conserved, the direction of movement, in the case of human beings, is subject to 'outside intervention'.

The distortions in the resultant conception of the mind tend to overshadow the no less important Cartesian misrepresentation of the concepts of the human body and of human behaviour.[39] Though Descartes conceded that 'I am not merely present in my body as a sailor is present in a ship', but am rather 'very closely joined and, as it were, intermingled with it, so that I and the body form a unit',[40] the

---

[39] I am indebted here to J. W. Cooke's 'Human Beings', in P. Winch (ed.), *Studies in the Philosophy of Wittgenstein* (Routledge and Kegan Paul, London, 1969), pp. 117 – 51.

[40] Descartes, *Meditations on First Philosophy*, 'Sixth Meditation', in *Philosophical Writings*, Vol. II, p. 56 (AT VII, 81).

intermingling is causal, and the unity contingent. I *have* a body; but according to Cartesians it is conceivable that I might not have had one, and it makes sense to suppose (for the sake of argument against hyperbolic doubt) that I do not have one. The body is explicitly conceived to be a *machine*. The mind or soul is the entity that has, owns, the body – and ownership consists in the two-way causal interaction between this pair of substances. The mind *controls* the body which it 'owns'. 'When a *rational soul* is present in this machine it will have its principal seat in the brain, and reside there like the fountain-keeper who must be stationed at the tanks to which the fountain's pipes return if he wants to produce, or prevent, or change their movements in some way.'[41] My body, therefore, is that body impact upon which causes me to have sensory experiences and which moves in compliance with my will. My behaviour consists in those movements of my body which are caused by me.

This conception could hardly help sowing the seeds of scepticism about other minds. In the *Meditations* Descartes wrote:

if I look out of the window and see men crossing the square, as I just happen to have done, I normally say that I see the men themselves . . . Yet do I see any more than hats and coats which could conceal automatons? I *judge* that they are men. And so something which I thought I was seeing with my eyes is in fact grasped solely by the faculty of judgement which is in my mind.[42]

The seeds duly germinated. Although Berkeley repudiated the Cartesian duality of mind and matter and rejected the attendant conception of material substance, he accepted without demur this picture of what is visible in the behaviour of human beings. 'A human spirit or person is not perceived by sense', he insisted;[43] 'We do not see a man, if by *man* is meant that which lives, moves, perceives, and thinks as we do: but only . . . a certain collection of ideas.' All we see of 'other spirits' are 'several motions, changes, and combinations of ideas'. For

is it not the soul which makes the principal distinction between a real person and a shadow, a living man and a carcass? . . .

By the person Alciphron is meant an individual thinking thing, and not the hair, skin, or visible surface, or any part of the outward form, colour, or shape, of Alciphron . . . And in granting this, you grant that, in a strict sense, I do not see Alciphron, i.e. that individual thinking thing, but only such visible signs and tokens as suggest and infer the being of that invisible thinking principle or soul.[44]

---

[41] Descartes, *Treatise on Man*, in *Philosophical Writings*, Vol. I, p. 141 (AT XI, 131).
[42] Descartes, *Meditations*, 'Second Meditation', in *Philosophical Writings*, Vol. II, p. 21 (AT VII, 32).
[43] G. Berkeley, *The Principles of Human Knowledge*, CXLV, CXLVII.
[44] Berkeley, *Alciphron*, 'Fourth Dialogue', §§4f.

Mill shared this conception:

> In the case of other human beings . . . I must either believe them to be alive, or to be automatons: and by believing them to be alive, that is by supposing the link to be of the same nature as in the case of which I have experience, and which is in all respects similar, I bring other human beings, as phaenomena, under the same generalization which I know by experience to be the true theory of my own existence.[45]

What grammar has put together, philosophers can only sunder at the cost of nonsense. Do we *believe* that other human beings are not automatons? Do we observe only physical movements and grimaces? And do we infer, on the basis of analogy with our own case, that our spouses and children are sad or joyful, amused or annoyed? Does the rich tapestry of human social life, of empathy and mutual understanding, of shared experience and emotion, hang upon an analogical thread?

Behaviourism is first cousin to 'the problem of other minds'. Cartesians pictured the soul's relation to the body rather like that of an immaterial hand within a visible glove. In one's own case, one can feel one's hand and see the movements of the glove; in the case of others one can see only a glove and its movements, and one infers the existence of an invisible hand by analogy. Behaviourism (by and large) rightly repudiated the Cartesian conception of the mind, but accepted the correlative conception of the body – as it were, an empty glove that moves in accord with the laws of stimulus and response (molar behaviourism), which are probably ultimately reducible to laws of physics (molecular behaviourism). But philosophical enlightenment, a surview of our concepts of both inner and outer, of psychological expressions and of behavioural ones, can be achieved only by repudiating *both* halves of the classical diptych.

Wittgenstein explicitly addressed the question of whether one believes other people not to be automatons. Characteristically, he faulted the question itself. In certain circumstances, one can say 'I believe he is suffering'. But can one also say 'I believe he is not an automaton' (PI p. 178)? No! – but not because I am *certain* that he isn't one. For what would it be like if he were an automaton? One might object that one can surely imagine this. Perhaps so, Wittgenstein replied, but then one would imagine him going about his business as if in a trance, with a glazed look in his eyes (cf. PI §420). But can one look at children playing and say to oneself 'Perhaps they are automatons'? Is one to suppose here that other human beings, behaving as they normally do, are unconscious (PI §418)? That is obviously absurd. Is it, then, that they are supposed to

[45] J. S. Mill, *An Examination of Sir William Hamilton's Philosophy*, ed. J. M. Robson, in *Collected Works of John Stuart Mill*, Vol. IX (University of Toronto Press, Toronto, 1979), p. 191.

lack consciousness? What does that mean? That they lack something which *I* have? 'I am conscious' has a use in special circumstances, but not as a report of an experience (PI §416; see 'The world of consciousness', §3). 'Consciousness' does not signify a private experience which I apprehend directly in my own case and problematically infer in the case of others; and to say that human beings are conscious or 'possess consciousness' is not to make an empirical statement at all (PI §418). When people behave *thus*, we say that they are 'fully conscious'; and when conscious they may further be conscious of a noise in the next room or of being overdressed for the party. People can, when drugged for example, behave like automatons, i.e. mechanically, moving jerkily, etc. But it makes no sense to ask of human beings behaving normally whether they may not be automatons for all that.

But surely, one may still object, human beings have bodies, and one *sees* their bodies (and not their souls). Does it not make sense to ask whether *those bodies* are not automatons? The question again is awry. One can ask whether those bodies (decaying corpses, for example) are human bodies as opposed to bodies of some other kind of primate. One can point at a person, indeed at the body *of* a person, and say 'That body is a human body' – which would be a grammatical explanation of the expression 'human body'. But the question 'Are those bodies automatons or human beings?' presupposes that it is legitimate, just like that, to say that human beings are bodies. This subtly distorts the grammar of 'a body', as well as that of 'human being' (or, indeed, 'animal') and 'mind' or 'soul'. (Do we *not* see a soul in anguish or a first-rate mind at work?) This distortion, in a philosophical context, is highly misleading. Human beings and animals *have* bodies; this is a grammatical proposition. And the grammar of 'having a body' has distinctive features which are obscured by replacing this phrase with 'being a body'. The grammatical distinction earmarks the qualitative difference between the living and the dead, the animate and the inanimate, the sensible and the insensate (PI §284).

I may be proud of my body without being proud of myself, and ashamed of myself without being ashamed of my body. It makes sense to say 'I am N.N.' on introducing myself to a stranger, but 'I am a body' is no introduction. Nor does it characterize me, as does 'I am a diabetic' or even the grammatical proposition 'I am a human being'. (Human *beings*, although they are space-occupants, are not human *bodies*.) Unless it is an emphatic insistence that I have physical needs, it is quite useless outside philosophy. And within philosophy its only use is as a misleading denial of the confused metaphysical claim that I am a mind.

One might venture another throw. If my body is healthy or, alternatively, out of condition, then I am healthy or out of condition, respectively. If my body is *n* stone in weight, then I weigh *n* stone; and when I die, my body will be a dead body, a corpse. So is it not correct to say that I *am* my body? But what is this supposed to mean? It surely cannot mean that I am *identical* with my body. For, first, it is no more an identity-statement than 'I am N.N.' (see 'I and my self', §4). Secondly, I will cease to exist before my body ceases to exist, for when I die I leave my remains behind. My body will then be a corpse, but I will not. Thirdly, although it is true that in some contexts 'I' can be replaced by 'my body', nevertheless, (a) the very phrase '*my* body' presupposes the distinctness of the grammars of 'body' and 'person' (or 'human being'); and (b) in most contexts the expressions are *not* intersubstitutable.

'I am *this* ↗ body' avoids the complications of 'my body' but otherwise fares no better. One cannot say, pointing at oneself, 'This body intends to go to London, has made up its mind, is trying to resolve a philosophical problem.' We must again call to mind Wittgenstein's remark that 'only of a living human being and what resembles (behaves like) a living human being can one say . . .' (PI §281). He did not write 'only of a living human *body*'.

The terrain here is strewn with mines, and one must tread with care. To repudiate the sentence 'I am my body', and to deny that a person is identical with his body or that a human being is a (human) body is not to affirm that I, or any other person, is identical with something else distinct from the body – a mind, soul, or self. 'Who am I?' is answered by 'I am N.N.'. 'What am I?' can be answered in various ways (soldier, sailor, tinker, tailor – or a miserable sinner, a misanthrope, etc.). But to deny the identity of myself or of another person with a body does not force one to adopt Cartesianism. It is noteworthy that even 'I am a human being', unless employed, for example, to remonstrate against maltreatment, has no function save as a grammatical explanation of the expression 'human being'. For as with 'He isn't an automaton', here too one might say: 'What information is conveyed by this and to whom would it be information? To a *human being* who meets [me] in ordinary circumstances? What information *could* it give him?' (cf. PI p. 178). 'He is a human being' would need a very special context to make any sense; but it is true that one might have occasion to explain that General Motors, unlike General Montgomery, is *not* a human being. Obviously something similar applies to 'I have a body'; it is more like 'this rod has a length' than like 'I have two hands'. But this rod may well have a length of two metres, and I may have a body of such-and-such characteristics.

Some human beings have beautiful bodies, others have ugly ones; but they are not their bodies. The grammatical form of ownership is doubtless misleading. To say that a person *has* such-and-such a sort of body is not to imply that the person is a Cartesian mind which owns that body. If it seems so, we should remind ourselves that a person is also said to *have* a decisive mind. To have a beautiful body, unlike having a beautiful car, is not to own or be in possession of something. Nor does 'having' here function in the same way as in 'I have two hands'. It makes sense to lose one's hand, but not to lose one's body. My hand is part of my body, but my body is not a part of anything. 'Having a body' does not signify a two-way causal interaction between a person and the body he has. A person's body is not like the car he drives, but not because he 'is more intimately intermingled' with it. The body of a living creature is not a machine, and a person does not control his body as a driver controls a car. Machines do not *have* bodies, and the bodies of living creatures, unlike machines, do not have intrinsic purposes. Only what is alive can be said to have a body, and not *everything* that is alive – for plants and trees, though they have branches and foliage, do not have bodies. Only animals, in particular self-moving, *sentient* creatures, have bodies (which become corpses on death). And it is not the body that is sentient, conscious, or unconscious, that sees or hears – but rather the creature whose body it is. Having a body, one might say, is a (formal) mark of *sentient life*. 'Our attitude to what is alive and to what is dead, is not the same. All our reactions are different' (PI §284). The same holds of what lacks life – of sticks and stones, and of what is not self-moving and is insensate – like trees and plants.

What then gives me the idea that living beings can feel (PI §283)? *Not* (as Mill thought) that I transfer the idea of feelings from my own case to objects outside myself. The idea that it must be either the body or the soul (or mind) that is conscious or unconscious, that sees or is blind, is excited or indifferent presents a misguided Cartesian dilemma – and it is this which must be repudiated. It is misconceived to think that categorially different properties, such as thinking on the one hand and walking on the other, must belong to categorially distinct substances, and equally erroneous to think that 'mind' and 'body' signify such substances. Sensation, perception, emotion, etc. are attributed to *human beings* and to creatures that *behave like them*; and neither minds nor bodies *behave*. Animals bark or purr, eat and drink, chase each other, search for food, etc; but these are not actions or activities attributable to their bodies. Human beings, unlike other animals, talk, ask questions and answer them, issue orders and obey them; but it is neither their *bodies* nor their *minds* that engage in these transactions. The category of human being, is, as one would expect, fundamental to our language-games. We react spontaneously in distinctive ways to other human beings, to our mothers and fathers, siblings and other children, long before we learn to speak. We are not of the *opinion* that our parents and companions are human beings. Our attitude towards them is an attitude towards *human beings*; and such attitudes come before opinions (alternative draft of PI p. 178 in MS. 169). Our language-games are rooted in these forms of pre-linguistic behaviour (cf. Z §545), and the question of whether 'these bodies' (of Mother and Father, and all the others) might not be automatons does not arise, nor can it intelligibly be raised.

Nevertheless, it might be replied, does the concept of a human being not stand in need of justification. Is not the attribution of pain, joy, and the rest based on *behaviour*? Do we not see the mere behaviour (which is, as Wittgenstein stresses, a *criterion* for the inner) and infer from it that such-and-such experience is being enjoyed? Does Wittgenstein himself not say that 'if one sees the behaviour of a living being, one sees its soul'?

Further confusions still need to be unpacked. First, as Wittgenstein remarks in a different context:

> Here we are in danger of wanting to make fine distinctions. – It is the same when one tries to define the concept of a material object in terms of 'what is really seen'. – What we have rather to do is to *accept* the everyday language-game, and to note *false* accounts of the matter *as* false. The primitive language-game which children are taught needs no justification; attempts at justification need to be rejected. (PI p. 200)

The child does not *learn* to respond to his mother's behaviour as to a human being. He responds – and later learns a language. Those responses might have been different, as they are in cases of autism. But had they generally been different, the human forms of life as we know them would not have arisen. The child does not see his mother's behaviour *as* the behaviour of a human being. For seeing human behaviour for what it is antecedes aspect-perception, which presupposes mastery of a technique. On the contrary, it is seeing human behaviour as the behaviour of automatons which could be said to be a limiting case of aspect-perception (PI §420).

Secondly, the relationship between behavioural concepts and psychological concepts is complex. Wittgenstein's analogy with the misconceived attempt to define 'material object' in terms of 'what is really seen' is apt. He noted elsewhere, apropos this very issue: 'It is like the relation: physical object – sense impression. Here we have two different language-games and a complicated relation between them. – If you try to reduce their relations to a *simple* formula you go wrong' (PI p. 180). One way in which this complicated relation gets oversimplified was built into Cartesianism *ab initio* and was inherited unquestioningly by behaviourism, logical and psychological alike. If one views the body as the vehicle of the soul, if one thinks that one does not really 'see the men themselves' but only 'hats and coats which could conceal automatons' (Descartes), then one is bound to think of human behaviour as 'several motions, changes' of 'the outward form, colour, or shape' of a 'mere body' (Berkeley). (This aberration is parallel to the thought that we do not even see 'the things themselves' but only their mere appearances, sense-data or impressions.) The consequent distortion of the concept of behaviour is the seed-bed of the philosophical problem of 'other minds'.

Disillusionment with Cartesianism bred behaviourism, which rightly rejected the Cartesian (and empiricist) conception of the mind, but accepted the associated conception of the body and behaviour. Hence the declared goal of C. L. Hull, for example, was to show how, from 'colourless movements' (as opposed to intentional, goal-directed behaviour) and 'mere receptor impulses as such', one can deduce or construct psychological concepts such as purpose, intention, desire, etc.[46] Logical behaviourists pursued, more or less self-consciously, a similar objective. And it has been thought that Wittgenstein differed from the Vienna Circle primarily in introducing a novel, and perhaps dubious, logical relation to mediate between (mere) observable behaviour and psychological state, viz. that of a criterion.

This is to overlook completely the fact that Wittgenstein repudiated the Cartesian and behaviourist conceptions of body and behaviour, as well as the Cartesian picture of the mind. Behaviour is indeed the criterion of the mental, but behaviour is not mere 'colourless movement'.[47] Wittgenstein parted company with the prevailing tradition in four crucial respects. First, when he wrote of the distinct criteria of thinking, pain, anger, joy, wish, fear, intention, etc., the term 'behaviour' includes not merely the play of facial expression and gestures, but also the surroundings, the occasion of these expressions and gestures (RPP I §129; cf. §314). Hence, for example, 'Pain-behaviour and the behaviour of sorrow. – These can only be described along with their external occasions. (If a child's mother leaves it alone it may cry because it is sad; if it falls down, from pain.) Behaviour and kind of occasion belong together' (Z §492). The behaviourist might go along with this. After all, he too describes behaviour in the context of a specific stimulus. But the characterization of the occasion in purely causal (stimulus) terms will obliterate or distort the crucial distinction between reason and cause, and hence too the difference between the causes and objects of emotions and the propriety of the behaviour (e.g. *obeying* an order) with respect to its occasion (viz. the issuing of a command).

Secondly, and connected with the latter point, behaviour which is, *inter alia*, a criterion for the mental includes not only what people do antecedently to learning, but also what they do, and in particular what they *say*, after having learnt. If someone has learnt to use the words 'I am glad' where others say 'I am frightened', then 'we shall draw unlike conclusions from like behaviour' (RPP I §131). So behaviour includes the use of the techniques of a language, and hence too what the speaker *means*

---

[46] C. L. Hull, *Principles of Behaviour* (New York, 1945), p. 25.

[47] It is noteworthy that in PR (Ch. VI) and even in BB (pp. 51f.) Wittgenstein drifted close to this position. (And this gave rise to Waismann's 'language strata' conception (F. Waismann, 'Language Strata', repr. in A. G. N. Flew (ed.), *Logic and Language*, 2nd series (Blackwell, Oxford, 1953).) Only gradually did he liberate himself from this misconception.

by what he says, and also whether he speaks *sincerely* or *plausibly* (cf. RPP I §287).

Thirdly, Wittgenstein denied that we see only 'colourless movements':

'I see that the child wants to touch the dog, but doesn't dare.' How can I see that? – Is this description of what is seen on the same level as a description of moving shapes and colours? Is an interpretation in question? Well, remember that you may also *mimic* a human being who would like to touch something, but doesn't dare. And what you mimic is after all a piece of behaviour. But you will perhaps be able to give a *characteristic* imitation of this behaviour only in a wider context. . . .

But now am I to say that I really 'see' fearfulness in this behaviour – or that I really 'see' the facial expression? Why not? But that is not to deny the difference between the two concepts of what is perceived. . . . 'Similar expression' takes faces together in a quite different way from 'similar anatomy'. (RPP I §§1066 – 8)

The supposition that we do not 'really' see the anger, sorrow, or amusement in a person's face is as absurd as the idea that we do not 'really' see the furniture in the room around us, but only sense-data or appearances. Behaviour, as Wittgenstein construes it, is indeed a criterion for the mental, but it does not follow that anger, sorrow, or amusement are, as it were, hidden behind the face that manifests them: 'In addition to the so-called sadness of his facial features, do I also notice his sad state of mind? Or do I *deduce* it from his face? Do I say: "His features and his behaviour were sad, so he too was probably sad"?' (LW §767).

The mind, human emotions and moods, desires and purposes, thought and belief are no more hidden behind their behavioural *expression* than the meaning of a word is hidden behind the utterance of a word. It is true that we may suppress our emotions, conceal our intentions and keep our thoughts to ourselves, but when we do not, when we express our feelings, manifest our purposes, and articulate our thoughts, they do not lie behind our expressive behaviour.

Fourthly, although what is 'outer' (behaviour) is a criterion of what is 'inner', far from the inner being describable only in terms of the outer, it is – a little paradoxically at first blush – the outer, or at least much of what is most important to us about it, that is essentially and unavoidably describable in terms of concepts of what is inner. The apparent paradox vanishes as soon as one recollects that, for example, we *recognize* facial expressions as joyous or sad, glum or preoccupied, amused or contemptuous, etc. And we describe facial expressions thus, in the rich vocabulary of the inner, of mood, emotions, attitudes, etc., and could not describe them in terms of *facial measurements* from which the character of the expression and hence too of what it manifests might be inferred (cf. PI §285). Indeed, not only the description of facial expression, but also of gesture and action, is run through with the vocabulary of the 'inner', something strikingly obvious when one remembers the character of adverbial modification of descriptions of action. We could not even describe (let alone distinguish) gesturing angrily or in despair, shuddering fearfully or in disgust, chortling joyously or with amusement, prancing expectantly, happily, or with surprise save in our psychological vocabulary. Our attributions of anger, despair, fear, disgust, joy, amusement, etc. do not rest on observations of 'colourless physical movements'. On the contrary, what we *see* is expressive behaviour – and we would be hard put even to describe the bare physical movements.

'The human body is the best picture of the human soul' (PI p. 178) not because the soul is something bodily (MS. 124, 7), but precisely because the soul is manifest in behaviour.[48] Only a creature with eyes can cast a loving look or a contemptuous gaze, weep with joy or grief. Only a creature with a mouth can smile, with sympathy or cruelty, in amusement or cold anger. But for these forms of expression to be possible a highly complex behavioural repertoire in widely varying circumstances is presupposed. The soul of a fish, if it had one, would be a poor thing. The articulations of the human face and body in the circumstances of human life are not externally related to what it makes sense to say of the human soul. Commenting on Fraser's report that the Malays conceive the human soul as a homunculus corresponding exactly in shape, proportion, and colour to the body in which it resides, Wittgenstein wrote: 'How much more truth there is in this view which ascribes the same multiplicity to the soul as to the body, than in a modern watered down theory' (GB 74).

---

[48] One must again bear in mind that 'Seele' does service for both 'mind' and 'soul'.

VII

THE INNER AND THE OUTER

1. Semi-solipsism

The traditional picture of the mental represented avowals of experience and expressions of thought as descriptions of inner states based on introspective scrutiny of private objects. A complement of that conception is an equally distorted picture of the nature of third-person psychological propositions. For a corollary of the idea of first-person 'privileged access' is the idea of 'indirect access' to other people's states of mind, thoughts, beliefs, or experiences. This aberration, which Wittgenstein referred to as 'semi-solipsism' (MS. 165, 150), is one of the targets of his critical investigations.

It is striking that few of the originators of the *philosophical* conception of the mind which we have inherited from the Cartesians and British empiricists dwelt at any length upon the nature of our knowledge of the 'inner world' of other subjects of experience. Berkeley was an exception, and his account of what he called 'our knowledge of spirits' is one of the more curious elements in that strange metaphysics which he constructed to replace the incoherences of representational idealism:

> It is plain that *we* cannot *know the existence of other spirits* otherwise than by *their operations* or *the ideas by them excited in us*. I perceive several motions, changes, and combinations of ideas, that inform me that there are certain particular agents *like myself*, which accompany them, and concur in their production. Hence the knowledge I have of other spirits is *not immediate*; as is the knowledge of my ideas; but depending on the intervention of ideas, by me referred to *agents or spirits* distinct from myself, as effects or concomitant signs.[1]

The 'intervening ideas', of course, are my ideas of the 'motion of limbs' of the body of another person, which ideas are conveyed to my mind by God. Indeed, Berkeley held, our knowledge of each other is less certain, more indirect, than our knowledge of God. If we cannot *see* God, we cannot see each other either, and our knowledge of others is mediated by God's activity in producing in us ideas.

> A human spirit or person is not perceived by sense, as not being an idea; when therefore we see the colour, size, figure, and motions of a man, we perceive only certain sensations or ideas excited in our minds; and these being exhibited to our view in sundry distinct collections, serve to mark out unto us the existence of finite and created spirits like ourselves.[2]

---

[1] Berkeley, *The Principles of Human Knowledge*, CXLV.
[2] Ibid., CXLVIII.

It is difficult to see how this form of 'semi-solipsism' can be prevented from collapsing. For if other people's bodies are merely collections of ideas in *my* mind, conveyed there by God's causal (volitional) activity, then *those ideas* cannot, contrary to Berkeley's insistence, be conceived as being 'accompanied' by 'certain particular agents like myself'. The only mental substances involved in this story are myself, whose ideas these are, and God, who causes them. In Berkeley's tale, there is only room for tea for two. An idealist cannot build anything upon an analogical argument.

Mill propounded a more explicit version of the analogical argument without the encumbrance of the Deity.

I observe that there is a great multitude of other bodies, closely resembling in their sensible properties . . . this particular one [viz. my own], but whose modifications do not call up, as those of my own body do, a world of sensations in my consciousness. Since they do not do so in my consciousness, I infer that they do it out of my consciousness, and that to each of them belongs a world of consciousness of its own, to which it stands in the same relation in which what I call my body stands to mine, . . . Each of these bodies exhibits to my sense a set of phaenomena (composed of acts and other manifestations) such as I know, in my own case, to be effects of consciousness, and such as might be looked for if each of the bodies has really in connexion with it a world of consciousness.[3]

This has a superficial cogency. But again, as with Berkeley, it is propounded in the context of an idealist metaphysics. For Mill argued that material objects, including human bodies, are no more than permanent possibilities of sense-experiences. Neither philosopher noticed the tension between his idealism and his account of knowledge of other people's experience.

The analogical argument sits more comfortably in a philosophical context which is not idealist. Like Berkeley and Mill, a proponent of such an argument conceives of the 'world of consciousness' as externally related to the 'world' of visible human bodies. We cannot *perceive* the minds or experiences of other people, but only their bodies and behaviour – and bodily behaviour *seems* to be just a matter of the movement of a physical object in space (see 'Behaviour and behaviourism', §4). The 'inner' therefore appears to be *hidden* behind the 'outer' and to be inferred from perceptible behaviour by analogy. Another person's pains, one is inclined to think, are hidden from me but accessible to him – I cannot feel them, but he can. Similarly, his thoughts are hidden from me, unless he reveals what he thinks. Hence, it seems, I can know only *indirectly* that he has a pain or thinks this or that, whereas he knows *directly*. For I have to *infer* that he has a pain, but he does not.

[3] J. S. Mill, *An Examination of Sir William Hamilton's Philosophy*, in *Collected Works*, Vol. IX, p. 192.

It seems obvious that what lies within is the *cause* of behaviour. For do people not cry out *because* they are in pain? And is pain not something 'inner'? They reach for a glass of water because they want a drink, and they make assertions because they believe what they say. So an inference from behaviour to a thought or experience that lies behind it must surely be an inference from an effect to a hidden cause. Hence we are prone to think of human behaviour as akin to the movements of a puppet manipulated by hidden strings, Cartesians conceiving of these strings as being controlled by the mind (via the pineal gland) and materialists conceiving of them as being pulled by the brain.

2. *Inside and outside*

Our knowledge of the experiences of others, in comparison with what philosophers think of as self-knowledge, seems distinctly shaky. Do I not know what I feel, want, or think directly, by introspection? But I know how things are with another person only on the basis of what he does and says, how he reacts and responds to circumstances. One is tempted to claim that one can never really know, but only *believe*, how things are with another person (PI §303). We are inclined to think that the belief or supposition that another person has a pain is just the belief or supposition that he has what I have when I have a pain (PI §350). I know what pain is, one wants to say, from my own case. To say that someone else is in pain just is to say that he has the same as I have so often had. This seemingly innocuous claim is one of the struts supporting the argument from analogy and also its updated version, the 'inference to the best explanation'. The *sense* of the third-person pain-attributions seems perspicuous and unproblematic. The philosophical problems appear to arise only with respect to knowing their truth. This is precisely where we go wrong.

'If one has to imagine someone else's pain on the model of one's own', Wittgenstein urged, 'this is none too easy a thing to do: for I have to imagine pain which I *do not feel* on the model of the pain which I *do feel*' (PI §302). For it is not as if I have to imagine that the pain I have in my knee is in my ankle, or even that I feel pain in someone else's ankle. Rather, I have to imagine someone else having *this*, which I now have. But what does it *mean* for another person to have *this*? This question antecedes any epistemological qualms. But surely, all one needs to suppose is that someone else has the *same* pain, and we have clarified that this is perfectly possible! Indeed so, but for an explanation in terms of *sameness* to get any grip, it must be determined what is to count as another person's being in pain. Wittgenstein elucidated the point by an analogy: one cannot explain what it is for it to be five o'clock on the sun by saying that it is five o'clock on the sun if it is five o'clock here and it is the same time there (PI §350). On the contrary, we can say that it is the same time on the sun as it is here if it is five o'clock here and also five o'clock there. But that presupposes an explanation of what it is for it to be five o'clock there. Similarly, if I have a pain and someone else has a pain, one can say that we have the same experience. But we have yet to explain what is to count as someone else having a pain. One's own pain does not furnish one with a criterion for being in pain, since one does not identify one's pain by criteria (PI §290); one just says 'I have a pain' (or groans), without any grounds or justification. A fortiori, one's own pain gives one no criterion for the identification of the pains of others.

But, of course, for one's *avowal* of pain to count as an avowal of *pain*, it must fit in with, be an extension and partial replacement of, one's natural pain-behaviour. For, just like natural expressions of pain, an avowal of pain is a criterion for others to judge that one is in pain. Hence ascription of pain (as well as sense-impressions, emotions, moods, desires, etc.) to others is rendered intelligible not by analogy with or by extrapolition from one's own case, but by reference to the behavioural manifestations of pain, etc. The behavioural *expressions* of the 'inner' are not mere symptoms (inductive evidence) of how things are, but critera. Hence it is a mistake to think that they are *mere* behaviour, nothing but externalities (just noises and movements). But as long as one is in the grip of the picture of the 'inner' and the 'outer', it is wellnigh impossible to think of the behavioural expression of the mental as anything other than an outward sign (symptom) of an inner, hidden state or experience.

It is noteworthy that one does not say, save when doing philosophy, that toothache is something 'inner' (LSD 18), any more than one says that pain is something mental. And that is right, for what would it be for toothache to be 'outer'? Indeed, what is toothache *in*? The mind? There is no such thing as mental toothache, and toothache is, by definition, in one's tooth. We talk of *physical* pain and contrast it with mental suffering, viz. anguish and grief. But we *compare* toothache and its behavioural expression with 'internal' and 'external' (LSD 18). The comparison is not silly, for it is true that I do not say that I have toothache on the grounds of observation, whereas I judge another to have toothache only in so far as I see him clutch his swollen jaw and hear him groan (cf. LPE 278). But, Wittgenstein observed, 'We must get clear about how the metaphor of revealing (outside and inside) is actually applied by us; otherwise we shall be tempted to look for an inside behind that which in our metaphor is the inside' (LPE 280).

Someone may have a pain and not manifest it; he can see something and not say what he sees; and he can think such-and-such and not voice his thoughts. But if he groans with pain, says what he sees, and expresses his opinions, then he has 'revealed' what is, *in our metaphor*, the inner. If he screams with pain as the doctor prods him, one cannot say 'Well, that is only behaviour – his pain is still concealed'. If he tells us, in no uncertain terms, what he thinks about so-and-so, we cannot say 'These are only words – he has kept his thoughts to himself'. And if he *shows* us what he sees, then we too can see what he sees, even though we do not look inside anything (LPE 279). This, in each case, is what we *call* 'exhibiting pain', 'expressing one's thoughts', 'showing what one sees'. For it is not as if, in such cases, he always leaves something behind which he keeps to himself.

There is indeed such a thing as concealing one's pain, hiding one's feelings, keeping one's thoughts secret. But to have a pain, feel annoyed, or think such-and-such is not *per se* to conceal anything. I hide my pain when I stifle my groans, but by the same token I reveal that I am in pain when a scream finally bursts from my lips. I conceal my feelings when I exercise self-control, but I reveal them when, e.g., I give vent to my anger. I do not conceal my thoughts merely by thinking them and not saying what I think, although it is true that that will often leave others bemused and may even mislead them (and hence it is *comparable* to hiding (RPP II, §§586ff.)). Rather, one hides one's thoughts by writing them down in code, by keeping one's diary under lock and key (LW §974), or by communicating them to one's wife in a language which the children do not understand (RPP II, §§563f.). But if the code is broken, the diary read, the foreign language understood, one's previously hidden thoughts are perfectly public.

Parallel to the confusions of 'inner' and 'outer', of 'concealed' and 'revealed', is a misuse of 'direct' and 'indirect'. It is wrong to say that I know only *indirectly* that he has pain, sees such-and-such, thinks this or that, whereas he knows directly. For, in the first place, it is wrong to say that he *knows*. Secondly, it only makes sense to talk of indirect knowledge if it also makes sense to talk of direct knowledge. For this distinction is meant to draw a contrast (and in *other* domains does). But there *is* no more direct way of knowing that another person is in pain than by seeing him moan and writhe. Similarly, there is no more direct way of seeing what he sees than by his showing what he sees, and no more direct way of knowing what he thinks than from his sincere confession. If a friend opens his heart to me, I cannot say 'I know only indirectly what he thinks and feels'. That would be appropriate if my information were *hearsay*, but a confession from the horse's mouth, so to speak, is not second-hand. Knowing indirectly that someone is in pain might be a matter of noticing the empty bottle of analgesics by his bedside or seeing that he has gone to lie down (as he always does when he feels unwell). But there is nothing *indirect* about witnessing the agony of childbirth. Not to have had such pains does not imply that witnessing them gives one only *indirect* knowledge of their severity, and to have suffered the pangs of childbirth is not to *know* anything directly, but to have *experienced* such pains, i.e. to have had them.

It is tempting to try to cash the metaphor of direct/indirect in the currency of inference. For one is inclined to say that he knows that he is in pain without inference, i.e. directly, whereas I know that he is pain by inference from his behaviour, i.e. indirectly. But this is in part nonsense and in part wrong. As argued, it is nonsense to say that he knows that he is in pain. What is true is that he does not say that he has a pain on the grounds of observation, whereas I do. But it is misleading to say that because I assert that he is in pain on the grounds of observing his winces, groans, or writhing, therefore I know that he is in pain by inference, i.e. indirectly (cf. LW §767). When someone writhes on the ground with a broken leg, one does not *infer* (draw the conclusion) that he is in pain from evidence; one *sees* that he is suffering. The doctor infers that his patient has an appendicitis from the character and location of the patient's *pain*, but it would be highly misleading to say that he infers that his patient is in pain from his screams of agony. If asked 'How do you know he is in pain?', one might answer 'I saw him writhing in agony', but it would be absurd to say 'I saw only his behaviour, but I inferred that he was in pain'. To see him writhing in agony *is* to see that he is in pain. But if I hear that someone has severe arthritis, then I might infer that he has pain.

One might object: to be sure, we can see *that* another person is in pain, but one cannot see his pain; surely that is inferred! The objection is incorrect. First, do we not say 'I could see his agony' or 'I was witness to his suffering'? Is it elliptical to say 'I saw the pain in his face'? (Although, to be sure, the pain I could see in his face may well be the pain of a broken leg.) Secondly, in so far as it is true that I cannot *see* or otherwise perceive his pain, neither can he. I see the manifestations of pain which he exhibits; but when he exhibits pain, it is *manifest*. It can be said that I cannot see his pain only in the sense in which I cannot see sounds or hear colours (LW §885). From the fact that I know he is in pain by observation or know his thoughts because I heard his confession, it does not follow that my knowledge is inferential, any more than the fact that I know that there is a picture on the wall because I can see it implies that I infer that there is a picture there.

Nevertheless, one may object, I may be wrong. I may see him writhing on the ground and say, 'He is in pain'; yet it might all be simulation and pretence. Similarly, he may confess that he thinks such-and-such and yet be totally insincere. And does this not show that his pain and his opinions are something 'inner', hidden behind his behaviour, and that my judgements about them are inferences from the 'outer', and hence that my knowledge is indirect and fallible? It is true that there is such a thing as pretending, that one can hide one's thoughts and feelings, even lie and dissimulate. Indeed, this is one thing that might legitimately be meant by saying that thoughts and feelings are private (RPP I §570). But under the spell of the misleading model of 'inner' and 'outer' we misconstrue the implications of these possibilities. For they no more show that our judgements about other people's mental states, etc. are inferential and our knowledge indirect than the possibility of illusion and hallucination show that our judgements about objects in our field of perception are inferential and our knowledge indirect.

The possibility of lying, deceit, and pretence shows that our judgements about other people are fallible; it does not show that their feelings, desires, and thoughts are hidden behind their behaviour as the movement of a clock is hidden behind its face. We judge another to be in pain, sorrowful, or overjoyed in as much as we take his behaviour to be an expression of pain, a manifestation of grief or joy. And we may, indeed, be deceived; for he may be pretending. But to be deceived here is not to think that there is something inner behind the behaviour when in fact there is not. It is to think that his groans are a manifestation of pain whereas they are mere pretence, that his sighs express grief whereas they are deceitful. That he is not in pain or not sorrowful is shown by *other things he does*, by what he said earlier or how he acts later, by subtle and barely noticeable deviations from the characteristic pattern of expression of pain or sorrow. These do not show the absence of something behind the behaviour, but the presence of something *in* the behaviour which is other than what one initially thought. It is misguided to think of moaning with pain as behaviour *plus* an inner experience, just as it is misconceived to think of saying something and meaning it as behaviour plus an inner act of meaning. One might rather say that moaning without pain or saying something and not meaning what one said is behaviour *plus* something, for here there is something which is absent in the case of sincere behaviour, viz. a dishonest purpose! We are systematically misled in this domain by our picture of 'outside plus inside' (LSD 10).

Expressions of pain, manifestations of sorrow, etc. are criteria for saying of a person that he is in pain, grieving, and so forth. The possibility of lying, deceit, and pretence shows that these criteria are, *in certain circumstances*, defeasible. It does not show that the observable criteria for being in pain, grieving, etc. are criteria for something hidden behind what is on view. But while agreeing that such criteria are defeasible, one must emphasize that their defeasibility is circumstance-dependent. Lying, deceit, and pretence are essentially parasitic activities, language-games that must be learnt and are learnt only after the 'host' activity has been mastered (cf. Exg. §§249f.). It would be unintelligible to suppose that the smile of an unweaned infant is pretence (PI §249);

indeed, 'it is senseless to say: the expression may always lie', for the language-games with expressions of feeling are based on games with expressions of which we do not say that they may lie (LPE 293). And that is not an *assumption* that might prove to be wrong. It makes sense to attribute deceit and pretence to a creature only within a highly complex weave of life, in which a wide range of other capacities is manifest. Hence one cannot attribute dishonesty and dissimulation to a dog (PI §250 and Exg.). Moreover, even if a creature does possess those capacities and has mastered those techniques, the intelligibility of attributing pretence to it is still circumstance-relative. If someone falls into a fire and screams with pain, it would be absurd to say 'He may be pretending' (cf. LPE 318). There are certain kinds of behaviour of which one may say 'One *can't* pretend like that' (Z §570), e.g. throwing oneself off the roof while pretending to be distraught. There are even circumstances in which one may say of a person 'He *thinks* he is pretending' (PI p. 229). The possibility of pretence gives no grounds whatever for the sceptical anxiety that maybe all behaviour is mere pretence (Z §§570f.). For here, as elsewhere, it is false that what happens sometimes might happen always (PI §§344f.).

One may still object: if Wittgenstein does acknowledge that 'pain' does not mean the same as 'pain-behaviour', that experience and thought are distinct from their public expression, must he not also acknowledge that what is 'inner' is the cause of the behaviour that we call 'its expression'? Is it not pain that causes me to cry out, desire that causes me to act, or fear that makes me blanch and tremble? And given that this is so, might it not be that the causal mechanism, with which I am intimately acquainted in my own case, is different in other people?

The causal conception of the mind and its relation to behaviour is too large to tackle comprehensively here; all that can be done is to sow seeds of doubt that may be cultivated elsewhere. We do say 'I asserted that because that was what I was thinking' or 'I insisted on that point because I remembered it happening'. But it does not follow that my thinking was an inner event or my recollecting an inner process which caused me to speak. Rather, such explanations are given in order to distinguish sincerely expressing one's opinions, from, e.g., pulling someone's leg, being deliberately provocative, or acting as devil's advocate, or, in the case of citing one's recollections, in order to make explicit the source of one's knowledge, viz. that one witnessed such-and-such and so was not merely repeating hearsay. 'Because' here does not identify a *cause*. One may concede that we often shrink from something because we are afraid or reach for something because we desire to have it. But it is not obvious that these explanations are causal. We contrast shrinking from something out of fear from shrinking from it out of disgust or disdain. These explanations *characterize* the action, but it is not evident that they do so by identifying a cause. It is as misleading to conceive of dancing with joy, chortling with amusement, or weeping with grief as behaviour plus inner process as it is to conceive of plaintive, joyous, or triumphant music as sounds plus plaint, joy, or triumph (cf. LSD 10f.). Similarly, saying something and meaning it is not saying plus an inner activity of meaning. In all these cases the inner/outer picture makes the causal model of explanation seem compelling, even inevitable. But if the grip of that mesmerizing picture has been weakened, we should examine afresh the plausibility and apparent inevitability of that model.

The dominant philosophical account of causation conceives of the causal relation as non-logical (external), inductive (hence requiring the possibility of independent identification of the relata), and nomic (instantiating a general law). The mental and its behavioural expression, however, do not unquestionably fit this account. Although one can have toothache and not show it or feign toothache without having it the behavioural manifestation of toothache is not logically independent of toothache (LSD 10). For the behavioural manifestations of toothache are the identifying criteria for toothache, not inductive evidence for it (LSD 134f.). It is not as if we can envisage the possibility of people having excruciating toothache but happily chewing their food, laughing, and joking. Nevertheless, when I have a toothache and inadvertently bite on the infected tooth, is it not the pain that makes me cry out? Of course; I *could not help* crying out, could not stifle the cry, so severe was the pain. But to admit that is not to admit that the pain caused me to cry out in the sense in which the sun causes wax to melt. If anything caused me to cry out in that sense, it was biting on the infected tooth. The pain is not a third object or event that *mediates* between the biting and the crying, even though it is true that one can feign toothache, i.e. bite and cry out without having a pain. But it is misleading to conceive of crying out with pain as crying out *plus* an inner experience that is its cause (LSD 10).

The sceptical supposition that the 'causal mechanism' might be different in other people, that they might cry out and moan when they injure themselves even though they have no pain but, perhaps, a pleasant sensation of warmth is as absurd as the supposition that they might all be automatons. If someone suggests that for all we know the blind really see, but only behave as if they do not, and that the sighted are really blind, but only behave as if they saw, it is obvious that his suppositions sever the concepts of seeing and blindness from their behavioural manifestation. In so doing, he deprives these words of any content; for such behaviour is what we *call* 'stumbling blindly', 'showing that one sees', etc. (LPE 286). These suppositions have no more content than the corresponding idea that maybe things cease to exist when no one perceives them. It is not, as some philosophers would have it, that everything speaks against such suppositions, but rather that nothing could *conceivably* speak for them.

3. The indeterminacy of the mental

We can know of the inner states, desires, and thoughts of another person, and often do. We can be as certain that someone else is suffering or joyful as that $2 + 2 = 4$. But to insist upon these platitudes is not to hold that the language-games that concern the 'inner' are logically of the same kind as those concerning the 'outer'. On the contrary, it was precisely because of a disposition to project the grammar of the 'outer' upon that of the 'inner' that philosophers were led to the sceptical absurdities that Wittgenstein exposed. But lurking behind those sceptical qualms is an important truth that characterizes the category of the mental.

We say of some people that they are transparent to us, that we know without a doubt what they are thinking or feeling, what mood they are in, or what they want. On the other hand, one human being may be a complete enigma to another – a phenomenon that is strikingly evident when one encounters an alien culture. Even if one speaks the language, one may fail to understand the people; their motives and reasons may be opaque to one, and their reactions puzzling. We cannot find our way around with them (PI p. 223). This is not because we do not know what they are saying to themselves. The phenomenon of opacity, though made vivid in alien contexts, is familiar at home too. For we often fail to understand someone, not only when he is successfully concealing his feelings, but also when he is doing his utmost to make himself intelligible (MS. 169, 86). The nexus between reason and action is elastic, and the transparency of reasons is both culture-relative and, to a degree, agent-relative.

We may agree with Hume that 'were there no uniformity in human actions, and were every experiment which we could form of this kind irregular and anomalous, it were impossible to collect any general observations concerning mankind; and no experience, however accurately digested by reflection, would ever serve to any purpose'.[4] Indeed, the behaviour would not be human, and our psychological concepts would get no grip, for their use depends upon a uniformity in the weave of life. Nevertheless, there is an *essential* unpredictability about the mental (MS. 173, 78). Not only are the important fine shades of behaviour unpredictable, but it is often impossible to foresee what another person will do *even though* one knows his beliefs and motives. It does not *follow* from the fact that he intends such-and-such, has

----

[4] Hume, *An Enquiry Concerning Human Understanding*, §65.

such-and-such beliefs, etc., that he will act. Two people may have the same beliefs and desires (even the same strength of desire by any available criterion of how much one wants such-and-such), and yet the one may act and the other refrain; and there may be no non-trivial explanation of why they behaved differently. One cannot say what the essential observable consequences of an inner state are, e.g. of someone's being pleased. There are, of course, characteristic consequences; but one cannot say exactly what is to be expected of him and what not (he may weep with relief, jump with joy, or just smile). His responses cannot be described in the same way as reactions characterizing the state of a physical object (MS. 174, 27). The limited predictability of human behaviour is not that of an only partly understood mechanism, and its unpredictability is not always a function of our ignorance, as if, were we better informed, we would always be able to predict with certainty.

Corresponding to this essential unpredictability of behaviour is a logical indeterminacy in explanation of behaviour, a feature upon which Kant dwelt in the Groundwork of the Metaphysic of Morals.[5] Wittgenstein did not elaborate this, but focused upon a related form of radical indeterminacy. We typically do not know what another person is thinking unless he tells us. Sometimes we guess, and the person may affirm (or deny) that that was what he was thinking. Yet in some cases he may be wrong; his memory may be deceiving him, or he may have let himself be talked into the conviction that he previously thought thus-and-so. And whether he really thought this or is merely imagining himself to have done so is essentially undecidable (RPP I §§568ff.; PI p. 222). The criteria for someone's guessing correctly what I thought consist in my confessing that he has guessed right; but one does not always have to believe such a confession, even if deception is ruled out (RPP II §692). Here, Wittgenstein suggested, there may be criteria, but none that are certain (MS. 174, 21), or criteria which some take as certain and others do not (MS. 174, 20). Our ignorance or uncertainty about what goes on in someone else is not uniform. We cannot read off what he is saying to himself from his behaviour, but must ask him. Sometimes we cannot understand what he says. Often we do not know what mood he is in, and his intentions may be obscure. In each case the ignorance is of a different kind, and is removed, if at all, in different ways (LW §957). Occasionally it cannot be definitively removed, for nothing counts in those circumstances as settling the matter beyond doubt. In certain circumstances, we cannot say whether one person feels more pain than another or merely gives stronger expression to his suffering (RPP II §647).

---

[5] Kant, Groundwork of the Metaphysic of Morals, Ch. II.

It is tempting to explain these various uncertainties by invoking the picture of the inner and the outer. Viewed from this perspective, one might naturally insist that 'While you can have complete certainty about someone else's state of mind, still it is always merely subjective, not objective certainty' (PI p. 225). But this is misleading. We can contrast subjective with objective certainty in the language-games with indirect, as opposed to direct, observation. I may be 'subjectively certain' that you have money in your purse, even though I cannot see it, while you are 'objectively certain', for you can. But there is no such contrast here, for it is not as if 'objective certainty' does not exist *because* we cannot see into another person's soul. He cannot see into his soul either, and his lack of doubt is not determined by his certainty; *both* are grammatically excluded. The claim that there is no objective certainty signifies the same as the claim that one cannot see into another's soul (MS. 169, 4f.). So 'Here I can't achieve objective certainty' is not like 'You can't know what is in a locked box', but is akin to 'You can't kick a goal in tennis' (RPP I §567). Of a clock one can say 'I don't know what is going on inside'; but with a human being, one might say, this indeterminacy or uncertainty is *postulated* (RPP II §§665f.) – it is impossible to look inside, i.e. there is no such thing. What looks like a defect in knowledge or a shortcoming in the available evidence, which we are inclined to express in the claim that there is no objective certainty, betokens a difference in language-games (PI p. 225). This uncertainty, if it is to be called such, might be said to be *constitutional* (RPP I §141). The *only* way to recognize pain is from the 'outer'; but that is no defect, for it lies in the nature of the language-game (RPP II §657).

One is inclined to say that one can be more certain about propositions concerning physical objects or about mathematical propositions than one can about the experiences of others. But that is wrong; I can be as certain that someone is in pain as of any mathematical proposition (PI p. 224). Nevertheless, one might respond, there is a difference in kind, even if not in degree. This is correct; but it would be wrong to represent the difference as a psychological one, e.g. a difference between objective and subjective certainty. In so far as there is an 'objective uncertainty' about the mental, it consists in an indefiniteness in the nature of the game, in the rules of admissible evidence (LW §888).

In conceding that there is a 'constitutional uncertainty' about the mental, Wittgenstein was not claiming that we can never know that another person is in pain (PI §246). On the contrary, there are indeed cases where only a madman would take an expression of pain to be insincere. There is an *unmistakable* expression of joy or sadness, and there are circumstances in which we *know* that someone is in pain or that he is not (MS. 169, 101). The 'uncertainty' in question, the philosophical uncertainty, does not relate to each and every particular case, but to the method of establishing the inner (Z §555; RPP II §682; LW §239). What are the peculiarities of the 'rules of evidence'?

One distinctive feature is that although the connection between the inner and the outer is not just empirical but logical (MS. 173, 73), our concepts of the mental do not bring behaviour, occasion, and inner process (or experience) into necessary connection (*zwangsläufige Verbindung*), for behaviour and occasion do not *entail* the inner process (MS. 169, 68f.). In certain circumstances I may be *certain* that someone is in pain, but another person in the same circumstances may not be convinced. I cannot offer him a *proof*, and neither he nor I will be judged to be irresponsible or incapable of judgement (RPP II §685; cf. MS. 169, 62f.). Of course, this discrepancy has its limits; but what is significant is that it lies in the logic of our concepts, not in ignorance of fact. Within this penumbra of indeterminacy there is such a thing as better and worse judgement, just as in art there are connoisseurs (LW §§917, 925, 927). In general, better attributions issue from the judgements of those who have looked at and compared numerous paintings, even though they might be unable to explain their reasons to a jury, as opposed to giving intimations to other connoisseurs. Similarly, those with a wide knowledge of mankind are more likely to give better *prognoses* regarding the genuineness of people's feelings than others. These judgements require experience. 'Learning' and 'teaching' here are peculiar, for though there are rules, they do not form a system. One does not acquire a technique, but learns correct judgements. A good teacher here does not impart a method, but teaches one to look, gives one *tips*, makes one sensitive to *imponderable* evidence, to subtleties of glance, gesture, and tone of voice (PI pp. 227f.). In judgements about the inner there is a dimension of particularity: one can judge the nuances of a person's behaviour better if one knows him well, and one can better judge the significance of a person's manifestations of feeling if he is an old acquaintance. And typically one cannot describe what it is in the conduct that is decisive (MS. 174, 27).

We operate in this domain with elastic, flexible concepts (LW §§244, 246; MS. 169, 74), and these concepts inform our behaviour and shape the contours of our lives. This does not, of course, mean that 'anything goes', that these concepts could be distorted as one pleases. But it does mean that there are phenomena of an essentially undecidable character (RPP I §568), that evidence for the inner is defeasible (cf. RPP II §692), that there is a logical indeterminacy in the concepts. How is this to be explained? Could we not replace these concepts with sharper ones? No; not without a fundamental change in our nature. For 'Concepts with fixed limits would demand a uniformity of behaviour. But where I am *certain* someone else is uncertain. And that is a fact of nature' (Z §374;

RPP II §683). Being sure that someone is in pain, doubting whether he is, 'are so many natural, instinctive, kinds of behaviour towards other human beings, and our language is merely an auxiliary to, and further extension of, this relation. Our language-game is an extension of primitive behaviour. (For our *language-game* is behaviour)' (Z 545; RPP I §151). We are all too prone to look upon our linguistic activities from the perspective of *thought* and the communication of thought. But our language-games are rooted in instinctive behaviour, and where there is lack of uniformity in that behaviour, it is reflected in our concepts: 'Instinct comes first, reasoning second' (RPP II §689), and 'There is uncertainty of behaviour which doesn't stem from uncertainty in thought' (RPP II §660). Our flexible, elastic concepts of the inner are not employed merely for *description* of the mental but for its constitutive *expression*; we manifest and give shape to our inner lives in these patterns of linguistic behaviour. The use of these concepts is part of our form of life. They are not concepts devised for the description and theoretical explanation of an independently existing reality (as are the concepts of physics); rather they *inform* the reality which they are *also* used to describe and (sometimes) to explain.

Wittgenstein conceived of the 'constitutional uncertainty' of the inner not as a consequence of defective evidence, but as a reflection in the rules of evidence of disagreement in human attitudes and responses that antecede our language-games. He recommends us to look at this uncertainty in the light of the (different) question of whether an insect feels pain (RPP II §661). For here too people react differently, and their disagreement is not resolvable by factual investigation. The non-uniformity in our instinctive reactions of trust and mistrust towards each other is one source of the constitutional uncertainty of psychological concepts. There is no such uncertainty in numerous other language-games, and that too is determined by the character of our reactions. Disputes over the correct result of a calculation are rare and can be settled conclusively (PI p. 225). Mathematicians do not in general disagree over the result of a calculation, and this fact determines our concept of mathematical certainty – not because 'mathematically certain' means the same as 'generally agreed by mathematicians', but because if mathematicians did not generally agree then we would not have our concept of mathematical certainty. Similarly, although there is such a thing as colour-blindness, there are ways of establishing it, and those who are *not* colour-blind generally agree in their judgements about colours (PI p. 227). There is no such agreement, however, in many applications of concepts of the inner.

It is still tempting to attribute the penumbra of uncertainty that characterizes these concepts to the fact that they signify what is 'inner', hidden 'behind' overt behaviour. Indeed, it is tempting to misconstrue the constitutional uncertainty of the mental as confirmation of the idea that the 'inner' is hidden. But this is a mistake. We do not disagree about other people's mental lives *because* their inner world is hidden from us; on the contrary, it is partly because of our (sometimes irresolvable) disagreement about people's motives, beliefs, and feelings that we cleave to the misleading picture of the 'inner' hidden behind the 'outer'. We need to be reminded that we recognize a sign of something inward to be trustworthy by reference to something outward, viz. antecedent or subsequent behaviour. So the distinction between what is certain and what is uncertain does not depend on the contrast between inner and outer (MS. 169, 101f.). Rather, the uncertainty depends upon the irregularity of the outer. Our inability to understand another person does not, in these cases, turn on our ignorance of what is going on within him, but on the consequences of his inner state. One aspect of our uncertainty consists in our inability to foresee his actions (MS. 173, 77); another turns on our inability to render his actions intelligible to ourselves (MS. 173, 87f.). For, given that a sincere avowal is a verbal reaction, rather than a description of an inner state which only the agent can observe, it is not determined what the consequences of this signal are (MS. 173, 94). An avowal is a behavioural manifestation of the inner, but it is a piece of behaviour that lies within a complex weave of circumstances, response, and consequence. This pattern is not wholly regular, and the irregularity of the pattern determines the penumbral uncertainty of our concepts of the inner (LW §211). The tapestry of human life is not machine-made. Irregularities are part of its texture. Some threads break off, others are knotted. These anomalies in the pattern are a feature of our nature, and their reflections in our concepts are not shortcomings.

VIII

THINKING: METHODOLOGICAL MUDDLES AND CATEGORIAL CONFUSIONS

1. *Thinking: a muddle elevated to a mystery*

It is natural to raise questions about thinking. Indeed, one who does not is lucky, or immune to puzzlement (LPP 236). It is noteworthy that anyone who does ask such questions is himself a thinking person; thinking is no novelty to him. And yet it will sometimes strike him as peculiarly baffling. When scrutinized from the wrong angle or when in the grip of a paradigm that does not fit the concept, thought appears to do very mysterious things.

If the dull substance of my flesh were thought,
Injurious distance should not stop my way;
For then, despite the space, I would be brought,
From limits far remote, where thou dost stay.
No matter then although my foot did stand
Upon the furthest earth remov'd from thee;
For nimble thought can jump both sea and land,
As soon as think the place where he would be.[1]

And when my thought of A traverses 'injurious distance', I think of *just him*, and my thought as it were nails him (Z §§13 – 17). So it is like a super-ballistic missile, only faster and more unerring than any physical missile could be! Even more mysteriously, I can think of someone even though he no longer exists – indeed, even if he never existed (PG 103). But I could not hit Santa Claus with a ballistic missile! Furthermore, just as I can think of someone even though he does not exist, so too I can think that such-and-such is the case even though it is *not* the case. But if what I think does not exist, if there is no such thing, how can I think it?

Not only can we readily generate the illusion that thinking can *do* mysterious things, but we also succumb to the idea that it operates in mysterious ways. It *connects* ideas in the mind, we say; and then we wonder how this strange connection is effected: by associative mechanisms, predicational glue, or whatever. Thinking sometimes seems to operate on images; but sometimes it seems to use words as its material. And when we mystify ourselves thus, it does indeed seem that thought is mysterious, that we need to find out what the materials of thought are and how the mind goes to work on them.

---

[1] Shakespeare, Sonnet XLIV.

It is equally easy to make thinking appear occult. In thought, we say things to ourselves – which no one else can hear, as in our imagination we picture things to ourselves – which no one else can see. One's thoughts can seem like super-private property: no one else can know what I am silently thinking; at best they can guess. One's thoughts seem hidden from the sight of all save oneself, hidden in the most secure hiding-place, one's own mind.[2] We all remark on the uncanny speed of thought; it

. . . can wing its way
Swifter than lightning flashes or the beam
That hastens on the pinions of the morn.[3]

Mozart was rumoured to be able to think through, 'hear', in a flash a whole concerto that he was composing. People often see the solution to a complex practical or theoretical problem in a moment. 'Now I have it!' they may exclaim, and it takes them half an hour to explain what they have thus grasped instantaneously.

Thought seems like an elusive, intangible material that is difficult to control. Thoughts often flit across our minds uncalled-for; occasionally they press in on us willy-nilly and we cannot banish them; sometimes they are apparently buried in the recesses of the mind and cannot voluntarily be brought to the light of consciousness. Hence thinking seems like a complex process undergone by an immaterial stuff in the receptacle of the mind. It then strikes us as being as mysterious as a flame, impalpable, in perpetual motion, endlessly fascinating and mesmerizing (Z §125).[4] So we are prone to conclude that 'thinking is an enigmatic process, and we are a long way off from complete understanding of it' (RPP I §1093).

It is characteristic of philosophers that having tied a knot in their reflections on thinking, they respond to the knot by constructing a theory. The apparent mysteries of thinking will be resolved, they fancy, by producing a good theory about the nature of thought. Frege notoriously conceived of thinking as a mysterious process ('perhaps the most mysterious of all' (PW 145)), a process of grasping immaterial objects that are like physical objects, only non-spatial and timeless (PW 148). It is the task of psychology, he proclaimed, to explain this mental process. Wittgenstein in the *Tractatus* entertained equally bizarre ideas (see 'Thinking: the soul of language', §1). His conception of

---

[2] The privacy of thought is further examined in 'Privacy', §2.
[3] J. G. Percival.
[4] But, Wittgenstein adds, why should something impalpable seem more mysterious than something palpable? Is it because we want to grasp it (Z §126)? And if so, is that not because of analogies between names of objects and expressions that superficially resemble names of objects but are not such names?

thinking as a kind of language (NB 82), stripped of its logical atomist elements, has an analogue today in the writings of cognitive scientists and speculative neurophysiologists. Thinking is conceived to be a mental process that is neurologically 'realized'. What this 'language of thought' is remains to be seen; it is a mystery that will be duly resolved by a good theory.

These programmatic theories, however, are but echoes of misunderstandings of conceptual articulations. The aura of mystery which thus surrounds thought is nothing more than a product of a distorted vision. The 'uniqueness' of thought, the mystery of understanding language through the medium of thought, is a *superstition* (not a mistake) produced by grammatical illusions (PI §110). The task of philosophy is not to construct theories about cognitive processes which scientists can then elaborate and test; it is rather to destroy those illusions.

It is noteworthy that thinking does not strike us as in the least mysterious when we think (PG 154; PI §428), but only when we think about our thinking, wonder what to say about our 'cognitive activities', let ourselves be guided by language along the smooth rails of a compelling analogy which leads us astray. Thinking (or understanding or meaning) is not a queer experience like the experience of weightlessness, but as commonplace and humdrum as walking or eating. Nor is it strange because it has curious and unanticipated *effects* (BB 5); on the contrary, the effects of thinking are typically transparent. X took an umbrella because he thought (believed) it was raining, and that is intelligible precisely because *that it is raining* is a *reason* for taking an umbrella. If anyone, even a child, is asked what he is thinking, he will answer with as much ease as if asked what he is doing. The question will not strike anyone as a question about a mystery. But one might wonder how he knows that what he is doing is thinking or that what he is thinking is that *p* rather than that *q* – and one is straightaway caught in a net of grammar.

One might respond by observing that there is nothing mysterious about things falling to the ground and other things floating or flying. This too is commonplace, but it needed the theory of gravity to explain the phenomenon. Water plays a familiar role in our lives, but the fact that it expands below 4° Centigrade is extra-ordinary, and its inner structure, which needed to be discovered, is what explains its properties, including this one. Is thinking (understanding, meaning, etc.) not similar? No; for what *mystifies* us about thinking is not anything that could be explained by a *theory* or by theoretical *discoveries*, any more than the beauty of a Mozart symphony could be explained by acoustics or psychology. There *are* discoveries to be made about our ability to think: e.g. how and why such-and-such capacities are impaired by alcohol, fail with age, or vary with gender. But these domains of relative *ignorance* are not what give us the (false) impression that thinking is mysterious. The 'speed of thought', the possibility of thinking about the non-existent or what is not the case, the transparency of thought and its privacy, are not features that could be demystified by the discovery of hidden inner structures (cf. LPP 236f.). They are, rather, muddles felt as problems (BB 6).

The sense of mystery here stems from *philosophical* bafflement. We know how to use the verb 'to think' (or 'to mean' or 'to understand') and how to teach its use to our children, to explain to them what it means. But we lack a surview of that use and of those explanations. When faced with questions about the nature of thought, we are as lost as when faced with parallel questions about the nature of the number 1 (PG 108). We sense a mystery because we lack a clear view of the grammar of such expressions, and hence naturally gravitate towards misleading grammatical analogies. Number-words resemble names of substances, so we think of numbers as objects, though we add that they are not concrete and are not located in space and time. Similarly, 'to think' *in some of its uses* resembles such activity-verbs as 'to speak' or 'to write', and we naturally conceive of thinking as an activity, though we add that it is an activity of the mind (as speaking and writing, crudely speaking, are activities of the body). We then project features of physical activity onto thinking, and then straight away (rightly) find thinking thus conceived to be a mystery. 'We interpret the enigma created by our misunderstanding as the enigma of an incomprehensible process' (PG 155).

Consequently, Wittgenstein argues, we do not need a theory or hypothesis to resolve our difficulties. We want to clarify the nature of thinking, but not as a physicist investigates the nature, the hitherto unknown structure, of water. It is not new empirical facts about thinking that will dispel the mystery that seems to surround thought, but a rearrangement of familiar *grammatical* facts. Recourse to laboratories *at this point* merely compounds confusion:

'Thinking is an enigmatic process, and we are a long way off from complete understanding of it.' And now one starts experimenting. Evidently without realizing *what* it is that makes thinking enigmatic to us.

The experimental method does *something*; its failure to solve the problem is blamed on its still being in its beginnings. It is as if one were to try to determine what matter and spirit are by chemical experiments. (RPP I §1093)

Will the philosophical clarification of thinking not rob us of an *appropriate* sense of mystery in the face of such things as thinking, dreaming, sensation? Not at all! What will disappear is the *bogus* mystery. And once that has gone, why should thinking or dreaming be any more mysterious than a table? Why should they not be *equally mysterious* (RPP I §378)? But *this* mystery is no longer ignorance or a conceptual muddle, but rather wonder before the contingency of all that exists.

2. Methodological clarifications

The suggestion that our sense of mystery about thinking is a pseudo-mystery, a mere mystification consequent on having a mistaken idea of the use of *words*, is repulsive (RPP I §§548f.). It seems to trivialize our inquiry; we want to investigate the essence of thinking, and Wittgenstein tells us to examine the use of words. Surely words are arbitrary; and that this word is used *thus*, that one *thus* is arbitrary too. Yet the nature of thinking is anything but arbitrary!

The objection rests on incomprehension. It is grammar that determines the essence of something (cf. Exg. §§371f.). The rules for the use of the word 'think' constitute what is to be called 'thinking', and that *is* the essence or nature of thinking. Of course, words are arbitrary; what is called 'thinking' could have been called something else. The use of the sign 'thinking' could have been different; but if it had been different, it would not have the meaning it has, and so it would not have signified *thinking*. Investigating the grammar of the word 'thinking' and seeking to lay bare the essential nature of thought are one and the same endeavour (cf. PI §370).

One should indeed concede that there is something wrong in saying that our philosophical bafflement stems from having the wrong idea of the use of the word 'thinking' (LPP 243f.). If someone has the idea that 'to think' means to be quiet, then he has a wrong idea of the use of this expression. He misunderstands the word, does not know what it means, and cannot use it correctly. But no philosophical troubles stem from such misunderstanding. Philosophical confusions typically arise when one does know how to use a word correctly, i.e. in accord with established use, but lacks a synoptic view of its use. Hence when called upon to resolve questions which seem factual but are not, e.g. 'Can machines think (perceive, wish)?' (BB 16, 47f. and Exg. §359), one flounders in a morass of confusion and in effect *misdescribes* one's own (correct) practice of using the word 'to think' in the bustle of daily life. This produces a philosophical conflict.

We might say that we form a wrong *picture* of thinking. This, Wittgenstein noted, sounds less repulsive than attributing our difficulties to misdescriptions of the use of mere *words* (RPP I §§548f.). But properly understood, this is no concession at all. It is *of* thinking that we thus form a wrong picture, and what makes it a wrong picture of *thinking* as opposed to something else is the association of the picture with the use of a word. We have a picture of thinking as an inner process or activity, a picture which is embedded in certain misleading aspects of the grammar of the verb 'to think'. We may even give it a concrete representation, e.g. in a drawing of a man with 'bubbles' coming from his head in which his thoughts are written. But is this sketch also a picture of the thoughtful tennis-player? Is the drawing of the thinking man also to be used with regard to one who speaks with thought or understanding? And while speaking can be called 'an activity', is the thought that informs it a *further* activity?

Why, then, do we form a wrong picture? Many factors contribute. We are misled by superficial features of grammar, and are impressed by the fact that 'thinking', like 'speaking', has the grammatical appearance of an activity-verb (forgetting altogether that 'sleeping' has too). We take figurative speech, e.g. 'Use your brains!' or 'I wonder what is going on in his head', literally, and imagine that it is an obvious fact that we think *with* our brains, *in* our heads. Metaphors such as 'A thought flashed through his mind' lead us astray. Partial convergence of different expressions, e.g. 'thinking' and 'saying . . . to oneself', induce the wrong *expectations*, and when we note that thinking does not satisfy them overtly, we conclude that it must be very mysterious! 'Here one tells oneself: "It must be like this! – even if I cannot immediately get rid of all the objections"' (RPP I §555). Wittgenstein gave an analogy for the way a wrong picture can play havoc with our philosophical reflections: imagine that the word 'giant' did service for 'big'. The picture we would form for ourselves of what it is to be big would be of a giant; and now imagine that one had to describe the queer employment of the word 'big' with this picture in mind[5] (RPP I §554)!

These grammatical sources of confusion feed, and in turn are fed by, more general culture preconceptions. Both the Greek and the Judaeo-Christian sources of European civilization foster the picture of thinking as an activity of the spirit or soul, part of the essential nature of humanity, separable from the body and its activities, hence more pure and incorruptible, enabling us to contemplate eternal truths that transcend the changing, destructible world of matter. This cultural mythology has partly philosophical origins, and it plays a role in strengthening philosophical prejudices and preconceptions. These are as evident among materialists as in the works of the dualist and idealist traditions. Since Wittgenstein's day, the computer revolution has set up fresh pressures, new sources of confusion. We use machines to carry out complex calculating tasks. Bedevilled by misconceptions about thinking, conceiving of calculating as 'pure thought' (cf. Frege's subtitle for *Begriffsschrift*), and divorcing thinking from its behavioural manifestations, many philosophers and artificial-intelligence scientists conceive of these machines as capable of thought. (Typically, those who demure object to this absurdity for the *wrong* reasons: e.g. because computers are

---

[5] E.g. big mouse/big elephant; big gap in the path/big gap in the argument; big smile, big fuss, big deal, big party.

not *conscious*). The more sophisticated these machines become, the greater the temptation to think of ourselves on the model of our creations (see 'Man, minds, and machines, §5). We understand (because we designed) the inner processes that occur in a computer; surely our own thinking must involve an analogous inner process! Like the Cartesian, the modern materialist has no qualms about the claim that thinking *is* an inner process. But, in his view, it takes place in the brain rather than in the mind.

We form a picture of thinking as an inner accompaniment of speech, which can go on alone and much faster. We suppose the concept of thinking to have a simple unified use with smooth contours (RPP I §554). But that is an illusion. The use of this expression is far more erratic than we expect, and also much more *specialized* (RPP II §234); hence the danger of using 'think' in a global, highly generalized way is great. The concept is a widely ramified one, like a traffic network connecting many out-of-the-way places (Z §110; RPP II §216). Compare, e.g., speaking 'with thought' (i.e. non-mechanically), speaking thoughtfully, thinking before speaking, speaking before thinking, thinking while speaking, speaking while thinking, speaking to oneself in the imagination, thinking of something or someone, thinking up a solution to a conundrum, a thought crossing one's mind in a flash, engaging in an activity attentively and with intelligence, etc. Of course, we are tempted to say that one feature unifies all these: viz. an activity of or process in the mind. In all these cases, the mind is not idle; something is going on inside it which does not occur when a person is in a stupor, and it is this that constitutes thinking (RPP II §§217 – 21). But it is precisely this idea which should be investigated. To be sure, the *picture* we all have of thinking is of an invisible auxiliary activity; but this may be just where we go wrong (RPP II §§226ff.). For this picture forces on us a wide range of *bad questions*, and in our attempts to answer them, we generate further confusion and mystification.

3. *Activities of the mind*

The verb 'to think' is multi-faceted, being connected with opining ('I think we ought to . . .'), believing ('I think she is in the garden'), conceiving, imagining, fancying, and envisaging ('That is just how I thought it would be). It is also bound up with doing things attentively, carefully, with due consideration. And, what is prominent in philosophical investigation, it is related to reflecting, musing, meditating (whether aloud or *in foro interno*), as well as to deliberating, speculating, reasoning, and inferring. Grammarians see in this latter use of 'to think' an 'activity-verb'. Like 'to run' or 'to talk', but unlike 'to know' or 'to understand', it has a progressive aspect, readily admits an imperative, can form a pseudo-cleft sentence with a Do pro-form ('What I did was to think hard'), can be qualified by manner-adverbs (e.g. 'quickly', 'laboriously', 'reluctantly'), and takes 'for . . . sake' constructions ('I thought hard for N's sake').[6]

Philosophers and psychologists alike find it natural to conceive of 'thinking' thus used as the name of an activity. (Moreover, they will be prone to generalize this categorial classification to all thinking.) 'What are you doing?' may get the answer 'Drawing a picture' or 'Thinking about tomorrow's party'. Thinking is something we engage in. It can absorb us; we concentrate on it; give ourselves over to it whole-heartedly. It often takes time, for though I may think of the answer to your problem in a flash, it may take an hour to think up the right solution, or I may spend a sleepless night thinking about it. One can think voluntarily or involuntarily, willingly or reluctantly. 'Thinking is a mental activity' seems a truism which no sane man would deny.

The concept of an activity, like the concepts of an act or an action, as well as those of happening, process, state, object, fact, etc., looks like a hard, clearly defined categorial concept, part of the bedrock of any conceptual scheme. But, Wittgenstein warned, 'these extremely general terms have an extremely blurred meaning. They relate in practice to innumerable special cases, but that does not make them any the more *solid*; no, rather it makes them more fluid' (RPP I §648; see Exg. §308(2); cf. LPP 265). Fluid though it is, the idea of an activity does involve the notion of a constituent series of successive (and occasionally simultaneous) acts systematically related to each other. Moreover, a detailed description of an activity will specify such acts and their manner of performance. Walking and running are activities, as are playing football or cricket. These are simple paradigms. However, as we move away from them, the concept blurs. Is talking an activity? One might well say so; but note that it would be something of a joke to answer the question 'What is your favourite activity?' by 'Talking', although one might reply thus to 'What is your favourite pastime?'. If talking is an activity, what of listening? At a piano recital, the pianist is hard at work at the keyboard; is the audience hard at work in their seats? And what of sleeping through a lecture or a concert? No one would call that 'an activity', even though the sleeper breathes, moves, and snores occasionally. 'Listen' and 'sleep' qualify as 'activity-verbs', and 'What is he doing?' can be answered by 'Listening' or 'Sleeping'. But the latter is certainly, and the former arguably, not what we call 'an activity'.

What of thinking? Someone who works with care and attention, concentrating on what he is doing and considering various options as he

---

[6] Cf. R. Quirk, S. Greenbaum, G. Leech, and J. Svartvik, *A Grammar of Contemporary English* (Longman, London, 1972), pp. 92ff.

goes along will typically intersperse his work with auxiliary activities (otherwise, at least in certain kinds of cases, he would be doing whatever he is doing mechanically). He will pause with X in his hand and examine it, stop periodically and consider things, frown, shrug his shoulders, and resume his labour, etc. However, these activities are *not* the thinking, any more than when one speaks with thought, the speaking *is* the thinking. But it is striking that the concept of thinking is formed on the model of an imaginary auxiliary activity (as the concept of the differential quotient is formed on the model of a kind of imaginary quotient). One imagines the thinking as that which must be flowing under the surface of these expedients if they are not, after all, to be mere mechanical procedures (RPP II §§226 – 8). Thinking seems to be the invisible stream which carries and connects these actions. And so we assimilate the grammar of 'thinking' to that of 'speaking', and this comparison plays havoc with our attempt to get a clear picture of thinking.

The conception of thinking as an activity of the mind that *may* (but need not) accompany certain physical activities is strengthened when we examine the notions of reflecting, musing, and pondering. Here, it seems, we have the activity of thinking pure and simple, unaccompanied by any physical activity. If we carefully scrutinize these phenomena, we will discover what this inner activity really is. So it seems that 'in order to get clear about the meaning of the word "think" we watch ourselves while we think; what we observe will be what the word means' (PI §316). As long as we do not think too fast, we should be able to discover what the real activity of thinking is by observing what happens in our minds when we cogitate. 'But', Wittgenstein retorts, 'this concept is not used like that' (ibid). We must compare the uses of 'thinking' with what are called 'activities'.

One engages in typical physical activities by doing things, acting in certain ways, with one's body, limbs, or other organs. One writes by moving one's hand, as one swims by moving one's limbs or sings by using one's mouth and vocal cords. If thinking is an activity, it is an activity we engage in *without using any organ at all*. I do not think up another verse to my poem by doing something with my brain, and when I am thinking my way through a difficult problem, I am not performing any constituent acts with my brain (cf. BB 6f.). Of course, thinking may be protracted, as when I struggle to think my way through a conundrum. Am I then engaged in an activity? One might reply that that is indeed so: I wrack my brains! But what exactly do I do then? I frown, very likely close my eyes, perhaps beat my brow with my fist. But *that* is not thinking, nor is it something I do with my brains (but rather with my face and fist). We must not be misled by the instruction 'Use your brain!'. Like 'Let your heart tell you what to do!', it is a metaphor. 'He's got a good brain' is like 'He's got a warm heart', not like 'He's got good teeth'. This is obvious enough when one recollects that the brain is not an organ one can move at all. One does *nothing* with one's brain, for it is not an organ over which one has any *control*. Might thinking then not be an activity of the brain, not after the pattern of writing's being an activity of the hand, but rather on the model of digestion's being an activity of the stomach? But this too is wrong. For while we say that I digest my food, for me to digest my food *is* for my stomach to do so, and I need know nothing about its chemical activities. But it is I, not my brain, that thinks. And when I think, I can say what it is that I think. It would be absurd to say 'My brain is thinking it over, but I don't yet know what conclusion it has reached!'

In response to this, one is inclined to shift ground. Granted that thinking is not an activity of the brain, surely, being a *mental* activity, it is an activity of the *mind*? Here we cast the mind in the role of an immaterial object. But the mind is not an ethereal appendage with which one can do things. 'It is a travesty of the truth to say "thinking is an activity of our mind, as writing is an activity of the hand" ' (PG 106). 'I think with my mind' is more akin to 'I love . . . with all my heart' than it is to 'I chew with my teeth'.

One might concede that the mind is not an organ with which one thinks, yet insist that mental activities, unlike physical ones, are engaged in without the use of any organ. For surely things *go on* in one's mind when one is thinking; one's thinking, like an activity, takes time, can be interrupted and resumed. The mind is not idle, but active, while one is engaged in thought.

These parallels between the grammar of thinking and the grammar of activities are misleading, for they induce us to overlook important differences. Nothing *need* go on when one thinks. First, when one speaks or writes with thought and concentration, nothing typically 'goes on' in one's mind, apart from the fact that one is thinking about what one says or writes. All one's attention is on what one is saying or writing, and any actual images or 'inward speaking' that may occur typically mark a lapse of concentration. Secondly, an interruption or break in thinking is altogether unlike a hiatus in an activity. A long pause in a speech is a period during which one is not speaking. But if one is thinking about rearranging a room, e.g. thinking whether this piece of furniture would look better there, and one gets a tape-measure and measures the size of this or that, and while doing so says nothing to oneself, one has not therefore ceased thinking about rearranging the room, that the chest will look better there, or how to hang the pictures (cf. PI §328). Thirdly, when one is reflecting on what to do or musing on a passage one has just read, interior monologue or mental imagery is neither necessary nor sufficient for the truth of 'He is thinking (musing, reflecting)', although they may and often do accompany the thinking. It is not sufficient, since reciting the multiplication-table or the alphabet in one's mind is not thinking (cf. RPP II §193). It is not necessary, since someone's report of what he has thought after musing or reflecting would not be undermined by his denying that he talked to himself in his imagination when he thought up the solution to such-and-such a problem. That is to say, the criteria which justify saying that someone is thinking about, over, or up something or other are not the criteria for someone's saying something to himself or for having an array of mental images; and the absence of criteria for the latter are not defeating conditions of the criteria for the former. We may indeed ask someone in a brown study what he is thinking, and he may tell us. But to tell us his reflections is not to report what images or words crossed his mind. The 'stream of thought' which so fascinated James (to whom we owe the memorable phrase) is largely a meaningless babble, and it is philosophical confusion to think that a description of the 'stream of thought' such as Joyce presented in *Ulysses* is a description of the real activity of (Bloom's) thinking. This is so far from the truth that a comprehensive description of any mental goings-on when one is thinking might well hardly *ever* even mention *what* one is thinking.

Of course, the answer 'He is thinking about . . .' can be given to the question 'What is he doing?' But note how it differs from answers that describe typical activities. Specifying an activity engaged in (e.g. playing cricket, negotiating a contract, building a wall) intimates what is going on, what kinds of things are being done (e.g. bowling, batting, or fielding; telephoning, drafting, or arguing; brick-laying, mortar-mixing, or pointing bricks). But when one is told that a person is thinking about, over, or up something or other, one does not and need not have the faintest idea of what is going on in his brain or what images or jumbled words flit across his mind (cf. Z §88). Rather, what one knows is what is *aimed* at, viz. a solution, answer, plan, or project. And if one is told what, after due reflection, he thought, one knows his conclusion, opinion, or considered judgement.

One might still object. Surely, at least in cases in which one thinks through an argument, one goes through a definite activity of thinking first that x follows from a and b, that given x and c, it follows that y, and y implies z. This is misleading. If one has thought through an argument, then the *expression* of what one thought will be an ordered sequence of thoughts or propositions. In so far as there is anything that can be called 'the structure of thought (or of thinking)' it is the structure of the expression of the argument which is thought through. But one must not conflate the *logical* stages of an argument with a psychological process or activity. Specification of the argument one has thought up or thought through is not a description of a psychological process. To report what one thought when one thought through an argument is not to describe what one *said* to oneself; nor is it to describe a series of *mental* images that crossed one's mind. A picture of what went on in one's mind, as it were, need not be a picture of the argument one thought of.

Nevertheless, one might respond in a reductive spirit, thinking is, at least in certain cases, an activity. It is not a *further* activity over and above talking (writing, engaging attentively in any non-mechanical task); rather, one might say that *in these circumstances* saying such-and-such or doing so-and-so *is* to think. But this too would be misleading, as if thinking is sometimes talking, at other times walking, sometimes singing, and occasionally diving! (Here we can see how the idea that thinking is an activity forces bad questions on us, for is it the *same* activity as talking, etc. or is it a *different* activity?) It is indeed correct that to do something thoughtfully, with attention or concentration, reflectively or with due care, is not to accompany the activity with an inner activity of thinking, concentrating, reflecting, or attending. But to say that in these circumstances the thinking *is* the doing is as misleading as to say that when one eats one's breakfast hastily, the hurrying *is* the eating; or that when one loiters with intent, the intending *is* the loitering. At best, the claim is an unclear gesture in the direction of what Ryle called the 'adverbial' character of thinking.[7]

Activities that are voluntary are typically taught, and thinking is indeed often voluntary. But there are not, and could not be, special lessons at school in thinking, over and above the run-of-the-mill lessons in arithmetic, physics, history, and so on. One learns to think, to use one's wits more effectively, in the course of learning these subjects. For, of course, thinking is not a specific technique with teachable procedures which one can learn. If one is faced with a difficult problem in arithmetic, physics, or history and asks a friend how to solve it, the reply 'Try thinking, it sometimes does the trick' is at best a poor joke.[8] There are indeed teachable procedures of a rigorous kind for certain types of problem-solving, e.g. code-cracking, but they typically eliminate or greatly reduce the need for thinking. Activities can be practised, but one cannot practise thinking *per se*; rather, one improves one's ability to think

---

[7] G. Ryle, 'Adverbial verbs and verbs of thinking', in *On Thinking* (Blackwell, Oxford, 1979). It is noteworthy that although Ryle's reflections in many respects run on parallel tracks to Wittgenstein's, they also diverge significantly. Where Wittgenstein stressed the misleading character of apparent categorial expressions and emphasized their indeterminacy, Ryle was prone to view them as sharp. Hence, where Ryle was inclined to categorize different uses of expression in apparently ready-made pigeon-holes, Wittgenstein described the irregularity and diversity of use. The temptation to 'systematize', to impose more order upon the untidy skein of our use of words than is actually there must be resisted on pain of distortion and falsification (RPP I §257).

[8] See J. F. M. Hunter, *Understanding Wittgenstein* (Edinburgh University Press, Edinburgh, 1985), pp. 173 – 85.

clearly by practising essay-writing or problem-solving in arithmetic or physics, etc. If thinking is an activity, it is, *at the very least*, atypical. Should we conclude that thinking is *not* an activity? Wittgenstein sometimes did (MS. 124, 215): 'Vom Worte "denken" konnte man sagen, es sei nicht ein Tätigkeitswort' ('One could say of the word "thinking" that it is not an activity word').[9] But one could – and Wittgenstein often did – take a gentler line. One might say that it is only *misleading*, not wrong, to say that thinking is an activity (cf. BB 6). It is misleading in as much as it commonly induces the wrong pictures of thinking, which then, *in certain contexts* – in psychology and philosophy – lead one astray, just as talk about 'imaginary numbers' once led many mathematicians astray (LPP 124 – 6, 244, 286). In some humdrum contexts there is nothing misleading about it at all: when the doctor explains my insomnia by saying 'Your mind is too active', he just means 'You lie awake thinking' (LPP 244). If one wishes to contrast stupor or mechanical action with the innumerable different kinds of cases of thinking and of thoughtful or intelligent action, one might well say that in all the latter cases the mind isn't idle, that something is going on in it. This is picturesque and draws a distinction (RPP II §217).

But when doing philosophy, one is prone to say 'Thinking is a mental activity', in order to distinguish it from *physical* activities. This *is* misleading, as misleading as saying that while numerals are physical objects, numbers are immaterial objects, real but non-actual, as Frege claimed. This makes the difference between numbers and numerals appear *too slight* (PI §339) and wholly obscures the role of arithmetical propositions, leading philosophers of mathematics up the garden path. Similarly, saying that thinking is a mental activity typically leads philosophers and psychologists into futile investigations about the 'materials' of thought (words, images, internal representations) and about mental operations allegedly constitutive of thinking (e.g. the psychologist's supposition that thinking about whether two drawings are of one and the same object at different orientations involves rotating images in mental space at constant velocity). It may generate wild mythologies of symbolism, such as pseudo-theories about the innate 'language of thought'. It induces the wrong pictures of thinking and generates misleading questions. It is, therefore, a move best avoided. Rather than locating the erratic and widely ramified concept of thinking in the deceptive, apparently determinate category of *activity*, we should, from case to case, investigate what are the criteria for someone's thinking. This will reveal *what* gets treated grammatically as an *activity* here (cf. PI §573), i.e. what in the superficial grammatical *form* looks like the name of an activity but has in numerous respects a quite different use from verbs signifying paradigmatic activities.

[9] Its grammar is *fundamentally* different from that of an activity, he wrote (MS. 179,12).

4. *Processes in the mind*

In philosophy and psychology we talk of thought-processes as little known and perhaps mysterious, certainly complicated, processes in the mind. The picture we have here (unlike the picture of thinking as an activity of the mind) is of a space in which these processes take place, as the fermentation of grape-juice occurs in a vat (cf. PG 100). We are then prone, rather inchoately, to conceive of thinking as a process of an ethereal 'mind-stuff' (as James called it). The picture is reinforced by the use of common phrases such as 'When I was talking to him, I didn't know what was going on in his head.' The sense of mystery associated with the idea of thought-processes is exacerbated by such phenomena as calculating prodigies, of whom neither we nor they can say *how* their feats are performed. Hence we suppose that hidden mental mechanisms are at work, mechanisms which must be investigated by psychology.[10]

It is almost universally agreed that thinking goes on in the head. The idea is far more compelling than the similar notion that one loves with one's heart. The latter is transparently metaphorical, but the former, we suppose, is a literal truth. However, if thinking really did take place in the head, then the question 'Where did you think that up?' would have answers such as 'Two inches behind my left eye', '39 mm below where I thought that we should go to London tomorrow', or 'Diffused right throughout the cranial cavity'. But these replies make no sense. The only licit kind of answer is 'In the train as I was going to London' or 'In the library'. Of course, it could be *given* a new sense: the cranial location of thinking might be stipulated to mean that part of the brain which, when probed with a micro-electrode, would cause one to cease to think of *A* (cf. BB 9). But that is not the sense of 'Where did you think of *A*? or 'Where did you think that up?' And note that by parity of reasoning, one might also stipulate a cranial location for digestion. If someone insists that thinking takes place in the head, one should press him to explain what it would be for human beings to think in their stomachs. For presumably it is an empirical truth that is in question, and hence contingent. The correlation between thinking and parts of the cerebral cortex had to be *discovered*. So what would creatures, otherwise akin to us in appearance and behaviour, be like if they thought in their stomachs? Is it that their *brains* would be in their midriff? Or is it that whereas we clutch our heads and groan 'Let me think!', they would clutch their stomachs?

---

[10] Under pressure from the alleged analogy between the workings of the brain and of the computer, many scientists hold that the hidden mechanisms are neural, forgetting that *whatever* neural mechanisms there are, they are not *thinking mechanisms*, and their operation is not a thought-process.

We are tempted to conceive of thinking as a process or activity which occurs in the head for a variety of reasons. (a) We draw an analogy between speaking, writing, and thinking. One does the first with the mouth and the larynx, the second with the hand, so surely one must do one's thinking with something, e.g. one's brain. But, as argued, this is wrong, for there is *no* organ of thought (BB 7). One does not think *with* anything – save with a pen in one's hand or with the wireless on! (b) We have a rather primitive picture of ourselves as located at the invisible apex of the cone of vision the base of which is our visual field, so we think of ourselves as looking *out* from our heads, and hence of our thinking as occurring in our heads (LWL 25). (c) We conceive of thoughts as the product of thinking and imagine them to be *stored* in our heads, for, after all, we remember what we thought, and how could we remember our thoughts unless we retained them? Memory, as Locke put it, is the storehouse of ideas, and the brain, the moderns add, is the storage depot. But, of course, this is confused. Whatever neural structures and events may be necessary for a person to think or remember that *p*, what he thinks no less than what he typically thinks about cannot be in the head (cf. PG 143). What one thinks, namely *that p*, is not an object and no more has a location, in the head or anywhere else, than does the fact that *p* which makes that thought true. It makes no sense to talk of *that p* as having a place; 'Where is the thought that *p*?' is like 'Where is your visual space?' (AWL 54).

Of course, the head is more closely connected with thinking than it is with digesting or walking, but not because one thinks with or in one's head as one digests food in one's stomach or walks with one's legs. Rather, it is because one clutches or beats one's head when one wracks one's brain, closes one's eyes to think better, and so forth. One reads a person's thoughts *on his face*, not on his feet; it is his *eyes* that light up when he has 'cottoned on', that twinkle when he is fondly pulling one's leg, and so on. This explains why we favour the *picture* of thinking as going on in the head. But when we proceed to claim that thinking literally goes on in the head, that the brain is the organ of thinking, or that thinking is a process or activity of the brain, we are misconstruing the use of the picture no less than when we conceive of thinking as an activity of or process in the mind (RPP I §§278f.; cf. PG 106, 143).

We would often like to know 'what is going on in someone's head', i.e. what he is thinking (PI §427). But that is no reason for being interested in what processes are going on inside him. What he is thinking is given by specification of a proposition, viz. he is thinking that such-and-such, not by a description of an inner process (RPP I §§579f.). And we find out what he is thinking by what he says and does. What goes on in his mind or brain while he is thinking almost never interests us when we are concerned with *what he thought* (Z §88). For to say what one is thinking, like saying what one intends, is not to describe an experience. And one does not read off what one thinks, any more than one reads off what one intends, from observation of any inner processes. It is a fundamental misconception to suppose that thinking is a mental, incorporeal process that accompanies talking with thought, and sometimes, as when one is musing or reflecting, goes on without it.[11] Though one may talk with thought or just babble, the thought is not detachable from the talking any more than when one eats with haste, the haste is detachable from the eating. They are not like Peter Pan's shadow (cf. PI §339). And likewise, a description of one's musing or reflecting is not a description of an 'incorporeal process'.

A superficial reaction to these claims would be to accuse Wittgenstein of propounding theses (which he is supposed to eschew) or of denying what we all assert (which he is committed to not doing). Furthermore, it may seem that he is a behaviourist in disguise. For is he not denying that anything goes on in the mind and insisting that thinking *is*, or is *reducible* to, just saying or doing? This is wrong. He is denying nothing but the misleading picture of an 'inner (incorporeal) process' that goes with the concept of thinking (cf. PI §305). 'Thinking' is not the name of an introspectible inner process; but to insist on that is not to deny that people think, nor is it to *equate* thinking with saying or doing. Wittgenstein does not deny that when one is thinking, a variety of things may cross one's mind – words, phrases, mental images, and the rest. But a description of *this* 'stream of consciousness' would *not* be a report of what one was thinking or of the *reasoning* underlying the conclusion reached. Nevertheless, is he not insisting (contrary to what we all know!) that nothing *has* to go on in my mind when I think, hence that thinking might be *nothing*? This misconstrues his argument: the images and jumble of words are indeed incidental to what I thought, but he is not denying that I was thinking about such-and-such, and that I concluded that . . . Should anything else have been going on (Vol. XII, 253)? What is repudiated is merely a misleading picture that is fostered by the similarities between the verb 'to think' and process-verbs such as 'to grow', 'to change', 'to deteriorate'.

As with 'Thinking is a mental activity', so too with 'Thinking is an inner process': one *can* say such things if thereby one wishes simply to differentiate thinking from corporeal processes like digestion (cf. PI §339) or (rather more profoundly) to point out that in as much as thinking is 'inner' (in as much as the concept is a psychological concept displaying first-/third-person asymmetry) the language-game with 'thinking' *begins* with the expression of thoughts and manifestations of thinking (cf. Vol. XVI, 134f.). But it is misleading, for thinking is not, as

[10] See James, *Principles of Psychology*, Vol. 1, Ch. VII, for an example of such confusion.

it were, just like a physical process, only mental! The physical analogues of engaging in thought are not physical processes like digestion or breathing, but the *soundness* of digestion, the *quickness* of breath, the *irregularity* of heartbeat (RPP I §661). Having 'a mental life', i.e. thinking, wishing, believing, doubting, having mental images, being sad or merry, and so on, is not analogous to: eats, drinks, walks, runs, but to: moves now fast, now slow, now towards a goal, now without a goal, now continuously, now in jerks (RPP I §284). Here Wittgenstein anticipated (but did not elaborate) Ryle's comparison of verbs of thinking to so-called adverbial verbs.

The concept of a process has a familiar application in the physical sphere, where we talk of physical, chemical, or biological processes, in the description of certain regulated human activities and sequences of actions, as when we talk of legal and constitutional processes, and in the characterization of industrial and other artefactual processes. But this model of a process, when applied to the mental in philosophical or theoretical contexts, distorts the phenomena, creating misleading pictures and giving rise to false expectations. In this respect 'Thinking is an inner, incorporeal, or mental process' is akin to 'Sensations are inner, mental objects'. The 'mental process of thinking' need involve no changes in or transformations of a substance (as the process of fermentation does) or any essential sequential array of acts by agents (as legal processes do) or the processing and transformation of particulars (as manufacturing processes do). What 'goes on' in thinking which is not inward talking, unlike what is manifest in its articulate expression, need not be and typically is not a sequential array of stages or phases in a 'process of thinking'. In short, we have here, one might say, the *form*, but not the substance, of a process. This is not to say that we do not have some use for the notion of a psychological (but not 'incorporeal'!) process; but it is highly specialized as in 'the painful process of coming to terms with the loss of a loved one'. When in philosophy we extend it beyond these rather narrow confines, confusion and obfuscation ensue.

Finally, to round off this discussion of thinking and its subsumption under putative categorial concepts, is thinking an *experience*? No, it is categorially quite distinct. We do not compare thoughts as we compare experiences (Z §96); the relation of thinking to duration is unlike that of experiences to duration (RPP I §105), and so is its relation to hedonic values. Two people think the same, their thoughts converge, if they both agree that such-and-such is the case or that if so-and-so, then probably such-and-such. They think the same thought, have the same idea, if the expressions of their thoughts say the same thing. But this is not like having the same experience. In one sense of that expression, two people have the same experience if they do or undergo the same things (which one may like, and the other may hate). In another sense, in which having a pain is said (perhaps misleadingly) to be an experience, two people can be said to have the same experience if, e.g., they both have a pain of similar intensity, duration, phenomenal character, and location. Experiences in this sense have a 'content': a pain, which may be sharp and throbbing or dull and nagging, or a perceptual experience, which may be enjoyable (smelling jasmine) or unpleasant (smelling hydrogen sulphide). But in this sense of 'content', the putative experience of thinking has *no* content. To say *what* I thought is not to specify the *content of an experience*; it is not to say 'what it was like'. Moreover, if one expresses a thought in speech, no one would say that the first word one speaks is the beginning of the experience of thinking that thought or that the experience of thinking occurred just then. And if one says that the beginning and end of the experience of thinking is the beginning and end of the utterance, one would not know how to answer the question of whether the experience is uniform throughout or constantly changing, like the words of the utterance (RPP II §257).

The moral of the tale is that there is no substitute in philosophy for the description of the particular case. The grammar of each concept needs to be examined in its own right. There are no short-cuts by way of invoking apparent categorial concepts to give us our bearings. On the contrary, if our first step is to take it for granted that, e.g., thinking is a mental activity (or remembering a mental process, sensation an inner object) the exact nature of which must now be investigated, then we go wrong at the very start. 'The decisive movement in the conjuring trick has been made, and it was the very one that we thought quite innocent' (PI §308). The concepts of activity, act, process, object, when invoked in philosophical psychology, lead us astray, imposing upon us misleading pictures, creating a false aura of mystery, and ensuring that we remain in a state of confusion (PI §339). 'One cannot guess how a word functions. One has to *look at* its use and learn from that' (PI §340).

IX

THINKING: THE SOUL OF LANGUAGE

1. *The strategic role of the argument*

The psychological hinterland of the austere logical doctrines of the *Tractatus* is notoriously obscure. The declared aim of the book is to set a limit to thought, or rather to the expression of thoughts (TLP, Preface p. 3). Only in language can that limit be set, and the *Tractatus* accordingly concentrates on delineating the essential nature of any possible represent-ation. The bare minimum about the psychological nature of thinking is given, for Wittgenstein believed that his task as a critical philosopher was purely logical. His study of language *corresponded* to traditional philo-sophical investigations, of a similarly critical nature, into thought-processes. But such enterprises typically got entangled in inessential psychological questions. With his method too, he was aware, there was a similar risk (TLP 4.1121), and he carefully screened out psychological concerns. The result is that the psychological presuppositions of the book are barely visible and must often be read between the lines or gleaned from the occasional remarks in the *Notebooks 1914 – 16* and correspondence.

This much seems clear: a propositional sign contains the possibility of expressing its sense (TLP 3.13).[1] It has that possibility in virtue of its logical multiplicity: the combinatorial possibilities in syntax of its constituent names, which must be logically isomorphic with what they represent. It only constitutes a proposition, however, if it is given a content. Tacit in the *Tractatus*, but explicit in the *Notebooks 1914 – 16*, is the idea that content is, as it were, injected into names by mental acts of meaning: '*By* my correlating the components of the picture with objects, it comes to represent a situation and to be right or wrong' (NB 33f.; cf. NB 53, 68, 70). Although there can be superficial vagueness in sentences, what one *means* by a constituent expression must always be 'sharp' (NB 68), for one can always explain that 'I *know* what I mean; I mean just THIS' and point with one's finger (NB 70). A proposition is not a Platonic object, but a propositional sign in its projective relation to the world (TLP 3.12). The method of projection is to think the sense of the proposition (TLP 3.11). When we use a propositional sign as a projection of a possible situation, i.e. use it 'thinkingly', with understanding, then it

---

[1] Here I follow A. J. P. Kenny's interpretation of TLP 3.13; see 'Wittgenstein's early philosophy of mind', repr. in his *The Legacy of Wittgenstein* (Blackwell, Oxford and New York, 1984), pp. 1 – 10.

is a proposition (*sinnvolle Satz*). It is, therefore, thought-processes (acts of meaning, thinking, understanding) that connect language with reality, link names with their meanings, and infuse sentences with life.

Further complications and irresolvable tension were added by the account of a thought as a psychological fact. A thought, like a proposition, is a picture or representation of a situation, although, unlike a proposition, it is not a perceptible one (TLP 3 – 3.1; NB 82). 'A thinks that *p*' is of the form ' "*p*" says that *p*' (TLP 5.542), which involves the correlation of *facts* by means of the correlation of their objects. The thought that *p* therefore is a psychical fact which, like a sentence, represents a situation. So a thought just is a kind of proposition, and thinking is a kind of language (NB 82). In response to Russell's queries, Wittgenstein wrote:

> I don't know *what* the constituents of a thought are, but I know *that* it must have such constituents which correspond to the words of language. Again the kind of relation of the constituents of thought and of the pictured fact is irrelevant. It would be a matter of psychology to find it out . . . [The] psychical constituents . . . have the same sort of relation to reality as words. What those constituents are I don't know. (R 37)

The tension in this account is between the idea that a thought is a representation and thinking a kind of language, on the one hand, and the idea (as Wittgenstein later put it) that thought 'is the last interpretation' (cf. BB 34). Whereas a language of perceptible signs may stand in need of an interpretation (in order to disambiguate, clarify vagueness, etc.), thought does not. For *me*, there can be no gap between what I think and what I mean. The underlying idea is both natural and mystifying.[2] It makes sense to ask what a sign 'N' (a name) means or to wonder what the sense of a sentence '*p*' is. But if I *think* of N or *think* that *p*, it makes no sense for me to wonder who I mean or what I am thinking. However, if a thought is a proposition in the language of thought, this remarkable power of transparent, unerring correlation between the thought-constituents and what they represent must itself be explained. Two moves might seem to be available, and it is unclear which Wittgenstein opted for. One might argue that thought-constituents *intrinsically* represent the objects they represent. To this there are two objections: first, that if so, then they do *not* have the same sort of relation to reality as words; second, that far from explaining how this mystifying relation is possible, the reply that it is intrinsic merely disguises the original

---

[2] It is mystifying if one lacks a surview of the grammar of 'thinking' and of the relation of thought and its expression. For how is it possible for me to think of just N? Even though he is not here, but in America, and looks just like his twin N.N., I can still 'nail him' with my thought! And how can I even think that *p*, if it is not the case that *p*? (See 'Thinking: methodological muddles and categorial confusions', §1).

question in the form of an answer. Alternatively, one might argue that thought-constituents *are* related to reality as words are, i.e. extrinsically. The mechanism of correlation would be by means of the Will, but not the Will as a phenomenon, rather the Will as an aspect of the metaphysical self. This, however, is mere mystery-mongering. As Wittgenstein was later to realize (see §3 below), this feature of our thoughts can be clarified only by relinquishing the ideas that thoughts are kinds of propositions and that there is any such thing as a language of thought. But if these ideas are abandoned, one must also relinquish the related idea that it is thought that breathes life into otherwise dead signs.

It is important to note that the conception of thoughts and of thinking in the *Tractatus* is exceedingly general. When Wittgenstein said that 'a logical picture of facts is a thought', his idea applied not merely, for example, to opining, but to judging, believing, wondering, guessing, and also to doubting, supposing, and assuming. In all these cases, and very likely also in the case of wishing, hoping, expecting, and so on, it seems that we *represent*, or *picture to ourselves*, a certain situation. The differences between these psychological verbs was of no concern to Wittgenstein; what was of logical (and metaphysical) importance was the nature of representation, and of thought *qua* psychic representation, in general.

It is natural for a philosopher to conceive of thought and of thinking in this generalized manner. It seems that a logical investigation into representation just is an investigation into the nature and limits of thought. Niceties about the differences between thinking, knowing, meaning, understanding, and judging seem irrelevant at this level of generality. Moreover, ordinary language (for what it is worth to such a philosopher) seems to support the natural philosophical intuition. In many contexts 'I think' *is* interchangeable with 'I imagine', 'I believe', 'I mean', and the possibility of expressing intentions, desires, and beliefs in the form 'I think I'll go now', 'I think I'd like a drink', or 'I think it's raining' suggest that all these are, or involve, thoughts and thinking processes. Finally, a venerable tradition in philosophy supports this generalizing penchant. The Cartesian use of *cogitare* subsumed almost the whole range of the mental; Kant's use of *denken* covered anything 'representable in thought'; and although Frege's *Gedanke* was a Platonic object rather than a psychological one, *thinking*, engaging with this timeless entity, incorporates or is a constituent of, conceiving, understanding, supposing, believing, and judging, as well as questioning.

Wittgenstein's anti-psychologism had induced him not to investigate the concepts that informed the psychological presuppositions of the *Tractatus*; only the essence of any possible symbolism seemed relevant to his concerns. Hence what it is to understand symbols and their use, what it is to mean something by a symbol, what kind of process (if any) thinking might be: these and related questions were allocated to psychology. When the edifice of the *Tractatus* collapsed, Wittgenstein started digging down to the foundations of the ruin. In the 'Big Typescript' (1932/3), his first effort at compiling a book incorporating his new ideas, Chapter 6 is entitled 'Thought and Thinking'. It is preceded by the following sequence of chapter themes: understanding, meaning, the proposition and its sense, instantaneous understanding, and the nature of language. It is evident that although in one sense his anti-psychologism is unabated, he now began to think that *philosophical* investigations into these psychological *concepts* is of paramount importance for the clarification of philosophical problems about meaning and representation.

The discussion of thinking in the 'Big Typescript' corresponds very roughly to that of Chapter V, §§63ff., of Rush Rhees's compilation *Philosophical Grammar*.[3] The aim of the chapter is to undermine the supposition that it is thought which lends life to mere signs, that makes sounds or marks mean something; and hence too to explode the idea that behind the intelligent use of any sentence lies a mental process of thinking the thought which that sentence expresses. For this destructive purpose, Wittgenstein continued to use the words 'thought' and 'to think' in the very wide sense sanctioned by the tradition of which the *Tractatus* had been the culmination. This is clear also from an opening passage of the *Blue Book*, where the same target is in view:

It seems that there are *certain definite* mental processes bound up with the working of language, processes through which alone language can function. I mean the processes of understanding and meaning. The signs of our language seem dead without these mental processes. . . . We are tempted to think that the action of language consists of two parts; an inorganic part, the handling of signs, and an organic part, which we may call understanding these signs, meaning them, interpreting them, thinking. (BB 3)

Despite this highly general and largely critical interest in thoughts and thinking, Wittgenstein's criss-cross journeys through this landscape led him into adjacent areas. Hence he also considered issues that bear only tangentially on his central theme: e.g. the location of thought, the purpose of thinking, and the possibility of a machine's thinking.

Few of the remarks from Chapter 6 of the 'Big Typescript' were incorporated into §§316 – 62 of the *Investigations* (though the discussion of the purpose of thinking in §§466 – 75 derives from those early reflections). Nevertheless, many of the themes recur: e.g. that thought is something ordinary and unmysterious, that thinking is not an inner

---

[3] For details of the relationship between the 'Big Typescript' and *Philosophical Grammar*, see A. J. P. Kenny, 'From the Big Typescript to the *Philosophical Grammar*', repr. in his *Legacy of Wittgenstein*, pp. 24 – 37, and S. Hilmy, *The Later Wittgenstein* (Blackwell, Oxford and New York, 1987), Ch. 1.

process, the absurdity of the idea that in French the order of words mirrors the order of thinking, and the question of whether machines can think. Moreover, the position of §§316 – 62 in the grand strategy of the *Investigations* has a similar rationale. Implicit in Augustine's conception of language is a beguiling picture of the nature of thinking and of the relation between thought and speech:

Augustine describes the learning of human language as if the child came into a strange country and did not understand the language of the country; that is, as if it already had a language, only not this one. Or again: as if the child could already *think*, only not yet speak. And 'think' would mean something like 'talk to itself'. (PI §32)

The misconceptions about thinking, meaning something by one's words, saying something with thought or understanding, that are implicit in this picture and which surface in sophisticated philosophical theories constitute Wittgenstein's target (and the presuppositions of the *Tractatus* are not far from the bull's-eye). Confusions about thinking in this very general sense contribute as much to our philosophical perplexities about the nature of language and linguistic representation as vice versa.

The strategic role of §§316 – 62 is likewise clear. The private language arguments have shown the incoherence of the idea that the foundations of language lie in private objects that constitute, or explain, the meanings of primitive indefinables of language. It is a natural extension of this classical philosophical picture that an inner process of thinking gives our discourse its life, differentiates it from mere noises, and is what we communicate to each other by means of a verbal vehicle when we talk. (It is no coincidence that the discussion of thinking here is followed by an examination of imagining, for part of the private language 'syndrome' is the idea that the imagination plays an essential role in language, for it seems that one must have an image of a sensation or experience if one is to understand the words that name them. And surely to understand what another person says is a matter of having the right array of images called up in response to his words!)

However, as in the 'Big Typescript', so too here, Wittgenstein's reflections carried him beyond the narrow confines of the immediate strategic purpose – e.g. in the brief discussion of machines' thinking – and of the restriction to human beings of predications of 'thinking' (a theme that links up with §§281 – 3). It is obvious that while writing the notebooks that are the immediate source of the bulk of this section, Wittgenstein's interests were moving markedly in the direction of themes in philosophical psychology. In his lectures on that subject in 1946 – 7, he dwelt more extensively on questions concerning the nature of thinking, and in the notes he wrote during the immediate post-war period on the philosophy of psychology (MSS. 130 – 8), his treatment of thinking is more fine-grained, concerned with the very specialized use of 'to think' and with its differences from other related psychological verbs.

In this essay, the later writings on thinking are treated as of a piece with those in *Investigations*, Part 1. They grew out of that seed-bed, and the only shift in the analysis of thinking is the sharpening of focus, the diminution of the global use of 'think', and the concentration on philosophical psychology. But there is no significant, discernible conflict between the 1944 – 5 remarks on thinking and those of 1946 – 8.

2. *The dual-process conception*

The idea that thinking is an inner process which accompanies speaking but may go on independently of it is indeed intuitively persuasive. The conception of thought as that which gives 'life' to otherwise 'dead' signs is compelling for quite mundane reasons. A machine can emit words, but they are, 'as far as it is concerned', just noises. A parrot can utter words, but it cannot *say* things or *tell* one things. It can croak 'Tea is ready' or 'Polly is pretty', but it cannot say *that* tea is ready or *that* Polly is pretty. It can utter words, but it does not *mean* them or *understand* them; it does not *think* what it utters. What a robot or parrot emits are just noises; the words are lifeless, without a soul. An alien script, prior to decipherment, is just a sequence of dead marks. Only when we can understand what thought they express do they come to life.

These observations, which are roughly right, make it seem plausible to suppose that what *animates* dead signs is something that lies behind them. And philosophers construct theories about the nature of this 'something'. On a Fregean view, it is a sense, an abstract entity distinct from the sign, which we attach to it. 'It rains' and 'Es regnet' are different signs to which the same sense is attached in the same context. If I, here and now, utter the English sentence and you utter the German one, we both grasp the same thought, which is neither English nor German. According to this conception, sense is logically independent of language, but it gives language life.[4] For language is 'alive' for one only in so far as one thinks or understands the senses attached to sentences. Thinking is a psychological process of coming into intellectual contact with, grasping, these lexical souls. Speech is the communication to others by means of a linguistic vehicle of the sense one has 'grasped'.

An alternative picture that has a similar rationale cuts out the Platonism. On this conception – e.g. in the *Tractatus* – a continual process of

---

[4] An economist of Fregean bent would think of paper money as paper with a value attached to it (cf. PG 106f.; BB 4). He might, absurdly, suppose that what gives a £5 note its value is its being attached to the value of £5, which is the *same* value (today) as is attached to $7.72. If he were a philosophical materialist rather than a Platonist, he might find incoherent the abandonment of the gold standard!

meaning or *thinking* accompanies one's cogent, non-mechanical speech and breathes life into otherwise meaningless signs. Yet another picture informs the tradition of the British empiricists, who conceived of thinking as a transaction with ideas or images which accompany intelligent speech. Speaking is accordingly a *translation* from the imagist 'language of thought' into word-language, which will generate in the mind of the comprehending hearer a similar play of representations.

It is indeed true that a sign can be lifeless for one, as when one hears an alien tongue or sees an unknown script. But it is an illusion to suppose that what animates a sign is some *immaterial thing*, abstract object, mental image, or hypothesized psychic entity that can be attached to it by a process of thinking (BB 4). One can try to rid oneself of these nonsensical conceptions by simple manoeuvres. In the case of the idealist conception, imagine that we replace the mental accompaniment of a word, which allegedly gives the expression its 'life', by a physical correlate. For example, instead of accompanying the word 'red' with a mental image of red, one might carry around in one's pocket a small red card. So, on the idealist's model, whenever one hears or uses the word 'red', one can *look* at the card instead of conjuring up a visual image in thought. But will looking at a red slip of paper endow the word 'red' with life? The word plus sample is no more 'alive' than the word without the sample. For an object (a sample of red) does not have *the use* of the word laid up within it, and neither does a mental image. Neither the word and the sample nor the word and the mental pseudo-sample dictate the use of a word or guarantee understanding.

In the Fregean (Platonist) case, one should ask of a given sentence, e.g. 'It is raining' (which allegedly has 'life' conferred on it by being associated with its sense), what sense it has. The reply 'Its sense is: that it is raining' does not animate the dead sign. The question 'What is the sense of the sentence "*p*"?' *if it is not a request for a paraphrase of 'p' into other symbols*, has no more sense than 'What sentence is formed by this sequence of words?' (cf. BB 161; PI §502). Explaining the sense or meaning of an expression is not to refer one to something extra-linguistic, i.e. to something other than an expression (Vol. IV, 237) or sample (which belongs to the means of representation). Understanding, according to Frege, 'would be something like seeing a picture from which all the rules followed, or a picture that makes them all clear' (PG 40). It seemed to Frege, Wittgenstein claimed, that no adding of inorganic signs, as it were, can make the proposition live, from which he concluded that 'What must be added is something immaterial, with properties different from all mere signs' (BB 4). He did not see that such an object, a sense mysteriously grasped in thinking, as it were a picture in which all the rules are laid up, 'would itself be another sign, or a calculus to explain the written one to us' (PG 40). If anything can be said to give a sign life, it is its *use* (as what gives a £5 note its value is what one can *do* with it). This is not something that *accompanies* a sign; hence to say what sense or meaning an expression has does not involve pointing at or ineffably showing some accompanying entity that is that sense, but rather to give *another expression* with the *same use*. To understand a sign, i.e. for it to 'live' for one, is not to grasp something other than the sign; nor is it to accompany the sign with an inner parade of objects in thought. It is to grasp the use of the sign itself (AWL 54; BB 4f.).

Recognizing such philosophical theories as confusions will not help unless one can free oneself from the urge to construct theories to dispel the apparent mysteries of thinking and meaning. One must locate the sources of the confusions and come to see that they can be dispelled only by grammatical clarifications, not by theories of thinking or of meaning. Many compelling considerations contribute to the idea that thinking is an inner process that accompanies speaking (which is not thoughtless) or listening with understanding.

(i) One can speak mechanically, without thought, or speak with thought. Surely thinking, the inner activity, is the accompaniment that makes the difference! One can think without speaking, and is that not to engage in the inner activity without communicating it to others in speech, for is not speech a matter of telling others what one has been thinking? Indeed, thinking often seems to be a kind of talking to oneself *in foro interno*, the soul conversing with itself (Plato). Moreover, one can say one thing and think another, so thinking is obviously quite different from saying. The one is an outer activity, the other looks like an inner activity that typically, but not uniformly, accompanies the outer.

(ii) A second array of factors contributing to the dual-process picture of thought and speech turns on the natural idea of a medium of thought. One can speak in English, French, or German; but is it not an open question what one *thinks in*? It is very tempting to suppose that some languages, especially one's own, have a word-order that corresponds to the order of thought, whereas others, such as German or Latin, say, do not (PI §336). Here it seems as if one thinks *in* a certain medium, perhaps in ideas or images, which one then translates into word-language. This picture is strengthened by our natural talk of having an idea before our mind, which we then express in words, as if we first think the idea and then translate it into English (BB 41). We sometimes look for the right word to express our thought, and superficial reflection on this suggests that we think the thought in 'Mentalese', as it were, and then look around for the right translation. For do we not sometimes exclaim 'What I said does not express my thoughts at all well! Let me try again!'? These considerations suggest a non-linguistic medium of thought, but others push in the opposite direction. Does the Englishman speaking German haltingly not think *in* English and then translate what he wants to say into German? And when he has thoroughly mastered the alien tongue, is one not tempted to say that he knows German so well that he even thinks in it?

(iii) We often understand something in a flash or think of a complex solution to a problem at a stroke. We naturally enough speak of the lightning process of thought. Hence it can seem as if thinking without speaking is a very rapid process (like the ticking of a clock with a broken escapement), whereas speech slows the thinking down (PI §318). We say 'Think before you speak!' like 'Wash before you eat!', and both orders appear to prescribe one activity before another (BB 148). As James noted, we ordinarily know what we are going to say before we say it, and this induces the idea that the thought must have been completed by the time the first word is uttered (PI §337). We use such phrases as 'What you really wanted to say was . . . ', which intimate the picture of the thought articulated in 'Mentalese' and of thinking as an inner activity of generating thoughts (PI §334).

The premises of the first array of considerations are correct, but they do not confirm the dual-process conception. Wittgenstein clarified this with a wide range of arguments, illustrations, and reminders. When one thinks without speaking, one is not doing what one does when one articulates what one thinks, only minus the speaking. For to speak with thought, i.e. non-mechanically, is not to speak *and* do something else as well (PI §332), as becomes obvious when one is asked to say something with thought and then just to do what one did when one said it with thought, only without saying it. What characterizes speaking without thought (viz. mechanically, unthinkingly, without understanding) is not the absence of an accompaniment. Indeed, it is sometimes the *presence* of an accompaniment which explains one's lack of thought, e.g. a violent headache or the distraction of one's attention ('I'm so sorry, I wasn't thinking when I said that, my mind was on the music'). One should compare speaking with thought not to singing and playing the tune on the piano as accompaniment, but to singing *with expression*, i.e. with modulation of the voice, accentuation, intensity, etc. These are obviously not *accompaniments* of singing (BB 148; cf. PI §341), and no more so is thinking when one speaks with thought. One can indeed imagine people who only think aloud (PI §331); but no one would imagine that when such people speak with thought, they say things twice!

The lack of thought in speech, in one sense, is manifest in the mechanical, monotonic mode of speech and in the lack of expression in voice and face. In another sense, it is marked by the inappropriateness or ineptness of what one says. In neither case, however, is the lack of thought a matter of the absence of an inner process accessible only to oneself. Lack of thought is characterized by one's inability or unwillingness to explain or justify what one said and by one's reluctance to stick by it. The function of 'When I said that, I wasn't thinking' or 'I didn't mean anything in particular when I said that' is not to make a report on introspected goings-on or their absence. If it were, it would make sense for the speaker to be mistaken as to whether he was thinking when he said what he said. But does it?[5] Even if certain ideas crossed his mind, indeed even if he *was thinking* (of something *else*), his words (viz. 'I wasn't thinking') are not nullified; for this utterance is a *disclaimer*, a denial of *intent* (cf. RPP II §§250ff.), not a report of mental happenings. 'I didn't mean anything by it, I was just saying it' is indeed, in a sense, indubitable or incorrigible, but not because it describes an experience (RPP II §253). 'I wasn't thinking' often means 'I didn't take *that* into account' (as I should have).

Any analytic investigation of the fine grain of the concept of thinking must distinguish the various ways in which an utterance may be thoughtless and in which something may be said unthinkingly. One may say something wholly mechanically (as when one repeats a line of poetry 500 times to commit it to memory), or one's words may be a spontaneous exclamation which one did not utter intentionally and, perhaps, should not have uttered at all. Here too one might say 'I wasn't thinking'. A remark is said to be thoughtless if it is indiscreet, insensitive, or inconsiderate; or, rather differently, if it is unreflective where reflection was meet, foolish where a little thought would have prevented the folly.

To be sure, saying that p and thinking that p are not the same, and one can say that p while thinking that not-p. But saying something and 'not thinking it' is not cutting out one activity or process. Saying something 'with thought', as opposed to saying it unthinkingly (in one or other of the *different* senses in which a remark may be thoughtless, mechanical, unthinking, unthoughtful), typically involves a *commitment*. One might compare it to playing a card in a game of cards. One must be prepared to defend what one says, to explain it, act on it in appropriate circumstances, take credit or incur debit for it, stand by it, and so on. One might say that to express one's thoughts, to say what one thinks, cannot be a description, report, or communication of an inner process or activity, because no such description of an inner process or activity could have the consequences in the language-game of the expression of thought.

Turning now to the second set of considerations, one should challenge the supposition that one thinks *in* anything, for it is highly misleading (cf. LPP 247f.). One speaks in a language, but does one think in a

[5] Some philosophers would argue that introspection, though a kind of 'inner' perception, is nevertheless infallible. But this purchases immunity to the above objection at the price of a mystery; for how can it be that a faculty of knowledge is guaranteed against error? See 'Privacy', §3, and 'The inner and the outer', §2.

language? Is the parallelism between speech and thought that simple? If I speak thoughtfully in English, am I at the same time thinking in English *in addition* to speaking? Enough has been said to make it obvious that this is erroneous. Of course, I may talk to myself *in foro interno* in English or in German. But, in the first place, not all 'talking inwardly' is thinking: reciting the multiplication-tables, going over one's speech in one's imagination to make sure that one knows it by heart, and 'counting sheep' in order to stop one from thinking and so to induce sleep are not. In the second place, one should note how peculiar and particular is the very notion of talking to oneself in the imagination. Talking audibly and talking in the imagination are no more two different ways of doing the same thing than experimenting in the laboratory and experimenting in one's imagination are two different ways of doing the same thing (cf. RPP I §574; PI §265). Reflect on the fact that we do not say 'After I said that to myself, I didn't talk to myself again for the rest of the day' or 'I am tired of listening to myself talking to myself', etc. We are inclined to think that talking in whispers stands to talking to oneself *in foro interno* as talking loudly stands to talking quietly, but this comparison is wrong. The last member of the series 'shouting, talking loudly, talking quietly, whispering' is 'moving one's lips silently', not 'talking to oneself in the imagination', let alone 'thinking'.[6] To be sure there *is* a close relationship between 'saying inwardly' and 'saying' (as there is between 'calculating in one's head' and 'calculating'). But it is not to be explained by saying that the 'inner' is just the same as the 'outer', only hidden from view (PI p. 220). It is manifest, rather, in the possibility of telling someone what one was saying to oneself (and that is *not* akin to relating a soliloquy one overheard!) and also in the outward actions that often accompany inward speech (e.g. I may sing inwardly and beat time with my hand).

Of course, one does say 'I can speak in German, but I can't think in German', signifying thereby that before I can say something in German, I must, by and large, first decide what I want to say and be *able* to say it in English, and then struggle to find the German words. But it does not follow that it makes sense to say of a native English speaker that he thinks *in* English, unless that just means that when he talks in his imagination what he thus says is in English (i.e. the answer to 'What were you saying to yourself?' is, e.g., 'I came, I saw, I conquered', not 'Veni, vidi, vici'). One may indeed say of an Englishman that he speaks German so well that he even *thinks* in German, but that just means that he *does not* first think of what he wants to say and then pause to try to think of the German word for such-and-such. Although it is in general true that the capacity for thought is bound up with the capacity to manipulate symbols, this is not

---

[6] Interestingly, Watson fell into this trap (see 'Behaviour and behaviourism', §1, and Exg. §330).

because unexpressed thoughts must be *in* a language, but rather because the *expression* of thoughts in speech must be. It is highly misleading to suggest that one thinks *in* anything, although it is both true and important that whatever one thinks must be *expressible* in words, images, or whatever.[7] We are doubtless deceived by the analogy between an English speaker hunting for the right German word in order to say such-and-such and an English speaker hunting for the right word in his own language to express his thought. But the analogy is deceptive; for in the first case he can *say*, in English, what he thinks, but in the second he cannot. And this is *not* because he has thought *in* images or 'non-linguistic symbols' and has not found the right translation, so that he, so to speak, knows what he thinks and is now looking for the words to express his subjectively perspicuous thought (cf. RPP II §565; PI §§335f.). 'The word is on the tip of my tongue' just means that the right word escapes me for the moment, but that I hope to find it soon (PI p. 219) and am on the verge of producing it. Similarly, 'I know exactly what I want to say, but I can't think of the words' is either nonsense or just means 'Give me another moment for the thought to crystallize and then I'll tell you what I think'.[8]

The third group of considerations ((iii) above) is equally confused. We do indeed speak of the lightning speed of thought, but this is a metaphor. One cannot literally *measure* the speed of thinking a thought, but only how long it takes someone to reach a conclusion (or a determinate phase of an argument) on a given occasion. Thoughts, like propositions, but unlike loaves of bread, do not come in slices; hence one cannot say 'Now he has thought half the thought, now two-thirds of it; now he has almost finished' (cf. PI §§318f.; PG 39). To say that thinking in a flash is the same as speaking with thought only very much faster is confused. The flashing of a thought, the sudden insight, is manifest in the exclamation 'Now I have it', followed by an expression of the thought or delineation of a scheme (PI p. 176). But 'Now I have it' is a jolt or glad start of sudden understanding. Though we say 'It flashed through my mind', we hardly ever ask 'How did it flash through your mind, what was it like?' (RPP I §239). What went on, if anything, is irrelevant to the thought's having flashed through your mind; what we are interested in is what you can now do, what conclusion you have reached in a flash. One should compare seeing or understanding a complex thought or plan in a flash not to running through it verbally at high speed, but rather to jotting down the whole theme of a lecture in a few key words: they are an epitome of those ideas in as much as I *can* run through the whole lecture on the basis of those jottings (PI §319).

[7] This point was further developed by Ryle in his essays on thinking.
[8] Searching for the right expression is *not* comparable to the efforts of someone who is trying to make an exact copy of a line which only he can see (RPP I §580).

It is perfectly correct to say that one typically knows what one is going to say before one says it. But one must not be misled by this turn of phrase. It does not imply that one has already said what one wants to say to oneself *in foro interno*. Nor does it imply that it *always* makes sense to ask 'How *long* before you said such-and-such did you know what you were going to say?' Rather, what it means is that when someone is interrupted, he can normally continue; and if he cannot, he says 'I've forgotten', not 'How should I know what words were going to follow?' Knowing what one was going to say is of a piece with knowing, being able to say, what one intended. One is no more surprised at what one ordinarily says than at what one normally does. And the intention to say such-and-such, like the intention to do such-and-such, does not 'contain' a model of what it is an intention of, from which one might read off what one meant (RPP I §§173ff.; Z §§1f.).

Equally, we do remark 'What you really wanted to say was . . . '; but that is not a guess at what he said to himself inwardly and failed to articulate overtly. Rather, this form of words is used to lead him (with his consent) to something *else*, which coheres in certain ways with the context and antecedent utterances, and so forth (cf. Exg. §334). It resembles certain uses of 'What you *really* want is . . . ', where it had never crossed one's mind that that was what one wanted, but which, once mentioned, crystallizes the will. Similarly, 'Think before you speak!' is not like 'Wash before you eat!' but more akin to 'Pause before you jump!' or 'Don't speak precipitously!' It is not an invitation to engage in an activity, but, e.g., *to take such-and-such factors into account* in one's reply.

The dual-procession conception of thinking is a mythology of the mind based on multiple misunderstandings. It exemplifies how, when doing philosophy, we misinterpret the very expressions we use comfortably in our daily transactions, 'like savages, primitive people, who hear the expressions of civilized men, put a false interpretation on them, and then draw the queerest conclusions from it' (PI §196). We are taken in by pictures embedded in language because we do not scrutinize their *use*.

The use of the word 'thinking' serves much more specialized purposes than its form suggests (RPP II §234). One must reflect on what role 'to think' has in characterizing people ('Yon Cassius has a lean and hungry look; he thinks too much: such men are dangerous'); what follows from the fact that when such-and-such occurred, I was thinking or musing; what are the implications of saying something with thought, as opposed to saying it mechanically (e.g. that I take responsibility for it, explain why I said it, justify my thinking thus as well as my saying what I think). If someone reads something with thought, i.e. attentively, then he may be impressed by it, he can say what he has read (Z §91), evaluate or criticize it, develop it further, and so forth. Someone who engages in a certain activity with thought (as opposed to doing it automatically) *considers* alternatives, makes choices, expects certain consequences, and so on (RPP I §§560ff.). The expression 'to think' is used as a very special sort of signal or indicator of antecedents and consequences, as well as of aspects or modes of speech and action, rather than to report on parallel covert activities or processes. And that, of course, is why *whether someone thought* on a given occasion is often determined by what comes before or after. Hence too it is only in very special circumstances that one can say that something was done without thinking (Z §95).[9] If thinking were an inner accompaniment of animated speaking, for example, then it would be intelligible that a highly animated, sophisticated conversation take place, only without any thinking. But this is not intelligible (Z §93; RPP II §238), not because it contradicts all our experience of human beings and their conversational capacities, but rather because what did or did not go on *in foro interno* is of no interest and has no bearing on whether the participants were thinking.

3. *Thought, language, and the mastery of linguistic skills*

It is tempting to wonder whether one can think without language. Indeed this question is a natural foil to the dual-process conception of speaking with thought or understanding, for one wants to get *behind* language in order to find what 'gives language life'. In connection with this confusing question, we harbour various conflicting pictures. On the one hand, we entertain the idea of wordless thoughts flashing across the mind in an instant; we suppose the play of images to constitute thinking; and we wonder whether, or fondly assume that, animals, especially our own pets, think even though they cannot speak. So we are inclined to advocate the intelligibility of thought without language. On the other hand, we are captivated by the venerable picture of thinking as the discourse of the soul with itself. For thought must be articulate; one must be able to distinguish the thought that *p* from the thought that *q*, even if one does not *say* what one thinks. And hence it seems that thinking that *p* must involve saying it *to oneself*. Therefore we are disposed to contend that only one who can talk, at least *in foro interno*, can think. Both pictures are given apparent support by scientific theorizing. On the one hand, psychologists try to collect evidence of 'wordless thought' by asking people to describe what happens when they think, and take their answers as evidence about the medium and process of thinking. On the other hand, theoretical linguists and 'cognitive scientists' argue that there must be an *innate* language of thought if human beings are to be able to learn a natural language.

[9] There is a parallel here with pretending.

Both pictures induce a conception of speech as a translation or encoding of thoughts. Hence we suppose, in conformity with tradition,[10] that given that we cannot directly transfer our thoughts to the mind of another, we translate our 'inner thoughts' into a natural language as an *indirect* means of communicating them. This confusion dovetails neatly with another, which turns on a muddle over the identity of thoughts (see 'Privacy', §2). According to one picture, successful communication consists in conveying to the hearer the thought that is in the mind of the speaker. Here the thought is conceived as an ethereal object and the sentence uttered as its vehicle, which will transport it from speaker to hearer. According to a different picture, the sentence is akin to a potion which will generate in the mind of another not the identical, but an exactly similar, thought to the thought in the mind of the speaker. These knots will be disentangled later.

The original question 'Can one think without language?' is doubtless as confused as the dogmatic answers 'All thinking is in language' and 'There is non-verbal thought'. As a first step towards clarifying matters we must side-step the original question, approaching it only indirectly by way of a different one: viz. whether the capacity to think is logically bound up with having mastered a language. This indirect approach will prove more fruitful than a direct strategy. William James cited the Ballard case as empirical proof that one can think even though one has not mastered a natural language and cannot speak one. Wittgenstein challenged the intelligibility of the story (PI §342 and Exg.). Given that the young Ballard could not speak any language, what would have *counted* as an expression of his alleged pre-linguistic thoughts about God and creation? If nothing in his behavioural repertoire would so count, then what would be the *criterion* for his having thought that *p* rather than that *q*, or indeed his not having thought anything at all? In the normal case the criteria for whether someone thinks such-and-such include his avowing this, i.e. his *expressing* what he thinks. And it makes sense to attribute unexpressed thoughts to a person only in as much as the possibility of his expressing them is intelligible. The question of how he *knows* that he thinks such-and-such cannot arise, for it is nonsensical, as is the question of whether he is certain or has doubts as to whether he thinks that *p* or that *q*.[11] But if, as in the Ballard case, we cut out the possibility of any behavioural expression of thoughts (viz. in avowals that *this* is what one is thinking), then doubts break out in respect of his memory-claim in later years. How could Ballard be sure that he had

---

[10] Cf., e.g. Hobbes, *Leviathan*, Ch. IV; Arnauld, *The Art of Thinking*, Introduction; Locke, *Essay Concerning Human Understanding*, Bk. III, Ch. i, Sect. 2; I. Watts, *Logick or the Right Use of Reason*, Pt. I, Ch. iv, Sect. 1. These confusions are equally evident in Frege (see FA §60; PW 105, 142, 269f.), Russell (AM, Ch. XI), and their current heirs.

[11] We are concerned here with ignorance, not indecision.

correctly translated those 'wordless thoughts' of his childhood into words? The question is absurd; but it points to something vital, viz. that with the abrogation of the normal language-game with the avowal of thoughts, we need a criterion of identity for what a Ballard might have thought, *and so does he*.[12] Since there is none, the question of how Ballard knows that that was what he thought, of whether he is sure that he has correctly translated his wordless thoughts, *does* arise – and can have no answer! And that shows not that he may be mistaken, but that the story is incoherent.

One might object to the drift of Wittgenstein's reflections. Do we not say of animals that they think? And yet they do not speak! But we must distinguish. For, first, we simply do not say of amoebas, crabs, or fish that they think, any more than we say it of chairs or tables. One would not know what it would be for a chair or a table to think, or even a fish (Z §129; PI §361); and this is not due to ignorance of fact or to epistemic qualms. Secondly, we must distinguish between thinking (opining, believing) that *p* and thinking (reflecting or pondering), e.g. thinking something over, thinking up a solution, thinking whether things are thus or not, or whether one ought to act in a certain way. In the former use, we do sometimes say of the higher animals that they think such-and-such (e.g. that a dog, hearing its leash being take off the peg, thinks it is going to be taken for a walk) – but only where their behavioural repertoire is sufficiently rich for something to *count* as an expression of such-and-such a thought or belief (e.g. the dog's joyful prancing at the door). This might be called 'primitive thought', describable via primitive *behaviour*, not via a 'thinking accompaniment of behaviour' (cf. Z §99); but the possibilities are very limited, as limited as the behavioural repertoire. Similar considerations apply to the second use: we do say, e.g. of Köhler's apes, that they found the solution to the problem of reaching the bananas – but only because their having solved the problem is expressed in their behaviour. (Note, however, that in Ballard's case *nothing* would count as behaviour expressing the fact that he thought that God created the universe, and furthermore that nothing would count as his thinking *about* or pondering on God and the origins of life.) Nevertheless, we hardly ever predicate 'is thinking' of any animal other than ourselves (Z §129). We do not say that, for all we know, dogs talk to themselves *in foro interno*, precisely because dogs do not talk; we only say of a creature that it talks to itself in the imagination if it is a creature that *can* talk (MS. 165, 200f.). For the criteria for someone's talking to himself thus consist in what he *says* when asked or when relating a certain

---

[12] A remark on thoughts in the spirit of *Investigations* §288. Note that this point is *not* *epistemological*, but logical. The question at stake is not 'How do we know?' but rather 'What counts as having such a thought?'

episode (cf. PI §376). Similarly, with rare exceptions, we do not say of an animal that it is thinking something over, thinking up a plan or project, or even just thinking about something. Köhler's apes could be seen as a limiting case (RPP II §224; RPP I §561), where we can discern a pale anticipation of *considering*, a glimmer of reflecting on options, even though the creatures have not mastered a language.

These arguments may impel us into the converse fallacy, viz. that if, with the exception of the above kinds of limiting cases, only a language-user can be said to think, then thinking must be inward speaking. But we have already shown that idea to be incoherent. One must not confuse the necessary capacity for the (outer) expression of thought with the actuality of inner vocalization. Mechanical 'inner' speaking is no more thoughtful than mechanical 'outer' speaking; moreover, one can think up, think about, reach the conclusion that something or other is the case without talking to oneself in the imagination at all. One may be inclined at this point to suggest that such 'wordless thoughts' are thought in images, for they must surely be *in* something! But that is just as confused. One does not think *in* images at all, although when one is thinking of something or about something, images may cross one's mind, and in certain cases conjuring up a mental image of *X* may serve a heuristic purpose (e.g. when solving problems in geometry). But having an image of *X* before one's mind is not thinking *in images* in the sense in which one speaks *in English*; 'thinking in images', like 'thinking in English', is not on the same level as *speaking in* a language. The words one utters when one speaks are the *expression* of one's thought; the images one may conjure up while thinking are *not* an expression of one's thought but an aid to thought or an accompaniment of thought.

There is, however, a deeper objection to the idea that thinking, taken in a wide sense, is inward speaking (as opposed to being occasionally accompanied by inner speaking): viz. that if it were so, then a report of thinking could not mention what or whom was *meant* (RPP I §180). For it is an essential feature of the linguistic expression of thought that the user of the linguistic sign can say whom he meant (e.g. by the sign 'N' in the sentence 'ϕN' or what he meant (by 'ϕN'). Of any sign one uses, it is always possible when the sign has been specified to raise the question of what one meant thereby (if anything). However, if thinking *were* just inner speaking, then a report of what one thought *would leave out what one meant*. All it could do would be to adduce further *signs*. But that is absurd, for there is no difference here between thinking that *p* and meaning that *p*. One can say of an expression one has used that 'By "N" I mean *this*', but one cannot say of a 'thought-constituent' 'By "N" I mean *this*'. For then it would not be a language of *thought* at all, but would have to be 'thought out' like any other symbolism. Signs have a use (and misuse). But thinking of something, thinking that things are thus-and-so, meaning or intending such-and-such *in foro interno*, is not a use of signs, even though it typically presupposes the mastery of the use of signs that would express what one thinks, means, or intends.

> The point is that one has to read off from a thought that it is the thought that such-and-such is the case. If one can't read it off (as one can't read off the cause of a stomach-ache) then it is of no logical interest. . . .
> If a thought is observed there can be no further question of an understanding: for if the thought is seen it must be recognized as a thought with a certain content; it does not need to be interpreted! – That really is how it is; when we are thinking, there isn't any interpretation going on. (PG 144f.)

Hence if one supposes the meaning, the thinking, to be a process accompanying the saying, and conceives of it as couched 'in the language of thought', i.e. as a further *sign*, one generates a dilemma. Either the meaning, the sentence-in-thought, can be interpreted, and the question of what one *meant* ('in thought') can, absurdly, arise; or, the meaning cannot be interpreted, and the question of what one meant (thought) cannot, absurdly, be answered (BB 34f.; PG 144ff.)!

To put the same point differently: the idea that I *interpret* my thought that ϕN as being a thought about N, is absurd. The thought is 'the last interpretation', it 'reaches right up to reality' (does not fall short of it). But the price one must pay for this is that thinking is *not* 'having representations' *in* a symbolism of any kind. And if thinking *is*, as some philosophers suppose, a matter of having 'internal representations', the question of what one means by such-and-such an internal representation must, absurdly, arise *in one's own case*.[13] Hence the contention that 'All thinking is *in* language', no less than 'There is wordless thought', is deeply confused.

These confusions can be made to disappear only when one abandons the conception of thinking (or meaning something) as an inner process or activity of any kind.

> If I try to describe the process of intention, I feel first and foremost that it can do what it is supposed to do only by containing an extremely faithful picture of what it intends. But further, that that too does not go far enough, because a picture, whatever it may be, can be variously interpreted; hence this picture too in its turn stands isolated. When one has the picture in view by itself it is suddenly dead, and it is as if something had been taken away from it, which had given it life before. It is not a thought, not an intention; whatever accompaniments we imagine for it, articulate or inarticulate processes, or any feeling whatsoever, it remains isolated, it does not point outside itself to a reality beyond.
> . . . We want to say 'Meaning is surely essentially a mental process, a process of consciousness and life, not of dead matter.' But what will give such a thing the

---

[13] This argument pin-points a fatal incoherence in contemporary speculation in cognitive psychology. Further investigation, however, would be out of place in this context.

specific character of what goes on? – so long as we speak of it as a process. . . . It could be said: we should call any process 'dead' in this sense. (PG 148)

Although *mastery* of a language is by and large a prerequisite of thinking, since what one can think is co-extensive with what one can express (although not necessarily only verbally), it does not follow that thinking is speaking to oneself in the imagination. And it does not follow from the latter point that 'wordless thought' is 'in' pictures or images.

Once these absurdities are dispelled, one can see how the classical pictures of communication by means of language are based on multiple misunderstandings. Both the 'vehicle' model, viz. that I convey the thought I have in mind to others by means of an uttered sentence that is its linguistic *vehicle*, and the causative or 'potion' model, that the sentence uttered *induces* in the hearer the same (exactly similar) thought that is in the mind of the speaker, conceive of speech as the *indirect* communication of thoughts in default of a direct means of apprehending or grasping the thought in question. It only makes sense to talk of communicating something indirectly if it also makes sense to talk of communicating it directly. The classical pictures labour under the misconception that I apprehend the thought I am thinking 'immediately', and that I could only communicate it directly to someone else by letting him 'see' what is in my mind. Since this is impossible, one must make do with indirect communication of thoughts. But this is a muddle. For, first, even if the hearer could look into my head or, *per impossibile*, into my mind, he would not discern there what I was thinking, i.e. what I *meant* (cf. PI p. 217). Secondly, the pictures confusedly suppose that the thoughts are *in* my head, and that communicating consists in transporting them to or generating them in your head. (The causative model is vividly, pictorially, manifest in de Saussure's famous 'speech circuit' diagram.[14]) But what I think, the thought I entertain, is no more *in* my head than the fact that makes what I think true is *in* the world. Is the thought in my *mind*? One may say that – although, for more reasons than one, it is highly misleading. But 'This is what I have in mind' or 'I have a thought in mind' are just ways of saying 'This is what I think' or 'I have thought of something'. Hence to conceive of communication as the transference of thoughts from my brain or mind to yours is a muddle. If I send you a letter, the letter which was in my possession will then be in yours, but I do not thereby lose the thoughts I expressed in the letter (unless I forget what I said). Communicating or expressing thoughts is not transferring or transporting objects of any kind. Thirdly, the alternative picture is no less confused. The causative model implicitly assumes that the thought allegedly generated in your mind by my utterance is not identical with

[14] F. de Saussure, *Course in General Linguistics*, tr. R. Harris (Duckworth, London, 1983), p. 11.

the thought in my mind, but only exactly the same, just as we are inclined to think that your headache cannot be identical with mine but only exactly the same (cf. PI §§253f.).[15] But this misguidedly projects onto thoughts a distinction between being identical and being exactly similar, which has application paradigmatically to material objects (see 'Privacy', §2). If I think that *p*, and you think that *p*, then we do indeed think the same (and not a 'just exactly similar' *or* a 'numerically identical') thought. Fourthly, for someone to understand what I say when I tell him what I think, it is not necessary that he should think what I think, 'have the same thought' as I, but only that he should *know* what I think (and said). It must be possible for him to *express* that thought, i.e. to say what *I* think; but it is not necessary that he should have or think it. The *pictures* underlying the concept of communication, viz. the pictures of *conveying* or *producing* thoughts, are deeply misleading. Finally, we can indeed distinguish various ways of communicating thoughts indirectly. We might call writing a letter 'indirect' by contrast with talking to the recipient; or we might contrast overtly telling someone something with communicating that message to him by a wink or a gesture; or we might contrast telling him something by word or letter with getting someone else to pass the message on to him. But in none of these cases is speaking to him conceived as *indirect* communication; there is no *more* direct way of letting someone know what one thinks than telling him!

4. *Making a radical break*

The pictures of thinking, of speaking with thought, of communicating our thoughts, mislead us in numerous ways when we are doing philosophy. One deep root of our troubles lies in a supposition which Wittgenstein criticized in the context of his discussion of the name/object model as misapplied to the concept of pain and its relation to pain-behaviour (PI §304). For of thinking too we might say that our paradoxes and bewilderment will only disappear 'if we make a radical break with the idea that language always functions in one way, always

---

[15] James writes:

. . . no one of them [thoughts] is separate, but each belongs with certain others and with none beside. My thought belongs with my other thoughts, and your thought with your other thoughts . . . each of these minds keeps its own thoughts to itself. There is no giving or bartering between them. No thought even comes into direct *sight* of a thought in another personal consciousness than its own. Absolute insulation, incredible pluralism, is the law. *Principles of Psychology*, Vol. I, pp. 225f.)

It was in response to such a muddle that Frege fell into the converse confusion of reifying thoughts (propositions, what we think) in order to ensure that different people can think the *numerically* identical thought.

serves the same purpose: to convey thoughts – which may be about houses, pains, good and evil, or anything else you please' (PI §304). This idea not only plays havoc with our endeavour to see utterances (*Äusserungen*) aright (not to mention ethical judgements); it also distorts our view of the very phenomenon from which it is derived, viz. the expression of thought. 'As if the purpose of the proposition were to convey to one person how it is with another: only, so to speak, in his thinking part and not in his stomach' (PI §317(b)). Numerous sentences we utter express a thought. But it does not follow that uttering such sentences is the outward manifestation of the inner state, process, or activity of thinking as a cry of pain is the outer manifestation of physical suffering (PI §317(a)). In saying '*p*', I may, *in certain contexts*, be expressing a thought; but it does not follow that I am communicating a thought that is 'in me', a thought that I am thinking or have in mind. We must remind ourselves how specialized is the language-game of saying what we think, of communicating our thoughts, of telling them to others.

You regard it much too much as a matter of course that one can tell (*mitteilen*) anything to anyone. That is to say: we are so much accustomed to communication (*Mitteilung*) through language, in conversation, that it looks to us as if the whole point of communication lay in this: someone else grasps the sense of my words – which is something mental: he as it were takes it into his own mind. If he then does something further with it as well, that is no part of the immediate purpose of language. (PI §363(b))

We are misled by the use of 'a thought' and 'to express a thought' into a too facile, smooth, and simple conception of the grammar of these expressions (RPP I §554). We say that a sentence 'S' expresses the thought that *p*, as we say that the sentence expresses the proposition that *p*. But it does not follow from the fact that a person uttered the sentence 'S' that he thought that *p* and expressed his thought in words in order to communicate his thought to his hearer. The phrase 'to express a thought', when applied to a person, has a quite particular grammar, which is abused when we take it for granted that every utterance of a sentence that can be said to express a thought (or proposition) involves the speaker's expressing his thought. (And something similar applies to the phrases 'to express a proposition' and 'to formulate a proposition'.[16]) So, for example, it would in most contexts be wholly misleading to suggest that one is expressing one's thoughts, saying what one thinks, or telling someone what one thinks, when one utters such sentences as 'Yes,

---

[16] For example, though one might say that the antecedent phrase of a conditional sentence 'If *p*, then *q*,' expresses the proposition that *p*, it would be quite wrong to say of someone who asserted the conditional (or asserted that not-*p*) that he expressed the proposition that *p*.

I'll go, 'I saw him yesterday', 'Then she burst into tears', 'No, I didn't', 'Really, how interesting!', 'It's the second on the left', 'I can see John over there', 'It's two o'clock', and so on. Even if we do wish to say that declarative sentences typically express thoughts or propositions (though not necessarily what the speaker is thinking), we are prone to be duped by failure to note the diversity of propositions and their functions. A *fortiori* the utterance of sentences expressing propositions does not have as its core, uniform function the conveying of the speaker's thoughts. It would be misleading to suggest that my saying 'But 25^2 is not 624' is an *expression* of my thinking (or of my thought) that 25^2 is not 624 (although I do think that 25^2 is not 624); rather, it is an expression of my thinking that you have made a mistake. The focal range of the phrase 'to express one's thoughts' is in the area of expressing one's opinions, reflections, and ruminations, in answering the question 'What do you think about this?' or 'What were you thinking just then?' It is in such contexts that we tell others what we think, express or confess our thoughts on this or that. These are very special moves in a language-game, and they call forth very particular kinds of response, e.g. agreement or disagreement, interest or amusement, admiration or disappointment. But reports, announcements, expressions of intent, declarations, repudiations, etc. are not, in that sense, expressions of thoughts. Romeo's passionate declarations of love communicate to Juliet not his *thoughts* but his passion; a war correspondent's reports from the front communicate to his readers what he has witnessed, what has happened, and only incidentally what he thinks about it.

Making a radical break with the idea that language always functions to convey thoughts enables us to recognize a familiar landscape distorted in our minds by misleading pictures. By reminding ourselves of the way such expressions as 'a thought', 'to have a thought', 'a thought's occurring to one', or 'a thought's crossing one's mind' are used, we can shake ourselves free of the philosophical illusions that pervade traditional reflections on this subject. By attending carefully to the use of 'thinking', 'confessing one's thoughts', 'telling someone what one thinks', and 'expressing (or communicating) one's thoughts', one will be liberated from the beguiling fallacies that beset one in this domain of philosophy.

X

IMAGES AND THE IMAGINATION

1. Landmarks

The family of concepts constituted by 'imagine' and such cognates as 'imaginary', 'image', 'imaginative', 'imaginable' is difficult to survey. Their contours merge imperceptibly here and there with those of the adjacent psychological concepts of thought and conception, perception and illusion, creativity and invention. The application of the concepts of the imagination is, like that of many other psychological concepts (e.g. understanding, thinking, feeling), heterogeneous. The natural philosophical impulse towards generalization and imposition of unity upon diversity, however, drives us to raise such questions as 'What is the hallmark of the imagination?', 'What does imagining consist in?', 'What is the process of imagining?' These questions invite oversimplification and mystification, and lead us astray from the very start.

Striving to find a simple characterization of the essence of the imagination, philosophers have argued that it consists in the power to call up before the mind mental images, either in recollection and recognition (the reproductive imagination) or in fancy (the productive imagination). These images, sometimes thought to be or to be constructed from faint copies of perceptual impressions, are (mysteriously) deposited in cold storage in the mind, the 'storehouse of ideas' as Locke put it. In more modern vein, it has been argued that imagining consists in the production and combination of 'mental representations', or that the raw material of all imaginings consists of 'reproductions' of visual, auditory, tactual, etc. experiences that one has previously had. It is then tempting to think that such 'mental representations' or images constitute private objects of comparison that guide us in our use of words.

Approaching the philosophical – i.e. conceptual (grammatical) – questions about the imagination from this vantage-point obscures one's view of the manifold facets of the imagination and leads to multiple distortions and oversimplifications. First, one will be prone to overlook grammatical facts. Many licit uses of 'imagine' fail to conform to the conception of the imagination as a kaleidoscopic faculty for combining images or 'representations'. That Columbus imagined he had reached the Indies does not imply that he had any mental images or representations of the Indies. That I can well imagine flying to New York does not mean that I must have flown there or elsewhere before or that I see myself in my mind's eye in a 747. That I can imagine N's delight (disappointment, surprise, embarrassment) at such-and-such news does not mean the same as being able vividly to imagine N's look of delight (etc.). It makes perfectly good sense to imagine much which it makes scant sense to picture to oneself, e.g. Queen Victoria's last thoughts, traditional virtues ceasing to be valued, new philosophical questions or confusions. Awareness of this typically leads philosophers to claim that there are multiple different senses of 'to imagine'. For to believe falsely (as Columbus did) is not an exercise of the faculty of the imagination, and the creative exercise of the imagination does not necessarily involve any mental imagery. The tie-up between *image*, *imagine*, and *imagination* is doubtless complex, although it is not obvious that one must conclude that there are many different concepts of imagining.

Secondly, philosophers are also prone to delineate the limits of the imagination in ways that are highly questionable. One cannot, it is sometimes argued, imagine something which one has not experienced or which is not decomposable into what one has experienced.[1] After all, it is *rightly* said, the congenitally blind cannot imagine the appearance of a bowl of flowers and the congenitally deaf cannot imagine the sound of a symphony. But must one explain this by reference to the supposition that their storehouse of ideas or neural repository of mental representations is inadequately equipped? Similarly, it has been argued that since the building-blocks of the imagination are experiences or their 'copies', nobody can imagine anything which does not essentially involve his experiencing something (e.g. being dead or asleep). Such suggestions arguably draw the limits of the imagination too narrowly. (It is improbable that Richard III could not have imagined being murdered in his sleep; but if it is true, it would have been due to lack of imagination, not to *logic*!) On the other hand, to claim that one can imagine being Napoleon or a bat arguably draws the boundaries too generously. I may be able to imagine what Napoleon thought or felt, and if I can do so, I may be able to *act* the role of Napoleon (like Charles Boyer) all the better. We also say, quite unproblematically, 'The disposition of forces at 11.30 a.m. at Waterloo was thus. Now, imagine you are Napoleon! What would you do?' Here one is invited to reflect on what one would do when faced by the options and predicaments that confronted Napoleon. But, this usage apart, is there anything else that can be understood by the order 'Imagine you were Napoleon (or a bat)!' What would it be for me to be Napoleon? If it does not make *sense* for *me* to be Napoleon (or a bat), does it make sense to imagine it? Is this any less absurd than imagining my clock's being a symphony, as opposed to its being a Tompion? For if it does not make sense, then there is nothing to imagine! Yet some people actually think, or believe, that they are Napoleon. Of course – but they are *mad*. Some lunatics think that they are pens (as in

---

[1] For Wittgenstein's ironic response to this conception, see Exg. §289, 2.

Peer Gynt). Is it so obvious that we understand what it is that they think? One might object that one can surely imagine what does not make sense – witness Lewis Carroll or much of science fiction! These are indeed nonsense. But there is nonsense and nonsense, some of it very entertaining. So one might say that to the extent that nonsense can be understood, to that extent it can be imagined.

Thirdly, and consequently, the boundary-lines between empirical and conceptual investigations are characteristically blurred. Investigations into the limits of the imaginable begin to look misleadingly like a curious kind of physics of the mind. One *cannot* imagine such-and-such, it is held, *because* one has not experienced anything like it, or *because* the building-blocks of the imagination are images, ideas, or representations. But one should query what this 'cannot' signifies. Are such claims meant to be empirical? Surely not, for then it would be at any rate logically possible, conceivable (imaginable?), that things be otherwise. Are they then non-empirical claims? If so, whence their necessitarian status? To attribute these alleged constraints to the 'essential nature of the mind' is to reproduce the very question in the guise of an answer. Whatever conceptual constraints there are upon the imagination are *conceptual* constraints, i.e. constraints laid down in our norms of representation, in what it makes *sense* to say and what it does *not* make sense to say. The conceptual limits of the imagination are the contour-lines, whether sharp or blurred, of the *grammar* of 'image', of the combinatorial possibilities of 'imagine' and its cognates which have a use in our language and for which we acknowledge certain explanations as correct explanations of meaning the giving of which constitute criteria of understanding.

Finally, we are prone to introduce questions about meaning in the form of questions about existence. There are heated debates among philosophers and psychologists alike over whether there really are such things as mental images, some insisting that there are, since they actually have them, others denying this, since 'introspection' in their own case reveals none. It is often held to be a simple fact of experience that certain people have mental images and others do not. But what is it the existence of which is being affirmed or denied? Does it make sense for psychologists to seek experimental confirmation for the existence of mental imagery in psychological laboratory tests? Should mental images be treated as theoretical constructs which must be 'postulated' as information-bearing structures, or 'data-structures', in the brain the existence of which would explain human behaviour? The dispute is not unlike classical debates over the existence of universals or continuing disputes over whether colours 'exist objectively'. The first question is not whether mental images exist, but rather what it means to say that someone has a vivid mental image of such-and-such and what the criteria are for having a mental image of something. Only when we have clarified what it would be for someone to have a mental image of something can we turn to the question of whether anyone does. And it might be hoped that the clarification of the first question will render the second as trivial as the question of whether any objects have shapes (or, for that matter, colours!).

The correct path through this morass was indicated by Wittgenstein:

> One ought to ask, not what images are or what happens when one imagines anything, but how the word 'imagination' is used. But that does not mean that I want to talk only about words. For the question as to the nature of the imagination is as much about the word 'imagination' as my question is. And I am only saying that this question is not to be decided, neither for the person who does the imagining, nor for anyone else – by pointing; nor yet by a description of any process. The first question also asks for a word to be explained; but it makes us expect a wrong kind of answer. (PI §370)

This is the route that will be followed in this essay. Before turning to the salient themes that preoccupied Wittgenstein, however, it is worth plotting some of the landmarks in the (English) terrain as a background against which to examine his observations. For not only is it difficult to 'look and see' how 'imagine' is used, especially if one thinks that one already has a clear picture of such a 'trivial' matter, but the temptation to tamper with the linguistic facts, the rules of grammar, is great:

> Mere description is so difficult because one believes that one needs to fill out the facts in order to understand them. It is as if one saw a screen with scattered colour-patches, and said: the way they are here, they are unintelligible; they only make sense when one completes them into a shape. – Whereas I want to say: Here *is* the whole. (If you complete it, you falsify it.) (RPP I §257)

The half-a-dozen foci of attention in this discussion are not the ground floor of a theory of the imagination, but rather poles of a description of grammar (cf. RPP I §633). One feature or aspect of the use of 'imagine', 'imagination', etc. is not offered as an explanation or justification of another; but there are multiple connections between them, some of which will be described. It should be noted that the grammatical web of 'imagine' and its cognates differs from that of the German 'vorstellen'. Hence, when we turn, in the next section, to examine Wittgenstein's remarks on the imagination, some strands in the network, e.g. the connection between 'imagine' and 'imaginative', will not be in view.

First, the concept of imagination is associated with the concept of a mental image. We are all familiar with the phenomenon of a tune 'running through one's head', and we commonly use such phrases as 'I can still hear his tone of surprise', 'I can readily call her face to mind', or 'I can visualize exactly what it should look like'. Hence we talk of visual, and sometimes of auditory, images, which may be vivid and clear or faint and obscure. The expression 'mental image' is, however, philo-sophically misleading, for it is constructed on the model of 'physical image' (cf. LW §442), i.e. a perceptible likeness (whether manufactured or natural), representation, or imitation of an actual or imagined form. A 'graven image' is a statue or bas-relief; a painted image is a figure in a painting. We also speak of a reflected image of an object in a mirror, and metonymically scientists speak of a pattern of light irradiation as 'an image'. Similarly, we refer to a counterpart, facsimile, or copy as 'an image', as when we say that a son is the very image of his father or that man is made in the image of God. It is all too easy to think of a mental image as a species of the genus *image*, i.e. 'just like a physical image, only mental'. This is no more illuminating than referring to the square roots of negative integers as being just like real numbers, only imaginary. The use of 'mental image' is no more closely related to that of 'physical image' than is the use of 'number' to that of 'numeral' (cf. LW §442). It is similarly misguided to think, as Hume and many after him did, that a mental image is a faint *copy* of a sense-impression.

Secondly, imagination is connected in *various* ways with perception. Although the august role given to the imagination by Hume and Kant in their very different accounts of perception and perceptual recognition of objects is arguably a case of miscasting, it is indisputable that it takes imagination to see or hear certain kinds of resemblances, forms of connectedness, or patterns of relationships. It takes imagination, for example, to hear a piece of music as a variation on a particular theme (PI p. 213); or to see certain kinds of 'quotations' in paintings, e.g. Michelangelo's *Isaiah* in Reynolds's *Mrs Siddons as the Tragic Muse*; or to see Marcel Marceau's Bip skating and skipping on ice where there is no ice in view and no skates to see. Although we can vividly imagine things disconnected from the physical space around us, e.g. call to mind the face of a childhood love or conjure up a vivid image of a long-vanished scene, we can also imagine things essentially connected with what we currently perceive. Here Leonardo's famous advice to painters is an apt reminder:

> I cannot forbear to mention among these precepts a new device for study which, although it may seem but trivial and almost ludicrous, is nevertheless extremely useful in arousing the mind to various inventions. And this is, when you look at a wall spotted with various stains, or with a mixture of stones, if you have to devise some scene, you may discover a resemblance to various landscapes beautified with mountains, rivers, rocks, trees, plains, wide valleys and hills in varied arrangement; or, again you may see battles and figures in action; or strange faces and costumes, and an endless variety of objects, which you could reduce to complete and well-drawn forms. And these appear on such walls confusedly, like the sound of bells in whose jangle you may find any name or word you choose to imagine.[2]

---

[2] Leonardo de Vinci, *Trattato della Pittura*, §508.

When we engage in such exercises of fantasy, we *see* the stain marks on the wall as hills and valleys, the cracks perhaps as winding paths or rivers, the crumbling plaster maybe as figures in a landscape. Hence too, it should not be surprising to find Wittgenstein connecting the concept of imagination with the capacity to *see aspects*, to see the duck-rabbit now as a duck, now as a rabbit, or to see a triangular figure as an object that has fallen over (PI p. 207).

Thirdly, the faculty of imagination is associated with artistic creativity and no less so with intellectual creativity, with originality, insight, and deviation from stock solutions to problems. The great painter, architect, or landscape-gardener is credited with outstanding visual imagination. Though this may be connected with his power to visualize things vividly, note that it does not *follow* that before he produces his highly imaginative frescoes, buildings, or gardens, he *must* first have vivid visual images of what they should look like, let alone that he *copies* these. His powerful imagination is visible in the spontaneity, originality, etc., of his product, not invisible in his mind, and it is exercised in its production and not in what precedes it in his mind's eye. Still less does our correctly crediting a Shakespeare or a Tolstoy with extraordinary imaginative powers, an ability to visualize a scene vividly, involve necessarily attributing to them vivid mental imagery. The creation of great fiction or great poetry needs imagination, but the only imagery it *requires* is verbal. Telling a good story needs imagination, but one may make it up as one goes along, rather than rehearsing it in advance in the imagination. Even less essentially connected with images is the employment of imagination in the solution of purely intellectual problems, e.g. in mathematics or philosophy itself. The power of intellectual insight, the capacity to see or create fresh analogies and intermediate cases, to find illuminating connections between *prima facie* unconnected phenomena, all these are no less exercises of the imagination than the creations of fiction or the visual arts.

Fourthly, 'to imagine' is connected not only with intellectual creativity, but also more generally with thought, conception, or supposition. For short stretches the concepts of imagination run cheek by jowl with these adjacent concepts, even though they diverge elsewhere. A bridge of well-imagined construction is well-thought-out, just as Gilbert Scott's frequently ill-imagined additions to medieval buildings are ill-conceived. A mind so noble as to be unable to imagine things contemptible cannot conceive of acting dishonourably. The nexus of 'imagine' with supposition is evident in such sentences as 'He never imagined that he could surpass them all', 'The town was further away than he had imagined', 'One would imagine it impossible that any creature could survive an Arctic winter'. Of course, that such sentences, in an appropriate context, might be paraphrased in terms of 'suppose' ('guess' or 'suspect') does not show that the expressions are *everywhere* interchangeable. The imagination is a faculty, but there is no faculty for supposition, any more than there are powers or skills of supposition. From the fact that one cannot imagine something, it does not follow that one cannot suppose it. One can vividly imagine but not vividly suppose, and one can imagine but not suppose the consequences of a supposition.

Fifthly, 'to imagine' is associated with false belief, mistaken memory, and misperception. We may imagine ourselves half-way to our destination when we have barely covered a quarter of the distance. Suddenly, we may think we see a friend in the crowd, only to realize on closer scrutiny that we merely imagined this. And so too, we may claim to remember having done this or that or having seen or heard such and such, only to be told that we are imagining things. Note that someone given to false beliefs, to making erroneous memory-claims, or to misperception is *not* said to be exercising his powers of imagination or to have a rich imagination (save ironically!). Such propensity to false beliefs is not conceived to be a feature of the imagination *qua* faculty, since as a faculty the imagination is not primarily concerned with literal truth and falsehood, but with invention, originality, and creativity. Whence then this connection between 'to imagine' and the false? Perhaps via the notion of the imaginary or fictitious as that which has no 'real existence', or (misleadingly) that which exists 'only in the imagination'. Also by reference to the relation between the concept of imagining and the concepts of finding and making up. What we imagine we make up. We find truths, but we make up lies. Furthermore, what we imagine we often think to be as we imagine it. And if we are wrong, then we are said to be *merely* imagining things, i.e. misconceiving or falsely believing. But note that while the imaginary is unreal, the imagined need not be. For things may be just as I imagine them to be.

Finally, the imagination is connected with make-believe, pretence, play-acting, or idle fancy. The actor imagines the character he is playing feeling this or meaning that, and how he imagines the character informs his acting. The child who can play happily alone with only a few blocks of wood to do service for bricks and yet builds castles in the air, who can ride his rocking-horse in the company of King Arthur and his knights, who can make an armchair into the cockpit of a Spitfire, is rightly said to be imaginative. But note that this imaginativeness *need* not be connected with originality, creativity, or insight. However, although imagination can contribute to successful pretence, one may be good at imagining, yet poor at pretending, because lacking the knack for acting or deceit. And conversely, many a charlatan has a poor imagination. It is mistaken to conceive of imagining as a kind of pretending (as Ryle did); for pretending, unlike imagining, is necessarily a performance. One must engage in some activity or perform certain actions as a means of pretending. Someone who is good at pretending is a good actor, for he must typically so behave that things seem to be as he pretends they are. Skill at imagining is not a skill in acting but in conceiving or envisaging. One can pretend without for one moment imagining that things are as one pretends them to be; and when one imagines something, one does not normally engage in any pretence. Confidence tricksters pretend; artists, writers, and neurotics imagine. Pretending is often deceitful, sometimes convincing and difficult to see through. Imagining may be clear, correct, or accurate. One can make mistakes when one imagines how things are, since one can imagine that things are so-and-so and also think (rightly or wrongly) that they are. But one cannot pretend that things are so if one actually thinks they are.

Wittgenstein's interest in the imagination focused upon six interrelated themes: (a) the relationships between seeing, imagining, and having visual (mental) images (*Vorstellungsbilder*[3]); (b) the analogies and disanalogies between mental images and pictures; (c) the similarities and differences between mental images and sense-impressions, including hallucinations; (d) the 'voluntariness' of the imagination and the relationship between a mental image and what it is an image of; (e) the irrelevance of mental imagery to meaning and understanding utterances (see Exg. §§390–7); (f) the connection between the imagination, perception, and the seeing of aspects. The latter theme, dealt with in *Investigations*, Part II, is too extensive to be discussed here.[4]

2. Seeing, imagining, and mental images

'The tie-up between imagining (*Vorstellen*) and seeing is close; but there is no similarity' (RPP II §70). The concepts of sense-perception in general and of vision in particular are used in the *expression* of our imaginings; we say that we *hear* speech or melodies in our imagination and that we *see* the faces of distant friends when we call them up before the mind's eye (cf. RPP I §885[5]). But though perceptual concepts are used here, they are used *differently*. What is or can be perceived can also intelligibly be imagined, and can also be imagined as being perceived (though these are

---

[3] It should be noted that the German 'die Vorstellung', 'eine Vorstellung', or 'Vorstellungen' are not always readily translated into English (see Exg. §300, 1). A very large number of the remarks on the imagination in RPP I and II and LW (sometimes perhaps unavoidably) are mistranslated (e.g. RPP II §§64f., 69f., 72, 75, 77f., 80, 82f., 88, 93, 110f., 116, 119 – 21, 125, 130f., 138f., 141f., 145). I am indebted here and elsewhere to A. R. White's writings on the imagination.

[4] A further issue that briefly concerned him is the connection between the imaginable and the logically possible, cf. Exg. §251.

[5] Here Wittgenstein remarks that it is *essential* to imagining that concepts of sense-perception are employed in its expression. It would be wrong to suggest, however, that whenever we imagine X, we imagine perceiving X.

different in important ways), but, nevertheless, much can be imagined that cannot intelligibly be perceived (e.g. A's having a right to appoint his successor or a number which is the sum of its prime factors). The same *description* can represent both what one sees and, in a different context, what one imagines (RPP II §69), but these identical descriptions are differently used, are embedded in very different language-games. What it makes sense to say in response to someone's giving such a description in one language-game (e.g. 'Are you sure?', 'Did you look again, more closely?', 'Did anyone else see?', 'Might you not have made a mistake?') makes no sense in the other. Bits of one language-game resemble bits of the other, but the bits which resemble each other are not homologous (RPP II §139). We must distinguish the phenomena of perceiving (and seeing in particular) from the phenomena of imagining (and visualizing or having visual images), as well as distinguishing the *concepts* of seeing from the concepts of (visually) imagining (RPP II §130).

The differences between the observable phenomena of seeing and of imagining are manifest in the difference in the criteria that justify saying of someone that he sees a house and the criteria that justify saying that he imagines a house. The faculty of vision is exercised by the use of the eyes in appropriate conditions of visibility. One who sees can find his way around his environment by using his eyes, can follow moving objects with his eyes. Hence seeing is conceptually bound up with looking, watching, observing, or scrutinizing what is publicly visible to others. One can observe a sighted person *trying* to see something, or trying to see it better, by looking over there ↗ , moving closer to get a better view, straining his eyes by screwing them up. By contrast, one who imagines something may imagine it in darkness no less than in light, with his eyes closed (save in 'Leonardesque' types of cases) or simply staring blankly into space (RPP II §134). Indeed, one may try to imagine more *clearly* by *closing* one's eyes (RPP II §§72, 77). One does not *observe* one's mental images when one visually imagines things (RPP II §885) or look at them more closely, although one may imagine seeing those things from closer to. What a person sees is, *ceteris paribus*, visible to others, and that he sees what is thus visible is evident in his reactions to it (including what he says). What a person imagines and how he imagines it is visible neither to himself nor to others, unless he displays or manifests it in drawing or mime. The criteria for what he imagines are what he sincerely says he imagines, what he draws or enacts in explaining what or how he imagines.

Hence the concept of the visual imagination is bound up with other psychological concepts quite differently from that of vision. One can *overlook* features of what one sees, look more closely and *notice* things one had not seen before. One cannot overlook features of what one imagines, any more than one can overlook (as opposed to forget) an aspect of (as opposed to a consequence of) what one intends. It makes no sense to notice or fail to notice an aspect of one's vivid visual image of a scene, for one does not observe it.[6] Looking informs us about objects in our environment; but imagining gives us no information, either right or wrong, about how things are (RPP II §63), even though things may turn out as we imagined they would. Imagining, unlike looking, is not a way of finding out how things are. Verbs of perception have a use as success-verbs: if A sees a tree in the quad, then there is a tree in the quad; but if he imagines a tree in the quad, it does not follow that there is one there. One cannot order someone to stop *seeing* what is before his eyes, only to stop looking at it; but one can order someone to stop imagining (or day-dreaming about) this or that and to get on with his work. One can cease to look at an object, but one cannot 'banish' one's visual impressions of an object while one is looking at it. By contrast, it *makes sense* to talk of 'banishing' or trying to 'banish' one's mental images (one shakes one's head, ceases to stare into space, and concentrates on the task at hand), even though they sometimes recur obsessively (RPP II §§89ff.). One may be surprised at what one sees, and a look of delight may spread over one's face, but one is no more *surprised* at the visual images that cross one's mind (RPP II §88) than at one's own intentions, although one may be pleased at the ideas that thus occur to one, and *others* may be surprised at what one imagines. When looking at a luminous object, one may be dazzled or blinded by the light it emits, and look away or shield one's eyes. While one can imagine dazzling objects or imagine being blinded by them, one's vivid mental images of a dazzling object do not bedazzle one and there is no such thing as being blinded by an imagined object. While it makes no sense for me to see something differently from how it appears to me (although I can *try* to see a double-aspect figure differently from how it *now* appears to me), I can certainly imagine something's being different from how it appears to me. Wittgenstein invites us to compare and contrast teaching someone to obey the order

[6] A. R. Luria in *The Mind of the Mnemonist* (Penguin, Harmondsworth, 1968) relates how the mnemonist explained an error in his mnemonic performance. The performance consisted in manifesting his ability to recollect a large number of random objects called out by his audience. His mnemonic device was to imagine himself walking down a street in St Petersburg, and as each object was called out, he would imagine himself placing it at a particular position in the imagined street. (The device is a variation upon an ancient one; cf. Frances Yates, *The Art of Memory* (Routledge and Kegan Paul, London, 1966).) When the audience had finished, he would recall the objects named by imagining himself walking down the street again, and would, as it were, read off the list of objects from his imagined scene. On one occasion he forgot an item, viz. a milk bottle. He explained this by claiming that he had imagined putting the bottle of milk in front of a white door, so that when he imagined walking down the street again, itemizing the objects in question, he did not *notice* the milk bottle against the white door! This makes *no sense*. (What would be the criteria for its *being there*, even though he did not 'notice' it?)

'Look!' with teaching them to obey the order 'Imagine!' These language-games must be taught quite differently (RPP II §139); they are played in altogether different contexts, for reflect when in real life we tell someone to imagine something! An actor may be having difficulty in interpreting the role he is playing, so the director may say 'Imagine Lear at this point being both hurt and furious, but determined not to reveal his feelings; and now speak the lines'; or, in narrating a series of events, we may say 'Can you imagine what would have happened if he hadn't done that?'; or, while choosing upholstery material, we may say 'Try to visualize the room! Will this colour go with the colours of the carpet?' Reactions and responses which belong to the language-games with 'Look!' do not belong to the language-games with 'Imagine!' or 'Visualize!' and the criteria for having complied in the one case are very different from those in the other. Imagining, unlike perceiving, is more akin to a creative, not a receptive, act (RPP I §111); and visualizing something is more closely akin to depicting than it is to seeing (cf. RPP II §115). It is comparable to an *activity* (RPP II §88), although this too can be misleading (RPP II §80).

The visual idiom dominates our discourse about the imagination. We talk of seeing things *in* (not 'with') our mind's eye, of visualizing or picturing things to ourselves.[7] We speak of visual images, perhaps of auditory ones, but not (in English) of gustatory or olfactory ones, although one can, of course, imagine tastes and smells. Those with the requisite facility draw things 'from the imagination' and not just what they currently see, and those who cannot draw can nevertheless describe how they visualize things. It is an interesting question, which Wittgen-stein raised (RPP II §§66, 144), whether there could be people who could draw 'from the imagination' or from memory, describe vividly how something looked or how they envisage something, and accompany these performances, as we do, by first staring into space or closing their eyes, exclaiming 'Ah, now I know what it is like', etc., but *not* use the visual idiom, finding such expressions as 'I see him vividly before me' wholly inappropriate. Indeed, he added, the really important question is whether this question itself *makes sense* (RPP II §144). For are these forms of behaviour not precisely the criteria for saying of *us* that we form visual images of things, visualize things clearly or vaguely, see things in our mind's eye?

3. *Images and pictures*

The multitude of grammatical similarities between the visual imagina-tion and visual perception is immensely deceptive. It inclines us to think

---

[7] Curiously, we do not speak of hearing things *in* (or *with*) the *mind's ear*, although we speak of hearing things 'in our head'. And, to be sure, there is no smelling things in the mind's nose!

of the 'inner picture' as differing from the 'outer picture' primarily in being private, as if the visual image were like a picture locked away in a room to which only the owner has the key. While it is true that in part of their uses 'visual image' and 'picture' run parallel, the concepts are very different. But the analogy which does exist tends to delude us (LPE 285). One must bear in mind that speaking of mental images as 'pictures in the mind' is only a metaphor (PR 82). It makes *sense* to see a picture and the object of which it is a picture (if it portrays an actual object or scene) juxtaposed; but there is no such thing as seeing a mental image of something actual juxtaposed with that of which it is an image. Hence too, the method of *comparison* of a picture (portrait) and what it is a picture of is altogether different from the relation between a visual image and what it is an image of. 'The room is quite different from how I imagined (visualized) it,' I may say, and I can tell you how – but not by comparing the room I see with my visual image of it (as I might compare the room with a picture of the room). Indeed, one cannot visualize – there is no such thing as visualizing – the room as it is,[8] any more than one can have a hallucination of it, *while* one is looking at it (cf. RPP II §63),[9] although I can say how I visualized it and how it differs from the way I imagined it as being.

One can imagine things which actually exist or things 'purely imaginary'. One can imagine existing things which one has previously perceived (as when one conjures up an image of an absent friend or childhood scene) or which one has only heard about. One can imagine fictitious things (the Olympian gods) and things which are as yet non-existent, but are to be made – as an architect imagines a building he is planning. In all cases of imagining what is depictable, there are obviously connections between the concept of a visual image that one conjures up when visualizing things and the concept of a picture. If asked 'What are you imagining?' one can sometimes (given the appropriate facility) give one's questioner a rough idea of what one is imagining by drawing a picture (PI §280; RPP II §63). But one does not *copy* one's visual image as one can copy a painting. A copy *reproduces* its original, but to reproduce one's visual image, if it means anything, would be to imagine or visualize *again* what one imagined previously.

Can one *draw* one's visual image? Certainly not as a *plein air* artist draws (but does not *copy*) the visible scene before his eyes. But artists also draw 'from the imagination', paint historical scenes as they imagine them (which is not necessarily as they imagine they appeared), produce

[8] But, of course, I can look at it and visualize what it will look like when redecorated.
[9] Although I might, while talking to an elderly man, suddenly imagine that I am talking to N. N., and he may actually *be* N. N. – but then I must not *know* his identity.

mythological and allegorical paintings, genre paintings of imagined scenes, paintings of imaginary objects, and so forth. Can one say in these cases that the artist depicts *his mental images*? That would be gravely misleading. To be sure, the artist depicts *what he imagines*; but he does not imagine his mental images, he imagines what his mental images are images of. Drawing what one imagines can be said to be drawing one's mental images only in so far as drawing what one perceives can be said to be drawing one's perceptions or sketching what one glimpsed can be said to be sketching one's glimpses. The *plein air* artist draws what his perceptions are perceptions of, and what the artist who draws from the imagination draws is what he imagines. It is confusing to call this 'drawing one's mental image'. Of course, one can draw 'from the imagination' – indeed, draw imaginary objects (think of Bosch doodling) – without having any mental images at all; but one nevertheless draws what one imagines. Even if one does vividly visualize the imaginary scene one means to depict, what one paints is what one's vivid mental images are images *of*.

A form of words can be used to describe what one sees or to describe what one imagines. A (naturalistic) picture of what one sees can be judged a good or poor likeness by visual comparison with its subject. *That* ↗ (and one points to the scene or person portrayed) is what is depicted, and the picture is compared with *that* for verisimilitude. If I draw a picture of what I imagine, perhaps to explain to my stage-designer what I have in mind, I may say 'That ↗ is what I imagined' – but then I point at my sketch, not at my mental image. A sketch of how I imagine something does not *resemble* the visual image I might have in imagining it, for it makes no sense to say that the sketch *looks like* the mental image. It *represents* what I imagine, as do *my words*.

Of course, how I imagine X may be similar to or identical with how X is. One may match one's imagination against reality in two ways, depending upon the direction of fit. One may imagine the Sistine Chapel vividly, and when one sees it, one may find that it is just as one imagined it to be, or, perhaps, far more splendid than one had envisaged. Here one imagined it rightly or wrongly. On the other hand, reality may be matched against what one imagined and be judged a more or less adequate *realization* of one's imagination. 'That is exactly how I imagined it', the director may say to his stage-designer who has made a set in accord with his instructions; or he may say 'I imagined the backcloth there a much deeper shade of green'. Here the relationship between the imagination and the artefact is akin to the relationship between an intention and its execution. Our judgement of match or mismatch (irrespective of direction of fit) is not like that of picture and pictured (which may fit either way too), for we compare the actuality with the person's *expression* of his imagination – with what he *says* or does in manifesting what he had in mind, not with his image (and this comparison is not a 'second best' either).

One may object that this account of the visual imagination and the actuality imagined, or the pictorial representation of what is imagined, is true for *others*, but not for the person who is imagining. Surely he *sees* the mental or visual image before his mind's eye! Hence *he* can judge whether something correctly *realizes* what he imagined (or only resembles it more or less adequately) and whether his sketch correctly *represents* what he imagined, not by comparing them with what he *says*, but by comparing them 'directly' with his mental image (cf. PI §280). This is confused; for when the director 'sees the set vividly before his mind's eye', he does not *see* a visual image, but rather vividly imagines the set as he intends it to be. He does not *know* how he imagines it by examining the visual image, which he can be said to *have*, and then reading off its features. For were that so, it would make sense to suppose that he might *err* and think that he imagines it thus, while really imagining it otherwise. But that makes no sense. His mental image does not *inform* him of what he has imagined, as the sketch he draws *or words he utters* may inform his stage-designer of what he has imagined. For were that so, it might misinform him, misrepresent what he imagines, and he might misunderstand what it tells him. But that too makes no sense. The 'inner picture', unlike the 'outer picture' which he might sketch, is not a representation of what he imagines (PI §280). And if he sketches a picture to represent what he imagines, he does not judge its adequacy *as* a representation by comparing it with a 'private image' (as an architect compares the finished edifice with his blueprint and elevations to assure himself of its adequacy), but rather as he judges what he says or writes to be an adequate expression of what he *thinks*. He imagines whatever he imagines, and says that *this* is indeed how he imagined things or that it is not quite right but approximates to what he had in mind. How does he know? He does not *know*; he *says* so, and what he says is decisive (cf. LW §811).

Because perceptual concepts and concepts of the perceptible play such a dominant role in the expression of our imaginings, we are prone to exaggerate the affinity of the imagination to perception and to overlook the extent to which and the manner in which thought suffuses the imagination. When a composer tells the musicians at a rehearsal that he had imagined *that* chord being played louder, that is not because it *sounded louder* in his imagination, any more than if I expected an explosion to be louder or thought that it would be louder, there was something louder in my expectation or thought (BB 40). Similarly, when a choreographer tells his dancers that he had imagined a particular *pas de deux* much faster than they danced it, that does not mean that they danced more quickly in his imagination. If someone insists that 'They danced more quickly in his imagination' just means the same as 'He imagined them dancing more quickly', then we should point out that what is important here is to note that it does not follow from 'They danced more quickly in his imagination' that they danced more quickly. And when people imagine a rotating figure, it does not make sense to try, as some experimental psychologists do, to measure the velocity of rotation.

Imagining is comparable to depicting in the following respect. One does not imagine whoever 'resembles' one's mental image, but rather one imagines whoever it is one *means* to imagine (RPP II §115), even though one may imagine him wrongly. Something parallel holds for paintings: the resemblance between Caravaggio's features and the features of the severed head of Goliath in his famous painting does *not* mean that the painting is not a painting of David holding the head of the Philistine, but is rather of David holding the head of Caravaggio! But there is this difference: that if I intend to paint a picture of M from memory and inadvertently paint a good likeness of N, it is doubtful whether the *portrait* could be said to be a poor portrait of M. Rather, one might say that I had meant to portray M, but, perhaps guided by unconscious forces, had produced a portrait of N (cf. RPP I §262). On the other hand, if I imagine how M looks and visualize him as having features that actually characterize N, not M, nevertheless the visual image I have is *of* M, not N – it is M whom I imagined, even though I can be said to have imagined him wrongly. Similarly, I can imagine a closed box, and I can draw a picture of a closed box, but a picture of a closed box could also represent several other things. For this configuration of lines on paper could represent a wire structure or three adjacent quadrilaterals, etc., hence it might need an interpretation. But a mental image does not, in that sense, consist of a configuration of lines; it is an internal property of my visual image of a closed box that it is *of* a closed box (LW §450).[10] A mental image is, as it were, all message and no medium – like a thought.

The idiom of 'picturing something to oneself' inclines one to think that visually imagining something is like giving oneself a picture of that thing. But this is misconceived (LSD 137), for we distinguish an object from a visual image of an object, and both of these from a picture of an object. Why should we say that when we visually imagine a robin, for example, we give ourselves a *picture* of a robin, rather than that we give ourselves a robin? For one can imagine (have a visual image of) a picture

---

[10] Wittgenstein compares this with knowledge in a dream (ibid.). I may dream that there is a desk in such-and-such a room, and, in the dream, I *know* that there is a book in the desk. Here it makes no sense to wonder whether I might not have been mistaken.

of a robin no less than one can imagine a robin, and these are by no means the same. If one objects that when one imagines a robin, one does not *really* 'give oneself' a robin, one may reply that that is obvious, but that, equally, one does not *really* 'give oneself' a picture of a robin either! To picture something to oneself is not to give oneself a kind of picture (viz. a 'mental' one).

'The "mental (visual) image" [*Vorstellungsbild*] does not enter the language-game in the place where one would like to surmise its presence' (RPP II §110). In particular, it does not enter the language-game of imagining in the place in which a picture enters the language-game of describing, evaluating, and judging the verisimilitude or interest of pictures. The beginning of the language-game of imagining is not the visual image, which one then describes, any more than the beginning of the language-game with 'pain' is the sensation, which one then describes (cf. PI §290). The language-games with the visual imagination begin with the *expression* of what one imagines and how one imagines it, and the description of what one imagines is *fundamentally* unlike the description of a picture which one sees, examines in good light, compares visually with what it depicts, and so forth.

4. *Visual images and visual impressions*

If the analogy between mental (visual) images and pictures is potentially misleading, that between visual images and visual impressions is even more confusing. 'Images seem to be dull reflections of sense-impressions,' Wittgenstein remarked (RPP II §142); but 'when does this seem to be the case, and to whom?' Paradigmatically to philosophers caught in the web of grammar. In a famous argument, Hume wrote:

> We find by experience, that when any impression has been present with the mind, it again makes its appearance there as an idea; and this it may do after two different ways: either when in its new appearance it retains a considerable degree of its first vivacity, and is somewhat intermediate betwixt an impression and an idea; or when it entirely loses that vivacity, and is a perfect idea. The faculty, by which we repeat our impressions in the first manner, is called the MEMORY, and the other the IMAGINATION. 'Tis evident at first sight, that the ideas of the memory are much more lively and strong than those of the imagination, and that the former faculty paints its objects in more distinct colours, than any which are employ'd by the latter. . . . in the imagination the perception is faint and languid, and cannot without difficulty be preserv'd by the mind steddy and uniform for any considerable time. Here then is a sensible difference betwixt one species of ideas and another.[11]

Later empiricists followed Hume in his confusions. But it is not *just*

---

[11] Hume, *Treatise of Human Nature*, Bk. I, Pt. i, Sect. 3.

philosophers who are thus confused. Francis Galton, pioneer of the psychological questionnaire, concocted the following:

> Before addressing yourself to any of the Questions on the opposite page, think of some definite object – suppose it is your breakfast-table as you sat down to it this morning – and consider carefully the picture that rises before your mind's eye.
> 1. *Illumination.* – Is the image dim or fairly clear? Is its brightness comparable to that of the actual scene?
> 2. *Definition.* – Are all the objects pretty well defined at the same time, or is the place of sharpest definition at any one moment more contracted than it is in a real scene?
> 3. *Coloring.* – Are the colors of . . . whatever may have been on the table, quite distinct and natural?[12]

Faced with these questions, 'men of science', as Galton called them, commonly protested that mental imagery was unknown to them. But much to Galton's relief, among lesser mortals a different disposition prevailed. As he reported:

> *Many men and a yet larger number of women, and many boys and girls, declared that they habitually saw mental imagery and that it was perfectly distinct to them and full of color . . .* They described their imagery in minute detail, and they spoke in a tone of surprise at my apparent hesitation in accepting what they said. I felt that I myself should have spoken exactly as they did if I had been describing a scene that lay before my eyes, in broad daylight, to a blind man who persisted in doubting the reality of vision.[13]

Galton concluded that 'scientific men', as a class, have feeble powers of visual imagination.[14]

Confronted by confused questions, it is hardly surprising that one gives confusing answers. To untangle the knots in one's understanding of these matters, one must first clarify what it is for a mental image to be clear and vivid or dim and faint, what it is for imagined objects to be well-defined, and what it is for the colours of an imagined scene to be distinct and natural. Superficial similarities between the grammar of 'mental image' and the grammar of visibilia derail us before we even start. Certainly there is such a thing as clarity and unclarity in visual images. If someone says 'My visual image of N is much less clear (or exact) than the visual impression I have when I see him', then this is true in so far as he cannot describe N nearly as accurately by relying on his

---

[12] F. Galton, *Inquiries into Human Faculty*; quoted by James, *Principles of Psychology*, Vol II, Ch. XVIII, pp. 51ff.

[13] Galton; quoted in James, ibid.

[14] He also thought that the French 'possess the visualizing faculty in a high degree', since they excel in ceremonials and *fêtes*, tactics and strategy. 'Their phrase "figurez-vous" or "picture to yourself" ', he concluded, 'seems to express their dominant mode of perception' (ibid.).

imagination as he can when he sees N before him. But in certain circumstances (e.g. if one is very short-sighted and one has lost one's spectacles) one may see a person much less clearly than one can imagine him (RPP II §142).

Similarly, there is such a thing as imagining the colours of a scene clearly, vividly, and distinctly. One who imagines a stage-set in clear, vivid colours can tell his stage-designer to paint the sky in the backcloth just a little bit more blue ('I imagined it bluer than this,' he might say) or to lessen the contrast between the red and the orange ('I did not imagine them as clashing,' he may add). By contrast, one who does not imagine the colours of a scene vividly will hesitate in judging whether the effect is right. 'Is that what you meant?', his stage-designer may ask, and he may reply, 'I'm not sure; let's try a little less blue and see what it looks like.' And if he says 'I did not imagine that these colours would clash thus,' that indicates a fault in his imagination.

Hume and his followers thought that the lesser vivacity of mental images as opposed to visual impressions was a datum. This invites the question: what would it be like if one's images were very vivid indeed? Would one then *mistake* one's mental images for sense-impressions, after-images, or hallucinations? If one imagined *very vividly* a red expanse with green dots on it, would it prevent one from seeing what is before one's eyes, as a vivid after-image disrupts one's vision (LPP 313f.)? Of course not, for then it would not be a case of imagining at all. The mental image and the visual impression (or after-image) are not in the same logical space, and it makes no sense to conceive of them as competing in the vivacity stakes. Conversely, if someone reports that his mental images are *less* vivid than perceptions, one might ask whether they are so much less vivid that he hardly *notices* them? On Hume's conception this question ought to make sense; but it does not, for one does not notice or fail to notice one's mental images, any more than one *notices* what one means to do. That they are 'less vivid' than perceptions does not mean that they are less noticeable, like faint stains on one's shirt after laundering, as opposed to vivid ones before a wash. What is at issue *is not that sense of 'vivid'* (LPP 313). Indeed, one might say that one's *perceptions* cannot be said to be vivid at all! What one sees may be vivid: e.g. a red rose against dark green foliage. I may see you vividly silhouetted against the sunset, but I cannot be said to see you vividly. Granted one may gain a vivid, i.e. memorable or striking, impression of what one looks at, nevertheless one does not *see* it vividly, only more or less clearly and distinctly.

No matter *how* vividly one imagines something, one's mental images are 'less vivid' than one's perceptions, for the so-called lesser vivacity is an ill-denominated and poorly understood array of *grammatical* features, not phenomenological ones. (An analogue here would be the claim that one's family obligations are weightier than any burden one might have to carry, in that one may not lay them down or transfer them to someone else.) The vividness or faintness of a mental image does not lie *on the same scale* as the clarity or unclarity of a visual impression. My mental image of A may be more vivid than my mental image of B, and I may be able to visualize such-and-such much more vividly than you can. But my mental image can no more be more vivid than my visual impressions than a negative attitude can be more negative than a negative integer.

What does the 'lesser vivacity' of mental images as opposed to perceptions amount to? Primarily to the different relations of imagining and perceiving to the will (see below), to the fact that what we perceive, in an important sense, is not voluntary, and to the unintelligibility of mistaking imagining for perceiving – hence also to the exclusion of certain kinds of epistemic expressions in connection with talk of mental images and sense-impressions. If someone were to say 'I don't know whether I am now seeing a tree or just imagining one', one would take him to mean 'or just fancying that there is a tree over there'. If this is *not* what he means, then one would not know what he is talking about, no matter how vivid his mental images are (RPP II §96). For it makes no sense to suppose that one might confuse discerning with inventing. Hence 'I fancy I can still see him in the distance' does not mean 'Maybe I am imagining him [conjuring up an image of him] in the distance' (RPP II §74).[15] One can think one is inventing when one is, unawares, plagiarizing; but one cannot think one is imagining the words one is *reading*. One cannot *mistake* a mental image for an after-image (or hallucination) or a sense-impression (any more than one can mistake a weighty obligation for a heavy load). It is not that mental images are less vivid than sense-impressions *and that is why we do not mistake our imaginings for perceivings*, but rather: there is no such thing as mistaking a mental image for a sense-impression, and that is *one* reason why philosophers are inclined to say that mental images differ in vivacity from sense-impressions.

The criteria for whether someone is imagining something are altogether different from the criteria for whether he is perceiving something or having a certain sense-impression. One who is imagining *behaves differently* from one who perceives something or other. And in one's own case, one could no more mistake an image for a visual impression than one could mistake drawing for seeing, even though what is drawn and what is seen may be the same thing (RPP II §113). Similar considerations apply to the contrast between imagining and having hallucinations. One

---

[15] But someone else might respond, 'Oh, you're just imagining it; he is no longer visible.' Here 'imagining' coincides with 'misperceiving', 'fancying', or 'thinking wrongly that you perceive'.

who has a hallucination typically takes himself to be perceiving what his
hallucination is a hallucination of, as Macbeth took himself to be
perceiving Banquo. But one cannot mistake – there is no such thing as
mistaking – a mental image for a reality. I can vividly imagine roses in
the vase on the table, but I cannot try to smell them (only try to imagine
their smell or to imagine smelling them). Hence Macbeth's dagger,
which he tried to clutch, was not an imagined dagger (RPP II §85),
although it was an imaginary one. He no more saw it in his mind's eye
than he imagined clutching it. Hallucinations are not subject to the will in
the sense in which images are (see below). It makes no sense to conjure
them up or 'banish' them (RPP I §653). Hallucinations, like after-
images, disrupt one's vision; imagining at most disrupts one's attention.

Finally, what should be made of the question 'Do mental images
exist?' Wittgenstein did not tackle this question, but his strategy suggests
the following tactics. We can clarify what it is for someone to visualize
things, to have a vague or clear mental image of something, to see things
vividly in his mind's eye. We can spell out what it is that someone who
has a good visual imagination can do, which someone who is a poor
visualizer cannot. We can describe the forms of words which a person
who vividly imagines a scene or object will be prone to use. In so doing,
we are also elaborating the *criteria* for saying of someone that he has a
clear mental image of such-and-such, that he visualizes things vividly.
Does it then follow that mental images exist? The question is misleading,
for it looks like 'Do unicorns exist?' If we deny the latter, at any rate it is
clear to us what it would be for a unicorn to exist. But those who deny
the existence of mental images or those who purport to be exercising
proper scientific agnosticism have no *coherent* conception of what it is
that they are denying or suspending judgement about – though they
typically have an incoherent one. The question is also *wrong*, for being
modelled on inquiries into the existence of objects, it invites spurious
questions about coming into existence and ceasing to exist, duration and
location. One can ask whether someone has a clear mental image of
such-and-such, whether he visualizes it vividly, and to this there are
typically answers. A vivid mental image may be before my mind's eye
for half a minute or so, but it would be misleading to say that the image
existed for half a minute; rather, my vividly imagining such-and-such
went on for half a minute. Does it follow that mental images do *not* exist?
No; it only follows that we should eschew this question. But whether
some people visualize things clearly, have vivid mental images of how
things were, are, or ought to be, of imaginary and fictitious objects, has
an obvious and straightforward answer.

5. *Imagination, intention, and the will*

One reason why we are so readily misled in our reflections on mental images and the imagination turns on misconceptions about what makes one's mental image of N a mental image *of N*. For if one has a vivid mental image of N, there is no doubt in one's mind that it is *N* whom one is imagining. So one is inclined to think that one knows that one is imagining N because one knows that one's mental image is a (mental) image of N. It then appears that one knows that it is of N because one *recognizes* it as such (how else could one know it?). But if that is so, then it must have certain (recognizable) features in virtue of which it is a mental image of N.

This is a misunderstanding of the use of the expression 'a mental image of . . .'. For what makes my image of him into an image of him is not its looking like him (PI p. 177). A mental image does not *look like* anything, and I can imagine him otherwise than how he looks. I then imagine him wrongly (with blue eyes rather than grey ones), but it is still him that I imagine! When I say that I am imagining him now as he was when I last saw him, I am not designating something as a *portrait*, i.e. something which one could *investigate* as to who it is of (LW §§308, 314).

It is true that a face can come before my mind (or a tune can run through my head) without my knowing whose face (or what tune) it is. This is akin to having a description in mind, but not knowing whom or what it fits (e.g. 'There was a tall fellow at the party with grey hair and a lisp; now remind me who that was'). It does not follow that when a face comes before my mind as I imagine N, I recognize it as N's face. What *makes* it N's face then? The question is misleading; for it is more like 'What makes this remark a remark about *him*?' (LW §317) or 'What makes the intention to write to him an intention to write to *him*?' than it is like 'What makes this photograph a photograph of him?' If I avow 'I see him now vividly before me', what makes my avowal into an utterance about N is not its being backed by a mental image which looks like him. If someone wants to know whom I meant, he can ask me (LW §317). And if someone wants to know of whom my mental image is an image, my sincere avowal provides the criterion. But what criterion do *I* use? None (cf. PI §377).

Might I not be wrong? If I imagine King's College on fire, how can I be sure that it is King's that I imagine? Could it not be a different building, but one which looks like King's? After all, one's imagination is not so exact that half-a-dozen buildings might not fit the bill! This misconceives matters: of course, I do not doubt that it is King's I imagine on fire, but not because I *recognize* it as an image of King's, have grounds for believing that it is King's I imagine. Rather, I *say* 'It is King's I imagined', and *this* makes the connection (BB 39), as I say whom I *meant* or to whom I am writing or what I intend. How do I *know*? Knowledge is not in question here, nor is ignorance. 'I imagine . . .' is not a description which may or may not fit an object. Rather, it determines the content of my imagination, somewhat as my avowals of intention determine (and constitute criteria for) what I intend. What is at issue is my ability to say whom or what I imagine, have in mind, or mean. One should bear in mind that we could replace 'I see him vividly before me' or 'I have a vivid mental image of him' by 'Now I know what he looks like' or 'Now I'll tell you what he looks like'; i.e. these forms of words could, for certain purposes, fulfil the same role. But the latter pair do not have the misleading character of the former (RPP I §360) and do not suggest that any 'act of recognition' is involved here. Mental images are not objects seen, as it were, through a private telescope.

There is a venerable tradition of associating perception with the category of passive receptivity and imagination with the voluntary. This is partly right and partly wrong. The various modes of perception are essentially connected with looking, listening, sniffing, sampling (food-stuffs), and fingering (as well as groping, prodding, touching, etc.). These are exploratory activities subject to the will. One can decide to look at *this* or smell *that*, and if ordered to listen to *that* or feel *this* material, one can obey the order or flout it (cf. RPP II §139). On the other hand, seeing (as opposed to looking), hearing (as opposed to listening), etc. are not, in that sense, voluntary. One cannot order someone to stop seeing what is before his eyes (only to stop looking at it) or to stop hearing what is audible (only to stop listening to it), let alone to stop tasting what is in his mouth. One's perceptual *impressions*, unlike one's perceptual *activities*, are not (save in the case of perceiving aspects) subject to the will.

To say that the imagination is dependent on the will is correct but potentially misleading. One can decide to imagine something, as one can decide to look at or listen to something, but not to see or hear what one looks at or listens to. One can stop imagining and 'banish' the mental images before one's mind in a way in which one cannot 'banish' one's visual impressions. But it is also true that images sometimes beset one against one's will, recur obsessively, and preoccupy one. Of course, one can struggle against them; yet to call such obsessive images voluntary would be like calling a movement of one's arm 'voluntary' when someone forces one's arm *against* one's will (RPP II §86). So the kernel of truth in the claim that the imagination is voluntary needs careful separation from the husks of falsehood. Our concern is with grammar, with what it makes sense to say, not with empirical descriptions of phenomena.

First, to say that mental images depend upon the will gives a wrong picture both of the will and of mental images. We do not first become acquainted with mental images and then learn that we can bend them to our will (RPP I §900). We do not 'direct' them with our will, for the will is not a kind of motor that puts them into motion (RPP II §78). It is not as if we had here a genuine case of psychokinesis, as it were!

Secondly, one cannot compare the voluntariness of the imagination with the voluntariness of one's bodily movements. For others can typically say whether I moved, but whether I imagine something moving or not is determined wholly by what I say (subject, of course, to the proviso that what I say makes sense). So really moving objects drop out of consideration, for no such thing is in question here (RPP II §123).

Thirdly, to say that mental images are dependent on the will whereas visual impressions are not makes it appear as if mental images are just like sense-impressions, only subject to one's control. But that makes *no sense* (RPP II §124). For it represents the difference between mental images and sense-impressions as an empirical one, viz. that one can voluntarily affect the former but not the latter (RPP II §§89f.). But that is altogether misguided. Even if one's visual impressions (e.g. one's impressions of what one sees in a peep-show) coincided exactly with what one wanted, one would not think that one was vividly imagining things, for one cannot even begin to take an impression for an image (RPP II §§96f.). Conversely, suppose that at will one could produce pictures on a screen visible to others as well. In this case, would 'I see such-and-such on the screen now' be equivalent to 'I imagine such-and-such'? Obviously not; for others have no less authority than I in saying what is on the screen, and, indeed, I might err in saying what I see there. But 'I see such-and-such on the wall' and 'I imagine such-and-such' are equivalent in the case of Leonardesque exercises of the imagination, and 'For me, what is on the screen now represents . . .' does correspond to imagining (RPP II §§119 – 20).

So what does the 'voluntariness' of mental images and of the imagination amount to? It boils down to an array of grammatical (conceptual) features characterizing the use of 'mental image' and 'imagine'. In this respect it is like the 'vividness' and 'faintness' of mental images. For in both instances distinctive aspects of the grammar of 'imagination' are confusedly captured by a characterization which appears to be phenomenological. What specific grammatical features are concealed by the slogan 'Images are voluntary'? Such things as that (a) imagining is not a way of finding out how things are and so is unlike perceiving; (b) imagining is not a matter of observing the 'inner'; (c) imagining is more akin to drawing than to seeing; (d) one imagines whoever one means to imagine; (e) it makes *sense* for one to 'banish' one's mental images at will, unlike one's sense-impressions; and so on.

Wittgenstein's treatment of the imagination is, to be sure, incomplete. Many questions remain unanswered, but then his aim was not completeness (Z §465). It was rather to teach us how to fend for ourselves when we get lost in the jungles of philosophy (cf. PI p. 206). For the right way of handling any of these puzzles concerning our psychological concepts casts light on the correct treatment of others (Z §465). So it is here; seemingly intractable problems about the nature of the mind are shown not to be empirical problems at all. Hence they are not amenable to experimental methods, but exemplify how 'in psychology there is what is problematic and there are experiments which are regarded as methods of solving the problems, even though they quite bypass the thing that is worrying us' (RPP I §1039). The questions with which we have been dealing are not solved, but dissolved. They yield to a patient examination of the grammar of expressions. Confused questions and muddled answers about the imagination are shown to be rooted in the misguided projection of one language-game onto another and in failure to note how an expression (e.g. 'vivid', 'voluntary', 'picture') used in one language-game may occur in another language-game with a very *different* use. Here, as elsewhere in the philosophy of psychology,

The difficulty is to know one's way about among the concepts of 'psychological phenomena'.

That is to say: one has got to *master* the kinships and differences of the concepts. As someone is master of the transition from any key to any other one, modulates from one to the other. (RPP I §1054)

XI

I AND MY SELF

1. *Historical antecedents*

Contemporary debates about the role of the first-person pronoun transpose onto a linguistic plane the discussion of the essential nature of a human being that stems, in modern times, from Cartesian metaphysics. Descartes took it for granted that there can be 'no act or accident without a substance for it to belong to',[1] and concluded correctly that a thought cannot exist without a thinking thing, a substance in which to inhere. Awareness of his own thoughts, he argued, 'proved' his existence as a substance named or signified by the word 'I'. But 'what this "I" is' must be investigated, since 'I must be on my guard against carelessly taking something else to be this "I" and so making a mistake in the very item of knowledge that I maintain is the most certain and evident of all'.[2] The *sum res cogitans* argument convinced him that 'this "I" – that is the soul by which I am what I am – is entirely distinct from the body',[3] and is an *immaterial substance*. Not being extended in space, it is indivisible and hence simple. Being simple, he thought it to be an indestructible, immortal substance[4] numerically identical through time.

Given the supposition that the word 'I' signifies a substance, it is perhaps understandable that Descartes had no qualms in using the expression 'this "I" '. But such a use of the indexical 'this' is as illegitimate as 'this "that" ', 'this "he" ', or 'this "now" '. It is not merely ungrammatical; if it is unclear which object one is speaking of in saying 'that ↗' or 'he ↗' (accompanied by an ostensive gesture), then adding 'this ↗ that ↗' can no more clarify things than pointing with one's left hand can clarify what one is pointing at with one's right hand. Moreover, in the special case of the word 'I' (whether accompanied by a reflexive gesture or not) there is no more *room* for disambiguating of whom I am speaking than there is room for disambiguating of what time I am speaking in saying 'Now . . .' – although, of course, I may still have to say who I am or what time it is.

---

[1] Descartes, 'Reply to the Third Set of Objections', AT VII, 175f.

[2] Descartes, 'Second Meditation', AT VII, 25.

[3] Descartes, *Discourse on Method*, AT VI, 33. To be accurate, the 'sum res cogitans' argument alone does not purport to prove this, but needs the additional argument of the 'Sixth Meditation'.

[4] There is an important equivocation on 'substance', signifying indestructible 'stuff' (material or immaterial) and also persistent particular.

Locke gave prominence to the perceptual model of inner sense, arguing that it is 'impossible for anyone to perceive without perceiving that he does perceive. When we see, hear, smell, taste, feel, meditate or will anything, we know that we do so . . . by this everyone is to himself that which he calls *self.*'[5] It is our consciousness of our experiences that 'makes everyone to be what he calls *self*; and thereby distinguishes himself from all other thinking things';[6] indeed, 'it is by the consciousness it has of its present Thoughts and Actions, that it is *self* to it *self* now, and so will be the same *self* as far as the same consciousness can extend to actions past or to come'.[7] It is noteworthy that this use of 'self' as an apparent sortal noun was an innovation, and arguably an aberration. Unlike Descartes, Locke did not think that a 'self' is a thinking *substance*, but only that it is 'annexed' to a substance, which may change without the self changing. For if I 'have the same consciousness' that I did such-and-such in the past as that I am writing now,

I could no more doubt that I . . . was the same self, place that *self* in what Substance you please, than that I that write this am the same *my self* now whilst I write (whether I consist of all the same Substance, material or immaterial, or no) that I was Yesterday. For as to this point of being the same *self*, it matters not whether this present *self* be made up of the same or other Substances.[8]

Linguistically tortured and philosophically confused as this passage is, one correct point shines through: to be in a position to say that I, who am writing this now, experienced this or that in the past, I do not first have to ensure that I am (or, perhaps better, my body is) made of the same stuff as he who had those previous experiences. But Locke sowed further seeds of confusion in suggesting that 'I' signifies a self, a thing distinct from the substance to which it is 'annexed', which is the 'bearer' of that consciousness 'which makes every one to be what he calls *self*'.

Hume sank deeper into this quagmire. He denied that we are 'every moment intimately conscious of what we call our SELF', i.e. a simple (indecomposable) continuant. The only object which would satisfy that specification would be a constant, invariable *impression*, which would give rise to the *idea of the self*. But, Hume observed, there is no such constant impression. Employing Locke's perceptual model of 'inner sense', he contended that 'when I enter most intimately into what I call *myself*, I always stumble on some particular perception or other . . . I never can catch *myself* at any time without a perception, and can never observe anything but the perception'.[9] Hence he concluded that what is

    [5] Locke, *Essay Concerning Human Understanding*, Bk. II, Ch. xxvii, Sect. 9.
    [6] Ibid.
    [7] Ibid., Bk. II, Ch. xxvii, Sect. 10.
    [8] Ibid., Bk. II, Ch. xxvii, Sect. 16.
    [9] Hume, *Treatise of Human Nature*, Bk. I, Pt. iv, Sect. 6.

called 'the self' is 'nothing but a bundle or collection of different perceptions which succeed each other with an inconceivable rapidity, and are in a perpetual flux and movement'. Hume's twentieth-century heirs would argue that the self (my self, the I) is a logical construction out of perceptions, and that these expressions are only apparent names, not real, logically proper names.

However, having abandoned the model of a subject of experience, Hume was faced with the problem of discovering a principle of unity that determines a series of experiences *as* the experiences that are *his*. Causal connectedness and resemblance seemed the only glue available to bind together the bundle of experiences; but such principles can be thought to unify a manifold only if it makes sense for the constituents of that very manifold *not* to be thus united. Causation and resemblance, in Hume's jargon, can provide no *real connection* among distinct existences; but that the 'perceptions' I have are *mine* is a 'real' (logical) connection, not an empirical one. For it makes no sense to query whether the perception I am now enjoying is really mine or perhaps someone else's, *a fortiori* to *find out* whether it is mine by detecting whether it stands in relations of causation and resemblance to my previous experiences. Hence Hume's confession of failure in the Appendix to the *Treatise*.[10]

Hume's account earmarks the stalemate between rationalism and empiricism, as is evident in Reid's objection to the 'bundle theory': 'Whatever this self may be, it is something which thinks, and deliberates, and resolves, and acts and suffers. I am not thought, I am not action, I am not feeling; I am something that thinks, and acts, and suffers.'[11] But, constrained by the misconceived framework of the debate, his objections falter, for the only alternative to Hume's subjectless associationism seemed to be a lapse back into a vague Cartesianism: 'My thoughts, and actions, and feelings, change every moment – they have no continued, but a successive existence; but that *self* or *I*, to which they belong is permanent, and has the same relation to all the succeeding thoughts, actions, and feelings, which I call mine.'[12] The bankruptcy of empiricism was definitive, and is evident a century later in Mill.[13]

An obscure alternative to the hopeless dichotomy emerged with Kant. His criticism of Cartesianism went deeper than Hume's, and he grasped some of the flaws in Hume's account. Rationalist psychology, he argued, confused the unity of experience with the experience of a unity, i.e. of a

---

[10] 'All my hopes vanish, when I come to explain the principles, that unite our successive perceptions in our thought or consciousness. I cannot discover any theory which gives me satisfaction on this head.'

[11] T. Reid, *Essays on the Intellectual Powers of Man*, Essay III, Ch. iv.

[12] Ibid.

[13] See J. S. Mill, *An Examination of Sir William Hamilton's Philosophy*, in *Collected Works*, Vol. IX, pp. 207f.

soul-substance. This illusory substance appears simple (and hence indestructible) because the rationalist confuses the absence of reference to a
complex object, a 'manifold' subsumable under the category of
substance, for a reference to a simple object. Kant did not abandon the
perceptual model of 'inner sense', but saw that within these constraints
the self-ascribability of experiences is a purely formal feature of concep-
tualized experience. It makes no sense to *look*, as Hume purported to do,
for a subject of experience in 'inner sense'. Rather, any 'experience' of
which I am 'aware in inner sense' must be such as I can attribute to
myself – the 'I think' must (analytically) be capable of accompanying all
my representations:

The renowned psychological proof [of the rationalist doctrine of the soul] is founded
merely on the indivisible unity of a representation, which governs only the verb in its
relation to a person. It is obvious that in attaching 'I' to our thoughts we designate the
subject of inherence only transcendentally, without noting in it any quality whatever
– in fact without knowing anything of it either by direct acquaintance or otherwise
. . . . The simplicity of the representation of a subject is not *eo ipso* knowledge of the
simplicity of the subject itself, for we abstract altogether from its properties when we
designate it solely by the entirely empty expression 'I'.[14]

Kant pin-pointed the source of error as the confusing of the purely
formal character of 'transcendental self-consciousness' with consciousness of a pure soul-substance. Awareness of the necessary self-
ascribability of experience, 'the "I think" that must be capable of
accompanying all my representations', is not an awareness of a Cartesian
self. He did not, however, deny that there is such a thing as empirical
self-consciousness yielding self-knowledge. His account is obscure and is
rendered incoherent by the demands of his transcendental idealism. The
first-person pronoun in psychological statements seemingly refers to an
empirical subject of experiences; but Kant fails to clarify what this
empirical subject, which is an object of possible experience, might be.
This empirical 'self' is indeed aware of fleeting experiences and conscious
of itself as so aware. Being an object with an autobiography, a history, it
must be part of the temporal, phenomenal world. Hence the 'self' that
appears to itself is itself mere appearance. So the 'self' as it is in itself, the
'noumenal self', must underlie it, as noumena underpin phenomena.
This entity must be both unknowable and also the known subject of the
moral law. For the moral 'self' must be free, subject to the laws of
practical reason, rather than to the constraints of causality. So it must be
super-sensible and atemporal and must also have a moral history, being
the subject of temporal moral judgements. 'I have an obligation to . . .'
seemingly refers to the ethical subject, the bearer of good and evil; but

---

[14] Kant, *Critique of Pure Reason*, A 355.

how, within the bizarre framework of transcendental idealism, that is possible is never made clear.

Substantialism, associationism, and transcendentalism, as William James classified them,[15] constituted the primary apparent alternatives for philosophical analysis of the nature of the 'self'. As James remarked, 'Terribly, therefore, do the sour grapes which those fathers of philosophy have eaten set our teeth on edge.'[16]

2. *'The I, the I is what is deeply mysterious'*

Wittgenstein's first attempt to grapple with the philosophical problems which cluster around the use of the first-person pronoun and which have bred such questionable expressions as 'the self' or 'the ego' (which, being Latin, sounds less offensive than 'the I') are to be found in the *Notebooks 1914 – 16*. A small selection of these reflections were incorporated in the *Tractatus* 5.6ff. Wittgenstein's familiarity with the history of philosophy was slight, and the tradition sketched above was transmitted to him primarily, if not exclusively, through Schopenhauer's *The World as Will and Representation* (which he had read as a teenager, and was perhaps re-reading during June and July 1916[17]) and through Russell.

Schopenhauer's philosophy was a version of transcendental idealism. Like Kant, he was critical of the Cartesian conceptions of 'the knowing subject' as a self-subsistent immaterial substance and of 'the external world' consisting of material substance set over against the subject as object of possible knowledge. The knowing subject properly conceived is indeed 'the supporter of the world, the universal condition of all that appears',[18] a presupposition of the possibility of experience and knowledge. But as such it cannot be a constituent of the world as we experience it – the world as representation. Rather, it is transcendental, and its relation to the phenomenal world is comparable to the relation of the eye to the visual field – for the 'eye sees everything except itself'.[19] Equally, the world as we experience it is not independent of our experience of it; it is, as Kant had argued, phenomenally real, but transcendentally ideal. The world as representation, is ordered in space and time, which are the forms of sensible intuition, and is subject to causality – the Principle of Sufficient Reason, which is the sole category of the understanding. The perceiving subject is as much a part of the

---

[15] James, *Principles of Psychology* Vol. I, p. 371.
[16] Ibid., p. 366.
[17] The evidence for this consists in the Schopenhauerian tenor (including metaphors and turns of phrase, as well as specific references) of the notebook entries for this period (cf. NB 72 – 91 and earlier remarks under 23 May 1915).
[18] A. Schopenhauer, *The World as Will and Representation*, tr. E. F. J. Payne (Dover, New York, 1966), Vol. I, p. 5.
[19] Ibid., Vol. II, p. 491.

phenomenal world as are the objects it perceives. But the noumenal subject, the thing-in-itself, which is the correlate of the world-as-representation, is not, as Kant had claimed, unknowable. For we have access in inner consciousness to 'the single narrow door to the truth': viz. the Will. Our subjective awareness of intentional action is an awareness of the objectified Will. The Will thus conceived is the noumenal reality underlying the phenomenal world. It is not to be viewed as one will among many, but rather as the metaphysical or World Will. It is unique, although it manifests or objectifies itself in the strivings and impulses of phenomenal particulars, inorganic and organic alike. In this (obscure) sense, individuality and plurality are illusory (phenomenal). Philosophical insight can penetrate the veil of Maya to apprehend that the plurality of individuals is merely the spatio-temporal objectification of the one, unique World Will.

Russell transmitted to Wittgenstein the predicament of classical empiricism. In *The Problems of Philosophy* (1912) he conceded to Hume that 'acquaintance with the contents of our minds', which, in accord with tradition, he termed 'self-consciousness', is not consciousness of a self, but only consciousness of particular thoughts and feelings. Nevertheless, he claimed, it is *probable* 'that we are acquainted with the "I" '. His argument was that

All acquaintance . . . seems obviously a relation between the person acquainted and the object with which the person is acquainted. When a case of acquaintance is one with which I can be acquainted . . . it is plain that the person acquainted is myself. Thus, when I am acquainted with my seeing the sun, the whole fact with which I am acquainted is 'Self-acquainted-with-sense-datum'.[20]

Consequently, the word 'I' is a logically proper name of this self with which one is aquainted. But, contrary to the rationalist tradition and to Reid's philosophy of common sense alike, 'it does not seem necessary to suppose that we are acquainted with a more or less permanent person, the same today as yesterday'.

The self thus conceived seems to be no more than a bare subject of predication demanded by the grammar of psychological verbs. It is not surprising, therefore, to find that in the manuscript *Theory of Knowledge* (1913) Russell shifted ground uncomfortably:

Hume's inability to perceive himself was not peculiar, and I think most unprejudiced observers would agree with him. Even if by great exertion some rare person could catch a glimpse of himself, this would not suffice; for 'I' is a term we all know, and which must therefore have some easily accessible meaning. It follows that the word 'I', as commonly employed, must stand for a description; it cannot be a true proper

---

[20] Russell, *The Problems of Philosophy* (Oxford University Press, London, 1967), pp. 27f.

name in the logical sense, since true proper names can only be conferred on objects with which we are acquainted . . . We may define 'I' as the subject of present experience.[21]

So the first-person pronoun is not really the name of an object given in experience, but rather does service for a definite description. What a 'subject' of experience might be is left obscure, and whether Russell really thought that one might 'catch a glimpse' of one's self is left equally opaque.

Wittgenstein approached the problems of the logical analysis of first-person propositions through an investigation of the very specific issue of belief-sentences. In 'A believes that p' and 'I believe that p', one proposition, namely 'p', apparently occurs non-truth-functionally within another, contrary to the thesis of extensionality. It looks as if such propositions describe a relation between an object and a proposition, and indeed Russell had construed them thus in his three articles 'Meinong's Theory of Complexes and Assumptions' in *Mind*, 13 (1906). In 'On the Nature of Truth and Falsity' of 1910,[22] Russell repudiated this dual-relation analysis in favour of a *multiple*-relation theory of belief (judgement or thought) on the grounds of ontological parsimony. For the dual-relation analysis committed him either to the existence of propositions in addition to facts or to the impossibility of false beliefs. For 'A believes that p' may be true even though it is not a fact that p, so 'p' must (apparently) exist if false judgements or beliefs are to be possible. But Russell denied that over and above facts there exists propositions. Hence, he argued,

If I judge that A loves B, that is not a relation of me to A's love for B, but a relation between me and A and love and B. If it were a relation of me to 'A's love for B' it would be impossible unless there were such a thing as 'A's love for B', i.e. unless A loved B, i.e. unless the judgement were true; but in fact false judgements are possible. When the judgement is taken as a relation between me and A and love and B, the mere fact that the judgement occurs does not involve any relation between its objects A and love and B; thus the possibility of false judgements is fully allowed for.[23]

Wittgenstein agreed with the repudiation of the dual-relation analysis (cf. TLP 5.541), but held the multiple-relation analysis to be likewise incoherent. For it does not ensure the preservation of sense; it does not suffice to mention just the constituents, or even the constituents and the form (unless in the proper order). For that will not exclude the possibility of, e.g., 'A believes that the table penholders the book' – i.e. the

[21] Russell, *Theory of Knowledge, the 1913 Manuscript* (Allen and Unwin, London, 1984), pp. 36f.
[22] Russell, 'On the Nature of Truth and Falsehood', in *Philosophical Essays* (Longmans, Green and Co., London, 1910), pp. 170 – 85.
[23] Ibid., p. 180.

possibility of believing nonsense (NB 96f.). This shows that the propositional form must occur in belief-propositions. In the 'Notes Dictated to
G. E. Moore' of April 1914, the analysis focused on the first-person
pronoun, and proposed a resolution that subsequently occurs in the
Tractatus: 'The relation of "I believe *p*" to "*p*" can be compared to the
relation of " '*p*' says *p*" to "*p*": it is just as impossible that *I* should be a
simple as that "*p*" should be' (NB 118).

This is partially clarified in the *Tractatus*. Propositions with two verbs,
as Russell called them (i.e. A believes (judges, thinks, says) that *p*) are of
the form ' "*p*" says *p*'. This does not correlate a fact with an object A (or
I), but rather correlates facts by means of the correlation of their objects
(TLP 5.542). More explicitly, Wittgenstein's idea seems to have been
that such propositions correlate the fact that constitutes a proposition (a
symbolizing fact, which may be a propositional sign in its projective
relation or a *thought* consisting of physical constituents (R 37)) with the
fact, or rather the state of affairs (possible fact) it depicts, by correlating
the constituents of each. This shows, he held, 'that there is no such thing
as the soul – the subject, etc. – as it is conceived in the superficial
psychology of the present day. Indeed a composite soul would no longer
be a soul' (TLP 5.5421). 'I' in 'I believe that *p*' is not a logically proper
name signifying a simple object, an empirical soul or substance. There
are indeed psychic facts, some of which constitute representations of
how things are in the world; they have psychic constituents, but there is
no soul-substance or simple object that 'owns' these psychic elements.

This neo-Humean strategy was subsequently synthesized with the
reflections on solipsism and the self of 1915 – 16 in *Tractatus* 5.63ff.
'There is no such thing as the subject that thinks or entertains ideas,'
Wittgenstein declared, for a description of 'the world as I found it' would
include my body, which parts of it are subordinate to my will, etc., *but
not the subject.* Thus far Hume was moving on the right lines – although
he was wrong to think that it was a matter of fact that he could not
encounter 'the self' in experience. For the *philosophical self,* which is the
concern of philosophy (TLP 5.641) is the *metaphysical subject,* not an
empirical object that could be given in experience (e.g. the body or the
psyche studied by empirical psychology), but a 'limit of the world' (TLP
5.632; NB 79), 'not a part of the world but a presupposition of its
existence' (NB 79). This Schopenhauerian thought[24] Wittgenstein tried
to clarify by means of a Schopenhauerian simile: the relation of the
metaphysical self to experience, to the world, is comparable to the
relation of the eye to the visual field (TLP 5.633f.). For, on the one hand,
'you really do *not* see the eye' (or, as Schopenhauer put it, 'the eye sees

---

[24] Schopenhauer, *World as Will and Representation*, Vol. I, p. 5.; Vol. II, p. 15.

everything except itself'[25]), and on the other hand, it is irresistibly tempting to argue that in some sense 'I also always find myself at a particular point of my visual space' (NB 86), even though the *I* is not an object I can confront (NB 80). The fact that the eye is not a constituent of the visual field (and, by implication, that the I is not given in experience) Wittgenstein connected with the fact that no part of our experience is at the same time *a priori* (TLP 5.634; NB 80) – whatever we see or experience could be otherwise. But, by implication, that *this* experience is *my* experience is no more a contingent fact than that *this* visual field is *my* visual field.[26]

With studied obscurity, Wittgenstein concluded that this shows 'that solipsism, when its implications are followed out strictly, coincides with pure realism. The self of solipsism shrinks to a point without extension, and there remains the reality co-ordinated with it' (TLP 5.64). Whether this is a repudiation of solipsism or a refinement and affirmation of *empirical realism and transcendental solipsism* is unclear. What is clear is that Wittgenstein thought that some aspect of solipsism is both true and metaphysically necessary (and hence ineffable): 'What the solipsist *means* is quite correct; only it cannot be *said*, but makes itself manifest' (TLP 5.62). And it is also perspicuous that Wittgenstein's Schopenhauerian reflections of 1916 reveal a commitment to the transcendental reality of the metaphysical self, which is identical with the willing self, the bearer of good and evil. On 5 August 1916, Wittgenstein wrote:

> The thinking subject is surely mere illusion. But the willing subject exists.
> If the will did not exist, neither would there be that centre of the world, which we call the I, and which is the bearer of good and evil.
> What is good and evil is essentially the I, not the world. The I, the I is what is deeply mysterious. (NB 82)

This mysterious metaphysical, willing self is not a human being, nor is it even a particular among others. Rather, as Wittgenstein put it in Schopenhauerian language: 'As my idea is the world, in the same way my will is the world-will' (NB 85).[27]

As far as the *Tractatus* programme of logico-linguistic analysis is concerned, it seems that Wittgenstein held that the first-person pronoun is not a 'name', but would disappear on analysis. In some cases, one might suppose, it would be replaced by body-referring expressions, themselves subject to further analysis. In other cases it would be

---

[25] Ibid., Vol. II, p. 491.

[26] The same point can be expressed by means of one of Wittgenstein's later metaphors, viz. that it is not a fact of experience that *this* visual field is seen by the 'geometrical eye'. The underlying idea, as he subsequently realized, is incoherent.

[27] For a more detailed examination of these obscurities, see P. M. S. Hacker, *Insight and Illusion*, rev. edn (Clarendon Press, Oxford, 1986), Ch. IV.

swallowed up in some detailed description of a field of psychic constituents, a Humean bundle, although again, this is not the final level of
analysis.

It is obscure what strategy he would have adopted with respect to
propositions about mental states of other people.[28] It is possible that he
thought that such references to other people would be analysable into
propositions about their behaviour, which in turn would decompose into
propositions about one's own current experiences. This would marry a
form of analytical methodological solipsism with ineffable transcendental solipsism. The truth that lies at the heart of solipsism, the centrality
of the metaphysical self, the bearer of good and evil, will ineffably be
shown by the *constant form* of all fully analysed sentences.

3. *The eliminability of the word 'I'*

When Wittgenstein resumed philosophical work in 1929, he jettisoned
the Schopenhauerian transcendentalism – no more is heard of 'the self of
philosophy' or of the metaphysical or willing self. Indeed, the aberrant
philosophical usage, 'the I' and 'the self', likewise disappears, except in
criticisms of misconceptions. Two important points, however, were
retained for a while. First, he continued to think that there is some
non-trivial sense in which the word 'I' can be eliminated from a language
without loss (WWK 49). He quoted, with approval, Lichtenberg's
contention that instead of 'I think' we ought to say 'It thinks', on the
model of 'It is raining' (M 309). This analytical claim, now severed from
the logical atomist doctrines of the *Tractatus* and embedded in the
methodological solipsism of the *Philosophical Remarks* (and the conversations with Waismann), can be seen as a logico-linguistic residue of his
earlier Schopenhauerian criticism of the Cartesian doctrine of the soul.
Secondly, Wittgenstein argued that first-person experiential propositions
– and their analogues in a language without a first-person pronoun –
have a special adequacy. They constitute 'primary language'. Indeed, it is
their special status which is reflected grotesquely in the distorting
mirrors of rational psychology, transcendentalism, and solipsism (cf. M
311).

The opening sentence of his reflections on the subject in the *Philosophical Remarks* earmarks the beginning of a change in method and
perspective: 'One of the most misleading representational techniques in
our language is the use of the word "I", particularly when it is used in
representing immediate experience' (PR 88). Traditional puzzlement
about the nature of 'the self' is to be resolved not by introspection,
metaphysical insight, or logical analysis into indefinables, but by scru-

[28] NB 49 is relevant, but opaque.

tiny of a representational technique. We must investigate the role of the first-person pronoun.

It is, he argued, an eliminable expression (WWK 49), and its role can be clarified by imagining how a language without this word might fulfil the same representational function. One can imagine a language of an oriental despot in which the despot himself is, as it were, at the centre of the language. When he has a toothache, he (and everyone else) says: 'There is toothache'. But when someone else, N.N., has a toothache, one says: 'N.N. is behaving as the Centre behaves when there is toothache.' This form of representation, Wittgenstein urged, is just as intelligible and unambiguous as ours. Indeed, given the form of analysis to which he now cleaved, it must have seemed *more perspicuous* than our language, for 'it would serve to show clearly what was logically essential in the representation' (PR 88). For it not only brings out the essentially 'subjectless' character of first-person experiential propositions, it also makes clear the logical character of 'hypotheses' about other people's experiences.

A mono-centred language can have anyone as its centre; but, Wittgenstein insisted, a language with *me* as its centre is privileged. However, its special adequacy cannot be stated. 'For, if I do it in the language with me as its centre, then the exceptional status of the description of this language in its own terms is nothing very remarkable, and in terms of another language, my language occupies no privileged status whatever. – The privileged status lies in the application' (PR 89). In conversation with Waismann he explained that a language of which I am the centre is one 'in which I can as it were say that I feel *real* pain' (WWK 50). The point where the particular status of these different languages comes to light is that when I say 'There is toothache' in the language of which I am the centre, what I say is *compared directly with reality* (cf. WWK 50, n.1).

This, as he later realized, is confused. But it is true that 'N.N. is behaving as the Centre behaves when there is pain' is no substitute, *as far as N.N. is concerned*, for *his* saying, in a language of which *he* is the Centre, 'There is pain' or, as we would say in our grammar, 'I have a pain'. One wants to be able to complain about one's pains even though one has *not* manifested them in behaviour and so cannot truly say 'N.N. is behaving as the Centre . . .'. A truthful avowal of pain ('There is pain' as said by the Centre) does not require the speaker to check *his behaviour* before he speaks to ensure that he speaks truly; but speakers other than the Centre can (in his language) only say 'N.N. is behaving as . . .', which will be false if N.N. is not behaving thus. Unlike the Centre's avowal of pain, in these cases there is room for error. Finally, in a language of which I am *not* the Centre, I cannot, as it were, say that I am in pain without saying who I am.

It is obvious that a mono-centred language is unsatisfactory for speakers other than the Centre. It lacks some of the articulations of our language. This is only to be expected, since it was designed expressly to highlight the first/third-person asymmetry *in our language*, and Wittgenstein's suggestion was that in effect *each of us* speaks, and is the centre of, such a (tacitly) mono-centred language. So the *explicit* asymmetry of the invented language allegedly makes clear something that is evident only in the application of ordinary language.

But is it obvious that, *for the Centre*, such a Lichtenbergian language *is* adequate? This question has two aspects. First, is it true that in *my* language alone 'I can as it were say that I feel *real* pain'? In a sense that is so, since *ex hypothesi* in another's language I, N.N., must say 'N.N. behaves as the Centre behaves when there is pain'. But the construction rests four-square upon the supposition that 'pain' in 'I have pain' (or 'There is pain' said by me in *my* language) is defined by reference to a private sensation and is privately verified by my having a pain. And it is equally supposed that 'pain' in 'He has pain' does *not* have the same meaning as in 'I have a pain'. So in attributing pain to others, one is, in some ineffable sense, *not* attributing *real* pain to them. From this bizarre perspective, a mono-centred language of which I am the Centre will obviously appear especially adequate. But the adequacy rests on an illusion.

Secondly, does this language, as Wittgenstein supposed, have the same logical multiplicity as the application of the appropriate first-person fragment of ordinary language by a particular person? Is it true that although it would not 'be in any sense more correct than the old one, . . . it would serve to show more clearly what was logically essential in the representation' (PR 88)? This seems more problematic than Wittgenstein envisaged in 1929. For 'I' has a use not only in 'experiential propositions', but also in sentences such as 'I am sunburnt all over' or 'I am *n* years old' or, even more significantly, in introductions ('I am N.N.'), in reports of one's activities ('I am writing a letter', 'I have read your essay'), in expressions of intention ('I'll go to London tomorrow'), and in the large and diverse class of performative utterances ('I promise . . .', 'I declare . . .').

It is *probable* that to the extent that Wittgenstein then reflected on this question, he thought that where 'I' was not eliminable in favour of a subjectless form, it can be replaced by 'this body'. In *Philosophical Remarks*, cheek by jowl with the claim that 'I' is eliminable, he wrote ' "I" clearly refers to my body, for *I* am in this room; and "I" is essentially something that is in a place, and in a place belonging to the same space as the one the other bodies are in too' (PR 86). In his lectures of 1932/3 (after he had abandoned his distinctive form of methodological solipsism), he argued that 'I' is used in 'two utterly different ways', one in which it is 'on a level with other people' and one in which it is not. Where 'I' is replaceable by 'this body', there 'I' and 'he' are 'on the same grammatical level'. The sentence 'I've got a matchbox' and 'I've got a bad tooth' are 'on a level' with 'Skinner has a matchbox' and 'Skinner has a bad tooth'. In these cases 'I have . . .' and 'Skinner has . . .' are both values of the same propositional function, and 'I' and 'Skinner' both denote 'possessors'. But in such sentences as 'I have a toothache' the word 'I' does not 'denote a possessor' and is not 'on the same level' as 'he' (M 308ff.).

The suggestion of a sharp dichotomy in the use of the first-person pronoun persisted, in transmuted form, in the *Blue Book*. There Wittgenstein distinguished between 'the use of "I" as subject' and its use 'as object'. Where 'I' is used as subject, as in 'I see so-and-so', 'I try to lift my arm', 'I think it will rain', 'I have a toothache', there is no recognition of a person, and there is no possibility of misidentification of a person, i.e. of mistaking another person for myself. But in such sentences as 'I have grown six inches', 'I have a bump on my forehead', 'My arm is broken', there is a recognition of a particular person, and the possibility of error has been provided for (BB 66f.)

It is significant that these claims sink from sight. It was plausible, within the phenomenalist framework of methodological solipsism, to suppose that there is a simple dichotomy between 'primary experience' (expressed in 'genuine propositions') and 'hypotheses'. Given that conception, 'I have a pain' will naturally be allocated to the former category, and 'I am six foot tall', like 'N.N. is six foot tall', will be allocated to the latter. But the idea that all first-person sentences are either concerned with 'the primary', which is logically independent of the body, or are about one's body (picked out as '*this* ↗ body') is a contaminated residue of Cartesian dualism. It presupposes the analysability of first-person action-sentences such as 'I am writing a letter' into 'This body is . . .' and 'There is a willing . . .', together, perhaps, with a causal rider. Similarly, expressions of intention such as 'I'll go to London today' must be decomposed into a *prediction* about my body and a *statement* about my will. But this is patently misconceived, as Wittgenstein later realized.[29] For statements about *behaviour* are not statements about bare bodily movements (see 'Behaviour and behaviourism', §4), and our concepts of intention and purpose are not of cogs that mediate between ethereal drive-shafts and physical axles. Not only is the analysis impossible, it wholly misconstrues the distinctive uses of such sentences. It is true that there are *some* first-person sentences which can be replaced by sentences

[29] This criticism of Cartesianism was independently elaborated by Ryle in *The Concept of Mind*.

about the body, e.g. 'I am sun-tanned all over' and 'My body is sun-tanned all over'. But it does not follow that the word 'I' sometimes means the same as 'this body' and sometimes does not – that would be highly misleading, suggesting an ambiguity where there is none. It would be more illuminating to say that 'I' and 'this body', for a short range of their use, run on parallel tracks.

The *Blue Book*'s attempt to salvage something from the flawed dichotomy of *Philosophical Remarks* is likewise erroneous. It is true that in the use of 'I have a pain' no room has been provided for misidentification of the subject, for there is here, as Wittgenstein later elaborated, *no* identification of a subject. But it is by no means clear that in such sentences as 'I have grown six inches', 'I have a bump on my forehead', or 'I have broken my arm' there is a *recognition* of a person (myself),[30] or that the possibility of misidentification has been provided for in the sense in which it has in 'N.N. has broken his arm'. I may be mistaken about whether my arm or your arm is broken or, in exceptional circumstances, whether *this* arm is mine or yours. But in such cases, when I mistakenly say 'I have broken my arm', for example, I do not *misidentify* myself or *mistake* myself for you; rather, I mistake my arm for yours, mistakenly attribute to myself something correctly attributable to you.

It is perhaps an awareness of these and similar points that partially explains why the idea of an essential duality in the use of 'I' lapses after the *Blue Book*, although, of course, that is not to say that the differences between 'I have a pain' and 'I am six foot tall' are not fundamental. Rather than a duality of essentially redundant uses of 'I' and essentially body-referring uses, as earlier envisaged, it would be better to think of a whole spectrum of sentences in the first person, ranging from avowals, through first-person reports, self-identifications ('I am N.N.', 'I am the so-and-so'), and first-person action-sentences, to a large variety of logically different kinds of description of oneself (including descriptions of one's mental state) and sentences which run parallel to bodily descriptions (e.g. 'I am six foot tall'). Similarly, the endorsement of a Lichtenbergian language as a more perspicuous representation of the logic of a sub-class of first-person sentences is dropped, although, of course, such a language may still be invoked as an illuminating object for comparison. To make clear how the use of 'I' differs from the use of proper names, descriptions, other personal pronouns, and demonstratives, it is not necessary to argue for its essential dispensability – although it is true that instead of saying 'I have a pain', one may say 'It hurts', whereas one cannot similarly replace 'N.N. has a pain' by such a sentence with a dummy pronoun and no person-referring expression. Nor need one argue that the 'special adequacy' of the first-person

[30] Unless, perhaps, I say this on looking at a photograph of myself.

experiential proposition is ineffably manifest in the application of a mono-centred language in order to clarify the special role of such propositions as *expressions* or *manifestations* of the inner, by contrast with their third-person counterparts, which are descriptions. But it was true to say that the logical peculiarities of such sentences are manifest in their *use*, as *Äusserungen* which are criteria for corresponding third-person assertions. And this, Wittgenstein noted in his lectures in 1946/7, would be visible even in a language with *no* personal pronouns, in which N.N. said not 'I am in pain', but 'N.N. is in pain'. For this, in his mouth, would be an utterance (*Äusserung*) of pain, not a description (LPP 49).

4. ' "*I*" does not refer to a person'

Throughout the 1930s, Wittgenstein persisted in his efforts to clarify the philosophical problems about the nature of 'the self'. These problems seem to limit us to a choice between three alternative types of solution: (i) Cartesian doctrines of the mind or soul – a substance, connected to the body, to which we refer by using the word 'I'; (ii) Humean theories according to which there is only a *fiction* of such an 'inner self' to which we *seem* to refer; (iii) Kantian accounts according to which 'I' on the one hand signifies the form of all experience, and on the other mysteriously refers to a noumenal object, the moral self. Wittgenstein came to think that these options, including their more recent derivatives such as his own transcendentalism in the *Notebooks 1914 – 16* and his 'no-ownership' conception in *Philosophical Remarks*, are all symptoms of grammatical misunderstandings. In his lecture notes in the mid-thirties, he wrote: 'I am trying to bring the whole problem down to our not understanding the function of the word "I" and "this ↗ "' (LPE 307).

He agreed with Cartesians that 'I' is not used 'because we recognize a particular person by his bodily characteristics' (BB 69), a feature particularly obvious in first-person experiential propositions. When I say 'I am thinking of such-and-such', the word 'I' does not refer to my body. But that 'I' is used differently from 'my body' does not imply that some new entity besides my body, viz. the ego, has been discovered (AWL 60). And it is an illusion to suppose that since in using 'I' we do not refer to our bodies, therefore we must be using it 'to refer to something bodiless, which, however, has its seat in our body' (BB 69). In an argument reminiscent of Kant's third paralogism, Wittgenstein observed that 'It seems that I can *trace* my identity, quite independent of the identity of my body. And the idea is suggested that I trace the identity of something dwelling in my body, the identity of my mind' (LPE 308). This idea arises from the fact that when I say that I did such-and-such in the past, I do not employ any criteria of subject identity; I do not check to see whether, as it were, I still have the same body. But that is not because I check on the continued identity of something other than my body. For suppose that 'I constantly change and my surrounding does: is there still some continuity, namely, by it being *me* and *my surrounding* that change?' (LPE 300).

But the neo-Humean reaction to Cartesianism that is evident in Russell is equally confused. For ' "Is my person (or a person) a constituent of the fact that I see, or not?" expresses a question about symbolism in the form of a question about nature' (LPE 282). Both Hume and Russell had pretended to look for their 'selves' in introspection, Hume supposing that if he found a persistent impression, it might be his self, and Russell thinking it possible that one might occasionally catch a glimpse of one's self, and that it is probable that one is acquainted with it. The *Tractatus* too erred in conceiving it to be a super-empirical fact or a truth of metaphysics that 'nothing *in the visual field* allows you to infer that it is seen by an eye' (cf. Exg. §402, 2.1). But to claim that one has looked for a self and not found it or to insist that such a search *must* be in vain presupposes the intelligibility of such searching. But the search is unintelligible – like 'looking for the East Pole', not like looking for the source of the Nile or even for Eldorado. It is not that one *cannot* find it, but that nothing *would count* as finding it.

The word 'I' is one symbol among others with a practical use, and it has that use in the context of pervasive, and therefore unremarked, facts about us. Although 'I' does not mean the same as '*this* body', it 'only has meaning with reference to a body' (AWL 62). If, when people spoke, all the sounds they made came from the same loudspeaker in the same voice, the word 'I' would have no use (AWL 24). The use of 'I' depends on the correlation between the mouth which says 'I' and the body from whose mouth the word 'I' is emitted. This is evident, for example, in avowals of pain; for a criterion for A's having a pain when *his* hand is pinched is that the *Äusserung* 'I am in pain' (or, what comes to the same thing, 'That hurt *me*') comes from *his* mouth (AWL 62).

It is immensely tempting to claim that the solution to these traditional puzzles is embarrassingly simple, viz. that although 'I' refers neither to a body nor to a self, it refers to a *person*, as 'he' and 'you' do. This Wittgenstein sometimes flatly denied: 'It is correct, although paradoxical,' he wrote (Vol. XII, 215); 'to say: "I" does not refer to [designate, *bezeichnet*] a person.' This contention undoubtedly goes against the grain and needs careful examination in order to discern what he was driving at. A simile Wittgenstein used with respect to the word 'today' may put one on the right trail: 'I' does not differ from person-referring expressions (e.g. 'N.N.', 'The so-and-so,' 'he') as a hammer from a mallet, but as a hammer from a nail (cf. BB 108). What must be done is to compare the use of the first-person pronoun with the uses of person-referring expressions to see whether the differences justify Wittgenstein's paradoxical claim.

The key to his conception lies in his often reiterated and *prima-facie* bewildering remark that *I don't choose the mouth which says 'I . . .'* (Vol. XVI, 25). When I express my pain in an avowal, I do not do so by choosing *this* mouth rather than another, any more than when I manifest pain by groaning I choose the mouth from which I groan. When I use the first-person pronoun, I employ no principle of differentiation to select one person from among others. Hence too, 'It has no sense to ask "How do you know it's *you* who sees . . . ?", for I don't *know* that it is this person and not another one which sees before I point. – This is what I meant by saying that I don't choose the mouth which says "I have toothache" ' (LPE 311).

That I do not *name* anyone when I say that it is I who . . . is obvious enough. 'I see X' does not mean the same as 'The person so-and-so sees X' (LPE 298), even though if I say 'I see X', *someone else* can on the grounds of this say 'The person so-and-so sees X'. But to grant that 'I' is not a name is still a long way from conceding that it does not refer to a person. 'He' is not a name either, but in saying 'He sees X', one is surely referring to a person.

It is tempting to claim that not only is 'I' a referring expression, it is a super-referring expression, for it is guaranteed success, being immune both to reference-*failure* and to referential *error* or *misidentification*. And if one so thinks, a simple explanation for these features is at hand; for, one will argue, the rule for the reference of the word 'I' is that it refers to whoever uses it. But one might be suspicious here; for is this not like arguing that an arrow stuck in the wall, around which one draws a bull's eye, has hit the target? Wittgenstein certainly was suspicious (and in the following passage expressed himself more cautiously than in Vol. XII, 215 (above)):

' "Ich" in meinem Munde bezeichnet *mich*.' Bezeichnet den dieses Wort in *meinem* Munde etwas besonderes? Ich wollte wohl sagen: ' "Ich" bezeichnet immer den Mensch der es ausspricht.' Aber was heisst das, es bezeichne ihn? Gibt es denn da nur *eine* Möglichkeit? (Vol. XVI, 230)

(' "I" in my mouth refers to [designates] *me*.' Does this word in *my* mouth refer to anything particular? I really wanted to say: ' "I" always refers to the person who utters it.' But what does it mean, it refers to him? Is there only *one* possibility?)

This suggests a more flexible way of challenging the idea that 'I' refers to a person in the sense in which 'you' and 'he' do, i.e. that the use of 'I' runs parallel to the use of 'you' or 'he'. Wittgenstein did not explicitly say what 'possibilities' he had in mind, and his point must be gleaned from his practice. 'Reference' is not a 'meta-logical' expression (in Wittgenstein's special sense of this term) with a sharply circumscribed use and strict *Merkmal*-definition. It is natural (although perhaps not to philosophers) and correct to explain it by reference to a range of simple paradigms which overlap but are not uniform. In this respect 'reference' is like 'name' or 'proposition'. And Wittgenstein's practice, in his extensive reflections on the first-person pronoun, was to compare its use with that of a central range, and a range of features, of expressions that are employed to refer to something.

One paradigm of reference is the use of an appropriate expression such as 'this', 'there', or 'he' in a sentence, accompanied by a deictic gesture. In such cases we typically refer to *this* ↗ thing, *that* ↗ place, or *this* ↗ person'. A sentence such as 'He has . . .', used on a particular occasion, has no sense unless it is related to a name, description, or ostensive gesture (Vol. XVI, 170). For an explanation of what was meant will specify by these means *who* was meant. And in the absence of such an explicit or implicit relation one will not understand, or fully understand, what was meant. In this sense, an ostensive gesture (name or description) belongs with 'he . . .' (Vol. XVI, 35). But do I, when I say 'I have . . .' *point at myself* (BB 67)? Do I even point figuratively, as it were? The mouth which says 'I' does not thereby point to anything (BB 68). It is not as if the very same pointer, so to speak, points now to him, now to me; 'I' and 'he' have very different functions in language (Vol. XVI, 171). Saying 'I . . .' is more like raising my hand to draw attention to myself than it is like pointing to someone. And when I raise my hand to do so, I do not thereby point to myself, any more than when I point to the sun, for example, I point to two things, viz. the sun and myself, just because it is I who am pointing (BB 67). And so too, when I say 'I meant him ↗ ', I am not *also* pointing to myself, although I am also drawing attention to myself. One might say that 'I' is the point of origin on the co-ordinate system of deixis, but not a point on the deictic graph (cf. BT 523); or that it is the centre of deictic reference and therefore not on its circumference. (One might say that all we are doing here is pointing out the difference between (○) and (⊖) .) An ostensive gesture does not, in this sense, belong with 'I'; and if I say to you 'I am tired', you will not fail to understand what I mean *because* I have not pointed to myself. In this respect the use of 'I' does not converge on this paradigm of reference.

It may be objected that one *does* sometimes point at oneself when one says 'I . . .'. But if I point at myself, I do not use the same gesture as in pointing to *him* ↗ , and my gesture does not have the same function. For it does not serve, as does the gesture accompanying 'he', to avert misidentification. Rather it *draws attention* to myself, like raising my hand or clearing my throat loudly before I speak (BB 67). I can *point him out* by pointing at him, but I do not *point myself out* when I point at myself. I do not *thereby* pick myself out from among others (except when I point at a photograph of myself in a group); and what looks like immunity from misidentification or reference-failure is in fact the absence of any reference at all. If, in saying 'I . . .' I do point at myself, I am, of course, modelling my use of 'I' on that of 'he ↗ ' or 'this ↗ person'. But, Wittgenstein notes, this makes 'I' similar to 'he' only in the way a degenerate identity-statement is similar to a genuine one. In proving that the sum of the angles of a triangle is 180°, we draw a diagram $\overset{\alpha' \diagdown \triangle \diagup \beta'}{\underset{\alpha \quad \beta}{\diagup \gamma \diagdown}}$ and say that α = α', β = β', and γ = γ (BB 68). In this way 'I' is referentially similar to 'he'. So one might say, although Wittgenstein does not, that the use of 'I', when accompanied by a reflexive gesture, is a case of *degenerate* reference, in the sense in which a point is a degenerate case of a conic section or a tautology a degenerate case of a proposition with sense.

A different line of attack seems equally plausible: one can surely say that the word 'I', in the mouth of a particular person N.N, refers to that person. For if N.N. says truly 'I ϕ', then others can say 'N.N. ϕs'. And equally, N.N.'s utterance 'I ϕ', if a candidate for truth at all, will be true if and only if that person, N.N., is ϕing. Hence, one might conclude, it is difficult to see how 'I' can be failing to refer if that is how it helps to determine the truth or falsity of the first-person utterance. Wittgenstein addressed the first limb of this objection. One can indeed say that in the mouth of a particular person 'I' refers to that person *in the sense that* if he rightly says 'I ϕ', then others can say truly 'N.N. ϕs'. But this transformation from first to third person is, so to speak, *for others*. For me, 'the word "I" is not a signal calling attention to . . . a person' (LPE 307). And one cannot significantly say that 'I' in my mouth refers to *me* (cf. Vol. XVI, 43), any more than one can significantly say that 'this' in my mouth refers to that (without pointing).

With respect to the second limb of the objection, different cases should be distinguished. Avowals (*Äusserungen*), at least at the most expressive end of the spectrum, are perhaps dubious candidates for truth, but for argument's sake we may disregard this. The utterance of 'I have a pain' is itself a criterion for the truth of 'He has a pain' said of the speaker. It is the fact that the utterance comes *from his mouth* that constitutes the ground for saying of him 'He is in pain'. But that no more shows that N.N.'s utterance 'I have a pain' *refers* to N.N. than the fact that his groan of pain comes from his mouth, and is likewise a criterion of his being in pain, shows that the groan *refers* to him. His saying sincerely 'I have a pain' does not rest on the criterion that *he* says this or on any other criterion, and he does not identify a person *for himself* when he avows his pain. Rather, he draws attention to himself, and *we* identify who is in pain.[31]

In other cases, where the utterance is not itself a criterion for the corresponding third-person assertion, e.g. 'I am seated' or 'I am locked out', the first-person assertion is, of course, true if and only if the corresponding third-person assertion is true. And if one wishes to call that a case of referring, one may do so. But one should still note, first, that 'what determines the truth' of what I say when I say 'I am locked out' is the fact that I am *locked out* (i.e. to verify it, I do not identify a subject), and second, that the fact that I used the word 'I' in saying what I said does *not* 'help to determine the truth or falsity of the *first-person* utterance'.

One might plausibly object that when one uses an expression to refer to a particular person, one distinguishes or intends to distinguish between that person and others. The role of the referring expression is to specify *which* person one is talking about. And surely, when I say 'I ϕ' ('am in pain' or 'am seated') I do just that! Wittgenstein again invites us to note *differences*. First, when I groan 'I am in pain' or exclaim 'I *am* tired', I am not distinguishing between myself and others by *identifying* a particular person. I am not selecting or picking out one person among others; and I am not saying that *this* person is in pain or tired, only that *I* am (cf. Vol. XII, 158). Rather, what I say *enables my hearers* to identify who is in pain.

Even in cases where, in using a first-person sentence, I do want to distinguish between myself and others, the use of 'I' is still subtly different from the use of 'he' or 'N.N.'. If I am among a group of people, and I, as opposed to others, volunteer for something or confess that I, and no one else, did something awry or announce that I alone know something, I am surely distinguishing between myself and others. But it does not follow that I do so by identifying myself as *this person*, N.N., who I am (cf. PI §406). For in numerous such cases I want to distinguish myself from others not by picking myself out from among them, but by obtruding myself upon them. And here, one might prefer to say, I draw attention to myself, but do not refer to myself. But if, while I was talking I said '. . . the ϕer . . .', believing myself to be the ϕer, I might later explain that I was, of course, referring to myself.

Proper names of people are one typical paradigm of referring expression, and it is instructive to recollect how differently the use of 'I' and the referential use of proper names is learnt. For the different mode of learning reflects the fact that one is learning to use very different

---

[31] Similar considerations apply to performatives. 'I promise . . .' does not say who promises; it is used by a speaker to *make* a promise. But 'I, N.N., promise . . .' *also* identifies me, says who I am.

instruments of language. One learns a proper name by being told 'He ↗ is N.N.', and one might be taught how to use a proper name to refer to a person by being told 'when *this person* ↗ has pains, you say "N.N. has pains" '. But does one learn how to use the word 'I' by being told '*This person* ↗ is I'? And is one taught the use of 'I' in the sentence 'I have a pain' by being told 'When *this person* ↗ has a pain, you say "I have a pain" ' (Vol. XVI, 153)? Similarly, if someone says 'He has a pain', one will not know what he meant unless one knows to whom he referred, viz. to N.N. or to *that person* ↗. So one will ask 'Who do you mean?' But if someone says 'I have a pain', can one still ask 'Who do you mean?' In short, one does not learn the use of the word 'I' in the way one learns the use of paradigms of referring expressions. 'I' is more like 'now' than it is like 'N.N.', 'the so-and-so', or 'he', and it shares some of its anomalous features relative to those paradigms. Failures of understanding, misunderstandings and misidentifications of reference that arise with respect to typical referring expressions, cannot arise in that way with 'I' (or 'now').

Even more marked differences come to light when one examines the sub-class of first-person sentences uses of which constitute *Äusserungen*. When I exclaim 'I have a pain' or 'I think that such-and-such', when I announce 'I say, . . .' or 'I'm going now', I am not *stating* that a certain person has a pain, thinks such-and-such, is speaking, or is about to go, I am manifesting my pain, giving my opinion, drawing attention to myself, or expressing my intention. I do so by using the first-person pronoun, but in so using it I do not pick out one person from among others. One might object that just as when I assert 'He is in pain' or 'N.N. thinks such-and-such', so here too I *know* or believe *of* a certain person that things are thus-and-so with him. But, as has been argued previously, this is misconceived. I do not *know* that I am in pain – although that is not because my evidence is slender. And I do not know, by being in pain, that someone else does not have the same pain (cf. PI §408; Vol. XVI, 43f.). 'I know' prefixed to an avowal, unlike 'I know' prefixed to a corresponding third-person sentence, does not signify an item of knowledge. Furthermore, a whole battery of epistemic terms – e.g. 'I doubt', 'I wonder', 'I suspect', 'I guess' – either cannot intelligibly be prefixed to first-person present-tense psychological sentences or, if they can, they function quite differently from cases where they are prefixed to third-person sentences. These differences too earmark the distinctive role of the first-person pronoun over this part of its range of use, a role which makes it fundamentally misleading to treat it as being on the same level as person-referring expressions.

Teaching differences was Wittgenstein's method for dissolving philosophical problems. For these problems typically arise through assimilat-

ing one type of expression to another which it superficially resembles or
through taking one simple paradigm to determine a certain kind of
speech-function where a whole family of distinct but overlapping
paradigms is more appropriate. The history of philosophical reflections
on 'the self' exemplifies the nature of these tangled knots in our
understanding. One thread that runs through these numerous knots is
the conviction that the word 'I' names, designates, or refers to something, a mental substance, a thinking thing associated with a substance, a
bundle of perceptions, or a transcendental subject. This century has
continued to dance to these classical tunes, but in the modern, jazzed-up
syncopation of logico-linguistic analysis. 'The self' has variously been
conceived of as an object of acquaintance or a logical construction, and,
more recently, the first-person pronoun has been thought to be a
super-referring expression guaranteed against reference-failure or misidentification, like a magic arrow that always hits the bull's-eye.
Wittgenstein's endeavour was to draw our attention to differences
between the word 'I' and proper names, descriptions, and other personal
pronouns, differences in function, in identification of the bearer, in
grammatical combination with other expressions, in verification, etc.
These differences are compelling, and they led Wittgenstein to deny –
paradoxically, as he admitted – that the word 'I' is a referring expression
at all. But, as he remarked in a different context, 'When white changes to
black some people say, "It is essentially still the same". And others, when
the colour darkens the slightest bit, say, "It has changed completely".'
(See Exg. of p. 46n.) What matters crucially is that one be aware of the
differences; and if thereafter, one still wants to say that 'I' is nevertheless
a kind of referring expression or, better perhaps, a degenerate referring
expression, nothing need hang on that preference as long as one does not
assimilate the function of the word 'I' to an inappropriate paradigm of
reference.

XII

THE WORLD OF CONSCIOUSNESS

1. The world as consciousness

In his lectures during the May term of 1932 Wittgenstein said that he himself had often been tempted to say 'All that is real is the experience of the present moment' or 'All that is certain is the experience of the present moment'. Anyone who is at all tempted to embrace idealism or solipsism, he added, knows the temptation to say 'The only reality is the present experience' or 'The only reality is *my* present experience' (M 311). Were the *Notebooks 1914 – 16* not available, one might have supposed these remarks to be a generous concession that it is intelligible how one can edge oneself into a solipsist or idealist frame of mind. But the Schopenhauerian passages in the *Notebooks* written between June and November 1916 suggest that Wittgenstein had indeed been tempted, and had succumbed to the temptation. In a strikingly sybilline passage, he wrote:

> What do I know about God and the purpose of life?
> I know that this world exists.
> That I am placed in it like my eye in its visual field.
> That something about it is problematic, which we call its meaning.
> That this meaning does not lie in it but outside it.
> That life is the world. (NB 73)

Some days later he elaborated:

> The World and Life are one.
> Physiological life is of course not 'Life'. And neither is psychological life. Life is the world. (NB 77)

And subsequently he added the Schopenhauerian thought that

> Only from the consciousness of the *uniqueness of my life* arises religion – science – and art.
> And this consciousness is life itself. (NB 79)

The equation of the world with 'life' and 'life' with consciousness ramified into the mysterious account Wittgenstein gave of the 'philosophical self' (see 'I and my self', §2). 'The philosophical I is not the human being, not the human body or the human soul [mind] with the psychological properties, but the metaphysical subject, the boundary (not a part) of the world' (NB 82). But, again echoing Schopenhauer, the philosophical self is stripped of all individuality, for 'I am my world'

(NB 84), and 'As my idea is the world, in the same way my will is the world-will' (NB 85).

The transcendental idealist (Schopenhauerian) drift is further evident in the claim that 'it is equally possible to take the bare present image as the worthless momentary picture in the whole temporal world, and as the true world among shadows' (NB 83), and in the contention that in death 'the world does not change but stops existing' (NB 73). What exactly Wittgenstein made of these apocalyptic pronouncements is very unclear, and likely to remain so. But there can be little doubt that they originate in Schopenhauer's *The World as Will and Representation*. There Schopenhauer adumbrated a strange, mesmerizing picture of consciousness. The concept of consciousness, he argued, 'coincides with that of representation in general'.[1] That the world is my representation is 'like the Axioms of Euclid, a proposition which everyone must recognize as true as soon as he understands it'.[2] The deep insight achieved by modern philosophy, according to Schopenhauer, is:

that the *objective existence* of things is conditioned by a representer of them, and that consequently the objective world exists only as *representation* . . . The objective as such, always and essentially has its existence in the consciousness of a subject; it is therefore the representation of this subject, and consequently is conditioned by the subject, and moreover by the subject's forms of representation . . .[3]

Actual or phenomenal individuality, according to Schopenhauer, is unreal; it is an aspect of our enslavement to the blind forces of the will. But in aesthetic experience and in contemplation of the sublime, we can free ourselves from our bondage and transcend our own particularity. Here one achieves 'pure contemplation, absorption in perception, being lost in the object, forgetting all individuality'.[4] Thus liberated, 'We are no longer the individual; that is forgotten . . . we are only that *one* eye of the world which looks out from all knowing creatures.'[5]

It is doubtful whether one can make sense of these dark sayings, and it is not to our present purposes even to explain why they might seem to make sense. What is important for the discussion of Wittgenstein's later reflections on the concept of consciousness is that he evidently sympathized with at least some aspects of this poetic metaphysics and had once been caught in this web of illusion. He had indeed experienced the seductive power of a certain form of solipsism ('What has history to do with me? Mine is the first and only world!' (NB 82)). It was surely with his own experience in view that, in response to his imaginary inter-

---

[1] Schopenhauer, *World as Will and Representation*, Vol. I, p. 51.
[2] Ibid., Vol. II, p. 13.
[3] Ibid., Vol. II, p. 5.
[4] Ibid., Vol. I, pp. 196f.
[5] Ibid., Vol. I, pp. 197f.

locutor's conception of the world as representation ('the visual room'), he later wrote:

'It is true I said that I know within myself what you meant. But that meant that I knew how one thinks to conceive this object, to see it, to make one's looking and pointing mean it. I know how one stares ahead and looks about one in this case – and the rest. (PI §398)

It is interesting that in his lectures in the early 1930s, Wittgenstein picked up the theme of consciousness as conceived by the metaphysician. Moore reports him as saying:

'In one sense "I" and "conscious" are equivalent, but not in another', and he compared this difference to the difference between what can be said of the pictures on a film in a magic lantern and of the picture on the screen; saying that the pictures in the lantern are all 'on the same level' but that the picture which is at any given time on the screen is not 'on the same level' with any of them, and that if we were to use 'conscious' to say of one of the pictures in the lantern that it was at that time being thrown on the screen, it would be meaningless to say of the picture on the screen that it was 'conscious'. The pictures on the film, he said, 'have neighbours', whereas that on the screen has none. (M 310)

It is doubtful whether he would later have said that there is a use of 'conscious' in which it is equivalent to 'I'.[6] But the principle of contrast which he invoked here by means of the phrase 'having neighbours' recurs both in the 'Lectures on "Private Experience" and "Sense Data" ' and in the brief, oblique riposte to solipsism and idealism in *Investigations* §§398 – 402.[7]

One is tempted, in moments of philosophical intoxication, to insist that 'Surely, if I'm to be quite frank I must say that I have something which nobody has' (LPE 283) – viz. my personal experience. This is surely unique – it has no neighbour! But, Wittgenstein replies, this 'uniqueness' is not the uniqueness of a single exemplar of something; it is rather the uniqueness of a *special position in grammar*. And in *that* sense, what is unique *has no owner*. One wants to say 'At any rate only I have got THIS'; but in reply one should ask

In what sense have you *got* what you are talking about and saying that only you have got it? Do you possess it? You do not even *see* it. Must you not really say that no one has got it? And this too is clear: if as a matter of logic you exclude other people's having something, it loses its sense to say that you have it. (PI §398)

Idealism leads solipsism, for if the *world* is idea, it is not anyone *else's* idea. But solipsism errs in thinking that the world thus conceived is *my*

---

[6] But he might have said that the misuse of 'consciousness' is akin to the metaphysician's misuse of 'I' as the name of a *res cogitans*. Equally, the illusory 'experience of consciousness' is similar to the illusory 'experience of the self'.
[7] Cf. also WWK 50; PR 85f.

idea, for *I* do not enter 'the world as idea'. In this sense 'the visual room' (PI §398), the 'world of private experience', has no owner.

Nevertheless, 'consciousness in general' (as Kant might put it) may still seem equivalent to the world experienced, the world as representation. And when Wittgenstein insists on the unintelligibility of private ostensive definition, on the incoherence of private ownership of experience, on the confusions surrounding epistemic privacy of experience, and when he denies that 'toothache' means *this* or 'fear' means *that*, it can readily seem as if he is neglecting the essence of the matter: ' "the experience or whatever you might call it? – Almost the *world* behind the mere words?" ' (LPE 296). In words reminiscent of his own reflections of 1916, Wittgenstein concedes that it *seems* that he neglects life, 'But not life physiologically understood but life as consciousness. And consciousness not physiologically understood, or understood from the outside, but consciousness as the very essence of experience, the appearance of the world, the world' (LPE 297).

What leads us into this strange illusion? After all, Wittgenstein distinguishes, as we all do, between saying 'I have a toothache' when one has a toothache and saying it without having a toothache, and so forth. So in what sense is he 'neglecting' something? 'Isn't what you reproach me of', he adds ironically, 'as though you said: "In your language you're only *speaking*!" ' (LPE 297). Does the illusion not stem from the idea of 'the world of consciousness' as the gold backing for our verbal currency? We conceive of this 'world' as a space peopled with experiences, sense-impressions, feelings, etc., which we *name* by private ostensive definition and observe *in foro interno*, describe in words for the benefit of others, etc. For we are indeed tempted to talk of the *content* of experience thus, to insist that:

I know what toothaches are like, I am acquainted with them, I know what it's like to see red, green, blue, yellow, I know what it's like to feel sorrow, hope, fear, joy, affection, to wish to do something, to remember having done something, to intend doing something . . . . I know, too, what it means to parade these experiences before one's mind. When I do that, I don't parade kinds of behaviour or situations before my mind. (RPP I §91)

Furthermore, one would like to say:

'I see red *thus*', 'I hear the note that you strike *thus*', 'I feel sorrow *thus*', or even ' *This* is what one feels when one is sad, *this* when one is glad', etc. One would like to people a world, analogous to the physical one, with these *thus*es and *this*es. (RPP I §896)

Such are the temptations. But enough has been clarified in previous essays for it to be obvious that they must be resisted. The concept of the content of experience thus invoked is no more than that of the 'private object', the sense-datum, the 'object' one grasps immediately in 'introspection' (RPP I §109). Do I really know what it means to parade these experiences before one's mind? Can I *explain* it, to others or to myself (RPP I §91)? The whole battery of arguments against the intelligibility of a private language demonstrates the vanity of this idea. One can only, as it were, 'people a world' with *this*es and *thus*es where there is a picture of *what is experienced* to which one can *point* as one gives such explanations (RPP I §896). But that is not intelligible here, in the *'world of consciousness'*.

The 'world of consciousness' does not belong uniquely to me, since it 'belongs' to no one. 'I can as little own it as I can walk about it, or look at it, or point to it' (PI §398). The 'contents' of this 'world' cannot be seen by others; but then neither can they be *seen* by me. To conceive of experience as 'a world', to think that it is in fact *the* world, is to construe a grammatical articulation as a quasi-physical phenomenon that one observes (PI §401). One can describe what one perceives, and also report the fact that one is perceiving what one thus perceives. But such a report is not a description of a unique, private, immaterial 'world of consciousness'.

2. The gulf between consciousness and body

If one is captivated by the picture of two 'worlds', the world of physical things, events, and processes and the world of consciousness peopled with mental objects, events, and processes (see 'Privacy', §1), then the nature of consciousness and states of consciousness is bound to seem mysterious. For these two worlds seem to be constituted of different *materials*, made of different kinds of substance. The physical world, as Descartes argued, is made of material substance, and the mental world 'is liable to be imagined as gaseous, or rather, aethereal' (BB 47). The latter evidently does not consist of material substance, so we are prone to think of it as consisting of immaterial substance. (Similarly, when we insist on the distinctness of numbers from numerals, we point out that numbers are not concrete objects, and are inclined to think of them as abstract objects.) But when asked to explain what this immaterial substance is, we falter. To say that its essence is thinking, as Descartes did, merely compounds the confusion – for the Cartesian concept of thinking is not coherent.[8] So we are inclined to insist that although we cannot point at this ethereal substance for others, each of us can, as it were, point at it *in foro interno* for himself. For surely we are, each of us, witnesses to our own consciousness (PI §416)? All *this*, we feel, is the world of my consciousness – it is indeed *my* world, and sometimes it seems to be *the* world.

[8] See A. J. P. Kenny, *Descartes* (Random House, New York, 1968), pp. 68 – 78.

Conceiving of consciousness as a private realm populated by private experiences, one is bound to be puzzled at its evolutionary emergence. Here we adopt a particular picture: 'The evolution of the higher animals and of man, and the awakening of consciousness at a particular level. The picture is something like this: Though the ether is filled with vibrations the world is dark. But one day man opens his seeing eye, and there is light' (PI p. 184). It seems, quite rightly, that consciousness, experience, emerges when phenomena in the physical world have evolved a certain degree of complexity (BB 47). For, to be sure, we do not attribute consciousness to plants or experience to an amoeba. A very complex biological substratum, a highly evolved nervous system, is a characteristic feature of conscious creatures. But here our picture of consciousness as an inner world, as light within the soul, leads us into confusion. For now the 'evolutionary emergence of consciousness' suddenly seems utterly mysterious. How could something so different from material things and their properties *emerge* from what is, after all, merely a more complex arrangement of matter? Could this whole, extraordinary world of consciousness spring into being through nothing more than an increase in the complexity of neural organization?

On the one hand, there seems to be 'an unbridgeable gulf between consciousness and brain-process' (PI §412). For how could *this*, my current experience, my present state of consciousness, be produced by a process in the brain? How could the ethereal emerge from the material? It is hardly surprising that a nineteenth-century scientist, Tyndall, should write:

The passage from the physics of the brain to the corresponding facts of consciousness is unthinkable. Granted that a definite thought and a definite molecular action in the brain occur simultaneously, we do not possess the intellectual organ, nor apparently any rudiment of the organ, which would enable us to pass, by a process of reasoning, from one to the other.[9]

And it is equally unsurprising that contemporary scientists and psychologists should concur, finding consciousness 'a great mystery',[10] and confessing that 'no one knows what consciousness is, or whether it serves any purpose'.[11]

On the other hand, it can seem equally baffling that we can attribute consciousness and states of consciousness to material things at all. For are living beings, animals and humans, not physical objects? And how can a

    [9] Tyndall, *Fragments of Science*, 5th edn, p. 420; quoted by James, *Principles of Psychology*, Vol. I, p. 147.
    [10] J. P. Frisby, *Seeing: Illusion, Brain, and Mind* (Oxford University Press, Oxford, 1980), p. 11.
    [11] P. N. Johnson-Laird, *The Computer and the Mind* (Fontana, London, 1988), p. 353.

mere physical object be conscious (cf. PI §283)? I *experience* my own consciousness, one is inclined to say, but how can I transfer this idea to objects outside myself? How can physical bodies in the physical world have something as alien to physical phenomena as consciousness? And if one thinks, as many philosophers and psychologists do, that it is the *brain* that is conscious, this exacerbates the mystery. For how can the mere matter inside the skull be conscious? Of course, when one attributes consciousness to things other than oneself, one does not attribute it to stones or plants. And if one is loath to attribute consciousness to a body as such, one is inclined to think that one must therefore attribute it to the mind or soul that certain bodies, e.g. human ones, have. For surely 'one has to say it of a body, or, if you like, of a soul [mind] which some body *has*' (PI §283)! But if we are puzzled at the idea that a body, a mere physical thing, could be conscious, we should surely be no less puzzled at the idea that *a body* might have a mind or soul.

These apparent mysteries reflect our mystification. We project our own misunderstandings of the conceptual or grammatical articulations of our language onto reality, and rightly find reality thus conceived to be unintelligible. When we insist upon the mysterious gulf between physical phenomena and facts of consciousness, when we hold with Tyndall that 'we try to soar in a vacuum the moment we seek to comprehend the connection between them', we in effect confuse the shadows of different grammatical rules for a cleft in reality.

The first step towards clarity is to remind ourselves that it is only of a living human being and what resembles (behaves like) a living human being that one can say that it is conscious or unconscious (PI §281). We do not attribute consciousness or lack of consciousness to stones, trees, or machines – not because they are insufficiently complex in structure or physical constitution, but because they are not living creatures that behave like us in circumstances in which we attribute consciousness to each other. We do not say of a tree that it is unconscious, for nothing would count as a conscious tree, and we do not say of a machine which is switched off that it will regain consciousness when it is switched on again.

Consequently, bafflement at the idea that the brain of a human being is conscious is misconceived. For the brain is no more a conscious being than a tree is. When a person who has been under an anaesthetic stirs, groans, and opens his eyes, we say that he has regained consciousness, that he is awake. But we do not say that his brain is awake. For it is not his brain that sits up in bed and asks for a drink, looks around, and gets out of bed. The brain, to be sure, is a highly complex organ – but it is not an organism. Consciousness is attributable to an organism as a whole, not to its parts, no matter how complex. And it is attributable to the organism on the grounds of its behaviour, its exercise of its perceptual faculties, its susceptibility to sensation, and its voluntary action (see 'Men, minds, and machines', §1).

One might object that surely the brain is the organ of consciousness. One can be completely paralysed, yet conscious for all that; but one could not be conscious without the brain. So must it not have some properties that confer consciousness upon it? This is confused. First, even if the brain were the organ of consciousness, it would not follow that the brain is conscious. For the eyes are our organs of vision and the ears our organs of hearing, but metonymy apart, our eyes do not see or our ears hear; rather, *we* see with our eyes and hear with our ears. Secondly, our brains are not organs of consciousness in the sense in which our perceptual organs are organs of perception. For we are not conscious, i.e. awake, *with* our brain. Nor does it make sense to talk of being conscious *of* something, e.g. the ticking of a clock or the disorder in a room, with our brain. The brain, unlike the eyes, is not an organ the movements of which we can voluntarily control or which we *use* as we use our sense-organs to perceive, since it does not move and we cannot control it. Nor is it the organ of consciousness in the sense in which the stomach, the functioning of which is likewise beyond our voluntary control, is the organ of digestion. For while digestion is a process that takes place in the stomach, being conscious is not a process, and it does not 'take place' in the brain. Although one can be paralysed yet still conscious, neither being conscious (as opposed to being unconscious) nor being conscious of something (i.e. having one's attention caught and held by something) are acts or activities of any bodily organ, since they are not acts or activities at all. It is true, of course, that unless the brain were functioning normally in certain respects, one would not be conscious, nor would one be enjoying states of consciousness, since one would be unconscious. But equally, unless the brain were functioning normally, one would not be able to talk; yet no one would say that the brain is the organ of speech.

To say that only living creatures which behave in certain respects like human beings can be said to be conscious or unconscious is to make a grammatical statement. But does this really solve our predicament? For are living creatures not *things*, physical objects? And how can a mere physical object be conscious? The question is misleading. For although it is true that human beings have bodies, they are not identical with their bodies (see 'Behaviour and behaviourism', §4). In the ordinary use of the terms 'thing', 'object', 'physical (or material) object', not only does one not say that human beings are things or physical objects – one *contrasts* them with objects or things. If asked to explain what the expression 'a physical object' means, no one would point at a human being and say 'That is a physical object'. And if someone were to over-value his chattels, giving preference to them at the expense of people, one would remind him that they are only things, mere physical objects. Used thus, the expressions 'thing', 'object', and 'physical object' are, as it were, demoting or derogatory terms.

If, when philosophizing, someone insists that human beings are physical objects, he is evidently diverging from this common use, and we should press him to explain what he means. If he means that human beings are not minds or souls causally linked to bodies, we should agree. A person, though not identical with his body, is not some other substance over and above his body. If he means that there are many properties (e.g. being sunburnt all over) with respect to which it is indifferent whether they are ascribed to the person or to his body, we should likewise agree. Human beings have physical dimensions, location, take up space, move or stay still, etc. As has been stressed, for part of their use, 'N.N.' and 'N.N.'s body' run along parallel tracks, *but only for a small part.* For even predicates of movement are not univocally attributable to a person and his body alike, and many (e.g. walks, runs) are indeed not licitly attributable to the body at all. To that extent it is both ill-advised and unnecessary to claim that human beings are physical objects; for the modest truths that are thereby intimated can be stated, as above, without this misleading form of words.

If the philosopher insists that at any rate a person's body is a physical object, we might go along with that. A corpse, the remains of a human being, can be said to be a physical object (although it is to be treated with a dignity which we do not generally accord to mere physical things). And we may concede that in certain respects a living human being is no different from a corpse: thus, if a corpse falls from a high cliff and a human being falls from a high cliff, the laws of physics will not discriminate between the two – the trajectory and the acceleration of both is described by reference to the laws of free fall. But a corpse is not a human being:

Our attitude to what is alive and to what is dead is not the same. All our reactions are different. – If anyone says: 'That cannot simply come from the fact that the living move about in such-and-such a way and the dead do not', then I want to intimate to him that this is a case of transition 'from quantity to quality'. (PI §284)

The categorial difference between what is alive and what is not, in particular between what is sentient and what is insensate, is marked in countless ways in our language, and is manifest in countless ways in our reactions and attitudes. One way in which it is marked is, as noted, in the peculiar locution of 'having a body'. We say that a person has a body, and speak of the body metonymically as 'a living body', as opposed to a corpse. A person's body, like all physical objects, consists of such-and-such quantities of chemicals; but one cannot say that a person consists of quantities of chemicals. ('He is flesh and blood' is no more a statement of what a person consists of than 'War is war' is an instance of the law of identity.) But it is the person, the living human being, that is said to be conscious. And no one would say 'My body is a human being'! So the very question of how a mere physical object like a human being can be conscious leads us astray from the start. A human being is not a mere physical object, but a living creature that acts and behaves, has goals and purposes of its own, perceives its environment, and responds in endlessly variegated ways to what it perceives.

We attribute consciousness to a creature on the grounds of its behaviour in the circumstances of its life, not on the grounds of its neural organization and complexity. There is no deep mystery about how a living creature can possibly be conscious; after all, the alternative, for a sentient animal, to being conscious is being asleep or unconscious. And there is nothing mystifying about the fact that the living are awake for most of the day. Consciousness does not 'emerge', like an ethereal halo or 'astral body', from inanimate matter. Rather, the biological constitution of living creatures becomes more complex as one ascends the evolutionary scale, and more forms of response and reaction to the environment are made possible. When these are manifest in certain forms of behaviour, the concepts of consciousness and states of consciousness get a grip; but these are not concepts of an inner realm. What particular neural structures make possible these forms of sentient and conative behaviour that manifest consciousness is a matter for empirical investigation – but no metaphysical mystery is involved.

That human beings and higher animals are conscious creatures is not an empirical truth, but a grammatical one. For just as one does not know what it would be for a stone or a tree to be conscious, so too one cannot picture what it would be like for human beings to lack consciousness (PI §418). Of course, one can, up to a point, imagine what it would be like if human beings were zombies; one can tell science-fiction tales about people walking mechanically, eyes glazed, speaking in a monotone. But this is not to the point; for what we are required to imagine is that human beings, behaving just as they normally do, are really not conscious at all, but mere automatons. This is not intelligible (PI §420). One cannot even entertain the thought, as one can in the case of being in pain, that these people might be pretending. For while one can pretend to be unconscious, as one can pretend to be in pain, there is no such thing as pretending to be conscious (Z §395). The assertion that human beings are conscious, like the assertion that human beings see, feel, and hear, only has a use as a grammatical proposition. It might be employed as part of an explanation of what the expression 'human being' or 'conscious' means.

What now remains of the 'unbridgeable gulf between consciousness and brain-process' (PI §412)? This is an illusion induced during philosophical reflection. For, after all, when we are told that A, who drank a

bottle of whisky, lost consciousness, we do not feel that something
strange and miraculous has occurred. It does not strike us that the
influence of alcohol involves crossing an unbridgeable gulf. That illusion
arises only when we think in terms of 'a realm of consciousness', of an
ethereal world populated with psychological objects. For then one is
prone to think that each of us has privileged access to this special domain,
that each of us is witness to the fact that we are conscious, as if being
conscious were a phenomenon that we experience. In the grip of this
picture, Wittgenstein suggests,[12] we are inclined to try to turn our
attention on to our own consciousness and to wonder how *this* could be
produced by a process in the brain. Part of what is awry about this
thought is the very notion of 'turning one's attention upon one's own
consciousness'. One is said to be conscious of something, e.g. the ticking
of a clock or a pain in one's back, when one's attention is caught and held
by that thing. But there is no such thing as being conscious of one's
consciousness, for being conscious is neither an experience nor an object
of experience. Rather, to have any experience at all, to enjoy any 'states
of consciousness' whatever, one must be conscious. Similarly, one can
attend to all manner of things, both perceptibilia and one's sensations,
moods, and feelings; but consciousness itself (unlike one's states of
consciousness) is not an object of attention or experience. So what does
one actually *do* when one thinks that one is 'turning one's attention on to
one's own consciousness'? Wittgenstein sketches one plausible possibility: one stares fixedly in front of one, with eyes wide open but a vacant
gaze. For one is not gazing at or attending to anything in particular, since
it is one's consciousness itself that one wishes to attend to, not something
else of which one might be conscious. But then 'turning one's attention
on to one's own consciousness' will not show one what consciousness is
or what the word 'consciousness' means, but only the very peculiar state
of one's attention when one says to oneself 'I am attending to my own
consciousness' (PI §413). And that state of attention is, to be sure, very
queer, since it involves, as it were, setting oneself to attend to something,
but not actually attending to anything!

Once one realizes that this curious illusion stems from a misuse of
words and misdirected attention (akin to trying to discover, as James
tried,[13] what the experience of the self is like), is it really mysterious that
specific brain-events should produce curious 'facts of consciousness'? In
an appropriate setting there is a perfectly decent, unparadoxical use for
the sentence 'This is produced by a brain-process'. In an experiment in
which part of the brain is stimulated by micro-electrodes, the patient
might report that a flashing of light on the periphery of his visual field

[12] This, of course, is not the only way in which we can engender this confusion.
[13] James, *Principles of Psychology*, Vol. I, p. 301; cf. Exg. §413.

resulted from the electrical stimulation (PI §412). And this is no more mystifying than the fact that certain pressure on the eyeball produces double vision. There may well be empirical ignorance about specific neural processes here, but no metaphysical mysteries.

3. The certainty of consciousness

A venerable tradition going back at least as far as Descartes conceived of consciousness as the immovable rock against which the waves of scepticism break. The fact of our own consciousness seems to be the one *indubitabile* that can never be shaken. Indeed, it was upon this foundation that Descartes endeavoured to construct the edifice of human knowledge. I cannot doubt that I am conscious, for in order to doubt anything at all, I must be conscious. So it seemed to Descartes that I must *know*, indubitably, that I am conscious; or, what for Descartes comes to much the same thing,[14] that I am thinking. And if I cannot fail to know this – if error here is impossible – then surely I have an indubitable foundation from which to infer my existence, and later my essential nature, and all the rest.

What Descartes failed to see is that here (as in the case of avowals (*Äusserungen*) of experience too) doubt is excluded by grammar, not by conclusive evidence. Far from each person being witness to his own consciousness, there is no such thing as observing or perceiving one's own consciousness (cf. PI §§416f.). One has, and can have, no grounds or evidence for claiming to be conscious. Indeed, one cannot *claim* to be conscious. For one cannot say 'He claims that he is conscious, but he is mistaken'.

Imagine an unconscious man (anaesthetized, say) were to say 'I am conscious' – should we say 'He ought to know'?

And if someone talked in his sleep and said 'I am asleep' – should we say 'He's quite right'?

Is someone speaking untruth if he says to me 'I am not conscious'? (And truth, if he says it while unconscious?) And suppose a parrot says 'I don't understand a word', or a gramophone: 'I am only a machine'? (Z §396)

It is not intelligible for it to *seem* to one that one is conscious, for 'It seems to him that he is conscious but he is mistaken' is nonsense. One can dream that one is asleep or dream that one is awake or conscious, but to dream that one is conscious is not to be conscious, nor is it to seem to oneself to be conscious. Descartes' Archimedean point is located beyond the bounds of sense:

---

[14] Descartes, *Principles of Philosophy*, Pt. I, Sect. 9: 'Hence thinking is to be identified here not merely with understanding, willing, and imagining, but also with consciousness.'

' "I am conscious" – that is a statement about which no doubt is possible.' Why should that not say the same as: ' "I am conscious" is not a proposition'?
It might also be said: What's the harm if someone says that 'I am conscious' is a statement admitting of no doubt? How do I come into conflict with him? Suppose someone were to say this to me – why shouldn't I get used to making no answer to him instead of starting an argument? Why shouldn't I treat his words like his whistling or humming?
'Nothing is so certain as that I possess consciousness.' In that case, why shouldn't I let the matter rest? This certainty is like a mighty force whose point of application does not move, and so no work is accomplished by it. (Z §§401f.)

'I am conscious' looks like, and is intended by the Cartesian-minded philosopher to be, an empirical proposition. But it has no intelligible negation; it admits of no doubt, and consequently actually precludes certainty too; it does not express something of which one might be ignorant but, by the same token, it does not say anything which one can be said to know. In this sense it can be said not to be a proposition at all, or to be a degenerate proposition. There is indeed *a* use for the sentence 'I am conscious', but this is not to make an epistemic claim, let alone to express an item of indubitable knowledge. Nor is it to convey to others my private observations or to report my current experience. It is rather akin to a signal. If, as I recover consciousness after an anaesthetic, I say to the nurse, whom I notice walking about the room, 'I am conscious again', I am giving her a signal. I do not say this after 'observing my own consciousness', but after observing the fact that she thinks I am still unconscious. I might just as well say 'Hello' (PI §416).

The Cartesian distortion of the use of 'I am conscious' is co-ordinate with an equally misguided distortion of attribution of consciousness and states of consciousness to others. Mesmerized by the inner/outer picture of the mind, we are inclined to think that we come to 'recognize' consciousness in ourselves and then 'transfer' the idea to others (cf. PI §283). Reflecting thus, it can readily seem as if what we observe is mere behaviour, and that we infer that there is, as it were, a consciousness behind it (cf. 'Behaviour and behaviourism', §4). What licenses this inference? Is it that when one is conscious and in a given state of consciousness, one notices the muscular movements of one's face, which one also sees in the faces of others? No; this is absurd. It is a piece of theorizing, an explanation, which is out of place when what is needed is a description of the use and circumstances of use of words:

Consciousness in another's face. Look into someone else's face, and see the consciousness in it, and a particular shade of consciousness. You see on it, in it, joy, indifference, interest, excitement, torpor, and so on. The light in other people's faces.
Do you look into *yourself* in order to recognize the fury in *his* face? It is there as clearly as in your own breast. (Z §220)

We *see* a human being giving angry, proud, ironical looks. We perceive the glimmer of amusement, the flash of anger, or the dull grief in a person's eye. This is how we speak and how we characterize what we see in another's face. To acknowledge this plain fact is not to make concessions to a behaviourist theory; nor is it to admit that one sees the glance in 'just the way' that one sees the shape or colour of the eye (Z §223). On the contrary, the shape or colour of an eye can be seen in an autopsy room – but the passionate look or loving gaze can be seen only in the face (Z §224) and in a context.

We do not see facial contortions and make inferences from them (like a doctor framing a diagnosis) to joy, grief, boredom. We describe a face immediately as sad, radiant, bored, even when we are unable to give any other description of the features. – Grief, one would like to say, is personified in the face.
   This belongs to the concept of emotion. (Z §225)

The countenance, Cicero remarked, is the portrait of the mind, the eyes are its informers.[15] Apropos Rembrandt's portrait of his friend, the poet Jeremias de Decker, Jan van Petersons wrote: 'O Rembrandt, you paint de Decker so that his soul shines through his face.'
   Of course, states of consciousness are not facial expressions, and consciousness is not behaviour. But they are exhibited, manifest, in behaviour, mien, and facial expression. We can see that a person is conscious, what he is conscious of, and often what state of consciousness he is in. We do not infer it 'problematically' from mere facial contortions and 'bare bodily movements'; although it is true and important that we can veil our eyes, conceal our feelings, pretend, and dissimulate. It is an absurdity, foisted on us by our own misconceptions and misconceived pictures, to think that we might be wrong in supposing other humans to be conscious beings. It is no more a *supposition* than it is a supposition that *I* am conscious (RPP I §930). The only kind of case in which one might be wrong about another person being conscious is when one sees an unconscious person stir and wrongly supposes that he has regained consciousness.

---

[15] Cicero, *De Oratore*, Bk. III, §59: 'Imago animi vultus est, indices oculi.'

XIII

CRITERIA

1. Symptoms and hypotheses

From 1932/3 the term 'criterion' crops up with moderate frequency in Wittgenstein's writings and lectures. It occurs in the course of reflections on logic (e.g. in emphasizing the differences between various criteria for the truth of general statements (LFM 270), which show that the grammars of 'All men', 'All the colours of the rainbow', 'All cardinal numbers', etc. are quite different). It crops up in discussions of mathematics (e.g. in examining the relation of proof to truth or in arguing that equinumerosity of finite sets and equinumerosity of infinite sets involve distinct concepts). It plays a prominent role in the elucidations of powers and abilities and also in Wittgenstein's investigations into meaning and understanding. And, most obviously, it occupies a salient position in his philosophical psychology.

Nevertheless, Wittgenstein's explicit explanations of what he meant by 'a criterion' are few and brief. Indeed, the main explanation in the *Blue Book* seems inadequate and ill fitted to his later use of the term. It is clear enough that he is concerned with a logical or grammatical relation which, at least in some forms, has gone unrecognized by philosophers and logicians. Certainly the formalization of logic that has flourished during the last century has made no room for a relation of presumptive implication or defeasible support; and to the extent that Wittgenstein's use of the term 'criterion' signifies such a relation, to that extent it falls outside the received scope of reflection on logical relations.

It is hardly surprising, therefore, that it should have given rise to controversy, bewilderment, and misinterpretation. It has been argued that it is a pivotal notion in Wittgenstein's later theory of meaning or semantics. Elaborating further, it has been suggested that it is embedded in an assertion-conditions or assertability-conditions theory of meaning which stands in contrast to Wittgenstein's earlier truth-conditional semantics. And this in turn is held to be an aspect of Wittgenstein's shift from a realist to an anti-realist theory of meaning and metaphysics.

If the discussions and arguments of this Analytical Commentary approximate to Wittgenstein's intentions even remotely, it is clear that such interpretations are wildly off course. Wittgenstein was not rejecting the philosophy of the *Tractatus* in order to replace it with an alternative metaphysics, and he was not engaged upon the construction of anything that could be called a theory of meaning, for he would have viewed any such enterprise as chimerical. It is doubtful whether there is any deep sense in which the *Tractatus* can be called 'realist' (save by contrast with nominalist), and it is evident that there is no significant sense in which the later philosophy can be viewed as anti-realist. Wittgenstein was not taking sides in the muddled controversies of the 1970s and 1980s, and his reflections cannot be fitted into the misconceived pigeon-holes currently in vogue. The premises upon which these latter-day controversies stand would all be rejected by him as dogmas, absurdities, and misunderstandings.

If we are to obtain a clear picture of his use of the term 'criterion', we must eschew theory and engage in patient description. It is far from obvious that it is a technical term or term of art. As we shall see, it converges substantially, though not uniformly, with the ordinary use of the word. It is not part of a *theory* of meaning, but a modest instrument in the description of the ways in which words are used. As we should expect if we have followed Wittgenstein thus far, it plays a significant role in his philosophy, but not by way of a premise in an argument, nor by way of a theory. 'An "inner process" stands in need of outward criteria' (PI §580) is not a thesis from which philosophical propositions are proved. It is a synopsis of grammatical rules that determine what we call 'the inner'.

Although it is not a theoretical term in Wittgenstein's philosophy, the word 'criterion' was the heir to an expression which could, with some justice, be called 'theoretical', one which was embedded in a philosophical account which might be viewed as a theory (even though its author did not see it thus). For part of the role fulfilled by the symptoms/hypothesis relation in Wittgenstein's brief 'phenomenalist' or, as he called it, 'phenomenological' phase in 1929/30 was taken over by the concept of a criterion. However, in the process all the theoretical baggage was shed, and at the same time the later conception of philosophy as descriptive in method and therapeutic in goal rapidly evolved (see esp. 'The Big Typescript', pp. 406 – 36).

It is illuminating to view the role of the concept of 'criteria' in Wittgenstein's later philosophy against the background of his earlier conception of symptoms and hypothesis. This serves to highlight similarities and differences. The notion of a hypothesis, as used in the *Philosophical Remarks*, is itself a remote heir to an undeveloped idea already present in the *Tractatus*. Hence it is from the latter work that the story must begin.

Elementary propositions, as conceived in the *Tractatus*, are essentially bipolar. They determine a logical space, which reality either occupies or leaves empty. If things are as an elementary proposition describes them as being, then the proposition is true; otherwise it is false. The fit between description and reality is sharp; there is no such thing as a vague elementary proposition which is neither clearly true nor clearly false.

Molecular propositions may indeed be vague; they may give reality a certain latitude as it were, but the vagueness must be determinate. For the freedom left to reality is a reflection of the fact that the relevant molecular proposition is disjunctive, leaving open various possibilities. But *which* possibilities are thus left open must be perfectly determinate. Whereas elementary propositions were held to be independent, molecular propositions enjoyed relations of implication, incompatibility, etc. All such logical relations between propositions were conceived as consequences of the combinatorial complexity of the molecular propositions.

Relatively little was said in the *Tractatus* about scientific propositions, and what was said was exceedingly obscure. What Kantian philosophy conceived of as metaphysical principles of nature, e.g. the principle of sufficient reason, the law of conservation, the laws of continuity and of least effort in nature (TLP 6.321, 6.34), are expressions of *a priori* insights concerning the forms in which the propositions of science can be cast. Such principles are not genuine propositions describing reality, but normative principles determining the general forms of laws. A particular scientific theory, such as Newtonian mechanics, 'determines one form of description of the world by saying that all propositions used in the description of the world must be obtained in a given way from a given set of propositions – the axioms of mechanics. It thus supplies the bricks for building the edifice of science, and it says, "Any building that you want to erect, whatever it may be, must somehow be constructed with these bricks, and with these alone" ' (TLP 6.341). Whereas the metaphysical principles of nature merely determine forms of laws, the so-called laws of nature are concerned, albeit indirectly, with the objects of the world (TLP 6.3431). They *construct*, according to a single plan (i.e. a chosen system of forms of laws, such as Newtonian mechanics), the true propositions that we need for the description of the world (TLP 6.343). These laws are not themselves descriptions of necessities in the world, however, for the only necessity is logical necessity (TLP 6.37). Nor are they explanations of why things happen as they do (TLP 6.371). Rather, in formulating natural laws within the constraints of a chosen physical theory, we are guided by the principle of induction, according to which we opt for the *simplest* law that can be reconciled with our experience (TLP 6.363). The law is then employed as a basis for predictions, on the *assumption* (which has no *logical* justification) of simplicity and uniformity. Hence, it seems, laws of nature are best viewed as rules for the derivation of predictions.

When Wittgenstein resumed philosophical work in 1929, he turned his attention to what in the *Tractatus* he had conceived of as 'the application of logic'. It is evident both from the 1929 manuscripts and from the lecture 'Remarks on Logical Form' that he did not see himself, initially at least, as overturning his first philosophy. The project of cooperating with Waismann on the production of *Logik, Sprache, Philosophie*, intended as the first volume of the Vienna Circle's *Schriften zur wissenschaftlichen Weltauffassung*, was advertised in the Manifesto of the Circle in 1929 and again in *Erkenntniss* (1930/31) as being 'in essentials a representation of the ideas of Wittgenstein's *Tractatus*. What is new in it and what essentially distinguishes it is the logical ordering and articulation of these thoughts.'[1] It seems, then, that his first efforts were conceived as further elaborations of the fundamental ideas of the *Tractatus*, together with what may initially have appeared to be modifications and improvements. What collapsed immediately was the logical atomism. The colour-exclusion problem led to the idea of a *Satzsystem*, and the independence of the elementary proposition was accordingly relinquished. Among these early modifications, which ultimately led to the disintegration of the philosophy of the *Tractatus*, was the introduction of the distinction between genuine propositions and hypotheses.

Genuine propositions are descriptions of what is immediately given (WWK 97). They are phenomenological statements (WWK 101) or judgements about sense-data (LWL 66) or 'primary experience'. Hence typical examples of genuine propositions are 'I have a pain' (or 'It hurts', 'There is a pain') or 'It seems as if there is a sphere in front of me'. Genuine propositions are conclusively verified or falsified by being compared with reality, i.e. immediate experience. They are either true or false, but not probable. Indeed, it is senseless to say 'There probably appears to me to be a sphere in front of me' (PG 222). Here there is no gap between appearance and reality, between seeming and being; for it makes no sense to say 'It looks as if there seems to be a sphere here' (PG 221).

Hypotheses, however, have a quite different grammar and constitute an altogether different kind of grammatical structure (WWK 210). They are not genuine propositions at all (or, one might say, they are propositions in a different sense), but rather, are laws for constructing genuine propositions (WWK 97, 210; PR 285). Propositions about material objects, about the experiences of other people, as well as laws of nature are hypotheses (PR 94f., 286; WWK 100f.). They stand in a different relationship to reality from genuine propositions, for they can be neither conclusively verified nor conclusively falsified (WWK 100). They are not true or false at all (PR 283), or not true or false in the same sense (PR 285), but only more or less probable. Nothing forces us to adopt a given hypothesis; but considerations of simplicity, con-

---

[1] *Wissenschaftliche Weltauffassung der Wiener Kreis*, published by Ernst Mach Society (Artur Wolf Verlag, Vienna, 1929), p. 47.

venience, and predictive power constitute good grounds for accepting a hypothesis.

Wittgenstein used various metaphors and similes to illuminate the relationship between genuine propositions and hypotheses. One can conceive of genuine propositions as sectional cross-cuts through the connected structure of a hypothesis (WWK 100). They stand to a hypothesis as determinate points on a graph to the straight line that connects them (PR 285) or as the different views or aspects of a material object to the material object *per se* (PG 220). Indeed, the latter comparison is not merely a simile, but an instance of the relationship. For the very notion of an object involves a hypothesis connecting the multiple phenomenal aspects which we experience. The descriptions of our immediate perceptual experiences are determinately true or false, directly verifiable by comparison with the given; but a hypothesis enables the prediction of future experiences. The genuine propositions that give evidential support to a hypothesis Wittgenstein sometimes called 'symptoms' (WWK 159; M 266f.).[2] Symptoms are grammatically related to the hypothesis which they support. They render it probable or plausible, but never certain; for there is no such thing as complete or conclusive confirmation of a hypothesis (PR 285). The probability of a hypothesis is measured by the amount of evidence needed to make it reasonable to relinquish the hypothesis (PR 286). But just as there is no conclusive verification of a hypothesis, so too there is no conclusive falsification; for disconfirmatory evidence can always be accommodated by auxiliary hypotheses (WWK 255).

A hypothesis can be viewed as a law unifying actual and possible experiences (LWL 16; PR 285). Unlike a genuine proposition, a hypothesis permits predictions. Thus, for example, the hypothesis that there is such-and-such an object here connects the perceived aspects of an object in a law-governed manner and licenses predictions about subsequent experiences (WWK 256).

It is plausible to suppose that when Wittgenstein introduced the distinction between genuine propositions and hypotheses he was generalizing his remarks about natural laws in the *Tractatus* while liberalizing the rigid, sharply defined conception of a proposition in that book. The bulk of our everyday propositions seemed clearly to be hypotheses, since the concept of an object inevitably involves the notion of a hypothesis to order, systematize, and simplify the description of the flux of experience.

---

[2] See also F. Waismann, 'Hypotheses', in his *Philosophical Papers*, ed. B. McGuinness (Reidel, Dordrecht, 1977), pp. 38 – 59. This essay was intended as a chapter for *Logik, Sprache, Philosophie*, and is derived from Wittgenstein's notes and dictations. The full German version is printed as an appendix to the German edition of *Logik, Sprache, Philosophie*, ed. G. P. Baker and B. McGuinness (Reclam, Stuttgart, 1976).

These propositions are not analysable into truth-functional combinations of elementary propositions or of sense-datum statements. But the relation between symptom and hypothesis is a grammatical, not an empirical, one. That such-and-such symptoms render a hypothesis probable is determined *a priori*, and is not a consequence of experienced (inductive) correlation. The support which a symptom or set of symptoms gives to a hypothesis always falls short of entailment, and a hypothesis can, in principle, always be overturned by subsequent experience. In this sense the evidential support is defeasible; although it would appear that whether defeating evidence suffices to undermine a hypothesis is conceived to be a matter of choice turning largely on considerations of simplicity and convenience. It is important to note that in the *Tractatus*, apart from the brief, undeveloped remarks on natural laws, there was no room for such a logico-grammatical relationship. The official doctrine there was that all logical relations are a matter of entailment, i.e. the inclusion (or exclusion) of the sense of one proposition in (or from) the sense of another.

2. *Symptoms and criteria*

Wittgenstein did not cleave for long to the conception of the relationship between evidential symptoms and hypotheses. Various considerations led to his abandoning it. The most important was his realization that what he had conceived of as genuine propositions describing immediate experience and conclusively verifiable or falsifiable by comparison with reality have a completely different role and status from that which he had supposed. They are not descriptions, but expressions, of experiences; they do not get compared with reality at all, and are not verified or falsified. For here truthfulness coincides with truth, and the truthfulness of an avowal does not turn on a comparison of a proposition with reality. Secondly, the claim that hypotheses are more or less probable, but can never be conclusively confirmed or rendered certain, has to be rejected on the ground that such a proposition can be said to be merely probable only if it at least makes *sense* for it to be certain. For 'probable' and 'certain' are correlative terms within the language-game of describing features of the world, and if there is no such thing as certainty, then 'probable' cannot have its ordinary sense. To be sure, this was implicitly recognized in the account of hypotheses, since they were not conceived to be descriptions, but rather rules for the construction of descriptions. But with the abandonment of the idea that first-person present-tense perception- and sensation-sentences are the genuine propositions, this conception of hypotheses inevitably collapsed. The assimilation of mundane material-object statements and statements about other people's states of mind to statements of laws in the natural sciences is fundamentally misleading, rendering such humdrum propositions as 'The curtains are red' or 'John has a toothache' hypotheses. Yet these are paradigms of ordinary descriptive, non-theoretical propositions that are verified or falsified by reference to experience.

The relation between a hypothesis and its evidential symptoms was displaced by that between a proposition and its criteria. The concept of a criterion is prominent in the 1932/3 lectures (AWL 17 – 19, 28 – 9, 31, 34 – 5, 59, 62) and is introduced with explicit explanation in the *Blue Book* (BB 24 – 5, 51ff.). Thereafter it occurs fairly regularly, both in Wittgenstein's philosophical psychology and in his philosophy of mathematics. Like symptoms in Wittgenstein's earlier writings, criteria are (a) fixed by grammar and (b) grounds or evidence for a proposition. In a shift of terminology, Wittgenstein now introduced the notion of a symptom as a foil for that of a criterion. Whereas a criterial relation is an *a priori* grammatical one, a symptom is a piece of inductive evidence discovered in experience. That *p* is a symptom for *q* presupposes the possibility of an independent identification of *q*, since the empirical determination of *p* as symptomatic evidence requires the inductive correlation of two distinct, externally related phenomena (AWL 34f.).

To specify the criteria for the truth of a proposition is to characterize ways of verifying the proposition (AWL 17, 19). It is one way of answering the question 'How do you know that *p*?' (AWL 18f.; BB 24). What distinguishes a criterion from a symptom in the new sense of the latter term is that criteria are fixed by grammar (PI §322), are laid down in language, in rules, charts, etc. (LPE 293), and in that sense are a matter of *convention* (BB 24, 57; AWL 28). These observations may mislead, and may have misled, philosophers. For the notion of a social convention comes to mind here, and with it the suggestion of choice, and often of relative unimportance ('a mere convention') and arbitrariness. With these associations in mind one may wonder how Wittgenstein can claim that the criteria for someone's being in pain are a matter of convention. For, to be sure, no committee resolved to *adopt* these criteria as conventions. That pain-behaviour is a criterion for a person's being in pain is not a matter of arbitrary decision which could just as well have been utterly different, like conventions of dress.

The objection is misplaced, however. Of course, in certain cases, e.g. in introducing new terminology in the course of constructing a theory about a certain phenomenon, one may stipulate criteria, lay down what evidential grounds are to justify the application of a new term (AWL 18). The stipulation of the criteria determines the grammar of the new expression in as much as it determines its use. But clearly these are not the cases Wittgenstein typically has in mind. His claim that the criteria for propositions about the inner or about powers and capacities are a matter of convention is intended to draw a contrast between what is normative and what is empirical discovery. To explain the criteria for toothache, for joy or grief, intending, thinking, or understanding is not to describe an empirical correlation that has been found to hold. For criteria, unlike symptoms (inductive correlations), determine the meanings of expressions for which they are criteria. To explain the criteria for the application of an expression 'W' is to give a grammatical explanation of 'W'. It explains what we *call* 'W', and so explains a facet of the use of the word (AWL 17 – 19). To say that *q* is a criterion for W is to give a partial explanation of the meaning of 'W', and in that sense to give a rule for its correct use.[3] The fact that the criterial relation between *q* and W may be neither arbitrary (in one sense at least) nor stipulated, that in innumerable cases we could not resolve to abandon this normative relationship without a change in our form of life, and in many cases could not abandon it at all, does not imply that it is empirical, let alone that it is a matter of *Wesensschau*. We may concede that certain concepts are deeply embedded in our lives, occupy a pivotal role in our thought and experience, yet still insist that their use is rule-governed, a matter of *nomos* rather than *phusis*.

Like the earlier symptoms/hypothesis relation, the criterial relation provides grammatically determined' grounds for a proposition. If a criterion for *p*'s being the case is exemplified in appropriate circumstances, then there are good grounds for judging *p* to be the case. This much, to be sure, is a feature of the ordinary use of the term 'criterion'. Wittgenstein's new use of 'symptom', however, is much wider than we would ordinarily countenance, since any inductive evidence for something counts as a symptom. Where the criterial relation *differs* from the earlier symptoms/hypothesis relation is in its connection with truth, verification, and knowledge. Hypotheses, Wittgenstein had earlier argued, are not true or false, or not true or false in the same sense as genuine propositions. They can neither be conclusively verified nor conclusively falsified. *A fortiori* they cannot be known to be true. Hypotheses are convenient, plausible, or probable, but they cannot, logically, be certain. Criteria, however, are said to be given in answer to the question 'How do you know?' (AWL 17 – 19, 28; BB 24f.), with the proviso that inductive grounds are symptoms, rather than criteria. Propositions the sense of which is partially determined by criteria, e.g. propositions about capacities or the experiences, thoughts, or intentions of other people, are true or false. Criteria constitute justifying grounds for their assertion, and hence are ways of telling whether they are true (BB 57; LPE 293; PI §182), reasons for judging things to be thus-and-so. The criteria for something's being the case, *at least in some instances*,

---

[3] Of course, that is not to say that any rule for the use of an expression is a criterion-specifying rule. Nor is it to say that every expression is used on criterial grounds.

establish decisively, with certainty, that that is how things are. This point will be examined further below.

It was an essential feature of the symptoms/hypothesis relation that there are multiple symptoms for any given hypothesis, just as there are multiple points on a line or multiple cuts through a geometrical structure. A criterion for a given proposition may, in certain cases, be unique. Wittgenstein's explanation of the distinction between criteria and symptoms in the *Blue Book* invokes an example of a concept, viz. angina (tonsilitis), which is defined by a single criterion (BB 25). The criterion for the truth of a mathematical proposition is its proof (LFM 131), and there is nothing unintelligible about uniqueness of proof. Nevertheless, in many cases (including mathematics) criteria are manifold; there may be multiple defining criteria (LSD 20); there are two different criteria for a method of projection coming before one's mind (PI §141); giving correct explanations and using an expression correctly are criteria for knowing what a word means (AWL 48ff.; LFM 20ff.; PI §75); and in different circumstances we employ different criteria for a person's reading (PI §164).

Characteristic of the symptoms/hypothesis relation is the fact that the evidential support which a symptom or set of symptoms gives to a hypothesis can be undermined by further evidence. This feature importantly distinguishes a symptom from a sufficient condition, and allocates to a grammatical (conceptual) relationship a property usually associated only with empirical (inductive) evidence. If *p* logically implies *q*, then no matter what other propositions are true, it still implies *q*. In this sense it is indefeasible. Inductive evidence is different, for however good the correlation between *p* and *q* may have been discovered to be (e.g. 99 per cent of Xs are men), an additional piece of evidence may undermine the support *p* gives to *q* (e.g. this X is a member of the YWCA). Wittgenstein did not, of course, use the (legal) term 'defeasible', but it seems apt to describe a feature of the symptoms/hypothesis relation. Similarly, defeasibility seems to characterize *some* domains in which Wittgenstein employed the term 'criterion'. This is evident in the case of psychological concepts. First, the circumstance-dependence of criteria implies that although *p* may give criterial support to *q* in certain circumstances, it will not do so in other circumstances. If someone hits his finger with a hammer and screams, assuages his finger, etc., that establishes that he has hurt himself. However, if all this takes place in a play, then this behaviour counts as acting as if he had so hurt himself. But the defeating evidence is itself defeasible (cf. RPP I §137); for if the actor leaves the stage with a bleeding finger, groaning, etc., then he has obviously accidentally hurt himself. Secondly, the multiplicity of criteria suggests, at least in some cases, the possibility of conflict of criteria. Using an expression correctly and giving a correct explanation of an expression are both criteria for knowing what the expression means. In most circumstances either criterion is a good reason for attributing understanding. But if someone uses an expression correctly, yet cannot explain what it means, or conversely, if he offers an adequate explanation, but misuses the expression, we would not say that he understands the word in question. Indeed, in some cases of conflict of criteria, we would not know what to say. Thirdly, in many circumstances the behavioural criteria for being pleased, annoyed, etc. may be manifest, only subsequently to be undermined by instantiation of the criteria for pretending. Though defeasibility seems to characterize Wittgenstein's construal of psychological concepts and their behavioural criteria, this feature is absent from his explicit explanation of the term 'criterion' in the *Blue Book* pp. 24 – 5 (although present in the subsequent discussion of perception (BB 57)) and from his use of the term in his mathematical writings (see below).

Though the distinction between a criterion and a symptom (inductive evidence) is as sharp as that between a rule and a fact, it is important to note that there is commonly, especially in science, a fluctuation between criteria and symptoms (PI §79). In the *Blue Book* Wittgenstein points out that where a variety of phenomena are found to go together in association with, e.g., a particular disease, it may be impossible in practice to say which phenomenon is the defining criterion of the illness and which phenomena are symptoms, except by making an arbitrary, *ad hoc* decision (BB 25). For most practical purposes it may be unnecessary to make such a decision, and indeed, doctors often use the names of diseases without ever doing so. This need not (though it may) signify a deplorable laxity, precisely because the various phenomena in question regularly coincide. We do not use language according to *strict* rules, and in many such cases it may matter little which phenomenon is taken as definitive and which as symptomatic, or indeed whether the matter is left undecided. Nevertheless, confusions sometimes result from this fluctuation. First, it may seem as if there were nothing at all but symptoms (PI §354). But this would be to confuse an indeterminacy in the rules for the use of an expression with lack of any rules for its use. The fluctuation between symptoms and criteria signifies an indeterminacy in the use, and hence the meaning, of the expression. What even one person takes as symptom and what as criterion will vary from case to case, and in particular philosophical or theoretical arguments concerning a given theory, what counts as criterion and what as symptom will have to be determined by examining or eliciting the manner in which a protagonist uses the relevant correlation on that occasion, viz. as definitive or as empirical. So too, for example, in an argument over the theoretical structure of, say, some part of Newtonian physics, it may well be impossible to determine once and for all what is a symptom and what is a criterion for a given phenomenon. Rather, in the context of that particular argument, it may be determined that if *this* is taken as a criterion for such-and-such, then *that* may be viewed as a symptom, and if that correlation is viewed as inductive, then *this* one should be seen as grammatical. Secondly, the regular coincidence of a variety of pieces of evidence and the absence of any explicit determination of what counts as criterion and what as symptom may in practice lead to confusions due to equivocation and lack of consensus. This may be a consequence of a fluctuation between symptoms and criteria in each person's usage of a term from occasion to occasion. But it may also result from different people using a different element out of a concomitant cluster of phenomena as the defining criterion. Either way, confusions may be engendered. This is nicely exemplified in medical debates over the concept of shock, an issue in which Wittgenstein himself was involved in the Second World War. Depending on how the concept is defined, i.e. what are determined as criteria and what as symptoms, a statement about shock may make good sense or be nonsense. Equally, diagnosis will vary according to the interpretation assigned by different doctors, precisely because the defining criteria vary from one authority to another (equivocation) and from occasion to occasion (fluctuation). Research will be hampered through lack of clear specification of defining criteria acceptable by all, especially in cases in which one is dealing with a set of overlapping but distinct syndromes.[4]

3. Further problems about criteria

The survey of the similarities and differences between the symptoms/hypothesis relation and criterial relations and of the distinction between criteria and symptoms (in the new sense of the term) has established the rough outlines of Wittgenstein's use of the term 'criterion'. To summarize: (a) criteria belong to, or are aspects of, the grammar of the expressions for the use of which they are criteria. Hence (b) they are aspects of, or partial determinants of, the meanings of such expressions; and (c) they are grounds for asserting a proposition, providing justifications for judgements, and hence connected with proof, verification, and knowledge. (d) In some cases at least, there are multiple criteria. (e) In some cases, criteria are defeasible. To sharpen the picture, more light needs to be thrown on the relation between criteria for the application of an expression (or, correspondingly, criteria for the truth of a judgement)

---

[4] See R. T. Grant and E. B. Reeve, *Observations on the General Effects of Injury in Man with Special Reference to Wound Shock*, Medical Research Council Special Report Series, No. 277 (HMSO, London, 1951). This was the project in which Wittgenstein participated at the Royal Victoria Infirmary, Newcastle, during the war. Although not mentioned by name, his hand is evident in the general discussion on the concept of shock.

and the meaning of the expression. That in turn will lead to further elucidations.

Wittgenstein often spoke of criteria as defining expressions. In the *Blue Book* example of angina, the presence of a certain bacillus is said to *define* what it is to have angina (BB 24). In his later lectures on sense-data and private experience he spoke of the defining criteria of something as constituting the nature of the thing (LSD 20). The criterion for carrying out a certain mathematical operation (e.g. adding two integers) defines what it is to perform that operation by reference to the result of the operation (RFM 319). In science we often choose phenomena that admit of exact measurement as the defining criteria for an expression (Z §438). More generally, the criteria for someone's being of an opinion, hoping for something, knowing something, being able to do something, determine what is to be *called* 'being of the opinion', 'hoping', 'knowing', etc. (cf. PI §§572f.).

Similarly, he held that the sense of, e.g., 'A has a toothache' is given by the criterion for its truth, for 'a statement gets its sense from its verification' (AWL 17). Its meaning is given it by the criterion (AWL 18). For 'Asking whether and how a proposition can be verified is only a particular way of asking "How d'you mean?" The answer is a contribution to the grammar of the proposition' (PI §353; see Exg.). To explain one's criterion for someone's having a toothache is to give a grammatical explanation about the word 'toothache' and, in this sense, an explanation of the meaning of the word (BB 24). It is these common criteria which give words their common meanings (BB 57).

A frequent manoeuvre in Wittgenstein's arguments is to show that the presuppositions of his adversary sever the connection between a certain concept and its criteria. When we reflect on visual experience, we are inclined to think that behaviour is no more than a fallible symptom of seeing, for the experience itself is private, and one can see something and not show it. So it seems that only the subject can really know whether he sees or is blind! This is wrong. 'It is clear that we in our language use the words "seeing red" in such a way that we can say "A sees red but doesn't show it"; on the other hand it is easy to see that we should have no use for these words if their application was severed from the criteria of behaviour' (LPE 286). Similarly, it is a crucial feature of the idea of a private language that it severs the concept of pain from the behavioural manifestations of pain that constitute criteria for third-person pain-ascriptions. The language-game with 'pain' involves the criterionless avowal of pain in one's own case, but that presupposes the criteria for third-person ascriptions. These include both natural pain-behaviour and the learnt linguistic extensions of natural behaviour, e.g. the verbal avowal of pain, which is itself a criterion of pain. Our concepts here are erected upon the *normality* of a web of connections, viz. between injury, reactive behaviour, avowal, and subsequent behaviour. The web is not seamless; but were it to unravel, the very concept of pain would blur (as it does in reported cases of lobotomy, where the patient insists that it hurts just as much as before, but that he doesn't mind) and ultimately disintegrate. Again, the sceptical supposition that all behaviour might be pretence severs pretending from its behavioural criteria, and that would make the concept of pretending unusable (Z §571).

These considerations make it clear that the criteria for the use of an expression are bound up with its meaning. Is the meaning of an expression *given* by specifying its criteria? Not necessarily. In some cases in which Wittgenstein employed the term 'criterion' it seems that one *can* say this, e.g. in specifying the criteria for being a triangle (LFM 164) or for having angina (BB 25). In others, he explicitly differentiated *giving* the meaning from *determining* or *helping to determine* the meaning of an expression (AWL 28f.). Screaming in circumstances of injury, assuaging one's limb after having hit it, etc. are criteria for being in pain; but 'to have a pain' does not mean the same as 'screaming and assuaging one's limb in such-and-such circumstances'. Rather, one crucial facet of the use of 'pain' is determined by the fact that this behaviour in these circumstances constitutes a justification for saying 'He is in pain'. Someone who has failed to grasp this does not understand what 'pain' means and does not know how to use it correctly. To specify the verifying criteria for someone's being in pain is to specify *a* rule for the use of 'pain', and in that sense, *part* of its grammar. But it is no less crucial an aspect of the grammar of 'pain' that 'I am in pain' is rightly uttered without grounds, that 'I doubt whether I am in pain' and 'I wonder whether I am in pain' make no sense, and so on.

In as much as the criteria for the use of an expression are in this sense determinants or partial determinants of its meaning, it is not surprising to find Wittgenstein explaining that a change in the criteria involves a change in meaning. For addition (or subtraction) of a criterion forges a new (or severs an old) grammatical link. When scientists find that a certain phenomenon belonging to a cluster of phenomena associated with something admits of precise measurement, they are prone to make it into the defining criterion. Here 'a measurable phenomenon occupies the place previously occupied by a non-measurable one. Then the word designating this place changes its meaning, and its old meaning has become more or less obsolete' (Z §438). Similarly, suppose that we accept a diagram as a proof that a pentagram has as many points as fingers on a hand (LFM 71 – 3). 'This means that we accept a new way of finding out that two things [viz. this hand and that pentagram] have the same number [of fingers and points]. We don't co-ordinate things one with the other now; we just look at this figure. I have now changed the meaning of the phrase "having the same number" – because I now accept an entirely new criterion for it' (LFM 73). Indeed, one of the functions of mathematical proofs is precisely to give us new criteria for equinumerosity or for equality of shape, area, volume, etc. A proof forges a new connection in grammar, and so licenses transformations of empirical propositions which could not antecedently be thus transformed. So too, introduction of new criteria for thinking, desiring, or having motives typically signals a conceptual change. Psychoanalysts erred in thinking that they had *discovered* new kinds of thoughts, desires, and motives, which are just like familiar ones only unconscious. In fact what they had done was to note an array of psychological reactions (e.g. patterns of behaviour and response characteristic of the Oedipal complex) which they brought within the ambit of the concepts of thinking, desiring, or having a motive by introducing a new convention or a new notation. For unconscious thoughts, etc. are not related to (conscious) thoughts as a newly discovered kind of apple is related to Coxes, Bramleys, etc. Rather, a conceptual shift has been stipulated (BB 22f., 57f.). A concept is determined by the rules for the use of an expression, and a change in the rules involves a modification of the concept. Whether we should say that such a change introduces a new concept or merely constitutes a novel extension of an existing one is to some extent a matter of choice, dependent upon what is at stake (BB 58). Failure to notice such conceptual shifts, e.g. in transposing the concept of 1:1 correlation from finite sets to infinite sets, can lead to disastrous confusions.

Criteria are determinants of meaning. They are grammatical or logical grounds for the truth of a proposition. But the kind of logical relation which is involved here is unclear and has been much disputed. Is a criterion a logically sufficient condition or a necessary condition or a necessary and sufficient condition? Or is it decisive for things being thus-and-so *without* amounting to entailment? And how could that be? Or are criteria kinds of evidence which, like empirical evidence, do not amount to entailment, but, like entailment, are determined in grammar? Is that intelligible, i.e. could there be any such thing as necessarily good evidence for something? And if so, could it be decisive?

If we survey Wittgenstein's use of the term 'criterion', we find *prima facie* conflicting accounts. In some cases it seems a criterion is a logically sufficient condition, or even a necessary and sufficient condition for something's being so. In the angina example in the *Blue Book* the presence of a particular bacillus in the blood is said to be *the defining criterion* of angina. 'A man has angina if this bacillus is found in him' is a tautology or a loose way of defining 'angina' (BB 25). In his lectures on the philosophy of mathematics, Wittgenstein spoke of the number of sides of a figure (viz. a closed rectilinear figure in a plane) as a criterion for its being a triangle, and conversely of a figure's being a triangle as a criterion for its having three sides (LFM 164). Similarly, he talked of the criterion of equinumerosity of sets (LFM 163) and of the proof of a mathematical proposition as being a criterion for its truth (LFM 131). These examples suggest that a criterion is a sufficient or necessary and sufficient condition.

On the other hand, in the subsequent employment of the term 'criterion' in the *Blue Book*, it is clear that it is so used that a criterion is non-inductive evidence distinct from entailment. One's tactile and kinaesthetic sensations are said to be criteria for one's finger moving from one's tooth to one's eye. Here, experiential or perceptual evidence is a criterion for a proposition about a physical object:

> The grammar of propositions which we call propositions about physical objects admits of a variety of evidences for every such proposition. It characterizes the grammar of the proposition 'my finger moves, etc.' that I regard the propositions 'I see it move', 'I feel it move', 'He sees it move', 'He tells me that it moves', etc. as evidences for it. (BB 51)

But, Wittgenstein insists, it is possible for it to *feel as if* my finger were moving from my tooth to my eye without my finger moving from my tooth to my eye. The former proposition might be true *without* that for which it is a criterion being the case. Indeed, we can imagine the visual criteria (e.g. when I look in the mirror) conflicting with the tactile and kinaesthetic criteria. If that were so, one might deny that one's finger had moved thus, even though it felt as if it had. Here it seems that criteria are conceived to be logical or grammatical grounds or evidence that are distinct from entailment. They seem to constitute presumptive evidence which is defeasible by countervailing evidence.

It is significant that this kind of example does not recur in later writings, with the possible exception of *Investigations* §354 (see Exg.). It arguably belongs to an earlier phase in his thought, the last remnant of his 'phenomenological' analysis, which subsequently disappears. This suspicion is strengthened by the fact that in the context in the *Blue Book* he still talked, as he later did not, of being 'handicapped in ordinary language by having to describe, say, a tactile sensation by means of terms for physical objects such as the word "eye", "finger", etc. We have to use a roundabout description of our sensations' (BB 52). It is true that in *Investigations*, Part 2, he compares the relation of behaviour to inner state with the relation of sense-impressions to physical object (PI p. 180); but the point of the comparison is not that in both cases we are dealing with criteria, but rather that in both cases there is a *complicated* relation which is distorted by any attempt to reduce it to a simple formula.

However, if we look at Wittgenstein's later use of 'criterion', especially in the context of his philosophy of mind, it is clear enough that there is generally a crucial point of continuity with the above passage in the *Blue Book*. The criteria for 'inner states' or 'inner processes' (PI §580) are behavioural, but one can behave in such-and-such ways and yet not be in the inner state, and conversely one may be in pain, for example, and yet not manifest it in one's behaviour. Hence the behavioural criteria for being in pain are neither necessary nor sufficient conditions for being in pain. Moreover, criteria are typically multiple, and conflicts of criteria can sometimes occur, typically leading one to withhold judgement. Finally, criteria are circumstance-dependent (Z §492). Hence the criterial support which p gives to q may be defeated. Evidence which in one context suffices to establish that q may fail to do so in another context. Or a subsequent event may defeat the support p gives to q.

How could Wittgenstein fail to notice this equivocation? It seems unlikely that he sometimes employed the notion of a criterion to signify a logically sufficient condition and sometimes to signify logically good evidence. To preserve consistency and to avoid the bewildering notion of *a priori* yet defeasible evidence, it is tempting to argue that one should view a criterion as a necessary constituent of a sufficient condition. For if p is said to be a criterion of q in circumstances C_1, but not C_2, etc., then the conjunction of p with a description of the appropriate circumstances and of the negation of the defeating circumstances would surely amount to a sufficient condition for q.

It is clear that Wittgenstein rejected this move. Two reasons seem to have weighed with him. First, such a manoeuvre presupposes that there is a definitely circumscribable list of conditions (both positive and negative) which is such that if it is satisfied, then it *must* be the case that the person is, say, in pain, sad, thinking, or whatever. But the range of defeating conditions is arguably indefinite, and the defeating conditions themselves are defeasible. Secondly, faithful to the methodological principle that the method of philosophy is purely *descriptive*, that we must look and see how expressions are used, and not construct *theories* about their use, Wittgenstein noted that expressions such as 'to think' are taught under certain circumstances, which the learner does not need to be able to describe. What he must learn is to recognize deviant circumstances as such, and realize that they constitute a reason for withholding a description. But any attempt to characterize the use, the grammar, of an expression by reference to features that have no normative functions in the practice of using that expression will inevitably distort it. Hence his observation

One learns the word 'think', i.e. its use, under certain circumstances, which, however, one does not learn to describe.

But I *can teach* a person the use of the word! For a description of those circumstances is not needed for that.

I just teach him the word *under particular circumstances*.

. . . I cannot enumerate the conditions under which the word 'to think' is to be used – but if a circumstance makes the use doubtful, I can say so, and also *how* the situation is deviant from the usual ones. (Z §§114ff.)

Our grasp of the meaning of psychological verbs, our mastery of their technique of application, is manifest in our using them on the basis of their defining criteria in appropriate circumstances, as well as in the manner in which we teach and explain their use. But a correct explanation of the meanings of these expressions does not require a description of the circumstances in which they are to be used. The complex normative practices that are constitutive of a language-game do not amount to calculi of rules, for 'in general we don't use language according to strict rules – it hasn't been taught us by means of strict rules either' (BB 25). Our explanations of the use of the verb 'to think' do not fall short of what it really means merely because we fail to give an enumeration of all the circumstances in which its use is justified by such-and-such behaviour; indeed, it is doubtful whether there is any such sharply determinate totality. On the other hand, our understanding is defective if, in particular cases, we cannot say or discriminate in what circumstances the expression is to be withheld, e.g. on grounds of pretence, play-acting, parrotting, etc.

If this correctly captures Wittgenstein's thought, then it is not possible to give a uniform account of his notion of a criterion. In some contexts a criterion amounts to a sufficient condition, whereas in others it constitutes grammatically determined presumptive grounds. But it is only if one is misguided enough to think that his conception of a grammatical criterion is part of a novel theory of meaning (perhaps an 'anti-realist' semantics as opposed to a 'realist' or 'truth-conditional' semantics) that one need find any incoherence here. What is constant in his use of this term is that criteria are laid down in grammar (in contrast with symptoms, which are discovered in experience), that they determine or partially determine the meaning, the use, of expressions, and that they are grounds for assertion, justifications for judgements, and answers to the question 'How do you know?' Given that constancy, the further grammatical features of criteria vary from one kind of language-game to another. It should not be expected that what counts as a criterion for the truth of a mathematical proposition should share all the logico-grammatical features of criteria for the truth of psychological propositions. For what it means to say that a mathematical proposition is true is quite different from what it means to say that an empirical proposition is true. The first signifies that a formula belongs to our system of mathematics, that it is a norm of representation integrated by a proof into the vast network of the grammar of number, etc.; whereas the second signifies how things happen to be in the world. There is no temporal dimension to mathematical propositions, hence no circumstance-dependent defeasibility. The contrast with the logical character of, and criteria for, psychological statements could not be greater and should not be at all surprising. These kinds of concepts belong to quite different language-games, and they fulfil very different roles and occupy very different positions in our lives.

Wittgenstein employed the notion of criteria in four distinct domains: (a) in his philosophy of mathematics, (b) in his brief allusions to the fluctuation between criteria and symptoms in science, (c) in his discussions of potentialities, powers, and abilities, both animate and inanimate, and (d) in his philosophy of psychology. There is a parallel between (c) and (d), since many crucial psychological expressions signify capacities rather than states, processes, or experiences. It is in these two domains that Wittgenstein used the term 'criterion' to signify grammatical grounds for a proposition which are distinct from entailment, yet in many cases justify a knowledge-claim. The remainder of our discussion will be concerned exclusively with this notion.

4. *Evidence, knowledge, and certainty*

It is noteworthy that in the discussion of the grounds for judging something to be possible, to have a power or capacity, as well as in discussing the outer criteria for the 'inner', one seems to be concerned with 'cross-categorial' support. Occurrent properties or past, present, and often subsequent performances are the criteria for potentialities and abilities; similarly, past, present, and subsequent behaviour – the 'outer' – constitutes the criteria for the 'inner'.[5] In both kinds of case it seems, when doing philosophy, as if there were a gulf between two different domains, between actuality and potentiality and between behaviour and the mental. Confused by this misconceived picture, philosophers have been tempted to reify powers on the one hand (and to conceive of them as occult causes of their exercise) and mental phenomena on the other (conceiving of sensations or sense-impressions as 'inner objects', these likewise being cast in the role of causes of their behavioural expression). When the *grammatical* differences between powers and their actualization and between the mental and the behavioural are construed as *reflections* of ontological realities, then the apparent gulf between distinct 'ontological realms' also seems to be reflected in a gap in our reasoning about powers or about the 'inner'. For our judgements rest on grounds which do not *entail* the existence of powers or experiences. We often judge a person to have the ability to ϕ, e.g., on the basis of his past performances. But one

---

[5] Whether someone had the ability to ϕ at time t is often manifest in what he does at time t_1, and what someone meant is frequently exhibited by what he later says.

cannot say that having ϕd n times in the past *entails* that the person has the ability to ϕ. We justify the judgement that a person is in pain by reference to his current behaviour. But one cannot say that this behaviour *entails* that he is in pain. Consequently, scepticism breaks out, and it seems that we can never really know whether a person is able to ϕ or is in pain, that our judgements are at best probable and never certain, for our evidential grounds are never really adequate.[6]

It was Wittgenstein's aim to cure philosophy of these diseases of the intellect. Ontology is only a shadow in the Platonic cave, a projection of grammatical structures. To resolve our philosophical difficulties, we must turn away from these shadows and examine the distinctive grammars of the problematic expressions, describe the language-games in which they occur. In both domains Wittgenstein employed the notion of a criterion, not as a technical term within a novel theory, but as a humdrum expression useful in the description of linguistic practice. His main discussion of powers and abilities is in the *Brown Book* (see Volume 1, 'Undersanding and ability', esp. §7). This will not be further examined here, save *en passant*.

Ascription of psychological predicates rests on behaviour in appropriate circumstances. It is what people do and say, how they act and react in certain contexts, that constitutes the justifying grounds for whether they are in pain, perceive things, are cheerful or depressed, are thinking or imagining, etc. The behavioural grounds for such judgements are evidently distinct from entailment. Equally clearly they are not symptoms. It is not an empirical discovery that people scream when they are in severe pain, that they avoid obstacles in their path which they see, and laugh when they are amused. These forms of behaviour, in context, constitute *logical* criteria (Z §466). Wittgenstein frequently explained that such behavioural criteria are *evidence* for sensations, experiences, emotions, or moods, for thinking, remembering, or imagining, and so forth. The use of the term 'evidence' here (e.g. BB 51; PI §641, p. 228; Z §439) is potentially misleading, for the concept of evidence is strongly associated with inductive support, i.e. symptoms. If p is inductive evidence for q, then it makes sense to identify q independently of p. To observe that p falls short of observing that q, as when one observes footprints or fingerprints. In judging that q on the basis of the evidence that p, one is typically inferring from the observed to the unobserved. Philosophical scepticism about other minds is rooted in the insight that the relation between behaviour and inner state cannot conform to the model of

---

[6] The next move on the philosophical treadmill is to espouse one form or another of reductionism, e.g. the reduction of powers to their exercise or to their vehicle or its structure (see Volume 1, 'Understanding and ability', §7) or the reduction of the mental to behaviour (see 'Behaviour and behaviourism').

inductive evidence for a phenomenon. It might be supposed that when Wittgenstein introduced the notion of criterial evidence for the inner as a novel logical relation, viz. as necessarily good evidence for something, he was stipulating or moulding a theoretical concept. The point of this theoretical innovation might then appear to be to demonstrate how one can, *pace* the sceptic, bridge the ontological gulf between the outer and the inner and close the gap in the problematic inference from behaviour to the mental.

This misconstrues Wittgenstein's intentions. There is no 'gulf' between the outer and the inner, any more than there is a 'gulf' between what one has previously done and what one is able to do. The wince of pain, the shriek of agony, the careful nursing of the injured limb are, of course, not themselves sensations. But they are not 'mere' behaviour either, but *pain*-behaviour, logically or grammatically bound up with the concept of pain. There is no 'gap' between criterial grounds for inner states and the propositions about inner states which they support. Hence it is neither necessary nor indeed possible to concoct new logical forms or relations to fill it. Rather, there is a distinctive language-game, which needs to be described in order to curb our tendency to confuse it with a different one and hence to view it as defective by reference to a wrong paradigm. The criterial evidence for the inner falls short of what it is evidence for only in the sense that it does not *entail* it, but not in the sense of falling short of direct observation. Hence 'I observed his behaviour but not his pain' is not like 'I observed the breadcrumbs left on the table, but not the loaf of bread'. If one denies that one can observe another's pain, this is at best like denying that one can checkmate in draughts and not like denying that one can checkmate Fischer. One might, perhaps, deny that one can observe the pains of another person; this is tantamount to emphasizing the grammatical proposition that pains are not visibilia, but are felt or had, not seen. But one cannot deny that one can observe *that* someone is in pain. Granted that pain-behaviour is not itself pain (behaviour is not a sensation!), to observe pain-behaviour is, *ceteris paribus*, to observe that a person is in pain.

We are tempted to think otherwise because we invoke the picture of direct, as opposed to indirect, knowledge and then contrast our judgement that another person is in pain with his avowal of pain, conceiving of the latter as an expression of direct knowledge. But this is misconceived (see 'The inner and the outer', §2). The behavioural criteria for pain are the best possible grounds for judging someone to be in pain; this is precisely how such judgements are justified. But it is misleading to suggest that, as with empirical evidence, i.e. symptoms, they are grounds from which one draws an inference or derives a conclusion. One does not say 'I saw him break his leg and scream, so I concluded that he was probably in pain' or '. . . so I inferred that he was in pain'. Rather, if asked how I knew he was in pain, I might say 'I heard him scream and saw him writhing in pain'. The pain is not identical with its behavioural expression, but it is not hidden behind it either.

As we have seen, our concepts of the inner do not bring behaviour, circumstances, and experience into necessary connection (MS. 169, 68f.). Similarly, our concepts of capacities do not bring past performances and current state, circumstances, and capacity into necessary connection. In both kinds of case we operate with flexible concepts. To imagine what it would be like to operate here with more rigid concepts, we would have to envisage a far greater degree of uniformity and predictability in respect of human behaviour. It is important that when human beings injure themselves and scream, etc., then normally they subsequently behave in such-and-such ways. Similarly, it is important that when people have previously behaved thus-and-so, have been taught in such-and-such ways, and now say 'Yes, I can . . .' or 'Now I understand', then they normally go on to do this or that. These normal regularities of phenomena are, as it were, the gravitational force that holds our language-games stable. Were these regularities in human life different, our language-games would lose their point. Nevertheless, the regularity is not mechanical, nor is it perfectly predictable. And our concepts reflect the irregularity in this pattern no less than the non-uniformity in our reactions to exemplifications of the pattern (see 'The inner and the outer', §3). For inflexible, rigid concepts to be appropriate, we would have to imagine human beings to be much more machine-like, akin to automatons. But they are not, and for that very reason, we would not know where to begin with analogous concepts which did involve necessary connection.[7]

In this area, criterial support is defeasible. But to insist on defeasibility is not to deny the legitimacy of knowledge-claims justified by criteria, let alone to open the door to philosophical scepticism. First, a claim to know that another person is in pain (or is sad or joyful, understands something, is able to read or multiply, etc.) cannot be undermined by the fact that the grounds supporting the claim are defeasible, but only by adducing countervailing grounds that defeat them. If the ordinary criteria for someone's being in pain are exemplified in an appropriate context, then the onus of disproof lies with the sceptic, and the logical possibility of defeat is not a defeating condition. Secondly, admitting the possibility of

[7] It is ironic that some contemporary philosophers and scientists yearn for a scientific millennium in which the 'unscientific', supposedly inadequate psychological concepts of ordinary discourse (absurdly referred to as 'folk psychology') will be replaced by allegedly more appropriate concepts devised by cognitive science. These concepts, derived from computer science, will have none of the elasticity, let alone constitutional uncertainty, of ours. They will be appropriate for the description of machines; and it is no coincidence that such philosophers and scientists talk incoherently of the 'mind/brain' and refer to the brain as the 'mind-machine'.

defeating conditions does not mean denying that there are any grammatical limits to defeasibility. In a particular case it may well be that sceptical
qualms can be rejected as unintelligible. If someone is thrown into the
flames, etc., it makes no sense to say 'Maybe he is not in pain, but just
pretending'. There are circumstances in which one may say that there is
no such thing as pretending. More generally, in certain circumstances,
nothing *counts* as a defeating condition. Hence we do, very often, know
when other people are in pain (PI §246); the truth of a confession is
guaranteed by the special criteria for truthfulness (PI p. 222); the criteria
for a capacity *demonstrate* (*beweisen*) that a person has a capacity (PI
p. 181). Here and in numerous other passages Wittgenstein suggested
that the criteria for the truth of a proposition justify a knowledge-claim.
Similarly, he insisted that propositions such as 'He is in pain' may be as
certain as '2 × 2 = 4' (PI p. 224). To be sure, there are logical differences
between the certainty of mathematical propositions and the certainty of
judgements about the inner, but not differences in the degree of
certainty. For 'I can be as *certain* of someone else's sensations as of any
fact' (PI p. 224). It seems, both from Wittgenstein's writings in the 1930s
and from the *Investigations*, that he conceived of criterial support as
decisive, conferring certainty, *ceteris paribus*, and as justifying a
knowledge-claim.

It is therefore interesting to discover that in his very last writings,
when he discussed the 'constitutional uncertainty' of the inner and the
role of 'imponderable evidence' (see 'The inner and the outer', §3), he
explicitly introduced the notion of uncertain criteria (*unsicheres Kriterien*).
His thoughts here were arguably fragmentary; different inclinations
jostle and conflict; and he did not live long enough to revise and polish
these final remarks.

Four related features were clearly uppermost in his mind: (a) the
relative unpredictability of human behaviour, the fact that what follows
from a sincere manifestation of an inner state or experience is, to a
degree, indeterminate; (b) the absence of agreement in our *reactions* to
other people's manifestations of the inner, something which stands in
marked contrast with our widespread agreement over mathematical
calculations on the one hand and perceptual judgements (e.g. about the
colours of things) on the other; (c) the cultural relativity of many of the
criteria for the inner (viz. not being able to 'find one's way around' with
members of an alien culture) and the individualized character of many
such judgements (e.g. if I know a person well, I may be absolutely
certain that things are thus-and-so with him, yet be unable to convince
another, even though I *can* cite the grounds that convince me (PI p. 227);
(d) the imponderability of much of the evidence for the inner, especially
in matters of subtle nuances of emotional response (thus I, who know the

person well, may be quite certain that he is sad or upset, but I may not be able to cite *any* convincing grounds (cf. PI p. 228).

It is the latter three points that disrupt the picture previously delineated. For it is they that are reflected in the fact that in certain circumstances the grounds of judgement for the inner are not decisive, or that they are decisive for me, but not for others who share the same concept. I may be certain that my friend is upset, yet another person may not be, and neither of us is being irrational. How can this be? Criteria are laid down in grammar and are constitutive of the concepts for which they are criteria, yet disagreement in certain cases, 'constitutional uncertainty', is possible! If the grounds of judgement for someone's inner state sometimes turn on intimate acquaintance with the particular person, on cultural differences, or even on imponderable evidence, it is not obvious in what sense they are laid down in grammar or in what sense they partly determine the meaning of the relevant expression. This can seem puzzling, but it is not really so. The grammar of the 'inner' is distinctive and must be described as it is, rather than measured against the yardstick of other, quite different language-games. What is laid down in the grammar of these concepts, in the 'rules of evidence' for the 'inner', is precisely this form of elasticity in application. The grammar here reflects the irregularities in the complex pattern of the outer and the non-uniformity in our reactions to other people's expressive behaviour. Our concepts are so moulded as to tolerate imponderable evidence (although, to be sure, that presupposes ponderable evidence), cultural differences, and better or worse judgement about, and insight into, human beings and their natures.

It was such factors which led Wittgenstein to point out that there can be complete certainty, yet no certain criteria (*kein sicheres Kriterium* (MS. 174, 22)). So too, there is constitutional uncertainty in the language-game. The uncertainty, for example, in recognizing someone's annoyance is not simply an uncertainty about his future behaviour, but 'lies much more in the concept of an uncertainty of criteria' (MS. 173, 92). To be sure, we say of an expression of feeling that 'it appears to be genuine'. But this only makes sense if there is such a thing as 'That is genuine', and if so, there must be a criterion for it. But does it follow that the criterion is certain (MS. 174, 21)? Of course, one may still *be* quite certain about the other person's feelings, yet be unable to cite anything that would justify one's certainty. Nevertheless, there is nothing irrational here. If one knows a person well, this is how one reacts. And although one cannot say what in his behaviour convinces one, one's certainty is taken seriously. For one's description of another person's psychological state, and the conviction with which one gives it, is itself a criterion for one's own response, for one's sensitivity, perceptiveness, and sincerity. One's response is not only or even typically a mere *opinion*, but a sincere (or insincere) reaction. Differences in the patterns of interpersonal reaction are part of the fabric of human life, and it is only to be expected that they should be reflected in our concepts.

The idea that in some cases there are no certain criteria did not, of course, lead Wittgenstein to espouse any form of scepticism. In so far as the concept of a criterion for the inner plays a role in his demonstration of the incoherence of scepticism, it is not because criteria are uniformly decisive. Rather, one salient flaw in the sceptical argument is that concepts of the inner are there severed from *any* criteria, whether they are, in this sense, certain or not. And Wittgenstein's last writings on philosophical psychology do not suggest that there are *never* certain criteria. Introduction of the notion of a penumbra of 'constitutional uncertainty' of the inner manifests his recognition of features in the grammar of the mental which are (at best) distorted and misrepresented in philosophical scepticism. In contrast to the sceptic, Wittgenstein wrote, 'I do not say that the evidence makes what goes on within us *only* probable. For as far as I am concerned, there is nothing missing from the language-game' (MS. 169, 131). The sceptic mistakes the limits of a language-game for shortcomings in the playing of the game. Wittgenstein's concern was to describe the rules of the game, with all their indeterminacy. Recognition of the fact that there can be criteria which are not certain earmarks a further elasticity in our concepts of the mental and characterizes an important facet of our language-game, and hence too of our lives.

INDEX

(Numerals printed in Bold signify a detailed discussion of the specified topic)

unity of science 105, 108
use 147

verification/verificationism 18, 107, 112,
    113, 246, 247, 248, 249
Vienna Circle 100, 102, 105, 124, 246
visual impression (*see also* Sense
    Impression) 198, 200f., 205
visualizing 186, 193, 202
vivacity 200f.

Waismann, F. 3, 105, 106, 107, 124n.,
    216, 217, 246, 247n.
Watson, J. 97–100, 101, 102, 105, 108,
    110, 171n.
Watts, J. 175n.
will 65, 163, 212, 230
Wundt, W. 66, 97

Yates, F. 192n.
Young, J. Z. 71